LAND TENURE IN SCOTLAND

AUSTRALIA
LBC Information Services—Sydney

CANADA and USA
Carswell—Toronto

NEW ZEALAND
Brooker's—Auckland

SINGAPORE and MALAYSIA
Sweet & Maxwell Asia
Singapore and Kuala Lumpur

LAND TENURE IN SCOTLAND

Professor Robert Rennie, LL.B, Ph.D., N.P., FRSA

Professor of Conveyancing, University of Glasgow, Partner, Harper Macleod

THOMSON

™

W. GREEN

Published in 2004 by W. Green & Son Ltd
21 Alva Street
Edinburgh EH2 4PS

Typeset by Servis Filmsetting Ltd, Manchester
Printed and bound in Great Britain by Cromwell Press Ltd, Trowbridge

No natural forests were destroyed to make this product;
only farmed timber was used and replanted

A CIP catalogue record for this book is available from the British
Library

ISBN 0 414 01548 7

ISBN 0-414-01548-7

9 780414 015487

CONTENTS

CHAPTER 3—FEUDAL REAL BURDENS—EXTINCTION AND REALLOTMENT—COMPENSATION

CHAPTER 4—FEUDUTIES

CHAPTER 7—PERSONAL REAL BURDENS AFTER FEUDAL ABOLITION

CHAPTER 8—ENFORCEMENT OF REAL BURDENS

CHAPTER 9—VARIATION AND EXTINCTION OF REAL BURDENS

CHAPTER 10—DEVELOPMENT MANAGEMENT SCHEMES

CHAPTER 11—SERVITUDES

CHAPTER 12—PRE-EMPTION AND REVERSION

CHAPTER 13—THE ROLE OF THE LANDS TRIBUNAL

CHAPTER 14—THE LAW OF THE TENEMENT

CHAPTER 15—SPECIAL RIGHTS—LAND REFORM ACT 2003

CHAPTER 16—HUMAN RIGHTS

PREFACE

It used to be said that conveyancers were a dull, predictable breed. Indeed Doctor Johnson is credited with the remark that lawyers knew no law but only practice. It would, I think, be fair to say that for many years conveyancing transactions ran smoothly without much reference to the law of property. I can recall as a humble apprentice in the late 1960s hearing a partner talk of a title being "good", "bad" or "difficult". As a young man fresh from the law faculty at Glasgow University I had some difficulty in understanding these terms in a legal context. What actually happened of course was that the partner exercised a judgement as to what could be accepted for a client without undue risk. In so far as the law of conveyancing was concerned there were at that time few up-to-date textbooks and, (apart from the badly drafted Succession (Scotland) Act 1964), the last major conveyancing statute was the Conveyancing (Scotland) Act 1924. Before that Act there was a gap to 1874. The United Kingdom Parliament had little time for legislation affecting Scotland and proposals for law reform were largely in the hands of a law reform committee. Imagine the shockwaves which went through the profession therefore when it was proposed to bring forward a flagship piece of Scottish legislation which would deal with some of the abuses of the feudal system and also reform the law of heritable security. I refer of course to the Conveyancing and Feudal Reform (Scotland) Act 1970. That Act also introduced some incidental conveyancing reforms and I recall even now the dire predictions of widespread fraud if the granter of a deed was required to sign on the last page only. Apart from the Land Tenure Reform (Scotland) Act 1974 there was not much legislative activity until 1979 when land registration was introduced in the Land Registration (Scotland) Act of that year. The Requirements of Writing (Scotland) Act 1995 further amended the formal requirements for written documents. The attitude of our profession is naturally conservative. I recall giving a two hour lecture to a local faculty of solicitors on the Requirements of Writing (Scotland) Act. At the end I sat down, exhausted, and invited questions. A gentlemen, I suppose in his late 50s, turned to me and enquired why we could not have left the law as it was. His reasoning was that everybody knew you needed two witnesses and everybody knew that a letter which was adopted as holograph was meant to be binding. He went home no doubt to examine his pension policies.

One of the great criticisms of the United Kingdom Parliament was that it paid little or no attention to reform of the law of Scotland. The excuse always was pressure of Parliamentary time. There are of course no votes in non-contentious law reform bills. With the advent of the Scottish Parliament however these excuses were no longer available and this has resulted in a steady flow of legislation. November 28 2004 (Martinmas) will be a significant day in the lives of all Scottish lawyers. On that day the main provisions of the Abolition of Feudal Tenure etc (Scotland) Act 2000, the Title Conditions (Scotland) Act 2003 and the

Tenements (Scotland) Act 2004 will come into effect. These Acts have been described variously as "a Conveyancing Revolution", "a New Play in Three Acts" and "Burdens and Bombshells". Perhaps the most important change will be a dramatic move away from law which is based on old statutes and decided cases to law which will be almost entirely statute based. The Land Reform (Scotland) Act 2003 is also in force. The challenge for those involved in conveyancing practice will be to interpret the new law and at the same time allow conveyancing transactions to proceed smoothly. The purpose of the legislative changes is to clarify and modernise the law, not to provide solicitors with a whole host of reasons for delaying transactions or a new raft of clauses in missives.

I am grateful to a number of people who have helped with this book. In particular I would like to thank Sheriff (formerly Professor) Douglas Cusine and Scott Wortley of the University of Strathclyde for reading the manuscript and making many helpful and pointed suggestions. I am also grateful to Professor Stewart Brymer of Thorntons, Dundee and Bruce Merchant of South Forrest, Inverness who were good enough to look over the drafts of the Deed of Conditions which is contained in the Appendices and point out several glaring inconsistencies. I should add a word of caution in relation to the Deed of Conditions. It is intended merely as an illustrative form and not holy writ.

Finally, I would like to thank my two secretaries, Alison Clement at the University who typed the manuscript and Mary Carey at Harper Macleod who typed the many drafts and re-drafts of the Deed of Conditions. Given the fact that Mary was largely responsible for the scanning and organisation of the Opinions which went into the recent collection of Professional Negligence Opinions I was surprised but grateful that she was happy to help again with this Book.

I suppose I should say that the law is as stated at November 28, 2004 or thereabouts.

Robert Rennie
September 2004

TABLE OF CASES

TABLE OF STATUTES

TABLE OF SCOTTISH STATUTES

TABLE OF STATUTORY INSTRUMENTS

TABLE OF SCOTTISH STATUTORY INSTRUMENTS

CHAPTER 1

HISTORICAL INTRODUCTION

ORIGINS OF THE FEUDAL SYSTEM

It might be said that the origins of the feudal system are lost in the **1–01** mists of time. The feudal system may have had its origins in the remnants of the Roman empire. What is probably true is that the feudal system was imported into England at the time of the Norman conquest in 1066. There is a story (probably apocryphal) to the effect that when William the Conqueror landed at Pevensey he stumbled and fell. The soldiers thought this was a bad omen and made to get back into the boats. However William, ever the pragmatic feudal superior, turned this awkward situation to his own advantage. He held up his hand and, showing the soldiers the sand which he had involuntarily clutched, declared that he was seised in the land. What he was effectively doing was taking symbolic delivery of England as feudal overlord. Initially therefore the feudal system was a system of government and it rested on the premise that the King owned all the land. Other feudal theories take this one stage further back and postulate that God owns all the earth and the sovereign, being His anointed, is God's vassal. This point was taken in a recent case involving the eviction of the Carbeth Hutters but rejected. Whatever the theory may be William the Conqueror used the feudal system to good effect by feuing out large tracts of land to nobles in return for services. The services would initially have been men at arms in time of war. There are doubts about exactly when the feudal system of landholding was introduced into Scotland but most writers are agreed that it came to Scotland when David I ascended the Scottish throne in 1124AD.[1] The nobles who held Crown charters of feu sub-feued smaller areas to lesser nobles again in return for men at arms. Effectively the men at arms were passed up the feudal chain to the service of the King. There was originally no limit in England or in Scotland to the number of sub-feus which could be granted so that the large estates became sub-divided and a feudal pyramid with the Crown at the apex was created. Essentially the sovereign was the paramount superior and the powerful nobles his immediate vassals. The lesser nobles were the vassals of the greater nobles who were mid-superiors and so on down to some lowly strip farmer at the bottom of the social and economic heap. The feudal system was an effective method of government in the sense that it effectively tied ownership of land with fealty or loyalty to the King. Breach of the conditions of the feu resulted in forfeiture of the lands which reverted

---

[1] Girvan, "Feudal Law" in *Sources and Literature of Scots Law*, The Stair Society, Vol.1, pp.192 *et seq.*

back to the King or the mid-superior as the case may be. Those nobles who dared to cross the King lost their lands (and probably their heads as well).

THE END OF FEUDALISM IN ENGLAND

1–02   Edward I used the feudal system to great effect during the wars of independence. Indeed it may be said that he obtained the fleeting allegiance of many Scottish nobles including the Bruce family by granting them charters of lands in England. However Edward I recognised that if unlimited sub-feuing was allowed then this increased the numbers who could form factions who might band together against the Crown. Accordingly in 1290 subinfeudation was prohibited.[2] After that statute the feudal system effectively withered on the vine in England and so far as heritable property was concerned it could be transferred without the consent of the feudal superior. Remnants of the feudal system in England were swept away by Cromwell during the Protectorate and these reforms were confirmed in England on the restoration of the monarchy in 1660.[3] The current position in England is that the Crown still holds a nominal superiority but with no practical or legal consequences.

THE END OF FEUDALISM ON THE CONTINENT

1–03   The feudal system persisted to a greater or lesser extent in Europe right up to the French Revolution in 1789. As the French empire expanded across Europe the feudal systems of other European countries were swept away. Feudal tenure was not reintroduced in these countries after the Congress of Vienna in 1815.

THE POSITION IN SCOTLAND

1–04   During the Protectorate in England there appears to have been an attempt by Cromwell and the Parliament to abolish feudal tenure in Scotland.[4] However Cromwellian legislation was repealed after the Restoration and the view is that the feudal system either survived that attempt or was revived. A series of Acts removed the last vestiges of feudal authority in the judicial and political sense.[5] So far as the law of heritable property was concerned the effects of feudalism were modified from time to time. Returns to the superior which had originally been in the form of men-at-arms and produce were abolished. Returns in commodities were finally abolished in 1924[6] but by that time the return or *reddendo* to the superior was mainly in the form of a money

---

[2] *Quia Emptores*, 1290 (18 Edw. I st. I).
[3] Tenures Abolition Act 1660.
[4] Ordinance of April 12, 1654.
[5] Highland Services Act 1715; Tenures Abolition Act 1746; Heritable Jurisdictions (Scotland) Act 1746.
[6] Conveyancing (Scotland) Act 1924, s.12.

payment known as feuduty. Returns by way of military service did not survive the Jacobite rebellions.[7] Feudal casualties, which eventually were one-off payments on the happening of certain events such as the entry of a new heir or singular successor were abolished in 1914.[8] The imposition of new feuduties (but not subinfudation) was prohibited in 1974.[9]

FEUDAL REAL BURDENS—A SYSTEM OF PLANNING

Although the feudal system disappeared as a political reality in Scotland it remained as the system of land tenure. In the latter part of the 18th century and in the 19th century it became what effectively was a private system of town planning. Land owners feued out large tracts or individual plots or steadings of land for development but subject to strict building and use conditions. The architectural character of the New Town of Edinburgh and the West End of Glasgow owe much to the stringency of these feudal conditions. It must be remembered that modern town and country planning was not introduced in Scotland until 1947. There is of course a crucial difference between a private system of development or planning and a public one. A local authority is supposed to have the interests of the whole community in mind when considering planning and development issues whereas a feudal superior, who may be a private individual or a private commercial concern, has no obligation to look at the wider public interest in coming to a view on what conditions are to be imposed or indeed on what conditions are to be waived. Nevertheless many of the feudal real burdens (and indeed non-feudal real burdens) imposed in the 18th and 19th centuries had a beneficial effect overall in the communities in which the properties were situated. In fact what happened was that the feudal system effectively reinvented itself   **1–05**

TERRITORIAL JURISDICTIONS

Originally the feudal system carried with it certain rights of jurisdiction where the superior held a regality or a barony. These territorial jurisdictions which were both civil and criminal were abolished after the 1745 rebellion[10] although there appears to have been a very limited jurisdiction remaining even after that date.[11]   **1–06**

SEPARATE ESTATES IN LAND

In feudal theory there could be any amount of separate ownership interests in one plot of land. Theoretically the Crown still owned all the land although in Scotland the paramount superiority is often held by the heir   **1–07**

---

[7] Highland Services Act 1715; Tenures Abolition Act 1746.
[8] Feudal Casualties (Scotland) Act 1914.
[9] Land Tenure (Scotland) Act 1974.
[10] Heritable Jurisdictions (Scotland) Act 1746.
[11] *The Laws of Scotland, Stair Memorial Encyclopaedia*, vol.18 at para.54.

to the throne as Prince and Steward of Scotland. Each mid-superior owns an estate in land which is known variously as the *dominium directum*, superiority, over-superiority or mid-superiority. The ultimate vassal or feuar who actually possesses the land is said to own the *dominium utile* of the land. In no other jurisdiction is there such a division of ownership in the same land. This division is in no sense common ownership but ownership of distinct interests or estates on different levels within the feudal structure. One would have some difficulty in justifying a land tenure system of this nature to anyone other than a Scottish lawyer who practiced in property and conveyancing. The fact that superiority or mid-superiority titles can be bought and sold without reference to the owner of the *dominium utile* title is also something which baffles laymen and non-legal professionals. In many ways this commercial trafficking in superiority titles for commercial purposes has prompted the current spate of property law reform.

ABUSE OF THE FEUDAL SYSTEM

1–08 Even in its guise as a private system of development and planning the feudal system was open to abuse by unscrupulous superiors. A feudal superior traditionally was thought of as a substantial landowner in an area who sought by the imposition of feudal real burdens to control development and land use within that area. Accordingly if the proprietor of the *dominium utile* wished to erect a new building or alter a building or change the use of a building contrary to the terms of a feudal real burden application had to be made to the superior for a waiver or a charter of novodamus. In theory the feudal superior gave consideration to this application taking into account the effect of the proposed development on the area and whether it would have an adverse effect on that superior's own land holdings. The superior could then grant or refuse the waiver. If the waiver was to be granted then the superior might expect to be relieved of legal expenses for the granting of any deed. However that is not how it has turned out in practice. Suburban development carried on apace after the Second World War and builders and developers were not slow to use the feudal system not just to control construction and use of buildings but also to provide a revenue stream by way of feuduty. It was not uncommon, for example, in the 1960s to find a reputable builder feuing out standard semi-detached five apartment houses in suburbs like Bishopbriggs subject to annual feuduties of £50. Most builders and developers eventually found that it was tedious and administratively costly to collect these feuduties although in the last analysis all vassals paid up. Not to do so was to run the risk of the feu being irritated if it remained unpaid for two years.[12] Many builders and developers simply sold the superiority title and with it the right to collect the feu duties and enforce the feudal real burdens after the development was completed. The purchasers of these superiority titles were not other landowners but tended to be safe and well established institutions who were looking for the safest of safe investments and a steady income stream. Insurance companies and

---

[12] Irritancy *ob non solutem canonen*; Feuduty Act 1597.

friendly societies were among those who acquired superiorities. However the owner of the largest number of superiorities was and is the Church of Scotland. It was thought that these superiority titles with the right to collect feuduties would be regarded as apolitical as well as safe investments. From a tenure or commercial point of view however there was no logical reason why a builder or developer should impose a feuduty; the feuduty was imposed not because strict feudal theory required a return or *reddendo* to the superior as a condition of the feu but simply to create an income stream which could be capitalised on the sale of the superiority. Those who bought superiorities calculated the price not just on the total amount of feuduties which could be collected from an estate but also on the likely waiver income from that estate. The fact that there was a waiver income to be derived illustrates how superiors had changed in character from the nineteenth and early twentieth centuries onwards. In a typical example a feudal condition relating to a house might prohibit further building and a feudal condition affecting a field might require that it be used solely in connection with agriculture. These feudal conditions might have been imposed in 1895 at a time when there was little development in the area. If the current owner of the house wished to sub-divide the large garden and sell off a building plot or if the owner of the field could make no income from agriculture and wished to sell it to a builder or developer then an application had to be made to the feudal superior for a waiver. In such a case the practice arose of the superior charging a fee or *grassum* for the grant of the waiver in addition to requiring relief from all legal expenses of the transaction. In some cases of course the superior resided in the locality and took a decision based on what was right for the amenity of that locality irrespective of the chance of financial gain. In many other instances however, especially where the feudal superior was some form of institution, it became normal and commercial practice to demand payment of a *grassum* for a waiver. These payments were sometimes on a sliding scale depending on the value of the proposed development or the nature of the alteration. On the one hand one can see why this commercial practice might be regarded as a complete reversal of all the principles on which the feudal system was based. Those who hold this view would simply regard the demand for payment in return for a waiver as a mild form of extortion. On the other hand the author has heard quite cogent arguments based on the commercial realities of the situation. One can argue that if a party holds an interest in land then it is an asset and accordingly there is nothing wrong in the owner of that interest in land realising money in a dealing with that asset. A superior who grants a consent or a waiver is giving up a right to enforce a legally binding obligation. In the real world people do not do this unless they are compensated. One can also argue that if the feudal superior is an institution, such as the Church of Scotland, which has paid out a capital sum for a superiority title based on the return from feuduty and the grant of waivers then it is unfair to prevent that institution from charging for waivers on a reasonable basis. After all no one is forced to buy a property and if they choose to do so they must accept the title with the feudal burdens attached thereto. Research indicates that ignorance of title conditions is not a factor which affects purchasers at the point of offering. The reality however is that many feudal conditions were laid down decades, if not more than a century ago, and purchasers of heritable property have little or no bargaining power when it comes to negotiation with the superior.

REDEMPTION OF FEU DUTIES

1–09   The income which superiors derived from feuduties diminished with the introduction in 1974 of voluntary and compulsory redemption of feuduty. Every vassal is entitled to redeem feu duty voluntarily.[13] The legislation also required allocated feuduties to be redeemed by the seller on the sale of a property.[14] Where property was compulsorily acquired the acquiring authority had to redeem the feuduty, allocated or not.[15] The redemption money which has to be paid to the feudal superior is calculated on the basis of fluctuations in the stock market from time to time. This reform had several results, some expected but others unexpected. In the first place there was a steady decline in feuduty income. That may have prompted some superiors to increase the amounts charged for granting waivers in respect of feudal real burdens. In the second place following on redemption of the feuduty there was little contact between the superior and the vassal simply because there was no need. Although the superiority title was a property title many superiors lost interest and failed to deal with the superiority title in their wills with the result that it became impossible to trace superiors. Other superiors simply changed address without advising any of their vassals. The result of this was to leave some vassals in difficulty if they wanted a permission or a waiver from a superior simply because they could not trace the party who was entitled to grant the permission or waiver. In the third place the framers of the 1974 legislation took the view that redemption of feuduties would inevitably mean that the feudal system itself would wither on the vine. The logic behind this proposition was that if there was no financial return by way of feuduty there would be little point in creating a new feudal estate for a new plot. However the framers of the legislation failed to reckon with the tenacity of the Scottish legal practitioner and his or her addiction to existing styles and forms. In fairness to the solicitors of the 1970s however it should be remembered that the title of a superior to enforce a feudal real burden was obvious; it was the superiority title itself. Moreover the interest of a feudal superior to enforce a real burden in a feudal deed was presumed at least in the first instance.[16] On the other hand the title of a disponer in a disposition or a co-feuar to enforce a burden based on a *ius quaesitum tertio* can be problematic and the interest of a disponer or co-feuar is not presumed but has to be established.[17] Only in a question between an original disponer and a disponee is the interest of the disponer to enforce the burden presumed.[18] Accordingly a solicitor advis-

---

[13] Land Tenure Reform (Scotland) Act 1974, s.4.
[14] *ibid.*, s.5.
[15] *ibid.*, s.6.
[16] *Earl of Zetland v Hislop* (1882) 9 R. (HL) 40.
[17] *Aberdeen Varieties Ltd v James F. Donald (Aberdeen Cinemas) Ltd*, 1939 S.C. 788; 1940 S.C. (HL) 52.
[18] *Scottish Cooperative Wholesale Society Ltd v Finnie*, 1937 S.C. 835.

ing a builder or developer as to the best method of securing enforcement of real burdens in a development might have been negligent if that solicitor had not recommended feuing as opposed to disponing the individual plots where real burdens were to be imposed.

VARIATION AND DISCHARGE OF REAL BURDENS

In 1970 the Lands Tribunal for Scotland was given power to waive or discharge real burdens in feudal and non-feudal deeds but only on one or more of three grounds set out in the legislation.[19] The three grounds are wide but no general power was given to the tribunal in the event that a particular case could not be brought within one of these grounds. Most applications were brought under at least two grounds. The Tribunal deals with such cases reasonably quickly, particularly if they are not opposed, but matters still take some months to be decided even where the application is unopposed. Where the application is opposed and there has to be a hearing the process takes longer. Because of this some parties have been unwilling, or unable, to wait for a decision. In any event success is not guaranteed. The Tribunal recognises the issues which come before it are essentially matters of private rights and interests as opposed to general or planning issues which affect the public interest.[20] Accordingly in many cases the party wishing a relaxation or a discharge of a burden simply pays the superior an agreed sum, usually after a horse trading process, in exchange for a waiver or discharge. This type of negotiation often occurs where the party seeking the waiver or discharge is a developer who cannot wait to get on site.

1–10

THE PRESSURE FOR CHANGE

In the late 1960s and particularly in the 1970s and 1980s criticisms were levelled at the feudal system. Many owners of properties did not understand why they needed to pay feuduty and further they resented the fact that although the local authority might have granted planning permission or building warrant for an alteration to a property the owner might still require the consent of some distant superior. Annoyance and frustration increased when that distant superior demanded money in exchange for the waiver. Furthermore if the superior could not be traced the owner might then be put to the expense of going to the Lands Tribunal to remove any possible difficulty in a sale of the property. Many owners simply took the chance that the superior (if such existed) would never find out. The practice of solicitors however in relation to conveyancing, has tightened over the years probably as a result of an increase in negligence claims. In many instances in the 1960s and early 1970s the standard reply to a request for production of a superior's consent was to the effect that the superior had no interest to enforce or had acquiesced in the breach of feuing conditions because the porch, gazebo or whatever had been erected some six months ago. However a detailed examination

1–11

---

[19] Conveyancing and Feudal Reform (Scotland) Act 1970, ss.1–7.
[20] see *Main v Lord Doune*, 1972 S.L.T. (Lands Tr.) 14; *Mercer v MacLeod*, 1977 S.L.T. (Lands Tr.) 14.

of the law relating to the interest of the superior and acquiescence shows that it is not as simple as that nor ever was. Accordingly many proprietors found themselves in awkward situations when they tried to sell in the 1980s and 1990s. This difficulty was exacerbated by the fact that a new breed of superior had grown up. Commercial entities have acquired the rump of old estates including all the superiorities. The purpose of this acquisition is purely commercial. In some cases these superiors carried out surveys of areas covered by the superiority title and noted extensions, alterations, changes of use and the like. These new age superiors then "invited" their luckless vassals to pay money for a consent or waiver under threat of legal action or irritancy.

IUS QUAESITUM TERTIO

1–12 In some developments there was a further complication and that was the existence, or possible existence, of a right in third parties to enforce the feudal conditions. The third parties were, of course, co-feuars subject to the same feudal real burdens. These rights caused and continue to cause considerable difficulty. In the first place, while it is competent to create such a right expressly, this has not been common and these rights are more frequently created by implication.[21] The law relating to implied third party rights is complex and in many cases it was extremely difficult to determine whether there was such a right and even if there was to identify exactly how many third parties had the title and interest to enforce. Even where such rights were created expressly those advising clients buying and selling were faced with a practical problem. If they advised the client that permission for an alteration, new building or change of use was requested from all of those, who, in theory had third party rights, it might not be obtained or at least not be obtained for a number of years. If one takes the example of a *ius quaesitum tertio* which is vest in two hundred proprietors in a standard housing estate then any attempt to obtain the consent of all the other one hundred and ninety nine proprietors is bound to fail. Some people will refuse, others will be absent or by reason of death or other causes unable to give consent. Some will offer to consent if they are paid. Even if third parties were willing to give consent, the consent of the third parties' heritable creditors might need to be obtained if the proposed change to the neighbour's property requiring the consent could adversely affect the property belonging to the third party. In practice what has happened is that while the feudal system exists lawyers have simply advised clients to obtain the superior's consent and ignored third party rights in their entirety. It can of course be argued that not every third party would have an interest to enforce in any event. However the title to enforce vest in a third party is not affected by a waiver from a superior.[22]

---

[21] See *Hislop v MacRitchie's Trs* (1881) 8 R. (HL) 95.
[22] *Dalrymple v Herdman* (1878) 5 R. 847.

THE REFORMS

Given these problems with the feudal system, both political parties at   **1–13**
Westminster in the 1960s and 1970s committed themselves to its
reform.[23] A systematic analysis of the problems surrounding the reform
was undertaken by the Scottish Law Commission in 1991 with the publication of its discussion paper.[24] In 1993 the author took the Chair of
Conveyancing in the University of Glasgow. It is the practice for new
professors to deliver an inaugural lecture which is open to the public.
The author entitled this lecture *The Feudal System: Going, Going, Gone?*[25]
Crowd control was not necessary despite the presence of Professor
Kenneth Reid in the audience. At the first lecture delivered every
session to third year conveyancing students at the University the author
has indicated that this might be the last year in which he is obliged to
give lectures on the feudal system. The words were beginning to wear
thin by 1999. In the late 1990s the Commission's interest in the reform
of the feudal system revived and in 1999 it produced a report on feudal
abolition.[26] An advisory group worked closely with the Commission
not only on the abolition of the feudal system but also on the issue of
real burdens. One of the questions which had to be addressed in relation to abolition was whether the whole notion that person owning land
could impose and enforce conditions on other land was appropriate in
a non feudal system of land tenure. On one view it could be argued that
such matters should be left in the hands of local authorities to be dealt
with through the planning and building control functions. Eventually
the Commission decided that there was still some merit in retaining the
concept of a real burden on land which was created for the benefit of
another party by virtue of that other party's ownership of other land
and which was praedial in nature in the sense of applying to the burdened land. Having taken that decision in principle the Commission
then had to look at the law in that area and examine and determine not
only the consequences of the abolition of the feudal system but also how
real burdens would be constituted and enforced in a non-feudal system.
The deliberations of the Commission following on the usual consultation are to be found in its report on Real Burdens.[27] This report was followed by a further consultation exercise carried out by the Scottish
Executive in May 2001. The Commission's report on feudal abolition
and the Executive consultation resulted in the introduction of the
Abolition of Feudal Tenure etc. (Scotland) Bill to the Scottish Parliament
and this received Royal Assent on June 9, 2000.[28] The Scottish Executive
then introduced the Title Conditions (Scotland) Bill 2003 to the Scottish
Parliament and it received Royal Assent on April 3, 2003.[29] Some provisions of these Acts came into effect immediately on Royal Assent or the

---

[23] *Conveyancing Legislation and Practice* (the Halliday Committee), Cmnd.3118 (1966);
Land Tenure: A Plan for Reform, Cmnd. 4099 (1969); *Land Reform in Scotland* (1972) (Green
Paper).
[24] *Property Law: Abolition of the Feudal System*, Discussion Paper No.93, July 1991.
[25] Published in 1995 J.R. 321
[26] Scot Law Com. No.168 (1999)
[27] Scot Law Com. No.181 (2000)
[28] The Abolition of Feudal Tenure etc. (Scotland) Act 2000, hereinafter referred to as the
"2000 Act".
[29] Title Conditions (Scotland) Act 2003, hereinafter referred to as the "2003 Act".

day after. However the bulk of the legislative proposals come into effect on the appointed day which is Martinmas (November 28) 2004. There will therefore be a seamless transition from a feudal system of land tenure to a non-feudal system of land tenure on that date. That at least is the theory.

LEASEHOLD TITLES

1–14   The prohibition of subinfeudation in England in 1290 resulted in the proliferation of leasehold tenure south of the border. In many ways leasehold tenure resembles feudal tenure with the landlord having some control over the use of the land. Leasehold tenure has not featured greatly in Scotland apart from certain areas.[30] One reason given for the existence of leasehold tenure in Scotland was that a lease could more easily be granted than a feu where the estate was entailed. The feudal abolition legislation expressly prohibits the granting of leases in excess of 175 years to avoid a repetition of the English experience.[31] It has been illegal in Scotland to create leases in excess of 20 years in respect of residential properties since 1974.[32] Although feudal casualties were abolished in 1914[33] leasehold casualties remained virtually unaffected although the feudal legislation would have allowed the Court of Session to apply that legislation to leaseholds by Act of Sederunt. The new age superiors in addition to acquiring superiority interests also acquired landlord's interests in areas where long leases (usually for 999 years) had been granted. They took advantage of the fact that some of these leases provided for a casualty or one-off payment on the entry of every new tenant based on the current market rent. New owners of leasehold properties in these cases found themselves facing bills of many thousands of pounds. The United Kingdom Government moved quickly and asked the Scottish Law Commission to look at the question of leasehold casualties as a matter of urgency. The Scottish Law Commission issued a report on April 30, 1998.[34] Because of the approach of devolution however it was left to the Scottish Parliament to pass the necessary legislation. A Private Members Bill (the first to be introduced) was the vehicle chosen and since the measure was non partisan it received full support. The Leasehold Casualties (Scotland) Act 2001 received Royal Assent on April 12, 2001. Leasehold Casualties were abolished with minimum compensation. The Scottish Law Commission is also looking at long leases in general and has published a discussion paper.[35] The scheme of the proposed reform is very similar to the scheme adopted in the feudal abolition legislation. Effectively long leases will be converted into ordinary ownership. The final report of the Scottish Law Commission together with a draft Bill is expected to be published towards the end of 2004.[36]

---

[30] Leasehold tenure features in certain parts of Lanarkshire and in other areas such as Blairgowrie where renewable leases have been common.
[31] 2000 Act, s.67.
[32] Land Tenure Reform (Scotland) Act, 1974 ss.8–10.
[33] Feudal Casualties (Scotland) Act 1914.
[34] Scot Law Com. No.165 (1998)
[35] Discussion Paper on Long Leases No.112 (April 2001)
[36] The timing of the introduction of a Bill will depend on the Parliament's timetable.

TENEMENTAL TITLES

One type of building which is very common in Scotland and, indeed, in   **1–15**
other countries is the tenement where there are a number of units,
usually residential, under one roof. It is obvious that certain things are
owned exclusively by the owner of an individual flat, but also that
owners share other things, such as the roof, the ground on which the
tenement is built and the outside walls. It is not uncommon to find that
all the flats in the building are governed by a single document (a deed
of conditions) which sets out who owns what exclusively, what is in
shared ownership and with whom, and the corresponding obligations
for maintenance and use. For example, the document might provide
that the roof is owned by all of the proprietors in common and consequently that they are required to contribute equally to the cost of
its maintenance. If, however, there is no such document or the document does not cover everything then ownership, common interest and
maintenance are governed by the common law. The Scottish Law
Commission undertook a separate consultation on the Law of the
Tenement which disclosed that the common law was unclear on certain
matters. Furthermore, it was thought that a building in respect of which
there was no governing document or no system of management might
benefit from having available a statutory scheme which would elimi-
nate the uncertainties of the common law. These matters were dealt with
in the Commission's report on the Law of the Tenement.[37] In connection
with this the Scottish Executive also published a consultation document
in March 2003. The Tenements (Scotland) Bill was introduced to the
Scottish Parliament in January 2004. It is expected to come into force as
an Act on November 28, 2004.

SERVITUDES

During its deliberations on title conditions the Scottish Law   **1–16**
Commission addressed another type of burden namely a negative servitude. Such a servitude achieves exactly the same result as a real
burden or condition by prohibiting a certain activity on the burdened
land. A prohibition of building or building[38] beyond a certain height[39]
could be the subject of both a real burden and a negative servitude.
Negative servitudes are abolished in the Title Conditions (Scotland) Act
2003 but are effectively converted to real burdens.[40]

LAND USE

The Scottish Executive have also looked at the more sensitive issue of   **1–17**
the use of land and in particular access to the countryside. The Land
Reform (Scotland) Act 2003 received Royal Assent on February 25, 2003.
This Act deals with three main things: access of the countryside, the

---

[37] Scot Law Com. No. 162 (1998).
[38] A servitude *non aedificandi.*
[39] A servitude *altius non tollendi.*
[40] 2003 Act, ss.79, 80.

ability of rural communities to buy land, and the ability of crofters to buy their crofts. Unfortunately land use issues have often been confused with land tenure issues in the past with every alleged abuse of ownership by landowners being blamed on the feudal system.[41]

---

[41] For a general introduction to the Land Reform Act 2003 see Ch.15 below.

CHAPTER 2

ABOLITION OF THE FEUDAL STRUCTURE

INTRODUCTION

The Abolition of Feudal Tenure etc. (Scotland) Act 2000 received Royal **2–01** Assent on June 9, 2000. The preamble states that the purpose of the Act is to abolish the feudal system of land tenure and a related system of land tenure and to make new provision as respects the ownership of land. Some provisions of the Act came into force on Royal Assent mainly to prevent superiors taking the opportunity to exact the maximum commercial benefit from their feudal estates prior to abolition. Similarly other anti-avoidance provisions also came into effect on Royal Assent. The most important of these is the prohibition of the creation of leases for any type of property in excess of 175 years.[1] The superior's right of irritancy was also swept away on Royal Assent.[2] The completely unconnected reform of the rules relating to descriptions and standard securities laid down in the Beneficial Bank cases[3] also came into effect on June 9, 2000.[4] A description in a standard security need only identify the subject although the description must meet the requirements of the Keeper. The remaining provisions relating to the abolition of feudal tenure as such do not come into effect until the appointed day.[5] In terms of the legislation the superior can preserve certain rights to enforce burdens even though the superiority title has gone. Some of these burdens will remain as real burdens attached to other land owned by the superior.[6] Other burdens which relate to a common facility or service used by a number of owners will remain but instead of being enforceable by a superior will be enforceable by all the owners using the facility.[7] The 2000 Act, as amended by the 2003 Act also allows the superior to retain burdens on a personal basis without the need to attach the right to enforce to other land. The concept of a personal real burden is rather difficult to understand and there is an argument for saying that a personal right should have no place in a system of land tenure. These burdens however might be said to have a commercial or community benefit and for this reason the view is taken that it would be unfair to deprive the superior of their benefit. The burdens are of course real in relation to the burdened land

---

[1] 2000 Act, s.67.
[2] 2000 Act, s.53.
[3] *Bennett v Beneficial Bank plc*, 1995 S.L.T. 1105; *Beneficial Bank plc v McConnachie*, 1996 S.C. 119; *Beneficial Bank plc v Wardle*, 1996 G.W.D. 30–1825.
[4] 2000 Act, Sch.12, para.30(23)(a).
[5] November 28, 2004.
[6] see Ch. 3 below and 2000 Act, ss.18–22.
[7] 2000 Act, s.23; re-enacted with amendments in the 2003 Act, s.56.

and if the personal real burden is negative it can have the appearance of a real right. In many cases the type of superior entitled to enforce this type of burden will be a recognised body such as a conservation body or a local or health authority and the burden will be peculiar to the function of that body as opposed to its ownership of any particular land. The personal real burden known as a conservation burden was introduced by the 2000 Act.[8] The other personal real burdens were introduced by the 2003 Act as burdens capable of creation after abolition but some of these have also been introduced into the 2000 Act as burdens which an appropriate superior may be able to preserve independently of the ownership of land. The new personal burdens which may be preserved by a superior are personal pre-emption burdens, personal redemption burdens, economic development burdens and healthcare burdens. The other personal real burdens which can be created after abolition are rural housing burdens and manager burdens. A rural housing burden will effectively be a pre-emption in favour of a rural housing body. Maritime burdens are in a rather odd situation. They could be regarded as personal real burdens. The 2000 Act preserves the right of the Crown to maritime burdens.[9] The Crown will retain the right to enforce these burdens albeit the Crown has no interest in any superiority or other land in the vicinity. However this right is reserved only to the Crown and cannot be assigned. The 2003 Act makes it clear that after abolition the Crown can create a real burden over the seabed or foreshore in favour of the Crown for the benefit of the public despite the fact that the Crown may not necessarily nominate any other benefited property as the land which is to have the right to enforce the notion that the burden must be for the benefit of the public suggests that the burden might be in respect of recreational rights.[10] Again however this burden can only be enforced by the Crown and cannot be assigned. Although the burden is for the benefit of the public the rights of the Crown appear to be exclusive.[11]

THE DEMISE OF THE FEUDAL SYSTEM

2–02   Section 1 of the 2000 Act states quite simply and somewhat dramatically that the feudal system, that is to say the entire system whereby land is held by a vassal on perpetual tenure from a superior is, on the appointed day, abolished. On a first reading it is a little unnerving to think that a system of land tenure which has been in operation for almost 900 years can be swept away in three lines of print. Perhaps this is because as a lawyer the author is not used to a statutory provision which takes the form of a blinding flash. One almost has a vision of a still photograph of hundreds or thousands of superiors, over-superiors and mid-superiors looking up in the direction of an approaching thunderbolt. Nevertheless it is refreshing to see a statute which opens with a simple but all embracing statement of what the Scottish Parliament is about to do. What the opening section makes clear is that the land tenure system whereby one party holds land of a superior on perpetual tenure ceases to exist. The

---

[8] ss.26–32.
[9] 2000 Act, s.60.
[10] See *Hope v Bennewith* (1904) 6 F. 1004.
[11] 2003 Act, s.44.

feudal system was essentially a contract between superior and vassal which was renewable by tenure each time the superiority or *dominium utile* titles were transferred eventually without the need for any consent from either superior or vassal.

OWNERSHIP AFTER ABOLITION

The Act goes on to provide[12] that on abolition an estate of *dominium utile* **2–03** of land shall cease to exist as a feudal estate. It will be transformed into ownership of the land subject to any subordinate real rights and other encumbrances which already affected the original estate of *dominium utile*. Accordingly existing standard securities and charges will continue as encumbrances on the newly created ownership. It is interesting to note that the framers of the legislation shied away from using emotive terms such as simple ownership or absolute ownership. The reason for this is obvious; ownership or more appropriately, the rights which flow from ownership, are not and never have been simple far less absolute. There are many restrictions both at common law and under statute which apply to owners in relation to their use of the land. To have used a phrase like "absolute ownership" might also have suggested that a party owning land need have no regard to his or her neighbours or the community at large. When the Justice Committee of the Scottish Executive took evidence from interested parties in relation to the provisions of the 2000 Act the fear was expressed by some groups that the removal of feudal fetters from the land tenure system would encourage land owners to pursue their own selfish interests more aggressively. One proposal which was put forward was that the paramount superiority of the Crown or Prince and Steward of Scotland should be retained presumably on the view that the Crown or Prince and Steward could in some way represent the public interest. The role of the Crown or Prince and Steward has never been a public interest role. The function has been exercised by the Crown Estate Commissioners on a quasi commercial basis. The Act makes it clear that every part of the feudal structure is to be dismantled apart from the original *dominium utile*. This means that all superiorities whether immediate, mid or over superiorities go[13] leaving only one estate of ownership. Even the paramount superiority of the Crown and Prince and Steward of Scotland goes.[14] After abolition it will not be possible to create a new feudal estate. Feudal deeds will be invalid.[15] The Act does not make it clear whether a conveyance of land by the owner of that land which takes the form of a feudal deed, presumably by disponing in feu farm with a *tenendas* clause, will be completely inept or whether it will simply be treated as an ordinary disposition transferring ownership without the creation of any feudal link. However the Land Registration (Scotland) Act 1979 is amended to take account of feudal abolition. That Act will, after abolition, provide that the Keeper of the Registers of Scotland shall not accept an application for registration if it relates in whole or in part to an interest in land

---

[12] 2000 Act, s.2(1).
[13] 2000 Act, s.2(2).
[14] 2000 Act, s.58.
[15] 2000 Act, s.2(3).

which has ceased to exist by reason of feudal abolition.[16] This suggests therefore that a feudal deed will be a complete nullity. In any event the Keeper will not be able to accept it for registration purposes and presumably will not be able to accept it as a link in title in any other application. Section 9 of the Land Registration (Scotland) Act 1979 which deals with rectification of the Land Register is also amended to the effect that the Keeper will be allowed to rectify to take account of anything done or purportedly done by virtue of the 2000 Act.[17] This will apply even though rectification might affect a proprietor in possession. This provision is strongly suggestive of the notion that any hint that a deed is a feudal deed will have serious consequences even though the grantee may have taken possession. Similarly the Keeper will not be required to pay indemnity in respect of any rectification which arises as a result of feudal abolition.[18] The Keeper will accordingly be able to delete superiority titles from the Land Register entirely although he may have to split off titles to minerals where these minerals have been reserved to the superior. Minerals run in a separate title and are not simply a pertinent of the superiority when to reserved the superior. Essentially a reservation of minerals to a superior created a separate *dominium utile* title to the minerals.[19] There may also be occasions where small strips of ground remain unfeued and the Keeper may have practical difficulties.

THE RIGHTS OF THE CROWN

2–04   During the law reform process a question arose as to whether or not it would be appropriate to retain the paramount superiority of the Crown and the Prince and Steward of Scotland. Although the feudal system withered on the vine in England and Wales a freehold title there is technically still held subject to a paramount superiority of the Crown. The view which was ultimately taken in relation to the feudal system in Scotland was that it would be inappropriate to retain any form of superiority, even the paramount superiority. If the Crown rights were preserved as a property law matter then the statement in the opening section of the abolition legislation would hardly have been accurate because the feudal system would still have existed albeit with a single paramount superior. Moreover it might have been necessary to define the role of the Crown as paramount superior and it has sometimes been difficult to separate the rights of the Crown as a matter of prerogative from the rights of the Crown as paramount feudal superior. On one view it would simply have been a matter of style and tradition but on another view the Crown might have been regarded as representing some form of general or public interest in all the land no matter who owned it. That appeared to be the view of those interest groups who wished to retain the paramount superiority of the Crown as a check on unfettered or absolute ownership by individuals. Accordingly the

---

[16] 2000 Act, s.3(a) inserting a new paragraph into s.4 (2) of the Land Registration (Scotland) Act 1979.

[17] 2000 Act s.3(b) amending s.9 of the Land Registration (Scotland) Act 1979.

[18] 2000 Act s.3(c) amending s.12(3) of the Land Registration (Scotland) Act 1979.

[19] see Rennie, *Minerals and the Law of Scotland*, para.1.8.

legislation provides[20] that the Act binds the Crown and more specifically that the provisions made for the abolition of the entire feudal
structure[21] will apply to the superiority of the Prince and Steward of
Scotland and to the ultimate superiority of the Crown. Accordingly as
a property law matter neither the Crown nor the Prince and Steward of
Scotland will have any tenure or ownership rights apart from rights of
ordinary ownership of land in the Crown estates. This is without prejudice to any other matter arising out of the Royal prerogative. The
Crown prerogative includes the prerogative of honour and the prerogative in unclaimed property and the *regalia majora*.[22] Where a limited
company is dissolved and struck off the register still owning property
that property falls to the Crown but it does not fall to the Crown by
virtue of the paramount superiority; rather it falls to the Crown because
it has become ownerless or at least may be treated as abandoned. The
maxim is *quod nullius est fit domini Regis* (ownerless property becomes
the property of our lord the King).[23] Prior to feudal abolition the Crown
would normally have disposed of land by way of a Crown Charter. The
abolition legislation now provides[24] that after abolition it shall be competent for the Crown in selling or disposing of land to do so by granting a disposition. On the grant of that disposition the Crown will be
divested of all property rights, title and interest in the land disponed.
The provisions relating to the abolition of feuduties[25] will apply to any
feuduties which are due to the Crown. However royalty payments in
respect of mineral workings which belong to the Crown[26] calculated as
a proportion of the produce will not be deemed to be a payment to the
Crown which is extinguished with feuduty or in terms of provisions
relating to the extinction of superior's rights and payments analogous
to feuduty.[27] The property rights of the Crown in relation to the foreshore and seabed are not directly affected by the abolition legislation.[28]
Nevertheless there are cases where the Crown has feued portions of the
foreshore or seabed in circumstances where it may not be in a position
to take advantage of the re-allotment provisions[29] because the Crown
does not actually own surrounding land. These title conditions would
of course have been enforceable by virtue of the Crown's paramount
superiority title. Special provision is made for this type of situation and
after abolition burdens of this nature will be known as maritime
burdens. In terms of the legislation[30] where before abolition the Crown
has enjoyed a right as superior to enforce a real burden against part of
the seabed or part of the foreshore then after abolition the Crown will
have both title and a presumed interest to enforce the burden subject to
any counter obligation the Crown may have undertaken. Effectively a
maritime burden will become a personal real burden enforceable by the

---

[20] 2000 Act, s.58.
[21] 2000 Act, s.2.
[22] 2000 Act, s.58(2).
[23] see Gordon, *Scottish Land Law* (2nd ed.) 13–26; Companies Act 1985, s.654.
[24] 2000 Act, s.59.
[25] 2000 Act, Part 3, ss.7–16 and see Ch. 4 below.
[26] By virtue of the Royal Mines Act 1424.
[27] 2000 Act, ss.54, 56.
[28] The Scottish Law Commission have published a report entitled *The Law Relating to the Foreshore and Seabed*, Scot Law Com. No.190 (2003).
[29] 2000 Act, ss.18–22.
[30] 2000 Act, s.60.

Crown but only by the Crown. The legislation makes it clear[31] that the Crown cannot assign the right to enforce this personal real burden. It should be noted that a maritime burden created in favour of the Crown as superior need not be for the benefit of the public. For the purposes of this provision "seabed" means the bed of the territorial sea adjacent to Scotland and "territorial sea" includes any tidal waters.[32] The provision in relation to maritime burdens only applies where these burdens were feudal real burdens as defined in part 4 of the 2000 Act. Such burdens do not require to relate to the seabed or maritime matters. They would include rights of pre-emption, redemption and rights (other than exclusive rights) of fishing or game but do not include pecuniary real burdens.[33]

BARONIES AND NOBLE TITLES

2–05   Barony titles are different from peerages. They are noble titles or dignities which attach to a title to the barony lands. Originally baronies were estates brought together and erected into a barony by the Crown. The owner of the land was entitled to the dignity of baron and there are different degrees of barony titles from earldoms to lordships. There were also certain jurisdictional rights to enforce civil and criminal law within the barony. Regalities had more extensive jurisdiction over all the baronies within the regality lands. Over time many of these baronies have been sub-divided by the grant of feus or dispositions but the dignity of baron remains with the *caput* or principal *messuage* of the barony.[34] When the title to the barony remained in the Sasine Register it was relatively easy to sell the barony title with the noble title. All that happened was that a disposition of the whole estate as originally described under exception of all the properties which had been conveyed away but including the superiority titles was granted to the purchaser with the benefit of the dignity. In many cases it would have been almost impossible to identify with absolute certainty the original *caput* of the barony or whether it remained as part of the rump of the barony land still able to be conveyed or whether it had been conveyed away with one of the exceptions. Since the Register of Sasines is simply a record of deeds which have been recorded with no guarantee of validity there was never any difficulty when deeds purporting to transfer a barony with the noble title were presented. Difficulties have arisen however where the land in which the barony is situated falls within an operational area for land registration purposes. It is the author's understanding that the Keeper has so far refused to issue any title sheet or land certificate in respect of a barony title with full indemnity as regards the dignity or noble title. An inordinate amount of time would have had to be spent by the Keeper analysing various exceptions and feus and other historical documents before he could say with any certainty that the noble title remained with the rump of the estate or indeed that it had been conveyed away with one part of the origi-

---

[31] 2000 Act, s.60(2).
[32] 2000 Act, s.60(3).
[33] 2000 Act, s.49.
[34] See *Spencer-Thomas of Bulquhollie v Newell*, 1992 S.L.T. 973.

nal barony lands. Noble titles are still much sought after not only by resident Scots who may feel they have some connection with a particular area but also by others including those in former British colonies who have Scottish ancestry. Substantial sums of money have changed hands for the more exclusive titles. When the legislation for feudal abolition was being considered some thought was given to whether or not baronial or other noble titles attached to land ownership should remain in a system of non-feudal land tenure. Baronial jurisdictions were very much tied to feudal notions of fealty and as such it would perhaps have been logical to abolish them on the appointed day. Nevertheless it was recognised that from a commercial point of view certain persons had paid a substantial sum of money to obtain such a title. The legislation adopts a compromise position.[35] It is provided that any jurisdiction and any conveyancing privilege incidental to a barony shall cease to exist on feudal abolition. However nothing is to affect the dignity of baron or any other dignity or office whether or not that dignity is of feudal origin. The dignity however will no longer attach to any land but will be treated as an incorporeal heritable right which presumably will be capable of assignation. Before abolition it was always necessary to own land to which the noble title was attached. It was a fundamental principle of the law relating to baronies that title to the land and the noble title itself were inseparable. After abolition the heritable title to the barony will cease to exist as a feudal estate and the separated dignity of baron which becomes an incorporeal heritable right will not be a heritable interest which can be registered in the Land Register nor will it be a right in respect of which a deed can be recorded in the Sasine Register.[36] This creates something of a difficulty for practitioners who regularly deal with barony titles in that there will be no public register of these titles after abolition. Obviously there will be nothing to stop an unscrupulous person selling a barony two or three times over and granting several assignations to different people resident in the four corners of the globe. Presumably the earliest assignation would prevail and the rule against offside goals would apply. At one point it was suggested that an informal register might be set up on a private basis which would allow for some sort of check to be made. As at the date of publication of this work no such register has been established. It is not thought likely or indeed appropriate that the Lyon Court set up a register. Presumably any informal register could only be a register of claims to baronies as opposed to a register with some sort of guarantee of title. In some cases the barony title will be burdened with a heritable security. The security would of course have affected not just the land but the noble title prior to the separation of the two on abolition. The Act provides[37] that where such a security exists over an estate to which is attached a barony, the security shall affect both the dignity and the land where the noble title is attached to a *dominium utile* estate. Where the noble title is attached to a superiority alone then the security is stated to attach to the dignity of Baron alone. This rather odd provision is necessary because the superiority title will have vanished on the appointed day. It is not clear to the author just what sort of security this will be but taking the view that the

---

[35] 2000 Act, s.63.
[36] 2000 Act, s.63(2).
[37] 2000 Act, s.63(3).

separated dignity of Baron is an incorporeal heritable right presumably the security is a heritable security. There is nothing however in the Act to suggest that after separation of the titles it will be possible to grant a standard security over the dignity itself. Plainly such a security (if in the form of a standard security) could not be registered in the Land Register or recorded in the Sasine Register because the title to the dignity cannot be so registered or recorded. It may be possible however to grant an assignation in security of the incorporeal heritable right applicable to the dignity.

Jurisdiction of the Lord Lyon

2–06　　The Lord Lyon, King of Arms, deals with matters heraldic at the Lyon Court. The Act makes it clear[38] that the provisions relate only to matters of land tenure and not to matters heraldic. The abolition of the superior's status has nothing to do with peerages or other matters relating to arms. The Lord Lyon may have some difficulty with baronies in that he will not be able to rely on the Land Register or Sasine Register as a check on entitlement to the noble title. Presumably other evidence of entitlement could be considered.

Non-feudal titles

2–07　　Various odd forms of tenure did exist alongside the feudal system.[39] One of these odd forms of tenure was vest in the King's Kindly Tenants of Lochmaben. The author has never met one and even in 1956 they appear to have been a scarce commodity. In the case of *Royal Four Towns Fishing Association v Assessor for Dumfriesshire*,[40] Lord Patrick observed[41]:

> "No good purpose would be served by considering in detail the origin and history of the King's Kindly Tenants of the four towns of Lochmaben. Much uncertainty surrounds these subjects and they have become matters of interest only to the historian and the antiquarian."

Effectively the tenants held land on a perpetual lease from the Crown without the need for any infeftment. Professor Halliday described this type of tenure as neither feudal nor allodial but nevertheless giving a right which amounted to ownership.[42] Professor Gordon on the other hand took the view that these were customary rights of a leasehold nature which resembled feudal tenure only because the tenant was a leaseholder of the Crown.[43] The tenancy was only evidenced in the rental book of the Crown Steward the Earl of Mansfield. On the

---

[38] 2000 Act, s.62.
[39] see O'Donnell and Rennie, "Non-Feudal Land Holdings in Scotland", 1998 S.L.P.Q. 31.
[40] 1956 S.C. 379.
[41] at 385.
[42] Halliday, *Conveyancing Law and Practice* (2nd ed.) para.31–17.
[43] Gordon, *Scottish Land Law* (2nd ed.) para.19–15; see also *Marquis of Queensbury v Wright* (1838) 16 S. 439 at 444.

appointed day this unusual form of tenure will be abolished[44] and converted into ownership along with any rights to salmon fishings which cannot be severed from the tenancy. The new right of ownership will be subject to the same subordinate real rights and other encumbrances as was the kindly tenancy.[45] Where the right of salmon fishing is inseverable from the kindly tenancy it shall remain inseverable from the new ownership of the land in question.[46] Allodial tenure such as udal tenure is not affected by the 2000 Act. Since all of Scotland is now an operational area for land registration purposes such tenure will on registration effectively be treated as ordinary ownership. True udal land held with no written title is rare in any event.

ENTAILS

There is still some land which is subject to an entail. An entail is not strictly a matter of feudal tenure but the 2000 Act makes provision for disentailment on the appointed day when abolition of the feudal system takes effect.[47] Entails are not abolished as such but on the appointed day they are treated as being disentailed. Section 32 of the Entail Amendment Act 1848 which provides for instruments of disentail to be executed and recorded applies to the statutory disentailment in the same way as it would have applied to an executed and recorded instrument of disentail.[48] In some cases the consent of an apparent or nearest heir of entail would have been required to any petition for authority to execute an instrument of disentail. The Act of 2000 provides that where such a consent would have been required the valuation of any expectancy or interest which, on a refusal to give consent prior to abolition, would have required to be valued in terms of section 13 of the Entail (Scotland) Act 1882 may be referred by that apparent or nearest heir to the Lands Tribunal for determination.[49] When the tribunal fixes a value then it must direct that any sum ascertained by it shall be secured on the land for the benefit of that person in such manner as the tribunal thinks fit.[50] Immediately before the appointed day the Keeper of the Registers of Scotland must close the Register of Entails and as soon as practicable thereafter transmit that register to the Keeper of the Records of Scotland simply for preservation.[51]

2–08

FEUDAL IRRITANCIES

Prior to abolition the main remedy or, in commercial parlance, bargaining tool of the superior was irritancy. If there was a breach of a feudal condition and the vassal was not prepared to pay the sum demanded by the superior for a waiver or consent the superior could threaten to bring an action of irritancy if there was an irritancy clause in the feudal grant.

2–09

---

[44] 2000 Act, s.64(1).
[45] 2000 Act, s.64(2).
[46] 2000 Act, s.64(3).
[47] 2000 Act, s.50.
[48] 2000 Act, s.50(2).
[49] 2000 Act, s.51(1).
[50] 2000 Act, s.51(2); see Gordon, *Scottish Land Law* (2nd ed.) para.18–54.
[51] 2000 Act, s.52.

Effectively this could result in forfeiture of the *dominium utile* title without any compensation in respect of the land, buildings thereon or any heritable security over the land. Feudal irritancies were abolished on June 9, 2000 when the abolition legislation received Royal Assent.[52] Such irritancies had to be abolished in advance of abolition of the feudal system because of the fear that superiors might attempt to enforce real burdens by means of irritancy in the run up to abolition on the appointed day. The abolition of the superior's right to irritancy applies to any proceedings already commenced prior to Royal Assent unless final decree has been obtained prior to that date. Final decree however is defined as a decree or interlocutor not subject to appeal or review. Presumably, therefore, a vassal, facing a decree by a Sheriff granted in May 2000 will have taken the opportunity to lodge an appeal so as to ensure that any appeal of further procedure took the matter beyond the date of Royal Assent.

EXTINCTION OF SUPERIOR'S ANCILLARY RIGHTS

2–10 Any ancillary rights which a superior may have and indeed any obligations which a superior may owe simply by virtue of the estate of superiority are extinguished on feudal abolition taking effect.[53] Any proceedings which have already been commenced prior to the abolition date are deemed to have been abandoned and decrees or interlocutors already pronounced are deemed to have been reduced or recalled with the exception of the superior's right of irritancy (which is dealt with in another section)[54] and the right to recover damages or the payment of money.

ANTI-AVOIDANCE PROVISIONS

2–11 The prohibition of subinfeudation in England and Wales merely resulted in the proliferation of leasehold tenure. Abolition of the feudal system in Scotland could have had the same result with the added problem of the imposition of ground rents. No lease could have been granted in respect of a dwellinghouse for a period in excess of 20 years[55] but commercial properties could be leased for any length of time. The 2000 Act contains a prohibition of the granting of leases for a period of more than 175 years.[56] This prohibition applies to leases of all subjects, residential or commercial. This provision came into effect on Royal Assent. The prohibition applies not only to a lease for a period of more than 175 years but also to a lease for a lesser term which requires the landlord to renew for a period which would take the total duration of the lease to a period in excess of 175 years.[57] For the purposes of the statutory prohibition subleases are included in the definition.[58] The prohibition only applies to leases entered into after the date of Royal Assent although where a lease

---

[52] 2000 Act, s.53.
[53] 2000 Act, s.54.
[54] See para.2–09 above and 2000 Act, s.53.
[55] Land Tenure Reform (Scotland) Act 1974, s.8.
[56] 2000 Act, s.67.
[57] 2000 Act, s.67(2).
[58] 2000 Act, s.67(5).

in excess of 175 years has been granted prior to Royal Assent it will remain possible to grant a sub-lease for the whole or any part of the land leased for the remainder of the term notwithstanding that may exceed the period of 175 years.[59] The prohibition however does not affect the renewal of a lease by tacit relocation or the extension of a lease by virtue of any other enactment such as the Tenancy of Shops (Scotland) Act 1949.[60] It should be noted that no such prohibition applies in England and Wales and there have been suggestions that commercial investment in Scotland may be adversely affected by this restriction. It is of course difficult to fix on any particular period in such a situation.

TRANSFER OF LAND AFTER ABOLITION

After abolition land will be transferred by ordinary disposition. In-   **2–12**
terestingly enough it is provided that ownership passes, in the case of a transfer which is registerable under section 2 of the Land Registration (Scotland) Act 1979, on registration in the Land Register.[61] In other cases where the conveyance is to be recorded in the Register of Sasines ownership passes on recording in that register.[62] It is made clear that even in land registration cases an actual conveyance or a notice of title must be registered.[63] These provisions are however without prejudice to any other enactment or rule of law by or under which ownership of land may pass.[64] The principle of ownership by registration has been reaffirmed in the Inner House of the Court of Session and in the House of Lords.[65] The decision of the House of Lords in *Sharp v Thomson*[66] is largely an interpretation of company insolvency legislation and is not regarded as one relating primarily to property law. The House of Lords has upheld the decision of the Court of Session in *Burnett's Tr. v Grainger.*[67] The House of Lords has not driven a coach and horses through Scottish property law by providing that ownership, or a beneficial interest in land, will always pass on delivery of a disposition. The special proviso in section 4, however is, in the view of the author, directed to the special rules in enactments whereby land can pass from one body to a successor body or from one party holding an office, such as the president or secretary of a club, to another party holding the same office without the need for any conveyance or deduction of title.[68] It will also apply to special destinations. Where deeds still require to be recorded in the Register of Sasines after the appointed day it shall no longer be necessary for there to be a registration warrant.[69] Scottish

---

[59] 2000 Act, s.67(4).
[60] 2000 Act, s.67(3).
[61] 2000 Act, s.4(1)(a).
[62] 2000 Act, s.4 (1)(b).
[63] 2000 Act, s.4(3)(a).
[64] 2000 Act, s.4(2).
[65] *Sharp v Thomson*, 1995 S.L.T. 837; *Burnett's Tr. v Grainger*, 2002 S.L.T. 699; 2004 S.L.T. 513.
[66] 1997 S.L.T. 636.
[67] 2002 S.L.T. 699; 2004 S.L.T. 513.
[68] The automatic vesting provisions for *ex officio* trustees are contained in the Titles to Land Consolidation (Scotland) Act 1868, s.26 and the Conveyancing (Scotland) Act 1974, s.45.
[69] 2000 Act, s.5(1).

Ministers may, after consultation with the Lord President of the Court of Session, make rules prescribing any form to be used for an application to record a deed in the Sasine Register and to regulate procedure relating to these applications.[70] Where a title is registered in the Land Register a clause of deduction of title is not required where a succeeding disposition is being granted by someone in a representative capacity such as a executor or trustee or a statutory successor of a public body. All that need be produced to the Keeper is the original land certificate and any links such as confirmation or a statutory instrument relating to vesting. Where the title is to be recorded in the Register of Sasines a deduction of title is still required. There are however some titles (mainly in favour of ancient universities) which are neither registered in the Land Register nor the recorded in the Sasine Register. These titles are generally in the form of Crown Charters which pre-date the Registration Act of 1617. The 2000 Act makes it clear that a clause of deduction of title will be competent in a deed granted by a party or body who holds such an unregistered or unrecorded title.[71]

---

[70] 2000 Act, s.5(2).
[71] 2000 Act, s.6.

CHAPTER 3

FEUDAL REAL BURDENS—EXTINCTION AND REALLOTMENT—COMPENSATION

INTRODUCTION

Following on the prohibition of the imposition of new feu duties in 1974[1] the main criticism of the feudal system related to the enforcement of real burdens and conditions by feudal superiors in an inappropriate manner. It was however not so much a question of enforcement as a question of a demand for a sum of money in return for a waiver or a consent by the superior. The view which was taken of the feudal system was that it was anachronistic to have a system of land tenure whereby someone who did not own the land, in the layman's sense of the word, could still regulate its use by virtue of some ethereal title known as a superiority. Accordingly the abolition of the feudal structure had to go hand in hand with the abolition of the superior's right to enforce real burdens or conditions laid down in the original feudal grant. This of course is logical because it has always been the law that a person (be that a superior or another proprietor) who wishes to enforce a real burden must have a title to enforce as well as an interest. If the feudal structure is removed then the superiority title ceases to exist and logically therefore the former superior would cease to have such a title. The 2000 Act makes it clear that the superior will, subject to certain exceptions, no longer be able to enforce real burdens as a superior.[2] However it was recognised that there could be situations where a party had been advised to feu land rather than dispone it because a feudal conveyance would be the best method of protecting other land which that party had retained. Perhaps the best example of this is the situation where a party (say a widow) has a large house and a large garden and with advancing years is unable to cope with the garden. In 1985 that party might have been advised, quite properly, to feu off the lower part of the garden as a building plot subject to stringent real burdens in relation to the number of dwellinghouses, height of dwellinghouse, use, erection and maintenance of boundary walls and others. In this context where the parties are to be neighbours it does make sense to allow burdens of this type to remain enforceable. However because these burdens are enforceable by the widow because she holds a superiority title over the ground feued as opposed holding an ownership title of her own adjoining ground, on abolition of the feudal system taking effect she would lose all enforcement rights. Accordingly there are provisions which allow a superior to reallot the right to enforce real burdens from the original superiority

3–01

---

[1] Land Tenure Reform (Scotland) Act 1974, s.1.
[2] 2000 Act, s.17.

title which will vanish on November 28, 2004 to an ordinary *dominium utile* or ownership title which that superior may own.[3] The superior must own the land nominated for reallotment purposes as sole owner and title to both the superiority and the nominated land must be in exactly the same name or names and be held in the same capacity.

EXTINCTION OF SUPERIOR'S RIGHT TO ENFORCE

3–02   It should be borne in mind that the 2000 Act deals with feudal burdens only and the superior's right to enforce these. The 2003 Act deals with real burdens after abolition of the feudal system. Burdens which are purely feudal in the sense of being enforceable only by a superior will be extinguished on the appointed day (November 28, 2004).[4] In some ways one might regard this provision as unnecessary given the fact that section 1 of the 2000 Act abolishes the feudal structure. Nevertheless it is, in the author's view, important to emphasise this fundamental point in a specific provision. The abolition of the superior's right to enforce is however subject to the reallotment provisions,[5] any express agreement to preserve burdens entered into with the vassal,[6] reallotment by order of the Lands Tribunal[7] and the preservation of facility and service burdens.[8] Extinction will not affect other existing feudal burdens which are converted into personal real burdens such as a conservation burden,[9] a personal pre-emption or redemption burden,[10] an economic development burden[11] or healthcare burden.[12] There are similar provisions which allow a superior to preserve existing sporting rights over a feudal estate of *dominium utile*.[13] The statutory provision however only affects burdens which are enforceable by a superior. In some cases feudal burdens are enforceable not just by the superior but also by co-feuars by virtue of *ius quaesitum tertio*. In such a case although the superior will lose the right to enforce the third party will not.[14] The law of a *ius quaesitum tertio* is dealt with in the 2003 Act.[15] No proceedings for enforcement of a real burden by a former superior can be commenced after the appointed day[16] and any proceedings already commenced prior to the appointed day shall be deemed to be abandoned without expenses being due.[17] Any decree or interlocutor already pronounced in proceedings for enforcement shall be deemed to have been reduced or recalled on the appointed day.[18] The exceptions to this are in relation to

---

[3] 2000 Act, s.18.
[4] 2000 Act, s.17(1)(a).
[5] 2000 Act, s.18.
[6] 2000 Act, s.19.
[7] 2000 Act, s.20.
[8] 2000 Act, s.23 (re-enacted in the 2003 Act s.56).
[9] 2000 Act, s.28.
[10] 2000 Act, s.18A.
[11] 2000 Act, s.18B.
[12] 2000 Act, s.18C.
[13] 2000 Act, s.65A.
[14] 2000 Act, s.17(1)(b).
[15] 2003 Act, s.49–58.
[16] 2000 Act, s.17(2)(a).
[17] 2000 Act, s.17(2)(b).
[18] 2000 Act, s.17(2)(c).

a right of irritancy already held by a superior and a right to recover damages for payment of money. Irritancies are dealt with separately.[19] This provision extinguishing superiors' enforcement rights is only likely to apply therefore to declaratory actions whereby a vassal is ordained to do something or to interdict where a vassal is restrained from doing something.

REALLOTMENT OF PRAEDIAL REAL BURDENS

Reallotment by nomination

Section 18 of the 2000 Act allows the superior to reallot the right to enforce a feudal real burden to other land or another heritable interest owned by that superior in three situations. Reallotment is effected by the superior executing and registering a notice in a form set out in the Act.[20] The notice must set out the title of the superior and describe sufficiently to enable identification by reference to the ordnance map the land which is burdened and the land which is nominated by the superior as the land which is henceforth to benefit from enforcement rights. Presumably a description by reference to a Sasine title containing a description or a postal address with a registered title number will suffice. If only part of the burdened or benefited land is involved then the part must be adequately described. The notice must also set out the terms of the real burden in question and the terms of any counter obligation imposed on the superior. The burden or burdens should be set out in full or by reference to the deed in which they were created and are set out in full. The notice must also state which of the three heads for reallotment applies.[21] The notice must be registered against both the dominant land (the nominated land for enforcement purposes) and the servient land (the land which is to remain subject to the burden).[22] The 2000 Act uses the terminology appropriate to servitudes namely dominant and servient tenements. The notice must be registered against both tenements and dual registration is a feature of both the 2000 and the 2003 Acts. The reason for this is obvious; part of the problem with real burdens in the past has been the difficulty of ascertaining just who has enforcement rights in any given circumstance. Burdens had to be registered against the burdened or servient property but not in the title of the dominant or benefited property. Before the superior submits any notice for registration that superior must swear or affirm before a Notary Public that to the best of his or her knowledge and belief all the information contained in the notice is true.[23] Where a superior is an individual subject to legal disability or incapacity and cannot therefore swear or affirm then the legal representative of such a superior may swear or affirm. Where the superior is a legal person such as a limited company then any person authorised

3–03

---

[19] 2000 Act, s.53.
[20] 2000 Act, Sch.5; and see Brymer and Wortley, "Preparing Superiors for Feudal Abolition", 2002 Prop. L.B. 60–6 and 2002 Prop. L.B. 61–1; Wortley, "Notices", 2003 S.L.G. 73.
[21] 2000 Act, s.18(2).
[22] 2000 Act, s.18(3).
[23] 2000 Act, s.18(4) "notary public" includes any person authorised to administer oaths in any county (2000 Act, s.49).

to sign documents on behalf of the entity may swear or affirm.[24] It should be noted that the right to reallot does not revive a burden which is unenforceable because it does not comply with the existing rules of constitution of real burdens. The reallotment provisions do not validate burdens nor make them real simply because the statutory procedure of serving and registering a notice has been correctly carried out. The legislation makes it clear that the burden must have been enforceable by the superior immediately before the appointed day although it is not necessary for the superior to have a completed title to the superiority on that day.[25] The term "enforceable" is not defined but it probably means more than not having title to enforce. Interest may have been lost or there may have been acquiescence. If these conditions are all complied with and the case fits one of the three scenarios envisaged then the nominated land becomes the dominant tenement with enforcement rights and the land subject to the burden will become the servient tenement. Effectively what happens is that a feudal burden enforceable by a superior in virtue of the superiority title will become a non-feudal burden enforceable by the former superior by virtue of that party's ownership of the other nominated land or of another heritable interest as the case may be. In addition to the requirement to register the notice it must also be served on the vassal.[26] The whole process of service on the vassal and registration of the notice against both dominant and servient properties must take place between the first appointed day (November 1, 2003) and the appointed day (November 28, 2004). A superior who fails to take advantage of the reallotment provisions for abolition will lose the right to enforce the burdens on the appointed day.[27] This would leave the superior with the faint hope of securing agreement under section 19 or an order under section 20.

The three reallotment scenarios under s.18

3–04   A superior will be able to reallot the right to enforce a real burden to another dominant tenement in three circumstances. The first of these arises where the burden is enforceable by one neighbour against another neighbour. The second is where the burden is a right of preemption or redemption in a feudal writ. The third is where the proposed dominant tenement comprises minerals or salmon fishings or some other incorporeal property and the terms of the burden were created for the benefit of that interest[28].

Adjoining properties—the 100 metre rule

3–05   The right to reallot here is justified by the need to preserve the amenity of adjoining properties. If the land which is to be nominated as the prospective new dominant tenement for enforcement of the real burden has on it a permanent building which is in use wholly or mainly as a place

---

[24] 2000 Act, s.18(5).
[25] 2000 Act, s.18(6).
[26] 2000 Act, s.41; see para.3–26 below.
[27] 2000 Act, s.17(1).
[28] 2000 Act, s.18(7).

of human habitation or resort then reallotment of the right to enforce the burden to that land will be possible. However the building in use as a place of human habitation or resort must at some point be within 100 metres, measuring along a horizontal plane of the land, which is subject to the burden.[29] In the case of flats the 100 metre radius may run vertically, up or down. The most obvious example of reallotment under this is the example of the widow who feus out the lower part of a garden for the erection of a single dwellinghouse. In such a situation it is reasonable that the widow should be entitled to protect the amenity of her retained property. In any event the only reason that the widow would not have been entitled to enforce the conditions would have been because she opted to feu the lower part of the garden rather than dispone it. The real burdens would have been enforceable even after feudal abolition if they had been contained in a disposition which had been properly framed with the retained land having enforcement rights as opposed to a superiority title. The 100 metre measurement is taken on a horizontal plane. That is to say it takes no account of dips or inclines such as valleys, hills, beds of streams, etc. even although the distance on foot or by vehicle taking into account these contours may be more than 100 metres.

Human habitation or resort

Although this provision is more likely to benefit superiors who have retained land with a house the provision would apply not just to retained residential properties but to commercial properties provided the building thereon could be said to be a place of human habitation or resort. Hotels, shops, factories, schools, universities, hospitals, cinemas, theatres and sports grounds are all places of human resort although they may not all be places of human habitation. Indeed it is almost difficult to think of a building which could not be said to be one to which humanity resorted. A graveyard springs to mind but live human beings resort to graveyards with a view to burying dead ones. What must be remembered however is that it is the building which is crucial. If a land owner owns thousands of acres and has feued a lodge house with grounds which adjoin the estate that superior will not be able to reallot a right to enforce the burdens under section 18 in the feu of the lodge house to the remainder of the estate unless there is a building for human habitation or resort on the estate within a 100 metres of the boundary. There may well be a large residence or manor house half a mile away but that will not permit reallotment. There were fairly cogent arguments put forward for land owners that different rules should apply in rural areas as the bill went through the Scottish Parliament but these were rejected. It should also be borne in mind that the words "wholly or mainly" qualify the requirement that the building is a place of human habitation or resort. There may be arguments here in relation to structures which are used mainly for the shelter of animals. It may well be that a farmer or some other agricultural worker will visit these structures from time to time to tend the animals. That would not however, in the opinion of the author, mean that these buildings were wholly or mainly places of

3–06

---

[29] 2000 Act, s.18(7)(a).

human habitation or resort. On the other hand a building or a complex of buildings comprising a fish farm to which the public had access might well qualify as would hotels, shops, factories, schools, universities, hospitals, cinemas, theatres, sports grounds, bus stations, railway stations and airports. Similarly although a temporary shelter for horses would not qualify a complex of buildings to which the public had access for riding lessons might well qualify. The term "building" is not defined in the 2000 Act. The term necessarily implies some form of structure or shelter. It would not, for example, include something like a wall or a fence.[30] The term would require to be construed bearing in mind the qualification that it must be a place of human habitation or resort. Presumably therefore it could not just be any pile masonry or brick.[31] It should of course be borne in mind that the term "building" always has to be construed with reference to its statutory context. The statutory provision refers not just to a building but to a permanent building. A tent or a towing caravan would no doubt be a place of human habitation or resort but it would not be a permanent building. Presumably it would not matter that the building was destroyed after the reallotment procedure had been completed or after the appointed day (November 28, 2004). The critical time is the date of registration of the notice. Notice must be served on the owner of the burdened or servient property.

Rights to enter and make use of property

3–07   A real burden may consist of a right in favour of the superior to make a certain use of property or take access to it. In certain circumstances although this right is reserved in a feudal deed to the superiority the use made of the burdened land by the superior will relate to other lands actually owned by the superior. Obvious burdens of this type would be rights of access which may of course be servitudes as well. In such a case the superior can reallot the right to enforce the burden from the superiority title to the title of other land owned by the superior. It should be noted that there is no requirement other than that the superior own the nominated land in his or her sole name as owner. In particular there is no requirement that the nominated land be within a certain distance from the land which is subject to the right preserved although in practical terms the two properties are bound to be close in such cases. There is no requirement that the nominated land has on it any building.[32] Notice must be served on the owner of the burdened or servient property.

---

[30] *Inglis v Blow*, 1959 S.L.T. (Sh. Ct.) 52.

[31] For examples of courts construing the term "building" see *Haig v Henderson* (1830) 8 S.912; *Partick Police Commissioners v Great Western Steam Laundry* (1886) 13 R. 500; *Duncan v Jackson* (1905) 8 S.323; *McCallum v Butters Brothers & Co. Ltd*, 1954 S.L.T. (Notes) 45; *Campbell v Invernairn's Trs*, 1955 S.L.T. (Sh. Ct.) 69; *Inglis v Blow*, 1959 S.L.T. (Sh. Ct.) 52; *Scottish Tar Distillers Ltd v Assessor for Stirlingshire*, 1960 S.L.T. 354; *University Court of University of Edinburgh v City of Edinburgh City Council*, 1987 S.L.T. (Sh. Ct.) 103; *Shipman v Lothian Regional Council*, 1989 S.L.T. (Lands Tr.) 82.

[32] 2000 Act, s.18(7)(b)(i).

Pre-emptions and redemptions

A right of pre-emption or redemption commonly attaches to a superior- **3–08** ity. Normally such rights are created real burdens on the *dominium utile* title and unless realloted to other land owned by the superior then the rights will be lost. The superior can reallot such rights to other land owned by that superior. There is no 100 metre requirement here nor is there any requirement that the other land must have any building on it for human habitation or resort. All that is required is the superior actually owns other land in sole name (not just by way of a superiority title).[33] In some cases of course the superior will not have any other land to which the right of pre-emption or redemption can be reallotted. In these cases it may be possible for the superior to preserve the right of pre-emption or redemption as a personal real burden.[34] Realloted pre-emptions or redemptions will be subject to the provisions of Part 8 of the 2003 Act. The notice must be served on the owner the burdened or servient property.

Minerals and salmon fishings

There may be situations where the superior owns minerals or salmon fish- **3–09** ings under or adjacent to land which is the subject of feudal real burdens which are plainly designed to protect the mineral or salmon fishing interests. Obvious examples of burdens of this type would be a burden preventing the erection of buildings of a certain height or weight which might result in increased pressure on the mineral strata. The superior may have imposed such a burden in the same deed in which the minerals were reserved. In the case of salmon fishings there may be a burden in favour of the superior in a feudal grant of property in the vicinity of the salmon river allowing access across that land to get to the salmon fishings or some other ancillary right. These burdens although created in a feudal deed and in favour of a superiority title are plainly not for the benefit of the bare superiority title but for the benefit of the other interest be that one of minerals or salmon fishings. In such a case the superior can reallot the right to enforce the burden from the superiority title to the title to the minerals or salmon fishings. There is no distance qualification vertically or horizontally in either case.[35] Although the Act specifically mentions mineral and salmon fishings this provision would also apply to any other incorporeal heritable right which benefited from a real burden. The only requirement is that it is apparent from the burden that it was created for the benefit of the minerals, salmon fishings or other incorporeal property. The notice must be served on the owner of the burdened or servient property.

Automatic reallotment—common facility or service burdens

Many feudal real burdens which are primarily enforceable by a superior **3–10** actually regulate the maintenance, management or the use of property which is a facility of or benefit to other property. The obvious example of such a common facility would be a common stair in a tenemental

---

[33] 2000 Act, s.18(7)(b)(ii).
[34] 2000 Act, s.18A; see para.3–12 below.
[35] 2000 Act, s.18(7)(c).

property. It may be that all the flats were feued subject to a burden enforceable by the superior that all the proprietors of flats should maintain the common stair at equal expense. In some circumstances of course this is the type of burden which would be enforceable by all the flat proprietors if a *ius quaesitum tertio* has been created. However there are situations where there is no *ius quaesitum tertio* and it would be to the detriment of all the flat owners if this obligation were to disappear with the feudal system. Accordingly the 2000 and 2003 Acts provide[36] that where immediately before abolition a real burden which is enforceable by a superior regulates the maintenance, management, re-instatement or use of heritable property which constitutes and is intended to constitute a facility of benefit to other land then the benefited land and the property which constitutes the facility shall each become a dominant tenement with rights to enforce the burden against the burdened land. Effectively what this means is that each flat will be a dominant tenement and servient tenement in respect of the maintenance obligation relating to the common close or other facility. This statutory provision which applies to all common facility burdens created before November 28, 2004 whether in a feudal writ or not, does not depend on either the existing law relating to *ius quaesitum tertio* or on the law as it will be under the 2003 Act. This provision stands on its own and is an example of automatic reallotment of the right to enforce a feudal burden. There is no need for the superior or any co-owner to take any action by way of service or registration of any reallotment notice. The original provision in the 2000 Act provided that where the facility had been taken over by a local or other public authority or a successor body then there would be no automatic reallotment. The 2000 Act also provided examples of common facilities. The examples quoted were a common part of a tenement, a common recreation area, a private road, a private sewerage system and a boundary wall. These provisions appear in the 2003 Act in the interpretation section.[37] A similar automatic preservation provision will apply where there is a feudal (or other) real burden regulating the provision of services to other land. On the appointed day the land to which these services are provided shall become the dominant tenement for enforcement purposes without the need for any reallotment procedure.[38] The obvious example would be a burden relating to the supply of water from other land. There does not seem to be a requirement that properties which benefit from the facility or service, such as unfeued units let out by a housing association, must already be subject to the burden in terms of existing titles.

PRESERVATION AS PERSONAL REAL BURDENS

Feudal real burdens preserved as personal real burdens

3–11   Between them the 2000 Act and the 2003 Act have introduced the concept of a personal real burden. In many ways this is, of course, a contradiction in terms. A real burden is supposed to be enforceable by

---

[36] 2000 Act, s.23 as re-enacted in the 2003 Act, s.56.
[37] 2003 Act, s.122(2) and (3).
[38] 2000 Act, s.23(2) as re-enacted in the 2003 Act, s.56.

the owner of heritable property by virtue of ownership and not by a person because that person is an individual or a specific body such as a conservation body or a health trust. Nevertheless it was felt that the right to enforce certain feudal real burdens should be preserved on a personal basis. The net effect is, the author supposes, that the burden will be real so far as the burdened land or servient tenement is concerned but will be personal so far as the right to enforce is concerned. Difficulties can of course arise when one considers whether or not the person with the right to enforce should have the right to assign the personal real burden to another party. The justification for some of these personal real burdens is a public interest one. In other cases the justification will be on the grounds that human rights may be infringed. It is appropriate to consider each case individually.

Personal pre-emption and redemption burdens

The 2003 Act amended the 2000 Act to allow a superior to preserve a **3–12** pre-emption or redemption right even in circumstances where that superior did not own any other land to which pre-emption or redemption could be reallotted in terms of section 18(7). In this case the superior must execute and register a notice in the form contained in schedule 5A of the 2000 Act. The requirements for the notice are the same as set out in section 18(2) except of course there is no requirement to describe any land to which pre-emption is to be reallotted. The superior must swear or affirm as set out in section 18(4). The pre-emption or redemption right is then converted into a personal real burden[39] and is personal to the superior despite the loss of the superiority but real in so far as the burdened land is concerned. Registration of the notice gives the superior the preserved right. The concept of this burden is further confused by the fact that the holder of a personal real burden who does not have a completed title (presumably someone who inherits the right of a trustee) may complete that title to the personal pre-emption or redemption by registering a notice of title or without completing a title may assign the right to the pre-emption or grant a discharge.[40] The fact that a notice of preservation must be registered before November 28, 2004 and that a notice of title (and presumably assignation) can be registered suggests that this personal real burden could require a title number. Alternatively it may just be regarded as an incorporeal heritable right which is not an interest in land capable of registration. It should be emphasised that reallotment and registration does not render an unenforceable pre-emption or redemption enforceable. The personal pre-emption or redemption right will be subject to Part 8 of the 2003 Act. Plainly this provision has been inserted from a human rights point of view in case a superior has no other land to which a pre-emption or redemption right can conveniently be reallotted. The concept makes no sense in pure property law terms, feudal or non-feudal.

---

[39] 2000 Act, s.18A(5)(a).
[40] 2000 Act, s.18A(8).

Economic development burdens

3–13   The 2003 Act introduces the concept of economic development burdens for the future but in an amendment to the 2000 Act also allows a superior to preserve an existing economic development burden after abolition. An economic development burden arises in a feudal context where the estate of *dominium utile* is subject to a real burden imposed for the purpose of promoting economic development and is enforceable by Scottish Ministers or a local authority as superior whether or not they have a completed title. It is not necessary to reallot this burden to other land although that may be possible within the terms of section 18 of the 2000 Act. It is simply preserved as a personal real burden if a notice is registered in terms of Schedule 5B. The interest of the local authority or Scottish Ministers to enforce the burden is presumed.[41] The notice must be registered before November 28, 2004 and the notice must state that the burden was imposed for the purpose of promoting economic development and provide information in support of that statement.[42] There are no assignation provisions here because only a local authority or Scottish Ministers can hold such a burden. There is no requirement to swear any oath or affirm. The notice must describe the burdened land and set out the terms of the burden. If the notice is served and registered then after the appointed day the real burden is converted into an economic development burden and Scottish Ministers or the local authority will have title to enforce it. Economic development burdens are dealt with in greater detail in the 2003 Act.[43] The 2003 Act provisions give some clue as to what an economic development burden might be by providing that it may comprise an obligation to pay a sum of money (whether fixed or ascertainable by a calculation set out in the deed) to the local authority or Scottish Ministers. The obvious type of burden envisaged would be some sort of clawback burden in favour of a local authority or Scottish Ministers where they have sold or feued land at a price based on some form of limited development but have made provision for an extra payment to be made in the event that increased or more lucrative development takes place. It should however be noted that the provisions in section 45 the 2003 Act relate to economic development burdens created on or after the day in which that particular section comes into force whereas the provisions contained in the 2000 Act for preservation of an existing feudal burden contained in section 18B relate to existing feudal burdens. There is no specific statement in section 18B of the 2000 Act to the effect that an economic development burden may comprise an obligation to pay a sum of money which may be fixed or calculable by some formula set out in the deed. Clearly under the existing law there would have been considerable doubt as to the enforceability of such a claw back burden especially one which was in respect of an uncertain sum of money. Accordingly the preferable view is that a typical claw back burden in a feudal writ registered prior to November 28, 2004 cannot be preserved in terms of section 18B of the 2000 Act. In such cases of course the obligation to pay the claw back may be secured in some other way such as by a standard security.

---

[41] 2000 Act, s.18B (1) and (4).
[42] 2000 Act, s.18B (2)(e).
[43] 2003 Act, s.45.

Healthcare burdens

The 2003 Act introduces the concept of health care burdens[44] and amendments to the 2000 Act allow a National Health Service trust or Scottish Ministers who are superiors entitled to a health care burden to preserve this as a personal real burden.[45] They do so by executing and registering, after service, a notice in the form contained in Schedule 5C to the 2000 Act. The notice sets out the title of the superior and describes the burdened land and sets out the terms of the health care burden. The notice must also state that the burden was imposed for the purpose of promoting the provision of facilities for health care and provide information in support of that statement.[46] On registration of this notice the real burden is converted into a health care burden and the Health Service Trust or Scottish Ministers are deemed to have title and interest to enforce.[47] There is no requirement to swear an oath or affirm that any statement in the notice is accurate. So far as the definition of a health care burden is concerned it is provided that the words "facilities for health care" include facilities ancillary to health care as for example accommodation for staff.[48]

3–14

Conservation burdens

The 2000 Act allows conservation bodies who are superiors to preserve burdens of a conservation type. It was recognised that certain real burdens in feudal writs had been imposed because of the nature of the superior and the type of property involved. The type of situation envisaged would be one where a conservation body such as the National Trust for Scotland acquired a row of derelict weaver's cottages, renovated the same in accordance with the original architectural style and then feued out the individual renovated cottages subject to very strict real burdens in relation to use, maintenance and above all prohibiting alteration. On abolition of the feudal system that conservation body would lose the right to enforce these burdens. Moreover unless that conservation body happened to own other land in the vicinity with a permanent building in use wholly or mainly as a place of human habitation or resort there would be no possibility of reallotting the right to enforce the burden in terms of the reallotment provisions in section 18. Accordingly the 2000 Act creates a new form of personal real burden known as a conservation burden.[49] Scottish Ministers have prescribed by regulation what bodies are to be regarded as conservation bodies for the purposes of this new type of burden. The list includes the John Muir Trust, the National Trust for Scotland and all local authorities. The object or function of the body or one of its objects or functions must be to preserve or protect for the benefit of the public architectural or historical characteristics of land or any other special characteristics. These special characteristics would include those derived from flora, fauna or the

3–15

---

[44] 2003 Act, s.26.
[45] 2000 Act, s.18C.
[46] 2000 Act, s.18C(2).
[47] 2000 Act, s.18C(3).
[48] 2000 Act, s.18C(5).
[49] 2000 Act, ss.26–32 (now repealed and re-enacted in the 2003 Act, ss.38–42).

general appearance of any land.[50] A conservation body can be a group of trustees.[51] Scottish Ministers have, in addition to the power to prescribe a body as a conservation body,[52] the power to prescribe that such a body shall cease to be a conservation body.[53] Scottish Ministers may be a conservation body.[54] In such a case the conservation body or Scottish Ministers may preserve the right to enforce a feudal real burden whether they have a completed title to the superiority or not if, before November 28, 2004 they execute and register a notice in the form contained in Schedule 8 to the 2000 Act. Such a burden will thereafter be known as a conservation burden.[55] It should be noted that only burdens which preserve or protect the architectural, historical or other special characteristics of the land can be preserved. The notice must be served on the proprietor of the burdened land in terms of the general intimation provisions.[56] On registration of the notice the burden is enforceable as a real burden by the conservation body or Scottish Ministers and interest is presumed.[57] A conservation burden may be assigned or transferred but only to another conservation body or Scottish Ministers. Such assignations are registerable.[58] A deduction of title will be competent as will the registration of a notice of title.[59] Again this type of burden appears to be personal and yet has some of the characteristics of an incorporeal heritable right not the least of which is that the right is registerable as is any assignation. However the right to enforce is very much tied to the conservation body and so if the body ceases to be a conservation body as when it is removed from the approved list by Scottish Ministers or where the body has simply ceased to exist then the burden is extinguished.[60] It is to be noted that the burden is extinguished in its entirety. There is no question of it reviving. Presumably therefore if there was a desire to preserve enforcement rights in respect of special burdens of this type the right to enforce would require to be assigned before the conservation body was removed from the list or ceased to exist. Although the right to enforce may be regarded as some sort of heritable incorporeal right it will not be competent to grant a standard security over the right to enforce.[61] The original provisions of the 2000 Act applied only to situations where the feudal superior was a conservation body or Scottish Ministers. As the 2003 Act was going through the Scottish Parliament it was recognised that there might be burdens which were designed to preserve architectural, historical or other special characteristics of land where the superior was not a conservation body. It was thought that it would be sensible to provide a mechanism whereby the right to enforce these burdens could be preserved but that the right to enforce be vest not in a former superior but in a conservation body or Scottish Ministers. Accordingly an extra section is

---

[50] 2000 Act, s.26(2); 2003 Act, s.38 (1).
[51] 2000 Act, s.26(3); 2003 Act, s.38(6).
[52] 2000 Act, s.26(1); 2003 Act, s.38(4).
[53] 2000 Act, s.26(4); 2003 Act, s.38(7).
[54] 2000 Act, s.26(1); 2003 Act, s.38(1).
[55] 2000 Act, s.27(1).
[56] 2000 Act, ss.41 and 42.
[57] 2000 Act, s.28.
[58] 2000 Act, s.29; 2003 Act, s.39.
[59] 2000 Act, s.30; 2003 Act, s.40, 41.
[60] 2000 Act, s.31; 2003 Act, s.42.
[61] 2000 Act, s.32; 2003 Act, s.38(3).

inserted by the 2003 Act into the 2000 Act.[62] In terms of these provisions where a person other than a conservation body or Scottish Ministers has a right to enforce a burden to protect architectural, historical or other special characteristics then that superior can, before the appointed day, execute and register a notice in the form contained in Schedule 8A to the 2000 Act and in that notice nominate a conservation body or the Scottish Ministers as the party who will have title to enforce the burden after abolition. It should be noted however that the consent of the conservation body concerned or Scottish Ministers is required before a superior can register such a notice.[63] Consent must be obtained before intimation to the owner of the burdened land. When such notice has been executed, served and registered then the nominated conservation body or Scottish Ministers have title to enforce the burden and is presumed to have an interest.[64]

PRESERVATION AS A SEPARATE INTEREST

Sporting rights

The 2003 Act inserts a new section into the 2000 Act in relation to sport-   **3–16**
ing rights which pertain to superiority titles.[65] This is an extremely odd provision and there may be difficulty over its interpretation in the future. There is a strongly held view that only salmon fishings are capable of separate ownership, feudal or otherwise. Other fishings and sporting rights of shooting over land owned by another person are not thought to be capable of separate ownership as tenements of land.[65a] It has however been recognised that such sporting rights of fishing and shooting can be leased provided they are not separated from owner-ship. Prior to the introduction of the 2000 Act the Scottish Law Commission considered sporting rights and the reservation of these rights in feudal grants. In many cases what was done was that on the grant of a feu rights of land shooting or fishings of a general nature were reserved to the superior. The view of the Commission was that non-exclusive reservations could be treated as real burdens and accordingly could be reallotted real burdens on the *dominium utile* title to other land owned by the superior.[66] There was however consider-able doubt as to the classification of the right so allotted. One thing is clear and that is that rights to fishings and shootings over another party's land are not servitudes. Moreover it is difficult to see such rights as real burdens in the land.[67] Presumably Scottish Ministers took the view that if the effect of the abolition of the feudal system was to extinguish rights of fishing and shooting which had been reserved to superiority titles then there might be a challenge under Article 1 of Protocol 1 to the European Convention on Human Rights especially

---

[62] 2000 Act, s.27A.
[63] 2000 Act, s.27A(2).
[64] 2000 Act, s.28A.
[65] 2000 Act, s.65A.
[65a] See Gordon, *Scottish Land Law* (2nd ed.), para.8–45.
[66] Reallotment provisions in s.18.
[67] Cusine and Paisley, *Servitudes and Rights of Way*, para.3.08; *Earl of Galloway v Duke of Bedford* (1902) 4F. 851.

since no compensation is payable to superiors for the loss of the superiority title as such. This presupposes a view that such rights can be
reserved to the superiority and in effect become a pertinent of it. The
new statutory provisions allow a superior to preserve sporting rights if
these were enforceable by a superior prior to the appointed day for abolition.[68] It should be emphasised however that the reserved sporting
rights must have been enforceable by a superior before the appointed
day. This is an interesting use of words. Presumably if one were to take
the view that prior to the passing of the 2003 Act it was not competent
to separate sporting rights (apart from salmon fishings) from ownership
of the *dominium utile* of the land then despite a reservation to a superiority title the superior would not legally have been entitled to enforce. It
might be argued of course that the original superior could have
enforced the reservation as a matter of personal contract as against the
original vassal.[69] However this would not necessarily have bound singular successors. It is fair to say that there may well be an alternative
view which is that although non-salmon fishings and shooting rights
cannot be separated from the ownership of land they can pertain to any
estate of ownership and in particular can pertain to a superiority title
which is or was at the time of the passing of the Act an estate in land.
While one can see why the Scottish Law Commission may have thought
that it was appropriate to treat these rights as real burdens capable of
reallotment it is difficult to see how they can fall within the existing
common law definition of a real burden. Real burdens consist of positive obligations to do something (to build or maintain) or prohibitions
(of nuisance, of trade, business or profession). Seldom do superiors
attempt to create a real burden which effectively gives the superior some
sort of right of entry on to land far less a right to do something on the
land. Rights of this nature are, generally speaking, servitudes and it is
of course quite clear that there cannot be a servitude of sporting rights.

Preservation of sporting rights by notice

3–17   To preserve sporting rights the superior must before November 28, 2004
execute and register against the *dominium utile* title which is subject to
the sporting rights a notice in the form contained in Schedule 11A of the
2000 Act. The superior must swear or affirm that the facts in the notice
are correct.[70] The notice must set out the title of the superior and
describe the land which is burdened with the sporting rights. The rights
themselves must be described as must any counter-obligation enforceable against the superior.[71] The superior must comply with the service
requirements for notice.[72] The effect of registration of the notice is qualified. On the one hand the new section provides[73] that if all the statutory
requirements in relation to the notice are complied with then provided
the sporting rights were enforceable by the superior prior to the
appointed day then on that day the sporting rights shall be converted

---

[68] 2000 Act, s.65A(1).
[69] *Scottish Co-operative Wholesale Society v Finnie*, 1937 S.C. 835.
[70] 2000 Act, s.65A(3).
[71] 2000 Act, s.65A(2).
[72] 2000 Act, ss.41 and 42.
[73] 2000 Act, s.65A(5).

into a tenement in land. However the section goes on to provide[74] that no greater or more exclusive sporting rights shall be enforceable by virtue of the conversion than were or would have been enforceable before. On one interpretation of these provisions all that they mean is that only the sporting rights which have been expressly reserved can be converted. On another interpretation if one takes the view that a reservation of a sporting right cannot actually be reserved to a superiority title[75] then no sporting right can be preserved. However this latter interpretation is perhaps inconsistent with the obvious intent of the legislation which is in some way to preserve sporting rights. Presumably the Scottish Parliament would not have enacted this if they held the view that sporting rights could not attach to a superiority title.

The nature of the preserved right

Professor Gordon's view was that sporting rights would go with the abolition of the feudal system but this may not now be the case. Reservations have in the past been expressed as to the theoretical possibility of reserving a right to shoot game to a superiority.[76] In the case cited a reservation of a right to all deer that might be found was restricted to deer which had already been killed and was not interpreted as a sporting right to hunt or stalk. It is apparent from the attempt to preserve a right to game as a tenement (whatever that may mean) that no-one was clear as to the property law concepts involved. The reservation of sporting rights therefore is probably best regarded as some sort of legislative compromise no doubt designed to avoid a claim by holders of sporting rights that their human rights in property have been infringed. The new statutory provision only applies to superiority titles as the sporting rights have to be enforceable by a superior of the feu. It is not clear whether the view was taken that sporting rights reserved in a disposition are not a separate heritable right but a personal license. Certainly there is no provision dealing with such reservations in a non feudal deed. It is perhaps odd, from a human rights point of view, to find that the superior may be in a better position than a disponer who has reserved sporting rights. It is also rather odd to find that sporting rights reserved to a superior if properly preserved are in some way a separate tenement whereas sporting rights reserved to a disponer presumably are not. This will of course lead to difficulties at the Land Register. Presumably if a superior reallots sporting rights and they become a separate tenement in land the Keeper will require to make up a title sheet in respect of the sporting rights. After registration one assumes that the holder of these sporting rights can then convey them by disposition. This will of course contrast with the situation where sporting rights which have merely been reserved in a disposition may be incapable of transmission as a separate tenement of land. Accordingly the new system of land tenure may allow ownership of sporting rights in only one sort of case and that is where these sporting rights have been reserved to a feudal superior. It seems to the author

3–18

---

[74] 2000 Act, s.65A(6).
[75] See Gordon, *op.cit.*, para.9–12.
[76] *Hemming v Duke of Athole* (1883) 11R. 93 at 97.

that this goes against the notion of a unitary concept of ownership. So far as the former vassal's title is concerned on registration of the appropriate notice the sporting rights will probably be removed from the title sheet of the vassal by a note in the property section. There already is a similar note in respect of reservations of minerals. The definition of incorporeal heritable rights[77] is expanded to include sporting rights as defined by the 2003 Act.[78] The definition of sporting rights in the 2003 Act is simply a right of fishing or game. The superior will preserve the right by service of a notice and registration of the same.[79] If the registration does not take place by notice prior to November 28, 2004 then the sporting rights will be extinguished with the superiority title. There is no suggestion that sporting rights shall be deemed to have existed as a separate tenement prior to abolition. The most that the legislation concedes is that sporting rights may have been a pertinent of the superiority. The Keeper will not require to determine whether the superior has notified the owner of the *dominium utile* before registration of the notice nor will the Keeper be required to determine whether the superior actually had the legal right to enforce the sporting rights prior to conversion. The Keeper will therefore not required to make the difficult decisions on interpretation of these rights which are inevitably bound to arise.[80] As with real burdens which have been extinguished on the appointed day where sporting rights are extinguished because there has been no notice of reallotment the Keeper will not be required to remove these sporting rights from the burdens section of the *dominium utile* title unless there is an application for registration or rectification or the Keeper is ordered to remove them.

COMPENSATION—RESERVED DEVELOPMENT VALUE

Development value burdens

3–19   The right to preserve a development value burden might be regarded as a right to convert such a burden into a personal real burden. Strictly speaking however the statutory provisions here attempt merely to safeguard the Scottish Executive against claims that human rights have been infringed. The burden is not preserved as such; merely the right to claim compensation. The Act does not provide for any compensation to be payable to a feudal superior for the loss of the superiority title, itself an estate in land, nor for the loss of the right to enforce burdens and conditions of the feu. At first glance this straightforward abolition of a property right without compensation might be said to contravene Article 1 of Protocol 1 of the European Convention on Human Rights which of course is now part of domestic law.[81] On the abolition of feuduties and similar monetary burdens a compensatory payment akin to a redemption payment is payable.[82] Some concern however was expressed in relation to land which had been feued for

---

[77] In s.28(1) of the Land Registration (Scotland) Act 1979.
[78] 2000 Act, s.65A(9).
[79] 2000 Act, s.65A(10) the notice will be under s.41 of the 2000 Act.
[80] 2000 Act, s.65A(11).
[81] Human Rights Act, 1998 s.1, Sch.1 Part II; and see Ch.16 below.
[82] 2000 Act, ss.8–10; and see Ch.4 below.

no consideration or for a reduced consideration, generally for some public or *quasi* public purpose where a burden had been imposed restricting the use of that land to that purpose. The obvious example would be the feu of an area of land in 1965 by a philanthropic land owner to a local authority for no consideration or for a reduced price subject to a real burden that the land was to be used in all time coming as a public park and for no other purpose. On November 28, 2004 the feudal system is abolished and the right of the feudal superior to enforce that burden goes. It may be that the local authorities feel that the public park is no longer necessary since it has provided more modern themed leisure facilities elsewhere. Moreover the public park is now surrounded by expensive residential developments. In terms of the 2000 Act no one has the right to enforce the burden so technically speaking there is nothing to stop the local authority from selling the public park to a developer for millions of pounds despite the fact that they may only have paid £100 to the superior in 1965. Of course in 1965 there may have been no development of any sort in the area and no planning permission would be likely to have been obtained for such a development. Nevertheless the fact that the burden is no longer enforceable and the land is freed up for development might be regarded as something of a windfall for the local authority at the expense, to some extent at any rate, of the original land owner who feued out the ground. The Act provides limited compensation in such circumstances.[83] There was a great deal of discussion of this matter when the Scottish Law Commission was considering feudal abolition. There was always going to be difficulty in framing a compensation provision which seemed to be fair in all circumstances. Prior to abolition the superior could have asked for a payment in exchange for a waiver and in many cases the payment would have been substantial, being a percentage of the value of the development. However against that an application might have been made to the Lands Tribunal for variation or discharge. In the example which I have quoted however that application would not have been straightforward given the fact that the local authority were the original vassals. In such a scenario therefore the feudal superior might have attempted to obtain a payment based on a percentage of the development value which would have been his if he had held on to the land in 1965 and simply awaited changes in the local structure plan. It should be noted of course that the provisions which allow a superior to claim a development value compensatory payment are most likely to be used where the superior does not have adjoining land to which the burden could be realloted in terms of the reallotment provisions.[84] If the feudal superior owns adjoining land on which there is a permanent building which is in use wholly or mainly as a place of human habitation or resort and that building is at any point within 100 metres of the burdened public park then the superior may find it more useful to reallot the burden and then demand payment for a waiver in the usual way. This would appear to be a far more commercial course of action than reserving a development value where the compensation is on any view minimal.[85] Before a superior can reserve the right to

---

[83] 2000 Act, ss.33–40.
[84] 2000 Act, s.18 and see paras 3–03—3–05 above.
[85] See para.3–23 below.

claim development value compensation it must be shown that the land was feued subject to an enforceable real burden which reserved to the superior the benefit of any development value of the land. Such a burden is referred to as a "development value burden". It must then be shown that the consideration paid at the time of the grant of feu was significantly lower than it would have been had the feu not been subject to the burden or that no consideration was paid because of the imposition of the burden. In such a case the superior may before November 28, 2004 reserve the right to claim compensation by executing and registering against the burdened land a notice in the form of Schedule 9 to the Act.[86] Development value is given a limited definition in the 2000 Act.[87] A development value is any significant increase in the value of the land which would arise as a result of the burden not being applicable. However the definition is subject to other limiting provisions in the Act.[88] It is easy to apply this definition to the example quoted above. Obviously the value of land which can only be used as a public park is significantly less than the value of the same land if it can be used for an upmarket residential development. However the development value is not the open market value of the property at the time of abolition and removal of the burden. The development value relates to the difference in value of the land with the burden imposed and without the burden imposed taken at the time of creation of the burden.

The mechanics of claiming reserved development value

3–20 To reserve a right to claim compensation for a development value burden the superior must before November 28, 2004 reserve the right to claim compensation by executing and registering against the burdened land a notice in the form contained in Schedule 9 to the 2000 Act. The notice must set out the title of the superior and describe the burdened land sufficiently to enable identification by reference to the ordnance map. The terms of the burden must be set out in full. It should be noted here that what must be set out is a specific burden which clearly indicates that it was reserving to the superior the benefit of any development value. There is no question for example of maintaining an argument that the overall effect of the reservation of minerals, the prohibition of trade business or profession, the obligation to make up a road and indeed all the other burdens which might be normal in any feudal writ collectively mean that the superior has somehow reserved a development value merely because he might obtain payment for a waiver of all or indeed any of these conditions. The notice must set out[89] the terms of a specific burden which has effectively reserved development value. The notice must also state in terms that the particular burden reserves development value and must set out information which is relevant to that statement. The notice must set out, to the best of the superior's knowledge and belief, the amount by which the original consideration was reduced because of the imposition of the burden.

---

[86] 2000 Act, s.33(1).
[87] 2000 Act, s.33(5).
[88] 2000 Act, s.37.
[89] 2000 Act, s.33(2).

This may not be as easy as it sounds. It may, in the example quoted, be obvious that the local landowner has made a gift of land for a public park where no price is stated to be payable. On the other hand if the feu was granted at the end of the nineteenth century for no consideration but subject to a feuduty at a normal rate it may be argued that the feuing of land subject only to a return by way of feuduty made perfect commercial sense at the time. Moreover if the public park was feued for a low consideration (in twenty-first century terms) it may not be easy to find a surveyor old enough to give a view on what the appropriate value would have been in 1965 if the land had been feued without the imposition of the burden. To put it simply a surveyor who was, let us say, regarded as experienced at the age of 30 in 1965 would be 68 in 2003 and presumably retired. Other evidence of comparable prices might be available from public records such as the Register of Sasines but it may not be easy to supply information which sets out "any information relevant" to the statement that a development value has been reserved. There may of course be minutes of the local authority which acknowledge the generous gift of the land owner or the fact that the land has been sold at a reduced or nominal consideration. Finally the notice must state in terms that the superior reserves the right to claim compensation in accordance with the Act. Before submitting any notice for registration the superior must swear or affirm before a Notary Public that to the best of his or her knowledge and belief all the information contained in the notice is true. Where the superior is subject to any disability or is a corporate entity then a legal representative or a person authorised to sign documents on behalf of the entity may swear or affirm. Registration of the notice is subject to the requirement to serve a copy on the owner of the land.[90] The effect of registration of a Schedule 9 notice is not to preserve the burden as such. The burden has not been realloted in terms of the reallotment provisions[91] and the burden will be extinguished on November 28, 2004. All that the notice does is preserve the right to claim compensation for a reserved development value burden. To that extent therefore it may be erroneous to think of this reservation as creating a personal real burden. Nevertheless the effect of registration is to give the superior the right to claim compensation. This right is a personal right in as much as it is not attached to any land. A purchaser of the property however would be put on notice that there is a former superior with a potential claim waiting in the wings. That will not have an effect on the title as such but a purchaser may want to know how much the superior will be able to collect because it is the owner at the time the claim is made as opposed to the owner at the time Schedule 9 notice is registered who is liable for the compensation.[92] As with burdens which are realloted the registration of a notice under Schedule 9 will not breathe legal life into a burden which was not enforceable in the first place. Some development value burdens provide a formula whereby the vassal is to pay a sum of money to the superior if the property comes to be developed in a particular way. While such a burden may be valid as between the original superior and vassal as a matter of personal contract[93] such

---

[90] 2000 Act, ss.41 and 42.
[91] 2000 Act, s.18.
[92] 2000 Act, ss.35 and 38.
[93] *Scottish Co-operative Wholesale Society Ltd v Finnie*, 1937 S.C. 835.

a burden being an obligation to pay an unascertained sum of money is not a real burden.[94] It may be an irony that the more specific the burden is in relation to the right of the superior to claim money if there is development the less chance there will be of the burden being valid and capable either of preservation by way of reallotment or compensation by way of reserved development value.

Who may serve the notice

3–21   It is remarkable that the Act gives no guidance on the question of the party who may serve the notice. One might say that this is obvious; the party is the superior. However superiorities change hands whether through inheritance or sale. If one is considering, for example, a feu of land for a public park in 1965 by an elderly landowner who wished to have a public park named after him, the chances are that he will not be the feudal superior in 2004 just before abolition takes effect. It may be a member of his family or it may be a completely independent party who has purchased the rump of the landed estate and the superiority. The question is whether such a successor to the original superior who imposed the burden and received the reduced consideration if indeed there was a price, is the party who can claim. On one argument of course the right to enforce the burden attached to the superiority and accordingly it is the current superior who should have the claim. On the other hand the party who suffered the original loss because of the imposition of the burden was the original superior and not the succeeding superior. If the superiority has been acquired for a commercial consideration then the new superior will have paid a market value and taken the title as it stands. The new superior may also have taken the title in the knowledge that the feudal system was to be abolished in the relatively near future and the calculated price accordingly. The only other statutory provision which is similar in effect is the existing provision in relation to payment of compensation where a land obligation is varied or discharged in terms of the Conveyancing and Feudal Reform (Scotland) Act 1970.[95] In terms of the 1970 Act provision compensation can be paid in two situations. The first situation is where there has been substantial loss or disadvantage suffered by the benefited proprietor in relation to the land obligation in consequence of the variation or discharge.[96] Clearly compensation could be claimed here by a successor to the superior or other benefited proprietor. The second situation is where the obligation produced an effect at the time it was imposed in reducing the consideration then paid.[97] In one case the tribunal suggested a singular successor might not be entitled to compensation under the second head because that party would not have suffered any financial loss at the time the burden was imposed, the price paid by that party to the original granter of the deed imposing the burden having been at market value.[98] Unfortunately the statutory provisions in the 2000 Act

---

[94] *Tailors of Aberdeen v Coutts* (1840) 1 Rob. App. 296.
[95] Conveyancing and Feudal Reform (Scotland) Act 1970, s.1(4); re-enacted with amendments in the 2003 Act, ss.90(6) and (7).
[96] Conveyancing and Feudal Reform (Scotland) Act 1970, s.1(4)(i).
[97] Conveyancing and Feudal Reform (Scotland) Act 1970, s.1(4)(ii).
[98] *Devlin v Conn*, 1972 S.L.T. (Lands Tr.) 11 at 14.

are unclear. Section 33(1)(a) refers to a situation where land was feued subject to a real burden "enforceable by *a* superior" (author's italics). It goes on to say that where a development value burden has been created and there was no consideration or a reduced consideration then "*the* superior" (author's italics) may before November 28, 2004 reserve the right to claim compensation. It may be that the use of the indefinite article in the first part of the clause and the use of the definite article in the second part of the clause indicate that the burden may have been imposed by any superior whereas the claim can be made by the current superior. Section 35(1) of the 2000 Act deals with the claiming of compensation and it provides that any person who has executed and registered a notice reserving a right to claim compensation can subject to the conditions of the section make the claim. The words "any person" may again suggest that the right to compensation can be reserved and the claim to compensation made by whoever the current superior happens to be. On the other hand, section 37 restricts the claim to the effect which the burden produced on the price at the time it was imposed. This suggests that compensation should be paid to the party who actually suffered the original loss.[99] Moreover the Act provides[1] in assessing the amount of compensation the entitlement of the claimant to recover any part of the development value of the land in any other way must be taken into account. Presumably this refers to a contractual arrangement between the original parties to the feu outwith the real burden. That would of course be a personal agreement which would not transmit to or against singular successors. The Act provides that once a section 9 notice has been served and registered the right to claim the compensation may be transmitted by assignation or by will.[2] However that is not the same as saying that someone other than the original superior can serve the section 9 notice. What can be transmitted or assigned is the personal right to claim compensation once the putative burden has been breached. Unfortunately the matter is unclear. If one takes the view that the abolition of the feudal system has no effect on the contractual obligation between the original superior and vassal despite the obligation ceasing to be a real burden[3] then the contractual obligation would subsist after abolition and a straightforward breach of contract claim would result. In such a circumstance the original superior would have no need to go through the procedure laid down in the 2000 Act to reserve and then claim development value compensation. On one reading of the statutory provisions therefore the only way in which a claim can arise is where the original superior who suffered commercial loss is dealing with a singular successor of the original vassal. That may not have been the desired result of the statutory provisions but it is the author's view that it is the most likely interpretation. The matter will probably be academic given the restricted nature of the compensation which can be claimed in any event.

---

[99] s.37(2).
[1] 2000 Act, s.37(3).
[2] 2000 Act, ss.34 and 40.
[3] 2000 Act, s.75.

Claiming compensation

3–22 The service and registration of a notice under Schedule 9 does no more than preserve the right to claim compensation. It does not give an immediate right to collect compensation. Before any claim can actually be made the development value burden (as it was pre-abolition), must have been breached. Moreover the right to claim only applies to burdens which have been extinguished by feudal abolition. A superior cannot reallot a burden and claim compensation at the same time.[4] The breach of the burden must have occurred either within a period of five years before November 28, 2004 or within a period of 20 years after that date. The breach occurring after November 28, 2004 will of course be a fictitious breach because the burden has ceased to exist. But that nominal breach will trigger the right to claim compensation.[5] Accordingly in the example quoted above the original feudal superior who feued the public park to the local authority would require in the first place to serve and register a notice in terms of Schedule 9 prior to November 28, 2004. If the local authority has already breached the burden (unlikely in the example quoted) within a period of five years prior to November 28, 2004 then the superior may take steps to claim compensation. Similarly if the local authority propose to sell the public park for residential development after November 28, 2004 and within a 20-year period from that date the superior can also claim compensation albeit there has been no actual breach of a real burden because the real burden has ceased to exist. In this case there must have occurred an event which would have been a breach. Where either of these events occurs the person entitled to compensation can claim that compensation by serving a further notice on the then owner of the land which was subject to the original burden. The notice must specify the amount of compensation claimed.[6] If the claim is based on a breach of the burden in the five-year period before feudal abolition then the claim itself must be made within three years after the appointed day.[7] If the claim relates to a putative breach within the 20-year period after feudal abolition then the claim must be made within a period of three years after the date of the occurrence which results in the putative breach.[8] If the pre-abolition breach or post-abolition occurrence is a continuing breach or occurrence then it will be treated as taken place when it first happens.[9] The notice claiming compensation must be delivered to the owner or sent to the owner by registered post or recorded delivery addressed to him or her at an appropriate place.[10] The former vassal may sign an acknowledgement in the form A of Schedule 10 or the former superior may produce a certificate of posting in the form B of that Schedule.[11] Alternatively if the notice is returned by the postal services with an intimation that it could not be delivered then the notice may be delivered or sent by post with that intimation to the Extractor of the Court of Session and an

---

[4] 2000 Act, s.35(2).
[5] 2000 Act, s.35(2)(c).
[6] As calculated in terms of 2000 Act, s.37.
[7] 2000 Act, s.35(4)(a).
[8] 2000 Act, s.35(4)(b).
[9] 2000 Act, s.35(5).
[10] 2000 Act, s.36(1).
[11] 2000 Act, s.36(2).

acknowledgement of receipt by the extractor on a copy of the notice is sufficient evidence of its receipt by him.[12] The date of service of the notice is the date of delivery or the date of posting as the case may be.[13] So far as the place of service is concerned it is to be at an appropriate place. This is defined in the Act[14] as being the owner's place of residence, the owner's place of business or a postal address which the owner ordinarily uses. If none of these are known at the time of delivery or posting of the notice then the appropriate place will be deemed to be whatever place is at that time the owners most recently known place of residence or place of business or the postal address then known as the one ordinarily used. In many cases the superior will not know the identity of the current owner and may serve notice on a party who was a previous owner. If that happens the person on whom the notice has erroneously been served is under a statutory obligation to disclose to the former superior the identity and address of the current owner or, if that is not possible, such other information as the former owner has that might enable the former superior to discover the identity and address of the current owner. The notice served in terms of section 35 has to refer to that requirement for disclosure. The 2000 Act makes it clear that it is the current owner at the time of the breach or the occurrence whether or not that party has a completed title.[15] In the case of a post-feudal abolition occurrence or putative breach then it will be the current owner at the time of the occurrence who is liable but in the case of a pre-feudal abolition breach it appears to be the party who was the owner at the time of the breach who is liable to pay the compensation.

The calculation of compensation

The method of calculation of compensation is provided in the statute.[16]   **3–23** The statutory provision begins by stating that the compensation is to be such sum as represents at the time of the pre-feudal abolition breach or post-feudal abolition occurrence a development value which would have accrued to the owner had the burden been modified to the extent necessary to permit the land to be used in the way which constituted the breach or occurrence. In the example used therefore that would suggest that it would be the difference between the value of the land subject to a restriction that it could be used as a public park and the value of the land with no such restriction preventing development. This part of the statutory provision emphasises the effect of removal of the burden on the owner of the property. However the section goes on to provide[17] that the amount payable as compensation is not to exceed such sum as would make up for any effect which the burden produced at the time it was imposed in reducing the price then paid. Accordingly the compensation is not the difference between the value of the land as a public park and the value of the land as a prime residential site. The compensation is restricted to the reduction in price achieved in 1965 when the landowner

---

[12] 2000 Act, s.36(2)and (3).
[13] 2000 Act, s.36(4).
[14] 2000 Act, s.36(5).
[15] 2000 Act, s.39(1).
[16] 2000 Act, s.37.
[17] 2000 Act, s.37(2).

feued the land subject to the burden that it could only be used as a public park. Accordingly if the land was feued then for £100 in 1965 and a surveyor can be found to say that if it had been feued without that burden in 1965 the price would have been £1,000 compensation is restricted to the figure of £900. It is obvious that this provision mirrors the existing compensation provision in respect of the variation and discharge of land obligation by the Lands Tribunal.[18] It would be fair to say that the Tribunal has not been keen to award compensation and those claiming compensation under the 1970 Act have found considerable difficulty in proving that the imposition of burdens in bygone deeds had any effect on the price paid.[19] Drawing the compensation claim back to the difference in value or price at the time the burden was imposed raises two interesting questions. In the first place there is the question of whether or not compensation, once calculated, should be increased to take account of inflation between the date of the imposition of the burden and the date of registration of the Schedule 9 notice or indeed the date the breach or occurrence resulting in a claim under section 35. In the second place there is the question of whether or not the former superior making the claim is entitled to interest on the amount of compensation. It seems to the author that the answer to both questions is in the negative. There is no provision in the 2000 Act for the compensation payment to be adjusted to take account of inflation nor for any interest to be paid. As far as inflation is concerned the approach of the Lands Tribunal when considering compensation following on the variation and discharge of a land obligation appears to be to ignore questions of inflation.[20] The rationale is obvious; before the burden is waived or discharged the superior has had the benefit of that burden and it is only when the burden is varied or discharged that the superior loses that benefit. Accordingly it is not logical to take inflation into account. The same reasoning applies to the argument over interest. It would follow that it is unlikely there will be many claims for reserved development value compensation except perhaps in relation to recently created feudal burdens. In such cases however it would be unusual for the parties to have left their commercial arrangements to a real burden alone. It is far more likely that there would be a complicated development agreement which would of course preclude a claim under the 2000 Act.[21]

References to the Lands Tribunal

3–24   The 2000 Act contains general provision referring any dispute in relation to any notice registered under the Act to the Lands Tribunal.[22] In determining the dispute the Tribunal may make any order it thinks fit discharging or restricting any notice. The Tribunal may also make such order as it thinks fit in relation to the amount of development value compensation to be paid.[23] In any application to the Tribunal whether

---

[18] Conveyancing and Feudal Reform (Scotland) Act 1970, s.1(4)(ii).
[19] See, *e.g.*, *Manz v Butter's Trs*, 1973 S.L.T. (Lands Tr.) 2.
[20] *Manz v Butter's Trs*, 1973 S.L.T. (Lands Tr.) 2; *Gorrie & Banks Ltd v Musselburgh Town Council*, 1974 S.L.T. (Lands Tr.) 5.
[21] 2000 Act, s.37(3)(a).
[22] 2000 Act, s.44(1).
[23] 2000 Act, s.44(2).

in relation to a reallotment notice or a notice preserving development value the onus of proving a disputed matter of fact is on the person relying on the notice or making the claim.[24] A vassal may feel aggrieved at a notice being registered against his or her title. If so the vassal can refer the matter to the Lands Tribunal. Any order made by the Tribunal may be registered and will take effect as regards third parties on registration of the extract.[25]

Transmission and discharge of compensation claims

Once a Schedule 9 notice has been served and registered the right to claim compensation can be assigned or transmitted by will or in accordance with the law of intestacy.[26] Where a claim has been paid in terms of section 35 then a discharge or a restriction in the form contained in Schedule 11 to the Act may be executed and registered. Schedule 11 also contains a form of assignation. An assignation or a discharge may be total or partial.

3–25

NOTICES OF REALLOTMENT AND PRESERVATION

Service of notices

Before any notice under the 2000 Act can be registered a copy must be served on the owner of the burdened or servient land. The registration of notices under the Act is a unilateral act on the part of the superior. Although the superior in most cases requires to swear or affirm that the facts contained in the notice are correct there is no independent assessment of whether or not the superior is entitled to serve the notice. Given the fact that the Keeper has no real duty to verify matters stated in the notice[27] it is essential that the content of the notice be made known to the burdened proprietor. The 2000 Act accordingly makes provision for service as a pre-registration requirement.[28] Before the superior executes the notice he or she must, unless it is not reasonably practicable to do so, intimate the notice to the vassal including whichever explanatory note is appropriate to the notice. When the superior executes and transmits the notice for registration the superior must state on the notice that appropriate service has been made or that it was not reasonably practicable to do so. There is no guidance given in relation to what is or is not reasonably practicable. Service is affected by sending a copy of the notice by post to the person who owns the *dominium utile* of the land to which the burden relates. The intimation should be addressed to "the proprietor" where the name of that person is not known.[29]

3–26

---

[24] 2000 Act, s.44(3).
[25] 2000 Act, s.44(4).
[26] 2000 Act, ss.34 and 40.
[27] 2000 Act, s.46.
[28] 2000 Act, ss.41 and 42.
[29] 2000 Act, s.41(3).

Choice of notice

3–27　The Act makes it clear that the superior will require to make a choice in relation to notices. It is not competent to register more than one notice in respect of the same real burden.[30] Accordingly a superior may have to decide whether it is more advantageous to attempt to reallot a burden restricting use of land away from the superiority to other land owned by that superior which qualifies under the 100 metre rule[31] or whether to attempt to reserve a claim to development value.[32] The only exception to this will arise where the superior has attempted to reach an agreement with a vassal whereby the right to enforce a real burden is voluntarily realloted to other land belonging to the superior.[33] If the superior has been unsuccessful in reaching such an agreement then the superior will be able to apply to the Lands Tribunal. Public authority type superiors may have the choice between preserving a burden as a conservation burden, healthcare burden or economic development burden (all species of personal real burdens) or preserving a burden as owner of adjoining land which qualifies under the 100 metre rule. Obviously a personal real burden may be better since enforcement rights are not tied to any land. If the Tribunal holds that a notice is for some reason ineffective or incompetent then the superior may try again. The same would apply where the superior has expressly discharged an earlier notice or agreement.[34] In some cases the superior will wish to preserve more than one burden. In such a case the superior can execute a single notice which specifies all of the burdens.[35] However where the original *dominium utile* title has been sub-divided so that all the sub-divided parts are subject to the same conditions the superior will have to treat each sub-divided part as a separate *dominium utile* and serve notice on the owners of each sub-divided part.[36]

REALLOTMENT BY AGREEMENT

Agreement to reallot real burdens

3–28　The legislation provides[37] a voluntary procedure whereby the superior and vassal can actually agree that a burden which is to be extinguished on feudal abolition will be preserved and the right to enforce realloted to other land owned by the superior. The superior can, before November 28, 2004 serve a notice in terms of Schedule 6 on the vassal to the effect that the superior seeks to enter into an agreement prospectively nominating other land owned by the superior as the dominant tenement for the future with the right to enforce an existing feudal burden. If the vassal agrees to this then the parties simply enter into an

---

[30]　2000 Act, s.42.
[31]　2000 Act, s.18(7)(a).
[32]　2000 Act, s.33.
[33]　2000 Act, s.19.
[34]　2000 Act, s.42(1).
[35]　2000 Act, s.42(4).
[36]　2000 Act, s.42(3).
[37]　2000 Act, s.19.

agreement which is registered against both titles.[38] The parties may modify the real burden and any counter-obligation in the agreement. The notice in terms of Schedule 6 requires to set out the title of the superior and describe the burdened land and the new nominated land. It must also set out the terms of the real burden and any counter-obligation.[39] The agreement must be in writing and must state that it is made in terms of the section.[40] A party may enter into this type of agreement even if that party does not have a completed title to the burdened land or the superiority or nominated land.[41] The agreement should be in self-proving wording.

REALLOTMENT BY THE LANDS TRIBUNAL

Application to the Tribunal

There may be cases where a superior wishes to reallot a burden but cannot meet the statutory requirements.[42] It may be for example that the superior does own adjoining land but there is no permanent building in use wholly or mainly as a place of human habitation or resort. In such a case the obvious course would be for the superior to attempt to enter into a voluntary agreement with the vassal.[43] However one must assume that few vassals would be keen to enter into an agreement which effectively prolongs the feudal system. The superior may of course offer some financial inducement. If there is such a refusal the superior may make application to the Lands Tribunal setting out that the superior has attempted to reach agreement with the vassal in terms of section 19. The application is for an order to reallot the right to enforce the burden to another nominated property owned by the superior. The application to the Tribunal must be made before November 28, 2004.[44] The applicant must include in the application a description of the attempt to reach agreement.[45] The Tribunal must on receipt of the application give notice of that application by advertisement or otherwise to any person who is an owner of the burdened property or indeed to any other person the Tribunal thinks fit.[46] Any person (whether they have received notice or not) who has right to the property subject to the real burden, or is affected by the real burden or by its proposed reallotment is entitled to oppose or make representations to the Tribunal in relation to the application. The Tribunal must allow any such person to be heard.[47]

3–29

---

[38] 2000 Act, s.19(4).
[39] 2000 Act, s.19(2).
[40] 2000 Act, s.19(3).
[41] 2000 Act, s.19(6).
[42] As contained in 2000 Act, s.18(1)(b) and s.18(7).
[43] 2000 Act, s.19.
[44] 2000 Act, s.20(1).
[45] 2000 Act, s.20(2).
[46] 2000 Act, s.21(1).
[47] 2000 Act, s.21(2).

Temporary preservation

3–30   It will be appreciated that it may take some time for the Tribunal to come
        to a view. Accordingly the superior may preserve the burden if he or she
        within 42 days or such longer period ending before November 28, 2004
        as the Lands Tribunal may allow executes and registers a notice in the
        form of Schedule 7. If such a notice is registered then the burden will not
        be extinguished in terms of the abolition provisions.[48] A Schedule 7
        notice must set out the title of the superior and describe the burdened
        land and the prospective dominant land which is to have the right to
        enforce for the future. It must also set out the terms of the burden and
        any counter-obligation and must be registered against both properties.[49]
        Such a notice must be served on the owner.[50] The effect of the Schedule
        7 notice is to temporarily preserve the real burden until the Tribunal has
        dealt with the application. Again the Keeper is not under any obligation
        to verify proper service of the notice, nor the information contained in
        the notice in relation to the attempt by the superior to enter into a vol-
        untary agreement with the vassal.[51] The Schedule 7 notice not only pre-
        serves the burden but temporarily at least gives enforcement rights to
        the proprietor of the prospectively nominated land for enforcement
        purposes.[52]

Criterion for reallotment and effect of order

3–31   If the Tribunal is satisfied that were the real burden to be extinguished
        there would be substantial loss or disadvantage to the applicant as
        owner of the proposed new dominant tenement it may order that the
        prospective dominant tenement is to become the dominant tenement
        with the right to enforce the burden against the burdened land.[53]
        Where a Schedule 7 notice has been served the order will simply con-
        tinue the enforcement rights of the proposed dominant tenement after
        the transitional period. If the Tribunal is not so satisfied it may order
        that the burden is to be extinguished or cease to be enforceable.[54] It will
        not matter that the order is registered before or after the appointed day
        for abolition. It should be noted that the question of substantial loss or
        disadvantage to the applicant relates to the applicant's ownership of
        the proposed new dominant land and not to the applicant's position
        as a superior. There may be circumstances in which the Tribunal feels
        that it would be wrong to extinguish the burden altogether and that
        there is some merit in the superior's argument. In such a case it will be
        open to the Tribunal to modify the burden in which event the modified
        burden shall be enforceable for the future by the proposed dominant
        tenement. A counter-obligation may also be varied.[55] There is no
        appeal from a decision of the Lands Tribunal.[56] The order of the

---

[48] 2000 Act, s.17(1).
[49] 2000 Act, s.20(3), (4) and (5).
[50] 2000 Act, s.41.
[51] 2000 Act, s.43.
[52] 2000 Act, s.20(5).
[53] 2000 Act, s.20(7)(a).
[54] 2000 Act, s.20(7)(b).
[55] 2000 Act, s.20(9).
[56] 2000 Act, s.20(10).

Tribunal must be registered against both the burdened land and the nominated dominant land.[57] It would be possible of course for a superior to use these provisions to create an artificial situation where the vassal, rather than contest the matter before the Tribunal simply paid an agreed sum of money to the superior for a discharge of the Schedule 7 notice. A person opposing an application by the superior incurs no liability unless his actings have been vexatious or frivolous in respect of expenses incurred by the applicant.[58] This provision may well have been inserted to deter superiors from seeking a commercial advantage by lodging an application to the Tribunal. As with other notices the superior must before submitting a Schedule 7 notice for registration swear or affirm before a Notary Public that to the best of his or her knowledge or belief all the information contained in the notice is true. The usual provisions in respect of disability and corporate entities apply.

REALLOTMENT AND PRESERVATION—GENERAL

The role of the Keeper

The provisions relating to notices and indeed agreements make it clear   **3–32** that they do not breathe life into burdens which were already unenforceable. That however would not preclude registration of a notice if the appropriate procedures have been carried out. The Keeper is bound to take notices at face value. In particular the Keeper is not required to determine whether the notice has been properly served on the owner of the burdened property.[59] Neither is the Keeper bound to determine whether the real burden is still enforceable.[60] Where there is a reallotment notice in terms of section 18(2)(c) the Keeper does not require to verify whether the proposed new dominant land has on it a permanent building in use wholly or mainly as a place of human habitation or resort nor whether that building is at some point within 100 metres of the burdened land.[61] Where a superior attempts to reallot a burden by agreement in terms of section 19 the Keeper will not be bound to verify that the superior has served the appropriate notice under Schedule 6.[62] Similarly, in accepting a Schedule 7 notice, the Keeper will not be required to determine whether or not the applicant to the Lands Tribunal did attempt to reach agreement with the vassal nor will the Keeper require to consider whether the description is correct and whether the notice has been executed and is being registered timeously or indeed any other matter as to which the Tribunal will have to be satisfied before making the order.[63] Where reserved development values are concerned, the Keeper will not be required to determine whether the original deed containing the burden did indicate a reserved development value or whether the statements made by the superior in the

---

[57] 2000 Act, s.20(11).
[58] 2000 Act, s.20(13).
[59] 2000 Act, s.43(1).
[60] 2000 Act, s.43(2)(a).
[61] 2000 Act, s.43(2)(b).
[62] 2000 Act, s.43(2)(c).
[63] 2000 Act, s.43(2)(d).

Schedule 9 notice in relation to development value and the amount of development value are in any way accurate.[64] The reason for this apparently negative approach is lack of resource at the Registers. In any event to decide on these issues would mean that the Keeper had to adopt a quasi-judicial position and possibly adjudicate between parties, something he has never done in the past and something which might have implications under Human Rights law.

Interest to enforce after reallotment or preservation

3–33   It has always been a principle of the law relating to real burdens that the party seeking to enforce the burden must have both title and interest to enforce. Where a burden is preserved or realloted as a personal real burden then interest is in many cases simply presumed. Where there is no such statutory presumption however the party entitled to enforce the realloted burden will still require to have an interest to enforce.[65] However whereas prior to abolition the superior's interest to enforce a burden was presumed[66] the position is now reversed in that the 2000 Act provides that the interest of the new dominant proprietor entitled to enforce a realloted burden will not be presumed.[67] Although the 2000 Act makes no attempt to further define interest to enforce this matter is to a certain extent dealt with in the 2003 Act. That Act provides that a real burden is enforceable by any person who has both title and interest to enforce it and that a person has title if that person is the owner of the benefited property or a tenant, non-entitled spouse or the holder of a proper liferent.[68] The 2003 Act goes on to provide that a person has an interest if in the circumstances of any case failure to comply with the real burden is resulting in, or will result in, material detriment to the value or enjoyment of that person's ownership of, or right in, the property which has the benefit of enforcement rights. The person will also be deemed to have an interest where the burden is one which obliges parties to defray or contribute towards some cost and the party seeking to enforce the burden seeks payment in respect of that cost. It may be that the statutory definition of interest does not take the discussion much further forward. Indeed cases relating to interest or the lack of interest to enforce a real burden are almost always fact-specific.[69]

Counter-obligations following reallotment

3–34   Where a real burden is reallotted in terms of sections 18, 19, 20 or 23 the right to enforce the burden as realloted shall be subject to any counter obligation enforceable against the superior immediately before reallot-

---

[64] 2000 Act, s.43(2)(e).
[65] 2000 Act, s.24.
[66] *Earl of Zetland v Hislop* (1882) 9R. (HL) 40.
[67] 2000 Act, s.24.
[68] 2003 Act, s.8(1) and (2).
[69] see *Macdonald v Douglas*, 1963 S.C. 374; *Howard De Walden Estates Ltd v Bowmaker Ltd*, 1965 S.C. 163; *Co-operative Wholesale Society v Ushers Brewery*, 1975 S.L.T. (Lands Tr.) 9; Halliday, *Conveyancing Law & Practice* (2nd ed.), paras 34–42 *et seq.*; Reid, *The Law of Property in Scotland*, paras 407 *et seq.*; Gordon, *op. cit.*, paras 22–32, 22–66, 23–15.

ment.[70] Reallotment therefore will apply not just to the burden but to the counter obligation so that the nominated new dominant land or tenement with the right to enforce will become burdened with the counter-obligation.[71]

Saving of personal contractual obligations

Whatever the status of a real burden might be (and many burdens   **3–35**
inserted in deeds do not qualify as real burdens)[72] they are enforceable as between the original superior and vassal purely as a matter of personal contract[73]. The Lands Tribunal has always been wary of discharging burdens where the application comes from the original vassal.[74] That does not mean however that the Tribunal cannot in appropriate circumstances vary or discharge a land obligation where the applicant is the original vassal.[75] The 2000 Act however preserves existing contractual rights. It provides as respect any land granted in feu before the appointed day that nothing in the Act shall affect any right (other than a right to feuduty) included in the grant insofar as the right is contractual as between the parties to the grant or as the case may be as between one of them and a person to whom any such right is assigned.[76] The view is therefore that feudal abolition will not affect an original superior's right to enforce burdens in a feudal writ against the original vassal. There is another possible interpretation and that is that where these conditions are expressly stated to be real burdens as opposed to personal conditions then they are extinguished on abolition but that is not thought to be the preferable view. Presumably the right of assignation would only apply while the original parties remain. Feudal superiors could not defeat abolition by assigning the original contractual right to someone else so that that party could then enforce against someone who was a singular successor of the original vassal.

---

[70] 2000 Act, s.25.
[71] 2000 Act, s.25.
[72] See Rennie, "The Reality of Real Burdens", 1998 S.L.T. (News) 149.
[73] *Scottish Co-Operative Wholesale Society Ltd v Finnie*, 1937 S.C. 835.
[74] *Murrayfield Ice-rink v Scottish Rugby Union*, 1972 S.L.T. (Lands Tr.) 20; 1973 S.L.T. 99; *Solway Cedar Ltd v Hendry*, 1972 S.L.T. (Lands Tr.) 42.
[75] *McVey v Glasgow Corporation*, 1973 S.L.T. (Lands Tr.) 15.
[76] 2000 Act, s.75.

CHAPTER 4

FEUDUTIES

INTRODUCTION

Payment of a *reddendo* or return by the vassal to the feudal superior was **4–01** an integral part of the feudal system. Originally the return would have been military service or produce. Latterly the return was commuted to a money payment known as a feuduty. The Land Tenure Reform (Scotland) Act 1974 provided for volutary and compulsory redemption of feu duties.[1] Moreover that Act prohibited the creation of new feu duties.[2] The framers of the 1974 legislation hoped that the lack of a monetary return would discourage developers from feuing out new plots and accordingly that the feudal system itself would wither on the vine. This did not occur and despite the redemption legislation some feu duties remain unredeemed. Since feuduty is a debt owed by the land or a *debitum fundi* it is not something that can be ignored in the course of an ordinary conveyancing transaction. Where the superior is known difficulties seldom arise in as much as the arrears of feuduty can be paid off and the feuduty redeemed if allocated. If the feuduty is not allocated then the feuduty can be allocated.[3] Obviously feu duties have no place in a non-feudal system of land tenure and the 2000 Act makes provision for the total extinction of feu duties subject to payment of a compensatory amount.

EXTINCTION ON THE APPOINTED DAY

Any feuduty which has not been redeemed and therefore extinguished **4–02** before November 28, 2004 is extinguished on that day and no payment can be collected in respect of that feuduty for that day or for any period after that day.[4] The extinction provisions apply not just to feuduties but to blench duties.[5] Blench duties are for nominal amounts. Extinction of feuduties does not affect the obligation to make payment of any arrears of feuduty due as at the appointed day. Any arrears of feuduty will fall due on the appointed day.[6] However, any sums due on the appointed day will simply remain as personal debts owed by the former vassal to the former superior. The Act makes it clear that neither the feuduty nor the

---

[1] Land Tenure Reform (Scotland) Act 1974, ss.4, 5 and 6.
[2] Land Tenure Reform (Scotland) Act 1974, s.1.
[3] Conveyancing and Feudal Reform (Scotland) Act 1970, s.3 (repealed 2000 Act, Sch.12, para.30).
[4] 2000 Act, s.7.
[5] 2000 Act, s.16(1).
[6] 2000 Act, s.13(1).

arrears shall remain as a *debitum fundi* or debt owed by the land itself.[7] Similarly if notice of the redemption of the feuduty has been given prior to extinguishment the redemption amount due in terms of the Land Tenure Reform (Scotland) Act 1974 shall not be a *debitum fundi* owed out of the land.[8] These provisions will of course remove much of the difficulty which surrounds arrears of feuduty and redemption payments in conveyancing transactions where, for example, the superior simply cannot be traced. The superior's hypothec is also abolished on the appointed day.[9] The effect of this is also to remove any suggestion that the superior or former superior will be left with any real remedy against the burdened land either in respect of arrears of feuduty or redemption monies.

THE COMPENSATORY PAYMENT

4–03   The former superior is entitled to claim a compensatory payment from the former vassal. However whereas the obligation was firmly placed on the vassal to redeem in terms of the Land Tenure Reform (Scotland) Act 1974 the obligation in terms of the 2000 Act[10] is placed firmly on the former superior. The former superior may within two years of the appointed day, serve a notice on the former vassal requiring the compensatory payment. The payment is calculated in accordance with the statutory formula.[11] One of the reasons why many feuduties remain unredeemed is because they are unallocated. In such a case a *cumulo* feduty was exigible from a whole tenement of flats and was informally apportioned among the flat owners. Under the Land Tenure Reform (Scotland) Act 1974 the feuduty had to be allocated before it could be redeemed. In terms of the 2000 Act however where the feuduty is a *cumulo* feuduty apportioned among various properties the superior must send a separate notice to each vassal liable for the *cumulo* in order to claim the compensatory payment. The notice is in the form contained in Schedule 1 or 2 and it must be accompanied by an explanatory note.[12] If appropriate notice is served the former vassal has a period of 56 days after service to make the compensatory payment.[13] The amount which has to be paid by way of compensatory payment is based on the formula already set out in the Land Tenure Reform (Scotland) Act 1974. The sum to be paid is the sum which would, if invested in two and half percent consolidated stock at the middle market price at the close of business last preceding the appointed day produce an annual sum equal to the feuduty.[14] Where the feuduty is a *cumulo* feuduty it is up to the former superior to determine the sum due for each apportioned part by allocation among the former vassals in such proportions as are reasonable in all the circumstances. The compensatory payment is then calculated on the apportioned part.[15] In most cases of course the *cumulo* feuduty will

---

[7] 2000 Act, s.13(2).
[8] 2000 Act, s.13(2).
[9] 2000 Act, s.13(3).
[10] 2000 Act, s.8.
[11] 2000 Act, s.9.
[12] 2000 Act, s.8(3) and (4).
[13] 2000 Act, s.8(5).
[14] 2000 Act, s.9(1).
[15] 2000 Act, s.9(3).

already have been apportioned informally in the split off deeds of the various flats or properties and in such a case for the purposes of a reasonable allocation the proportions set out in the split off deeds shall be presumed to be reasonable.[16] Where the compensatory payment is not less than £50 the former superior must serve with the notice an instalment document in the form of Schedule 3 for signature and dating by the former vassal and an explanatory note. If the former superior does not do this there is no requirement to make the compensatory payment. This additional document if completed and signed by the former vassal allows him or her to pay by instalments.[17] If the property is sold or transferred for valuable consideration after the instalment document has been served then if the option to pay by instalments has been obtained it is lost and if the option has not been obtained it cannot be obtained.[18] There are detailed provisions in relation to payments and arrears.[19] The instalment document must be returned by the former vassal within the 56-day period and it must be accompanied by a payment equivalent to one tenth of the compensatory amount. This initial payment is in addition to the total compensatory payment which will be due. If the option is lost because of a sale or transfer the whole balance is payable within seven days.[20] The former vassal may pay the outstanding balance at any time.[21] If an instalment is unpaid for 42 days the balance of the entire compensatory payment falls due.[22] The obligation to make a compensatory payment will be subject to the short negative prescription of five years.[23]

SERVICE

The documents claiming the compensatory payment require to be served on the former vassal and may be delivered or sent by registered post or recorded delivery addressed to the former vassal at an appropriate place.[24] The former vassal may sign an acknowledgement in the style of form A of Schedule 4. Alternatively a certificate of posting in the terms of form B of Schedule 4 is evidence of service.[25] If the notice is returned service may be made on the Extractor of the Court of Session and acknowledgement obtained from the Extractor.[26] The date on which service is deemed to have taken place is the date of delivery or in the case of posting the date of posting. Service should be made to an appropriate place which in the case of a former vassal is construed as a reference to his or her place of residence, place of business or a postal address which he or she ordinarily uses or if none of these is known at the time of delivery or posting a reference to whatever place is at that time his or

4–04

---

[16] 2000 Act, s.9(4).
[17] 2000 Act, s.10(1) and (2).
[18] 2000 Act, s.10(3).
[19] 2000 Act, ss.10(4) and (5).
[20] 2000 Act, ss.10(4)(d)(ii).
[21] 2000 Act, s.10(4)(d)(iii).
[22] 2000 Act, s.10(4)(d)(i).
[23] Prescription and Limitation (Scotland) Act 1973, s.6 and para.1(aa) of Sch.1 as introduced by 2000 Act, s.12.
[24] 2000 Act, s.11(1).
[25] 2000 Act, s.11(2).
[26] 2000 Act, s.11(3).

her most recently known place of residence or place of business or postal address ordinarily used.[27] Were a property held in feu is owned by two or more vassals as common property they are severally liable to make the compensatory payment but as between them are liable only in the proportions in which they own the property. For the purpose of service they are treated as a single vassal.[28]

PRACTICE

4–05 The difficulty which many former superiors will face here is the difficulty of obtaining information. Some superiors may frankly feel that the trouble and expense of serving notices, working out apportioned parts of *cumulo* feuduties and the like far outweigh the amount of compensatory payment which will be due. Some help is afforded to former superiors in the legislation. A superior or, after the appointed day a former superior who receives payment of a *cumulo* feuduty from a third party such as a factor may require that third party to disclose the identity and address of the vassal or former vassal and where the amount paid by the third party is only part of the feuduty the amount collected from the vassal or former vassal. The third party has a legal requirement to disclose this information.[29] Similarly where the former superior serves a notice requiring a compensatory payment on the party he regards as the former vassal but the person on whom it is served is no longer the former vassal because immediately before the appointed day the property has been transferred then the party on whom the notice is served must disclose to the former superior the identity and address of the new owner or such information as he has which might enable the former superior to trace the party liable.[30]

---

[27] 2000 Act, s.11(5).
[28] 2000 Act, s.16(4).
[29] 2000 Act, s.14.
[30] 2000 Act, s.15.

CHAPTER 5

PRAEDIAL REAL BURDENS—CONSTITUTION, CONTENT AND INTERPRETATION

INTRODUCTION

On one view, possibly an extreme view, there should be no place for real burdens in a non-feudal system of land tenure. The idea that one party having an interest in land can control the use of other property owned by another party where there is no personal contract voluntarily entered into between these parties smacks of feudalism. Nevertheless it has to be accepted that for decades now many real burdens have been validly created outwith a feudal context. The most famous case of all related to burdens in a disposition.[1] Moreover real burdens or title conditions enforceable by one proprietor against another are a feature of most other jurisdictions. Ultimately it was considered that there should still be a place for the private regulation of the use of land by title conditions in a non-feudal context and that matters should not simply be left to local planners. The difficulty was to frame a sensible code of law for real burdens in a non-feudal context. If one analyses the existing law it is still very much centred on feudalism. For example for a party to be able to enforce a real burden that party must have both title and interest. In the case of a feudal real burden, title is obvious; it is a superiority title itself. So far as interest is concerned the interest of the superior is presumed.[2] It does seem that the existing rules relating to non-feudal real burdens are really tacked on to the rules relating to feudal real burdens. The right of a singular successor of a disponer to enforce a real burden created in a disposition is a complicated matter and the case law has never been clear.[3] When it comes to the question of interest to enforce the interest of the original disponer appears to be presumed but only against the original disponee.[4] When it comes to co-feuars or co-disponees the position is even more complicated. Accordingly it was necessary to set out new rules relating to the constitution and interpretation of real burdens in a non-feudal context. This is done in Part 1 of the 2003 Act which deals with real burdens in general. By and large the existing common law is restated with some welcome clarification and amendment. It should be noted at the outset that most of the Act, and this part of the Act in particular, is retrospective in that, unless a contrary intention appears, or unless otherwise specifically provided in the Act the provisions apply

5–01

---

[1] *Tailors of Aberdeen v Coutts* (1840) 1 Rob. App. 296.

[2] *Earl of Zetland v Hislop* (1882) 9 R. (HL) 40.

[3] *JA MacTaggart & Co. v Harrower* (1906) 8 F. 1101; *Braidhills Hotel Co. Ltd v Manuels*, 1909 S.C. 120.

[4] *Scottish Co-operative Wholesale Society v Finnie*, 1937 S.C. 835.

to all real burdens whenever created.[5] Thus, for example, the provisions relating to the manner in which real burdens are to be interpreted[6] will alter the way in which courts interpret real burdens created prior to November 28, 2004. Having said that, the changes to the existing common law are minimal.

PRAEDIAL REAL BURDENS—DEFINITION AND TERMINOLOGY

The praedial rule

5–02 For a burden to be real under the existing law it had to be praedial both as regards the land subject to the burden (the burdened land) and the land to which enforcement rights attached (the benefited land). The classic statement of the praedial rule is to be found in the leading case of *Tailor's of Aberdeen v Coutts*.[7] In that case it was stated:

> "To constitute a real burden or condition, either in feudal or burgage rights, which is effectual against singular successors, words must be used in the conveyance which clearly express or plainly imply that the subject itself is to be affected and not the grantee and his heirs alone."

The common law however did not require any particular form of words nor indeed any labels. It was not necessary for example to state in terms that the burden was to be real. What had to be shown was that the obligation pertained to the land and not first to individual parties who were essentially entering a personal contract. The difficulty with rules of this type is that they are general in their expression but particular to individual cases in their effect. Thus it has been held that an obligation to pay a share of the cost of construction of a road which had already been made was not binding on a successor.[8] The provision was simply construed as a personal obligation. This rule has recently been applied in relation to a purported real burden which prohibited playing tennis on a Sunday. It was held, admittedly in the Sheriff Court, that the burden was not praedial in the sense that it had more to do with the day of the week than the use of land.[9] One of the difficulties which has surrounded the existing law results from a use of real burdens to deal with essentially personal matters. Many such title conditions have laudable social aims such as a provision to the effect that a house cannot be sold in a sheltered housing complex to anyone other than a disabled person or a person over a certain age. Under the existing law however there must be doubt that such a burden could ever be praedial.[10] Part of the difficulty with many of such burdens is relating a praedial benefit directly to the land to which enforcement rights attach. One could argue, for example, that provisions in a tenemental title in relation to meetings of

---

[5] 2003 Act, s.119(10).
[6] 2003 Act, ss.2(5) and 14 and see para.5–27 *et seq.* below.
[7] (1840) 1 Rob. App. 296 at 306.
[8] *Magistrates of Edinburgh v Begg* (1883) 11 R. 352.
[9] *Marsden v Craighelen Lawn Tennis and Squash Club*, 1999 G.W.D. 37–1820.
[10] See Rennie, "The Reality of Real Burdens", 1998 S.L.T. (News) 149; such a burden would be valid under the 2003 Act, s.54(5)(c).

proprietors, property committees, property councils, etc. are purely mechanisms dealing with how people manage their affairs as opposed to praedial burdens. The alternative view of course is that without such mechanisms other burdens relating to the maintenance of the property would be difficult to enforce and accordingly that such management type burdens have an indirect praedial connection with the property. Even under the existing law it has sometimes been difficult to distinguish between a title condition which is essentially personal and one which is, directly or indirectly praedial.[11]

Burdened and benefited property

The 2003 Act uses the terminology "burdened" and "benefited" prop-   **5–03** erty whereas the 2000 Act used the term "dominant tenement" for the purposes of re-allotment of feudal burdens. "Land" is defined in the 2003 Act as including all heritable property both corporeal and incorporeal capable of being held as a separate tenement including land covered by water.[12] Accordingly heritable incorporeal property such as salmon fishings and tenemental properties are included within the definition. The expression "owner" is defined as a person who has right to the property whether or not that person has a completed title and this could include a person who has most recently acquired a right if more than one person could fall within the definition. A heritable creditor in possession is an owner for certain purposes.[13]

The expression "real burden"

The expression "real burden" is defined in the opening section of the   **5–04** 2003 Act. There it is provided that a real burden is an encumbrance on land constituted in favour of the owner of other land in that person's capacity as owner of that other land.[14] Thus the praedial rule is essentially preserved. The encumbered land is known as the "burdened property" and the other land with enforcement rights is known as the "benefited property".[15] This definition would of course rule out many of the personal real burdens which are permitted under the 2003 Act. These burdens are conservation burdens, rural housing burdens, maritime burdens, economic development burdens, healthcare burdens, manager burdens, personal pre-emption burdens and personal redemption burdens. These burdens are not constituted in favour of benefited property but in favour of a person. However the 2003 Act caters for this by providing that notwithstanding the praedial rule the expression "real burden" will include these personal real burdens.[16] The concept of a praedial real burden is further expanded in the 2003 Act. It is provided that a real burden must relate in some way to the burdened

---

[11] See, for example, *Aberdeen Varieties Ltd v James F. Donald (Aberdeen Cinemas) Ltd*, 1939 S.C. 788; 1940 S.C. (HL) 45, where the distinction between a personal commercial benefit and a praedial benefit is explored to some extent.
[12] 2003 Act, s.122(1).
[13] 2003 Act, s.123.
[14] 2003 Act, s.1(1).
[15] 2003 Act, s.1(2).
[16] 2003 Act, s.1(3).

property.[17] However the relationship may be direct or indirect provided that the relationship is not just to the burdened party as owner of the burdened property.[18] Accordingly burdens which might have been doubtful under the existing law because they were ancillary or management type burdens will now be praedial even if they are only praedial indirectly.[19] Where there is a definite benefited property then the burden must be for the benefit of that property and no other property except in the case of a community burden.[20] The obvious example would be a situation where a widow dispones half her garden as a building plot because the garden has become too much to manage. In the disposition there will no doubt be several burdens to preserve the amenity of retained property. These burdens would obviously be wholly for the benefit of the retained property. The 2003 Act contains provisions which create a new category of burden known as a "community burden".[21] These provisions are designed in part to replace the unsatisfactory law of third party rights. Indeed some existing third party rights will become community burdens. However in such cases the burdens might be said to be for the benefit of the whole community as opposed to one particular property. Accordingly the 2003 Act further relaxes the praedial rule by providing that a community burden may be for the benefit of the community to which it relates or of some part of that community as opposed to a particular property.[22]

Affirmative, negative and ancillary burdens

5–05   Most burdens in existing titles might be said to be either affirmative, negative or ancillary. An affirmative burden contains an obligation to do something such as erect a dwellinghouse within a certain time and to a certain specification. It may also be a continuing obligation such as an obligation to maintain common parts in a tenemental title. A negative obligation normally takes the form of some type of prohibition generally of a specified use. The titles to residential properties commonly have prohibitions of the carrying on of trade, business and profession as well as prohibitions of nauseous trades and the like. Very often there is a general prohibition of nuisance. More modern titles have more detailed prohibitions relating to the parking of commercial vehicles, powerboats and the keeping of certain pets. In addition to affirmative and negative burdens many titles contain some sort of framework for management of the property or at least the common parts and this framework is often ancillary to the main affirmative or negative burdens. The 2003 Act retains this classification. It provides that a real burden can only be created as an obligation to do something (which will include an obligation to pay or contribute towards some cost) or an obligation to refrain from doing something.[23] The former type of burden is

---

[17] 2003 Act, s.3(1).
[18] 2003 Act, s.3(2).
[19] This is emphasised by the creation of a separate category of ancillary burdens in 2003 Act, s.2(3).
[20] 2003 Act, s.3(3).
[21] 2003 Act, Part 2, ss.25–37 and see Ch.6 below.
[22] 2003 Act, s.3(4).
[23] 2003 Act, s.2(1).

to be known as an "affirmative burden"[24] and the latter type of burden is to be known as a "negative burden".[25] However this strict classification is modified to the effect that a real burden may also be created which consists of a right to enter or otherwise make use of property or makes provision for the management or administration of property provided the burden is for a purpose ancillary to those of an affirmative or negative burden.[26] This type of burden is to be known as an "ancillary burden".[27]

The rules of constitution

The combined effect of sections 1, 2 and 3 is to restate by and large the common law relating to the rules of constitution.[28] Under the existing law if a purported burden did not conform to these rules then it could not be real and did not affect singular successors. The rules in relation to interpretation and construction of real burdens tend to merge with the rules of constitution. On the one hand if the rules on constitution are not complied with the burden is not real; on the other hand even if it can be said that the rules on constitution have been fulfilled if the burden is too inspecific it cannot be enforced. In many ways it might be said to come to the same thing. Under existing law real burdens are construed very strictly *contra proferentem* and in accordance with the presumption of freedom.[29] This rule of constitution is relaxed in the 2003 Act which provides that in determining whether a real burden is created as an affirmative, negative or ancillary burden regard is to be had as to the effect of the provision rather than to the way in which the provision is expressed.[30] This provision should be read together with another provision of the 2003 Act which provides in relation to the construction of real burdens, as opposed to their constitution, that they are to be construed in the same manner as other provisions of deeds which relate to land and are intended for registration.[31] Presumably this means that real burdens and conditions will no longer be subjected to the malign construction which has been applied in some cases.[32]

5–06

PRAEDIAL REAL BURDENS—CONTENT

Rights of pre-emption, redemption, reversion and options to acquire

A real burden may consist of a right of pre-emption. Normally this will be a pre-emption which pertains to a benefited property although personal pre-emptions are possible under the re-allotment provisions of the

5–07

---

[24] 2003 Act, s.2(2)(a).
[25] 2003 Act, s.2(2)(b).
[26] 2003 Act, s.2(3).
[27] 2003 Act, s.2(4).
[28] Reid, *op. cit.*, para.386 *et seq.*
[29] *The Walker Trustees v Haldane*, 1902 4 F. 954 at 596; *Anderson v Dickie*, 1915 S.C. (HL) 79 at 89; Reid, *op. cit.*, para.390; Halliday, *Conveyancing Law and Practice* (2nd ed.), pp.24–27.
[30] 2003 Act, s.2(5).
[31] 2003 Act, s.14 and see para.5–27 *et seq.* below
[32] See *Lothian Regional Council v Rennie*, 1991 S.C. 212.

2000 Act.[33] It will not however be possible to create a right of redemption or reversion after November 28, 2004 nor a real burden which purports to create some other type of option to acquire the burdened property.[34] A right of redemption is effectively a right to buy back at any time or on the occurrence of a particular event. There has already been some statutory reform in relation to redemptions. After September 1, 1974 a right of redemption cannot last more than 20 years.[35] Accordingly as the law stands at the moment any right of redemption created between before September 1, 1974 will remain valid subject to the termination provisions in the 2003 Act for real burdens in general. Redemptions created between September 1, 1974 and November 28, 2004 will be subject to the 20-year limit and it will not be possible to create rights of redemption after November 28, 2004. It has never been very clear what a right or reversion actually is. The author has come across a number of reversions. Some of these are statutory such as those under the School Sites Act 1841 but others simply appear in deeds. Commonly they may appear in deeds granted for some sort of public of quasi-public purpose. It may be that property is conveyed to a public body for use as a hospital subject to a clause which states that it will revert in the event that the property ceases to be used for that purpose. The difficulty with such clauses of course is often to decide to whom the property is to revert, especially if the reversion is created in a non-feudal deed. On one interpretation it might be that the reversion is personal to the granters of the deed; on another interpretation it might be vest in the granters of the deed and their successors in remaining lands. On the other hand it might be that the reversion is simply an irritancy by another name. Feudal irritancies were abolished on June 9, 2000 by the 2000 Act[36] and non-feudal irritancies were abolished as at April 4, 2003 by the 2003 Act.[37] The final position is:

(a) Rights of reversion created after September 1, 1974 are subject to the 20-year rule and can only be exercised once.[38]

(b) Rights of reversion created prior to that date do not appear to be subject to any rule and will remain although there are still likely to be problems in relation to the identity of the parties who are entitled to the reversion. They can only be exercised once.

(c) It will not be competent to create a right of reversion after November 28, 2004.[39]

Legality, public policy and monopolies

5–08   It has always been the law that a real burden must not be contrary to law or public policy nor useless or vexatious nor inconsistent with the nature of the property.[40] The 2003 Act restates the existing common law

---

[33] See para.3–12 above.
[34] 2003 Act, s.3(5).
[35] Land Tenure Reform (Scotland) Act 1974, s.12.
[36] 2000 Act, s.53.
[37] 2003 Act, s.67.
[38] Land Tenure Reform (Scotland) Act 1974, s.12.
[39] 2003 Act, s.3(5).
[40] *Tailors of Aberdeen v Coutts* (1840) 1 Rob. App. 296 at 307.

by providing that a real burden must not be contrary to public policy as for example in unreasonable restraint of trade and must not be repugnant with ownership nor illegal.[41] The Act goes on to provide that except in so far as expressly permitted by the Act a real burden must not have the effect of creating a monopoly as for example by providing for a particular person to be appointed as the manager of property or the supplier of any services in relation to property. This latter prohibition which would of course strike at some factorial or property management appointments is subject to the detailed provisions in the Act relating to manager burdens.[42]

A burden which is contrary to the existing law would not be enforce-   **5–09**
able. Thus it has always been clear that a prohibition of selling or sub-feuing without the superior's consent is illegal.[43] The spread of anti-discrimination laws however has extended the category of burden which might be illegal. A burden which, for example, prohibited ownership or occupancy of property with reference to race or sex would clearly be illegal.[44] The same presumably would apply in relation to a burden which discriminates against disabled people. There might be, for example, an interesting argument over a prohibition of lifts.

Public policy—sheltered housing and retirement complexes

Many burdens which are illegal would presumably also be contrary to   **5–10**
public policy but this is perhaps a more fluid term. Prior to the 2003 Act one might have argued, for example, that a burden in the title to a sheltered house within a retirement complex to the effect that the house could only be owned and/or occupied by someone over a certain age or having a particular level of disability was unenforceable either on the grounds that it was not sufficiently praedial or on the grounds that to restrict ownership or occupancy to a particular section of the community is contrary to public policy. The alternative argument of course would have been that it was positive discrimination in favour of a section of the community which required certain special facilities. Under the 2003 Act it seems to the author however that such burdens will be enforceable even if they are not to be regarded as essentially praedial because a sheltered housing or other complex would be regarded as a community and the burden therefore would be a community burden. A community burden may be for the benefit of the community to which it relates or some part of that community as opposed to being for the praedial benefit of other land or heritable property.[45] In so far as public policy is concerned it is the author's view that it is by no means contrary to public policy to have special burdens which pertain to the particular type of property. The only point which is perhaps worth making is that the provision relating to age or disability should relate to occupancy rather than ownership. The author has known

---

[41] 2003 Act, s.3(6).
[42] See 2003 Act, ss.28 and 63 and para.6–26 *et seq.* below.
[43] Tenures Abolition Act 1746, s.10; Conveyancing (Scotland) Act 1874, s.22; Conveyancing Amendment (Scotland) Act 1938, s.8.
[44] Race Relations Act 1976; Sex Discrimination Act 1975.
[45] 2003 Act, s.3(4).

situations where a younger member of a family has purchased sheltered housing in his or her own name for the occupancy of an ageing parent. A provision relating to ownership as opposed to occupancy might be more difficult to justify on public policy grounds.

Manager monopolies

5–11　　Under the existing law a real burden could not confer a monopoly.[46] The 2003 Act reiterates the common law but provides an example. A real burden cannot (except so far as expressly permitted by the Act) have the effect of creating a monopoly by providing that a particular person can be or can appoint the manager of property or the supplier of any services in relation to that property. This provision strikes at provisions in titles to residential and commercial estates whereby the original developer attempts to retain control over the management of common parts. There are transitional provisions which allow these monopolies to continue for a maximum of five years in most cases or 30 years in the case of burdens imposed in deeds by local authorities in right to buy sales to sitting tenants. In the case of common schemes involving sheltered housing the period is three years. These periods however do not run from the coming into force of the 2003 Act but from the day on which the burden creating the monopoly has been created by registration.[47]

Unreasonable restraint of trade

5–12　　Under the common law there appears to be a distinction between a burden which is designed purely to preserve or protect a personal commercial benefit and one which is designed to protect a praedial or patrimonial interest.[48] The focus of discussion however has tended to be in relation to the benefit conferred on the property to which enforcement rights attach rather than the burden imposed on the burdened property. Titles to residential property contain a large number of real burdens which prohibit all sorts of commercial activity. The reason that these are enforceable appears to have nothing to do with the fact that they may be in restraint of trade in relation to the burdened property but more to do with the fact that the parties entitled to enforce the burden are not doing so to protect a commercial interest but rather to protect an amenity interest in a larger area which interest could of course be said to be praedial.[49] Problems arise where the right to enforce a prohibition of trade or commerce pertains to other commercial property which happens to be in close proximity. In *Philips v Lavery*,[50] a party owned two grocery shops and sold one subject to a burden in a disposition that it could not be used as a butcher's shop or a grocer's shop. The court held that the burden was unenforceable as being in restraint of trade. The court took this view despite the fact that

---

[46] *Yeamen v Crawford* (1770) Mor. 14537; *Orrock v Bennet* (1762) Mor. 15009.

[47] 2003 Act, ss.28 and 63 and see para.6–26 *et seq.* below.

[48] *Aberdeen Varieties Ltd v James F. Donald (Aberdeen Cinemas) Ltd*, 1939 S.C. 788; 1940 S.C. (HL) 52.

[49] See the discussion in Reid, *op. cit.*, para.391.

[50] 1962 S.L.T. (Sh. Ct.) 57.

the parties to the action were the original parties to the disposition. The court took the view therefore that the obligation was unenforceable as a personal obligation as well as a burden. The court came to a similar view in *Giblin v Murdoch*[51] where the business in question was that of a hairdresser. Nevertheless one cannot say with certainty that under the existing law a burden which protects a commercial interest cannot at the same time protect a praedial or patrimonial interest. In the leading case of *Aberdeen Varieties Ltd v James F. Donald (Aberdeen Cinemas) Ltd*[52] a party who owned two theatres conveyed one under a burden which effectively prevented the use of the building as a theatre for the performance of stage plays of a certain type. The burden was held not to be enforceable but if one looks at the judgements in the Court of Session and in the House of Lords the basis on which the decision was taken is far from clear. Indeed different judges may have come to the same conclusion for different reasons. Certainly the short distance between the two properties was a factor. In the more recent case of *Co-operative Wholesale Society v Ushers Brewery*[53] a small shopping precinct had been constructed in 1966 within a council housing scheme. The shopping precinct comprised a public house, a licensed betting office and a supermarket. One might describe these units as providing the essentials of modern life. The land had been made available by the local estate trustees who feued each plot to separate purchasers under restrictions as to use which were declared to be enforceable not only by the trustees as superiors but also by the proprietors of the three plots among themselves. The proprietors of the supermarket were required to use their plot for the purpose only for a retail shop and were prohibited from selling excisable liquor. In 1973 a co-operative society who had succeeded to the interests of the original feuar applied to the Lands Tribunal for a discharge of the relevant restriction. Their application was later amended to seek a discharge to the extent only of allowing alcoholic liquor to be sold in the supermarket under an off-sales certificate. The application was opposed by a brewery company who had become the owners of the adjoining public house. They claimed compensation in the event that the burden was discharged. The Lands Tribunal did not have any jurisdiction to decide that the burden in question protected a commercial benefit and accordingly was in restraint of trade and unenforceable. However they did take the view in granting application that there was an enforceable real burden to be varied. They also awarded compensation, presumably taking the view that there was some praedial interest which would be adversely affected by the grant of the application. The Tribunal considered the *Aberdeen Varieties Ltd v James F. Donald (Aberdeen Cinemas) Ltd*[54] case, and the passage in *Tailors of Aberdeen v Coutts*.[55] The Tribunal posed the question whether or not the burdens in all the titles were purely trading conditions divorced from the land or whether patrimonial interests were involved. Crucial to the decision was the small nature of the shopping precinct and the fact that all the properties were subject to the same type of restriction.

---

[51] 1979 S.L.T. (Sh. Ct.) 5.
[52] 1939 S.C. 788; 1940 S.C. (HL) 52.
[53] 1975 S.L.T. (Lands Tr.) 9.
[54] 1939 S.C. 788; 1940 S.C. (HL) 52.
[55] (1840) 1 Rob. App. 296 at 307.

The owners of the public house could not have turned their property in to a supermarket. The Tribunal stated that[56]:

> "... it was not entirely clear to the Tribunal whether we were also being asked by the applicants to hold that the restrictions in the present case were unenforceable as being contrary to public policy. We do not think they were imposed by the superiors in restraint of trade. Nor do we consider that a restriction could be invalid as being contrary to public policy, *quoad* co-feuars or co-disponees but valid merely *quoad* and superiors ... In the present case it appears to the Tribunal that the restrictive conditions were wholly connected with adjacent heritable properties which formed part of a distinct small neighbourhood. The public house, as dominant tenement, is a one-storey building comprising nothing else but lounges and public bars; and it was to protect the owner's interest in this property that the superiors first imposed these obligations along with a number of other obligations. In these whole circumstances the Tribunal considered that the owners of the dominant tenement do have a patrimonial interest sufficient in law to entitle them to enforce the restriction and that the latter is capable of elevation into a real burden as opposed to a personal contract enforceable only between the contracting parties."

The view which the Tribunal presumably took was that the burdens were there not so much to protect an individual commercial interest but to protect the overall commercial viability of the small development. There was therefore a link between the commercial businesses carried on in the properties and the properties themselves. Put in commercial terms two supermarkets would presumably have struggled and accordingly the values of the properties would have been affected. Accordingly there was a praedial or patrimonial interest.

5–13　　The 2003 Act simply states that a real burden must not be contrary to public policy as for example being in unreasonable restraint of trade.[57] Only the word "unreasonable" might be said to be an addition to or modification of the existing law. The addition of this word however might suggest that there can be a real burden which is in "reasonable" restraint of trade. In other words a burden which restrains a trading activity will not necessarily fail for that reason alone. It seems to the author that the law remains very much as it was set out in the *Co-operative Wholesale Society v Ushers Brewery* case. It seems to the author that there will still require to be some sort of praedial or patrimonial interest being protected even if indirectly protected by the commercial burden. In circumstances such as arose in *Philips v Lavery*[58] a court would be likely to come to the same decision after the coming into effect of the 2003 Act.

---

[56] 1975 S.L.T. (Lands Tr.) 9 at 12.
[57] 2003 Act, s.3 (6).
[58] 1962 S.L.T. (Sh. Ct.) 57.

Repugnancy with ownership

The common law rule was expressed by that serial dissenter, the **5–14**
redoubtable Lord Young, in *Moyes Trustees v McEwan*.[59] Lord Young
stated:

> "I think that to insert in a proprietory title—a feu-charter conferring
> a right of property in fee-simple—a prohibition against letting alto-
> gether would be bad from repugnancy, just as a prohibition against
> selling would be bad for repugnancy. You cannot make a man pro-
> prietor and yet prohibit him from exercising the rights of proprie-
> torship."

This principle is restated in the 2003 Act.[60] Plainly prohibitions of what
might be regarded as ordinary juristic acts such as the granting of leases
or dispositions would be struck at but prohibitions of certain types of
use or trade especially in residential properties presumably would not
even though they are fetters on the rights of ownership.[61] It has, for
example, been held that it is not competent to create a real burden which
restricts a common owner's right to the ultimate remedy of division and
sale.[62] Professor Reid draws a distinction between restrictions which are
expressed in negative terms such as prohibitions and those which are
expressed in positive terms which set out the use which is allowed.[63]
The distinction is between an obligation not to sell alcohol and an obligation that alcohol must be sold. The former would be enforceable but
the latter would not, presumably on the ground that the latter is in practical effect a far wider prohibition than the former in that it prohibits all
uses except one.[64] The 2003 Act simply states that a real burden must not
be repugnant with ownership. In the author's view the law remains
very much as it was.

Waiver or discharge by third party

In terms of the 2003 Act it is not competent to provide in the deed creat- **5–15**
ing a burden or importing the burden a provision to the effect that a
party other than a holder of the burden can waive compliance or mitigate or vary a condition of the burden.[65] Although many builders or
developers have abandoned the feudal system as a means of conveying new housing those same builders and developers often wish to
retain control over the development as a whole. Indeed they were
perhaps encouraged to take the position of a quasi-superior where they
had granted a deed of conditions and then followed this up by simple
dispositions. The practice in the legal profession when looking for a
consent or a waiver in respect of a burden in such circumstances is still

---

[59] (1880) 7 R. 1141 at 1145; and see Reid, *op. cit.*, para.391.
[60] 2003 Act, s.3(6).
[61] *Earl of Zetland v Hislop* (1882) 9 R. (HL) 40.
[62] *Grant v Heriot Trust* (1906) 8 F. 647.
[63] Reid, *op. cit.*, para.391.
[64] See *Burnett v Great North of Scotland Railway Co.* (1885) 12 R. (HL) 25, a decision which
Professor Reid doubts.
[65] 2003 Act, s.3(8) (as prospectively amended by the Tenements (Scotland) Bill 2004,
s.22(2)).

to write to the original builder or developer as if they were a superior. In a case where the builder or developer has sold all the plots and retained no meaningful heritable interest then the consent of that builder or developer would have been worthless. However in some deeds of conditions there is an express provision which allows the builder or developer to grant waivers or consents even although they have no remaining title. The builder or developer may of course retain enforcement rights if some ownership rights in the development are retained. Community burdens created in terms of the 2003 Act[66] are in a different position. There is specific statutory provision in relation to waiver or discharge of these burdens and accordingly an exception is made which in certain circumstances may allow waiver or discharge even without the consent of all those in the community entitled to enforce the burden.[67] Some existing burdens created prior to the appointed day will become community burdens. The most obvious example would be burdens covering a whole estate or a block of flats. The new provisions in section 3(8) of the 2003 Act apply to burdens created after the appointed day. There is provision to a similar effect in respect of burdens created before the appointed day.[68] That provision is to the effect that in construing a burden created before the appointed day any provision to the effect that a person other than the person entitled to enforce the burden may waive compliance or mitigate or vary the burden is to be disregarded. Accordingly if a superior has reserved a right to himself as developer to vary or discharge burdens then on abolition of the superiority title the former superior will not be entitled to rely on that provision as developer and only those who have legal enforcement rights after the appointed day will be able to waive or discharge. Unfortunately there does not appear to be the equivalent exclusion in respect of community burdens and the special rules relating to waiver or discharge of these burdens. There, are certain circumstances, where waiver or discharge may be granted by majority. Perhaps the correct view is that the provisions in the 2000 Act were meant to deal with the situation of the superior whereas the provisions in the 2003 Act are meant to deal with the ongoing situation. Burdens contained in pre-appointed day deeds of condition will not be community burdens until after the appointed day and, having assumed the character of community burdens and the legal consequences of that character it may be argued that the provisions of the 2003 Act will then apply to these pre-appointed day burdens as they become community burdens after the appointed day. If that interpretation is not correct then the situation (presumably unintended) will be extremely messy with there being a different regime for the waiver of community burdens created prior to the appointed day from that applicable to community burdens created after the appointed day. That certainly cannot have been the intention.

---

[66] 2003 Act, ss.25–37.
[67] 2003 Act, s.3(9).
[68] 2000 Act, s.73(2A).

REAL BURDENS—DEED OF CONSTITUTION

Creation of real burdens by deed

Under the existing law a real burden has to be created in a deed. The **5–16** rules for the constitution of real burdens in a deed are set out in the standard texts.[69] The basic principles may be summarised as follows:

a) The burden must affect the land; this is simply the praedial rule.
b) There must be a separate dominant or benefited property and a servient or burdened property.
c) The burdened land must be precisely identified.
d) The burden must appear at length in the original infeftment generally speaking in the dispositive clause although there has always been a view that a feudal burden need not be in the dispositive clause.[70]
e) The burden must be specified with such a degree of precision that anyone looking at the record of the deed on the register will be able to understand the nature and extent of the burden.
f) The content of a burden must not be contrary to law or public policy nor useless or vexatious nor inconsistent with the nature of the property.

Requirement for double registration

In practice burdens have been created in a conveyance or a deed of **5–17** conditions. Where they are created in a conveyance the universal practice is to insert them in the dispositive clause after the description even in feudal deeds. The facility of a deed of conditions was introduced as early as 1874.[71] Burdens in a deed of conditions are imported into the title of the burdened property either on registration of the deed of conditions[72] or when the deed of conditions is first referred to in a subsequent conveyance.[73] In either case the burden must appear in the recorded or registered title of the burdened property. There is under the existing law no requirement for the burden or the right to enforce the burden to appear in the title of the benefited property. This of course has led in many cases to difficulty in ascertaining the identity of the parties entitled to enforce especially where the burdens are created in non-feudal deeds and cover or bear to cover more than one property. The framers of the 2003 Act therefore took the view that one of the main aims of the legislation must be to provide greater transparency in relation to the identity of those who have rights of enforcement. This is achieved in large measure by introducing the concept of

---

[69] Halliday, *Conveyancing Law and Practice* (2nd ed.), paras 34–20 *et seq.*; Reid, *op. cit.*, paras 386–392; MacDonald, *Conveyancing Manual* (6th ed.), paras 10.8–10.14.
[70] Gordon, *Scottish Land Law* (2nd ed.), pp.22–33.
[71] Conveyancing (Scotland) Act 1874, s.32 as amended by the Land Registration (Scotland) Act 1979, s.17.
[72] Under s.17 of the Land Registration (Scotland) Act 1979.
[73] Where s.17 of the Land Registration (Scotland) Act 1979 is disapplied.

double registration against the title of both the burdened and benefited properties. Apart from this however there is a relaxation in the type of deed which may be used to create a real burden. The main provisions are contained in section 4 of the 2003 Act.

The constitutive deed

5–18   A real burden will be created after the appointed day by duly registering a constitutive deed containing the burden. This is defined[74] as a deed which sets out the terms of a title condition (or of a prospective title condition). The expression however includes any document in which the terms of the title condition in question are varied. Title condition is given a very broad definition.[75] A title condition means a real burden or a servitude or an affirmative obligation imposed on a servitude. It can also mean a condition in a registerable lease and Scottish Ministers may by order prescribe that other conditions relating to land are to be title conditions. A constitutive deed must state that the conditions are to be real burdens.[76] In conveyances and deeds of condition which contain real burdens it is of course common to end the burdens clause with a statement that the burdens are created and declared to be real liens and burdens upon and affecting the subjects. After November 28, 2004 it will be essential to use the term "real burden" unless the burdens are of a named type and are described by reference to that name. For example instead of stating that the burdens are to be real burdens the draftsman could state that they are to be community burdens as opposed to real burdens. The same would apply to other named burdens such as health-care burdens, conservation burdens and the like.[77] The constitutive deed must be granted by or on behalf of the owner of the burdened land.[78] The term "owner" is defined the Act[79] as the person who has right to the property whether or not that person has a completed title. If there is more than one person in that situation then any one of them can grant a constitutive deed creating real burdens.[80] This is a change in the law in that a party granting a deed of conditions had to have a completed title. Where the title to the burdened property is in the Sasine Register and the party granting the constitutive deed containing the burdens is uninfeft then the constitutive deed will require to contain a deduction of title clause. If the title is in the Land Register then obviously no deduction of title clause is required.[81] For the purposes of granting a constitutive deed a heritable creditor in lawful possession is specifically included in the definition of owner.[82] The constitutive deed must nominate and identify both the burdened land and the land which is to be the benefited property.[83] This latter requirement will not apply in the case of personal real burdens where the requirement will be to identify the person in whose

---

[74] 2003 Act, s.122(1).
[75] 2003 Act, s.122(1).
[76] 2003 Act, s.4(2)(a).
[77] 2003 Act, s.4(3).
[78] 2003 Act, s.4(2)(b).
[79] 2003 Act, s.123.
[80] 2003 Act, s.123(1)(a).
[81] 2003 Act, s.60; Land Registration (Scotland) Act 1979, s.15.
[82] 2003 Act, s.123(2).
[83] 2003 Act, s.4(2)(c).

favour the burden is to be constituted.[84] The requirement to identify the burdened and benefited land mirrors the existing law although the legislation does not give any guidance in relation to the degree of identification required. In one case it was held that a description of land as "the ground occupied as a lawn" was insufficient.[85] Given the requirement to register the constitutive deed against the titles of both burdened and benefited properties however it seems clear that the description of the benefited land should be sufficient to allow the Keeper to identify that land. Where the titles to the burdened and benefited properties are registered then the reference will be to the respective title numbers. Where the titles or one of them are in the Sasine Register then a description by reference to a particular description in an earlier deed will be appropriate. In other cases there will require to be a plan. The burden becomes real only on registration against the titles of both burdened and benefited properties.[86] Where community burdens are created there is also an additional requirement to nominate and identify the community in the constitutive deed.[87] Where the burdened land is owned in common *pro indiviso* then all common owners would require to grant the constitutive deed. A deed granted by only one or some of the *pro indiviso* owners cannot be used for the creation of real burdens.[88]

Reference to outside documents—maintenance obligations

The basic rules relating to content have already been discussed.[89] The requirement of the existing common law that the burden appear at length in the infeftment is repeated.[90] The rule was put succinctly by Lord MacMillan in this way:[91]   **5–19**

> "I need not remind your Lordships of the importance of the requirement that any burden or restriction to be effectual must enter the records. In Scotland the purchaser of land buys on the faith of the records. He obtains for his protection a search of the Registers and is entitled to rely on the land being unaffected by any burdens or conditions other than those contained in the deeds found on record to relate to the subject-matter of his purchase."

Thus burdens contained in ancillary but related documentation and simply referred to in the infeftment cannot be real.[92] Despite this rule there are many instances of purported burdens in existing titles which make reference to outside documents. For example it has been quite

---

[84] 2003 Act, s.4(2)(c).
[85] *Anderson v Dickie*, 1915 S.C. (HL) 79.
[86] 2003 Act, s.4(5).
[87] 2003 Act, s.4(4).
[88] 2003 Act, s.4(6).
[89] See paras 5–07—5–16 above.
[90] 2003 Act, s.4(2)(a).
[91] *Kemp v Magistrates of Largs*, 1939 S.C. (HL) 6 at 13.
[92] *Croall v Magistrates of Edinburgh* (1870) 9 M. 323—burdens in articles of roup; *Liddall v Duncan* (1898) 25 R. 1119—building conditions in a contract among proprietors of land; *Botanic Gardens Picture House v Adamson*, 1924 S.C. 549—burdens in the title of another property; *Aberdeen Varieties Ltd v James F. Donald (Aberdeen Cinemas) Ltd*, 1939 S.C. 788—burdens referring to an Act of Parliament relating to theatres.

common in the framing of maintenance obligations in tenemental property to provide that each party will bear a share of the expense of common repairs in proportion to respective rateable values as shown in a valuation roll. Similarly it has been quite common in commercial developments to provide that the property can only be used for any of the uses set out in a particular clause of the Use Classes Order. Other deeds provide for committees of proprietors or property councils who are given the power to make regulations which are to bind all the proprietors and their successors. Obviously the regulations are outwith the infeftment and in most cases would post-date that infeftment. The 2003 Act provides in general terms that the burden must appear at length in the constitutive deed. There is however an exception in the case of common repairs. In such a case reference may be made to another document outwith the constitutive deed provided that document is a public document such as an enactment or a public register or a record or a roll to which the public readily has access.[93] However this concession only applies where the burden is in respect of payment of or a contribution to some cost. The most obvious example would be a title which provided that each proprietor would pay a share of maintenance costs based on rateable value. This provision is retrospective. This concession would not allow a reference to the Use Classes Order in a burden which purported to restrict use.

Burdens for uncertain sums of money—maintenance obligations

5–20   One of the basic principles laid down (at least by some of the judges) in *Tailors of Aberdeen v Coutts*[94] was to the effect that where a burden provided for payment of money then the amount of money had to be specific and the creditor identified.[95] This has caused difficulty in relation to provisions in many deeds of conditions relating to tenemental property and blocks of flats where each unit is often burdened with a share of the cost of maintenance. In many cases the share is stated as a fraction or a percentage. In a tenement each flat might be burdened with a one eighth share. The difficulty is that the actual amount payable each year (as opposed to the proportion) will change depending on the total cost of repairs and maintenance during the year. On one view therefore burdens which imposed an obligation to pay by reference to a fraction or percentage might not be enforceable at least as against singular successors. There is of course no good policy reason why a burden which sets out a method of calculation should be unenforceable and indeed there have been arguments that even under the existing law such a burden would be enforceable for practical or policy reasons.[96] The 2003 Act clarifies matters by providing that it shall not be an objection to the validity of a real burden (whenever created) that an amount payable in respect of an obligation to defray some cost is not actually specified in

---

[93] 2003 Act, s.5(2).

[94] (1840) 1Rob. App. 296.

[95] See also *David Watson Property Management v Woolwich Equitable Building Society*, 1992 S.L.T. 430.

[96] See *Wells v Newhouse Purchasers Ltd*, 1964 S.L.T. (Sh. Ct.) 2; *Sheltered Housing Management Ltd v Cairns*, 2002 H.L.R. 126 *per* Lord Nimmo Smith at para.22; Rennie, "The Reality of Real Burdens", 1998 S.L.T. (News) 149; Reid, *op. cit.*, para.418.

the constitutive deed. Similarly it shall not be an objection to the validity of a real burden (whenever created) that a proportion or share payable in respect of an obligation to contribute to some cost is not specified provided the method of calculation of the proportion of share is specified.[97] This provision is expressly stated to be retrospective. The net effect of this provision and the other provision allowing reference to outside documents[98] is that a maintenance obligation expressed as a burden to pay a share of the costs based on rateable value will be valid assuming the public continue to have access to the valuation roll.

Clawback burdens

In commercial transactions involving prospective development with a 5–21 so-called "hope" value it is common to provide that the seller of ground will be entitled to an additional payment if the purchaser obtains a certain planning permission or a planning permission on certain terms to do with density and the like. A common provision of this type would be one which provided that the seller would obtain an additional payment based on a certain formula if planning permission is granted for a certain number of additional units. Generally speaking in such cases the additional consideration is based on a sum per unit over and above a fixed ceiling. In some cases this provision may be left to rest on a personal agreement or even on missives. In other cases there may be a standard security granted by the purchaser to the seller in security of the obligations to make the additional payment. In such cases care should be taken to ensure that the obligation or the security is not destroyed by the expiry of missives in accordance with a time limit expressed in a non-supercession clause.[99] In addition to these contractual or security arrangements it has been the practice to insert the obligation as one which binds singular successors to pay additional consideration as a burden on the title of the subjects conveyed. Whatever the arguments may have been surrounding the enforceability of a maintenance obligation in a tenemental title for a share of the cost of common repairs there is no doubt that a burden which purports to set out some sort of formula entitling the granter of a deed to additional consideration or clawback cannot be a real burden. Even if it was for a specific amount it might be regarded as a real burden for money which on one view is outlawed by legislation.[1] In most cases of course there is no specific sum because the amount of the clawback or additional consideration is dependent on a calculation based on some complicated formula involving the number of extra units or an increased floor area for a particular planning use. In such cases the burden falls foul of the rule which requires precision. There is nothing in the 2003 Act which changes this rule. Accordingly although a clawback burden of this type may be effective as a matter of personal contract between the original granter and grantee of the deed containing that burden[2] it will not be valid as a real burden and

---

[97] 2003 Act, s.5(1).
[98] 2003 Act, s.5(2).
[99] See for example *Albatown v Credential plc*, 2001 G.W.D. 30–8.
[1] Conveyancing and Feudal Reform (Scotland) Act 1970, s.9(8)(c); Halliday, *op. cit.*, para.50–01.
[2] *Scottish Co-operative Wholesale Society v Finnie*, 1937 S.C. 835.

accordingly will not bind a singular successor of the original grantee. The only exception to this is where the burden is constituted as an economic development burden or a healthcare burden.[3] In these cases it is specifically provided that the burden may comprise an obligation to pay a sum of money provided a specific sum or a method of determining the sum is specified in the constitutive deed. An economic development burden can only be granted in favour of a local authority or Scottish Ministers and a healthcare burden can only be granted in favour of a national health service trust or Scottish Ministers.

PRAEDIAL REAL BURDENS—TIMING AND ENDURANCE

Effective date

5–22   In the normal way a real burden will become effective when the constitutive deed is registered against the titles of both the burdened and benefited properties.[4] However it will permissible to specify another date such as a fixed date in the future following registration or a date in the future which can be determined by reference to the occurrence of an event or the date of registration of another deed.[5] This provision is similar to the provision relating to deeds of condition under the existing law[6] which allows a party granting a deed of conditions to suspend the enforceability of the burdens until the deed is actually referred to in a conveyance. In some cases developers have run into difficulties where burdens have been set out in relation to a whole estate at the outset and then, following on the grant of several conveyances the developers have wished to change the overall development plan. The obvious example is where a deed of conditions makes provision to the effect that the whole estate is to be used only for the erection of detached or semi-detached dwellinghouses and subsequently the developer wishes to erect a block of flats in one part of the estate. If the burdens have become enforceable immediately on the registration of the deed of conditions then there may be a problem especially if enforcement rights are vest in the owners of plots which have already been conveyed. Accordingly the new provisions would allow a developer in these circumstances to provide that the deed of conditions would only affect each plot at the time it is conveyed rather than the whole estate at the outset. In effect the burdens would only apply to each plot at the time a disposition of the plot is registered leaving the developer free to alter the conditions for the remaining parts of the estate. If this is what is desired care should be taken to ensure that there are no provisions of any missives in respect of the sales of plots or in a deed of conditions which binds the developer to insert the same or similar conditions in the titles of every plot as this might give rise to some sort of contractual liability.

---

[3] 2003 Act, ss.45 and 46.
[4] 2003 Act, s.4(1) and (5).
[5] 2003 Act, s.4(1)(a) and (b).
[6] Land Registration (Scotland) Act 1979, s.17.

Transitional provisions

There will be deeds of condition granted prior to the appointed day which exclude the application of section 17 of Land Registration (Scotland) Act 1979. In such cases the burdens are not effective until the deed of conditions is referred to in a conveyance. Section 32 and Schedule H of the Conveyancing (Scotland) Act 1874 and sections 17 and 18 of the Land Registration (Scotland) Act 1979 are repealed.[7] The transitional provision provides that a real burden can be created by importation in a subsequent conveyance even though it is created in a deed of conditions prior to the appointed day. A form of words for importation is provided.[8] This transitional provision cannot be used to create a burden over a *pro indiviso* share.[9]

5–23

Duration of burdens

Under the existing law real burdens are perpetual. Although the right to enforce a burden in respect of a particular breach may be subject to the long negative prescription the burden itself is not affected by lapse of time. This principle is reaffirmed in the 2003 Act subject to the proviso that it will be possible to provide in the constitutive deed that the burden is to last only for a specified period.[10] The 2003 Act does contain provisions which may result in the extinction of real burdens which are at least one hundred years old.[11]

5–24

Reference to burdens in future deeds

For the avoidance of doubt the 2003 Act provides that any provision in a deed which requires the terms of burdens to be repeated in subsequent conveyances and that failure to do so will result in nullity is of no effect.[12]

5–25

Personal contractual obligations

Under the present law even if a real burden is unenforceable as such it may well be enforceable as between the original parties to the conveyance in which the burden is created as matter of personal contract.[13] Whereas the 2000 Act appears to have preserved existing contractual rights as between the original superior and the vassal[14] the same does not appear to be the case in relation to burdens in non-feudal deeds. The 2003 Act provides,[15] that incidental contractual liability which a constitutive deed (or a deed into which a constitutive deed is incorporated)

5–26

---

[7] 2003 Act, s.128 and Sch.15.
[8] 2003 Act, s.6(2) and Sch.1.
[9] 2003 Act, s.6(3).
[10] 2003 Act, s.7.
[11] 2003 Act, ss.20–24 and see para.9–14 *et seq.* below.
[12] 2003 Act, s.68.
[13] *Scottish Co-operative Wholesale Society v Finnie*, 1937 S.C. 835.
[14] 2000 Act, s.75.
[15] 2003 Act, s.61.

gives rise to ends when the deed has been duly registered and the real burden has become effective. Accordingly a burden will either be a real burden or a personal obligation but cannot be both. It would seem however that if the burden cannot be a real burden because it does not comply with the new rules for the creation and content of a real burden then this particular provision will not apply and the burden may still have contractual effect as between the original parties to the constitutive deed.

PRAEDIAL REAL BURDENS—INTERPRETATION

The existing law

5–27   Professor Halliday set out the existing law in relation to the construction and interpretation of praedial real burdens in the following terms:[16]

> "... a real condition which imposes obligations or restrictions upon land which will be binding upon each successive owner of it should be expressed in clear and unambiguous terms. It must not be indefinite either as to the land affected or the nature of the restriction which cannot be one which is determinable as a matter of taste or by a subjective test on which there could be legitimate difference of opinion."

The overriding presumption is in favour of the freedom of the owner of land to use the property as he or she wishes and accordingly any praedial real burden is construed very strictly against the party entitled to enforce.[17] Thus where a real burden provided that villas or dwellinghouses were to be erected it was held that this did not prevent the erection of tenements of dwellinghouses because a flatted dwellinghouse in a tenement falls within the general definition of a dwellinghouse and the obligation was not to be restricted to a villa type dwellinghouse.[18] Similarly where a real burden contained a positive or affirmative obligation to erect a dwellinghouse with suitable offices within a set period of time and went on to provide that no buildings of any other description were to be erected it was held that this did not preclude the erection of a stable years after the original dwellinghouse and offices had been completed. The superior may have intended that consent to the original buildings coupled with the prohibition of buildings of any other description would mean that consent would be required for any additional building. The court however held that a stable was within the definition of "suitable offices" and that the prohibition did not apply where the additional buildings could fall within the original definition. In other words the prohibition was not against any other buildings of any description.[19]

---

[16] Halliday, *op. cit.*, pp.34–31.

[17] Reid, *op. cit.*, para.416; Halliday, *op. cit.*, pp.34–32; *The Walker Trs v Haldane* (1902) 4 F. 594 at 596; *Anderson v Dickie*, 1915 S.C. (HL) 79 at 89.

[18] *Bainbridge v Campbell*, 1912 S.C. 92.

[19] *Wyllie v Dunnett* (1899) 1 F. 982.

The attitude of the courts

Both Professor Halliday and Professor Reid have formulated lists of subsidiary rules which illustrate the *contra proferentem* type of construction or interpretation employed by the courts. It must be remembered however that under the existing law each case was decided very much on its own facts. It is almost always possible to mount an argument to the effect that a real burden lacks precision in some way. This is sometimes known as adopting a malignant construction.[20] It is difficult to escape the conclusion that the attitude of the court to the interpretation of a particular real burden may to a large extent depend on the view which they take of the nature of the dispute which has arisen and the motives of the parties to that dispute. A court may adopt a less strict interpretation of a burden which is clearly designed to protect the genuine amenity of an adjoining property where the adjoining proprietor entitled to enforce the burden has a reasonable and proper reason for so doing. On the other hand a court might adopt a stricter or even malignant construction where it is plain that a speculative superior with no real connection with the local area is trying to extract money from the burdened proprietor in exchange for a waiver or consent.[21]

5–28

The subsidiary rules[22]

There are risks in formulating a series of rules setting out the existing law in relation to the interpretation of real burdens given that the 2003 Act only contain a single section in relation to how real burdens are to be interpreted.[23] Nevertheless it does seem to the author that the new statutory provision which is to the effect that real burdens are to be construed in the same manner as other provisions of deeds which relate to land and are intended for registration does not alter the law dramatically. The subsidiary rules for interpretation under the existing rules may be stated briefly as follows:

5–29

    (a) A positive obligation (affirmative burden using the 2003 Act terminology) to do something such as erect a dwellinghouse will not carry with it an implied prohibition of doing anything else. Accordingly an obligation to erect a dwellinghouse does not imply a prohibition of erecting another dwellinghouse or indeed another form of building once the first dwellinghouse has been built.[24]

---

[20] *Ewing v Campbells* (1877) 5 R. 230 at 233; *Hunter v Fox*, 1964 S.C. (HL) 95 at 99; and see the dissenting judgement of Lord McCluskey in *Lothian Regional Council v Rennie*, 1991 S.C. 212 where burdens requiring a person to maintain a supply of water to provide an adequate flow to the reasonable satisfaction of the party entitled to enforce the burden was held to be imprecise because the test of reasonable satisfaction was subjective rather than objective.

[21] See the general discussion in Gordon, *op. cit.*, pp.22–41 *et seq.*

[22] Reid, *op. cit.*, para.416 *et seq.*; Halliday, *op. cit.*, pp.33–34 *et seq.*; Gordon, *op. cit.*, pp.22–41 *et seq.*

[23] 2003 Act, s.14.

[24] Halliday, *op. cit.*, pp.33–34 *et seq.*; Reid, *op. cit.*, para.417 *et seq.*; *Fleming v Muir* (1896) 4 S.L.T. 26; *Kemp v Magistrates of Largs*, 1939 S.C. (HL) 6.

(b) An obligation to construct or erect a building on its own will not imply a further obligation to maintain that building.[25] However if there is an obligation to maintain a court will more readily interpret that obligation as requiring a reasonable standard of maintenance having regard to the nature of the building or other structure which is to be maintained.[26] Accordingly while the courts will not rewrite a burden by inserting words which simply are not there with a view to expanding the burden or adding a further restrictive element to it where the burden appears to have a reasonable object such as maintenance courts are unlikely to adopt a malignant construction.

(c) A burden which requires a particular type of building to be erected may be construed as importing an obligation in relation to original construction rather than a continuing obligation restricting the use of that building to the original use for which the building was designed.[27] Accordingly if there is a burden which binds a proprietor to erect a single self-contained dwellinghouse but that burden is not coupled with a prohibition of sub-division then provided the burdened proprietor initially erects a self-contained dwellinghouse that burden will not prohibit the sub-division of the dwellinghouse into two self-contained properties.[28] The cases which attempt to apply this subsidiary rule are both confused and confusing.[29]

(d) Some real burdens are so ambiguous as to be wholly unenforceable.[30] However it is probably more accurate to state that the least favourable construction to the party seeking to enforce the burden will be employed in cases where there is any degree of uncertainty.[31] It does appear to be fairly clear that the interpretation of a positive or affirmative burden to do something is likely to be stricter than the interpretation of a prohibition because a party subject to a positive or affirmative burden must know precisely what is to be done in order to comply with the terms of that burden. Prohibitions and restrictions on the other hand can be more general. It has never been doubted for example that a general prohibition of anything which might cause a nuisance is enforceable.[32] It appears that courts find it easier to accept that a particular activity may be prohibited under a general name or category.[33]

---

[25] Halliday, *op. cit.*, para.34–33; Reid, *op. cit.*, para.417; *Peter Walker & Son (Edinburgh) Ltd v Church of Scotland General Trustees*, 1967 S.L.T. 297.

[26] *Church of Scotland General Trs v Phin*, 1987 S.C.L.R. 240; Reid, *op. cit.*, para.417.

[27] Halliday, *op. cit.*, para.34–33; Reid, *op. cit.*, para.421.

[28] *Porter v Campbell's Trs*, 1923 S.C. (HL) 94; *Fraser v Church of Scotland Trs*, 1986 S.L.T. 692.

[29] See the comments of Professor Reid, *op. cit.*, para.421, especially at fn.7.

[30] As in *Lothian Regional Council v Rennie*, 1991 S.L.T. 465.

[31] Reid, *op. cit.*, para.419.

[32] See *Mannofield Residents Property Co. Ltd v Thomson*, 1983 S.L.T. (Sh. Ct.) 71.

[33] See Reid, *op. cit.*, para.418.

The effect of section 14

Section 14 of the 2003 Act runs to two lines and it provides that real   **5–30**
burdens shall be construed in the same manner as other provisions of
deeds which relate to land and are intended for registration. The section
should of course be read in conjunction with section 2(5) which deals
with one of the rules of constitution of a real burden. That latter provision is to the effect that in determining whether a real burden has been
created regard is to be had to the effect of the provision rather than the
manner in which the provision is expressed. One could say with a
degree of certainty that the days of a malignant construction being
applied to the interpretation of a real burden, whether created before or
after November 28, 2004, are gone.

Comparison with other deeds relating to heritable property

Other deeds which relate to heritable property and are intended for   **5–31**
registration would be dispositions, standard securities, deeds of servitude, discharges, boundary agreements[34] and the like. Attempting an
analogy from the terms of a disposition does not really help because a
disposition is a straightforward conveyance of an interest in land.
Similarly a standard security will not normally contain any form of
burden but will simply be a grant of a security over an interest in land.
Admittedly there are standard conditions which apply to securities
and these may be varied. To that extent they are obligations which
require to be interpreted and there could be an analogy drawn with the
interpretation of these conditions. Registered leases of course can
contain a great many obligations and there was a view at one time that
the obligations of the tenant in a lease were to be construed strictly
contra proferentem against the landlord.[35] However this strict method of
construction was rejected in the case of *Marfield Properties Ltd v
Secretary of State for the Environment*.[36] In that case landlords sought
payment from tenants in relation to a share of the expense of maintenance of common parts. The sheriff had decided that the roof and external walls of the building did not fall within the definition of common
parts in the lease because they were not specifically named as being
common parts. It was argued for the tenant that a clear and precise stipulation was required in order to impose on the tenant an obligation
which would otherwise fall upon the landlord at common law. Counsel
for the defender referred to an observation by Lord Cameron[37] to the
effect that it would require clear and precise stipulation in a contract to
provide the laying on the landlord's shoulders of the burden of re-
instating property in the event of destruction because the common law
did not imply such an obligation. In the *Marfield Properties* case the
Inner House took the view there was no lack of clarity in the provision
in the clause of the lease whereby the tenants undertook to pay a proportionate share of the expense of the maintenance and cleaning and

---

[34] Under s.19 of the Land Registration (Scotland) Act 1979.
[35] See Rankine, *The Law of Leases in Scotland* (3rd ed.) 98.
[36] 1996 S.L.T. 1244.
[37] In *Cantors Properties (Scotland) Ltd v Swears & Wells Ltd*, 1978 S.C. 310 at 322.

lighting of the common parts. The obligation was plain and the only issue was whether or not the roof and walls were common parts. The Inner House took the view that this was a question of construction of the words used. The court took the view that the expression "common parts" simply meant that a part had to be common to the premises let and other parts of the overall development. The court also took the view that parts of the structure of the building such as the roof and external walls fell naturally within the scope of the expression "common parts". The only requirement was that the part was not designed for the exclusive benefit of one unit. The Lord President said[38]:

> "For these reasons, as we do not consider that the roof and external walls require to be mentioned expressly, and because we consider that the definition of the common parts is wide enough to include them by implication, we have decided that we must allow this appeal."

Effectively the court held that the terms "common parts" was not a term of art in Scots law but had to be interpreted sensibly against the background of the particular building and the nature of the obligations undertaken. This method of interpretation is a far cry from a *contra proferentem* interpretation. It must be borne in mind however that a real burden will, in the normal case, place an obligation on the ownership of the burdened property in perpetuity whereas an obligation in a lease will last only as long as the lease.

5–32 Another analogy might be taken from the law of servitudes. It is clear law at the moment that a servitude is not interpreted in as strict a manner as a real burden. In the case *McLean v Marwhirn Developments Ltd*[39] a servitude was granted of a right to use all existing reservoirs, tanks, systems, works, springs, wells, rivers, water streams, water courses, pipes, connections, drains, sewers and others in and under adjoining lands which were at present used. It was argued that the servient tenement was insufficiently described. This argument was based on the law relating to real burdens as set out in *Anderson v Dickie*.[40] The court rejected this argument. The Lord President made the following comment:[41]

> "So far as we are aware it has never been held that the exceptionally strict tests of the sufficiency of a real burden proper apply to the description of a known servitude contained in an express grant. It must be recognised that a servitude is in its nature essentially different and a real burden proper rests upon the record and the record alone. The peculiarity of a servitude is that it rests not upon the record for its validity but upon its being well known to the law."

Nevertheless the argument in *McLean v Marwhirn Developments Ltd* was not so much as to the extent of the burden of the servitude but the identification of the servient tenement. The Lord President did accept that

---

[38] At 196 S.L.T. 1247.
[39] 1976 S.L.T. (Notes) 47.
[40] 1914 S.C. (HL) 79.
[41] For a more detailed discussion of the Lord President's comments, see Cusine and Paisley, *Servitudes and Rights of Way*, para.2.38.

there was some attraction in the view that where a positive servitude was constituted in an express grant in a deed it must be unambiguously described.[42]

Taking the two provisions of the 2003 Act together[43] there does certainly   **5–33** appear to be a shift in the law away from a very strict construction of the actual words used to one which focuses on the object or effect of the burden. Only time will tell how the courts choose to interpret real burdens in the future. It must be assumed however that the new rules will apply to existing burdens as well as those created after November 28, 2004.[44]

---

[42] See also the remarks of Lord Jauncey in *Alvis v Harrison*, 1981 S.L.T. 64 where he indicated that where a servitude was constituted in a deed by express grant then the words used in the deed were the measure of the servitude.

[43] 2003 Act, ss.2(5) and 14.

[44] 2003 Act, s.119(10).

CHAPTER 6

COMMUNITY BURDENS AND MANAGER BURDENS

INTRODUCTION

The 2000 and 2003 Acts introduced new forms of real burden. The 2000   **6–01**
Act, as amended by the 2003 Act, allows some of these new burdens to be
preserved by superiors as well as created as real burdens after abolition.
The new burdens are community burdens, conservation burdens, personal pre-emption burdens, personal redemption burdens, economic
development burdens, healthcare burdens, rural housing burdens and
manager burdens. Common facility and service burdens are also placed
in a separate category.[1] Certain other burdens are categorised as maritime
burdens which will pertain to the Crown.[2] Of these new named burdens
some would have to be regarded as proper real burdens in the sense
that they are praedial both as regards the burdened property and the
benefited property. Community burdens, common facility and service
burdens and to some extent maritime burdens created post-abolition by
the Crown fall within this category. The other named burdens are more in
the nature of personal real burdens in that they are burdens constituted in
favour of a person other than by reference to that person's ownership of
any land.[3] In some ways of course the concept of a personal real burden
is a contradiction in terms. Part of the reason for the introduction of this
concept was the effect of the extinction of superiority titles. In some cases
it was thought unfair to deprive the superior of a right to enforce a burden
merely because that superior did not have any other heritable interest to
which the burden might attach.[4] One can of course argue that a personal
real burden is real at so far as the burdened property is concerned in the
sense that the burden runs with the burdened land. If properly constituted the burden will apply no matter who owns the burdened land. The
conceptual problem is emphasised when one considers that the right to
enforce some personal real burdens can actually be assigned.

COMMUNITY BURDENS

Community burdens and third party rights

The 2003 Act attempts to deal with the vexed question of implied third   **6–02**
party rights to enforce. These rights are usually stated to be based on the
law of *ius quaesitum tertio* but the legal basis for enforcement of real

---

[1] 2000 Act, s.23; re-enacted with amendments in the 2003 Act, s.56.
[2] 2000 Act, s.60; 2003 Act, s.44.
[3] 2003 Act, s.1(3).
[4] See para.3–10 above.

burdens by co-feuars or co-disponees is frankly unclear. On one view the right of a co-feuar to enforce a real burden in a feudal title is akin to a servitude.[5] The 2003 Act contains transitional provisions in relation to existing implied rights to enforce real burdens.[6] These provisions are some of the most difficult to interpret. Indeed in some ways the provisions of section 52 do not sit easily with the provisions of section 53.[7]

Definition of community burdens

6–03   The 2003 Act defines a community burden[8] with reference to a common scheme. It is provided that a community burden is a real burden imposed under a common scheme on two or more units where each of these units is, in relation to some or all of those burdens, both a benefited property and a burdened property. It is also provided that burdens imposed under a common scheme on units in a sheltered or retirement housing development[9] are community burdens notwithstanding the fact that the development may contain accommodation such as a warden's flat which by its very nature is not subject to the burdens which pertain to the actual sheltered or retirement housing units.[10] Section 25 and sections 52, 53 and 54 all refer to a common scheme. However that term is not defined in the 2003 Act. Given the confusion which has existed over the existing law relating to implied third party rights to enforce real burdens this is perhaps an unfortunate omission although the author supposes that a common scheme must relate to two or more units which are subject to the same or similar burdens. The difficulty really arises when one considers the extent to which the new provisions will apply to existing burdens which cover or are meant to cover a number of properties.

Application to pre-2004 burdens

6–04   There seems little doubt that the new provisions relating to community burdens set out in the 2003 Act apply to burdens which were created prior to November 28, 2004.[11] However for the new provisions in Part 2 of the 2003 Act to apply to existing burdens they would have to fall within the statutory definition of a community burden. In the first place therefore there must be two or more units. In the second place the properties must already have mutual enforcement rights.[12] There is a provision to the effect that where the deed creating the burden states that the burdens are to be community burdens then each unit shall be both a benefited and burdened property.[13] However it is very unlikely that the term "community burden" will have been employed in any pre-2004

---

[5] *Hislop v MacRitchie's Trs* (1881) 8 R. (HL) 95 *per* Lord Watson at 102; for discussion of the legal basis of a co-feuar's right see Reid, *op. cit.*, para.4.02.

[6] 2003 Act, ss.49–53.

[7] For a detailed discussion of these provisions, see para.6–04 *et seq.* below.

[8] 2003 Act, s.25.

[9] 2003 Act, s.54(1).

[10] 2003 Act, s.25(2).

[11] 2003 Act, s.119(10).

[12] 2003 Act, s.25(1)(b).

[13] 2003 Act, s.27.

deed. In some cases there will be express provision to the effect that all burdened proprietors can enforce against each other but in others it may be left to implication. Accordingly in these cases any pre-2004 existing deed creating burdens will require to be examined to see if these burdens are indeed community burdens. This unfortunately brings us back to the existing law relating to implied third party rights of enforcement as amended by sections 52 and 53 of the 2003 Act. There is no doubt that the new statutory provisions are far more important than the existing law in coming to a clear understanding of the position of existing burdens designed to benefit a community. In some ways it might have been preferable if section 53 had come before section 52 because it has been suggested that there is a tension between the two sections.[14] On one view section 53 is by far the more important of the two sections with section 52 being merely a general mop-up section which would cover situations not covered by section 53.[15]

Related and unrelated properties

The main difference between sections 52 and 53 is that section 53 uses the term "related properties" whereas section 52 does not. In many ways section 52 is a restatement of the existing law relating to implied third party rights however unlike section 53 section 52 is not restricted to related properties. The term "related properties" is defined to an extent in the 2003 Act.[16] The definition is illustrative rather than exhaustive. Whether properties are related properties is to be inferred from all the circumstances. However circumstances giving rise to such an inference might include obvious physical conditions such as being part of a tenement or block of flats or an individual house or unit in a development or estate[17]. Other factors mentioned in the subsection are the convenience of managing the properties together because they share a common feature or an obligation for the maintenance of a common facility. A common facility could be a common yard, storage area, a refuse collection area or parking area. If these areas are owned in common then this would be a clear indication that the properties owning in common are related. However even if the subjects are not owned in common the fact that there is an obligation of common maintenance on a number of properties would also imply that the properties are related.[18] Another factor which would infer that the properties are related would be that the properties are all subject to burdens contained in the same deed of conditions,[19] in other words that the properties were all subject to a common scheme. It is easy to understand the concept of related properties when one considers an individual tenement of eight flats. It is less easy to apply the concept to a commercial development comprised of large units of different sizes and different designs. Nevertheless if such a development is governed by a single deed of conditions with uniform burdens

6–05

---

[14] See the excellent commentary on these two sections in Reid, *The Abolition of Feudal Tenure in Scotland*, paras 5.01–5.17.

[15] That is the view of Professor Reid with which the author agrees.

[16] 2003 Act, s.53(2).

[17] 2003 Act, s.53(2)(d).

[18] 2003 Act, s.53(2)(a) and (b).

[19] 2003 Act, s.53(2)(c).

and there are also common facilities such as private access roads then it is likely that such units, despite any physical disparity, will be related properties. The burdens must have been imposed under a common scheme in terms of section 53. If that is the case and the properties are related then all units comprised within the group of related properties subject to the common scheme are benefited properties in relation to the real burdens. They will of course also be burdened properties because to qualify as related properties the units must all be subject to the burdens. Effectively therefore for related properties subject to a common scheme any burdens contained in a pre-2004 deed will become community burdens within the meaning of section 25 of the 2003 Act.

Mixed estates of owned and leased properties—council houses

6–06   The scheme for related properties set out in section 53 works well enough if the owner of the properties comprised within the scheme or community, be it a developer or a local authority or other social land-lord, has set out the burdens in a deed of conditions covering the community executed prior to November 28, 2004. Some landowners, contemplating the sale of individual units however have proceeded by the grant of individual conveyances (usually feudal but not necessarily so) of the individual units all containing the same or roughly similar burdens. In the normal case under the existing law these burdens would be enforceable by co-feuars or co-disponees.[20] The difficulty here is that the retained land remaining in the ownership of the developer or local authority will not be subject to the existing burdens which affect the sold units. If a deed of conditions has been granted then in the normal course of events[21] these burdens will affect all the land whether sold off or not at the point of registration of the deed of conditions. If however individual conveyances containing burdens have been granted then the unsold units are not subject to any burdens. No doubt after November 28, 2004 individual conveyances could still be granted containing these burdens but the difficulty would then relate to the enforcement rights. The developer or local authority cannot be a feudal superior and even under section 53 as originally drafted the developer or local authority as owner of the residual land would not be able to enforce burdens against units already sold. There are also obvious difficulties in relation to mutuality where the right to enforce is based on implication. It is dif-ficult to see how, for example, owners across a development or housing estate could have mutual rights based on implication after November 28, 2004. Any deed creating or purporting to create a real burden after that date must identify the property which is to be the benefited prop-erty for the purposes of enforcement of the burden.[22] This problem is perhaps more acute for local authorities or other registered social land-

---

[20] See *Hislop v MacRitchie's Trs* (1881) 8 R. (HL) 95 for a general discussion of third party rights under the existing law see A. J. McDonald, "The Enforcement of Title Conditions by Neighbouring Proprietors" in D. J. Cusine (ed.), *A Scots Conveyancing Miscalleny: Essays in Honour of Professor J. M. Halliday* (1987), pp.16 *et seq.*; Reid, *The Law of Property*, para.399 *et seq.*

[21] Assuming s.17 of the Land Registration (Scotland) Act 1979 has not been disapplied.

[22] 2003 Act, s.4(2)(c) and (5); existing implied rights of enforcement are abolished by 2003 Act, s.49 in general terms.

lords subject to right to buy legislation than builders or developers holding an incomplete and partially sold estate or development. On one view of course parties developing and selling land may have little or no interest in who can or cannot enforce the real burdens or title conditions. However for local authorities and registered social landlords there is another dimension. These bodies owe obligations to their tenants who occupy the unsold units. Moreover the conditions of let very often mirror the real burdens which apply to any sold units. Accordingly it is more than usually important that a local authority as an owner of retained properties which are let can enforce the real burdens which have been made applicable to the units which have been sold. The dilemma is best illustrated by way of example. It would be a fairly normal provision in a title to a local authority house sold under the right to buy legislation that the purchaser is allowed to keep one dog or one cat provided that animal does not prove to be a nuisance. A similar provision would also be likely to appear in a tenancy agreement between the local authority and a tenant. From a property management point of view it is essential that the local authority can enforce not only the condition in the tenancy agreement but also the real burden in the title of a sold unit. The problem for local authorities and other registered social landlords is that they are still looked to as the focal point of property management. Accordingly a tenant may complain to the local authority or other landlord if an owner occupier in a formerly tenanted property has three Alsatians which are allowed to roam wild over the common courtyard terrorising the children of existing tenants and other owners. In situations where the local authority or other landlord granted individual feu dispositions without a deed of conditions then on the abolition of feudal tenure taking effect there will be no enforcement rights which vest in the local authority or other landlord unless these rights are realloted to one or all of the retained let units under the re-allotment provisions contained in the 2000 Act.[23] Certainly where the burdens relate to common facilities or services they may be automatically preserved and may be enforceable by all those using the facility.[24] However where the burden relates to the use of a sold unit there is no automatic re-allotment and so in the example quoted above the local authority or other residual superior would require to consider reallotting the burden in relation to pets in terms of the re-allotment provisions.[25] The re-allotment provisions are however designed in the main for one-off situations involving neighbouring properties and not for developments or estates or groups of flats in tenemental or high-rise property. Moreover the holder of the retained land would require to decide whether or not to reallot to one individual retained unit such as a single flat or to all of the retained properties still tenanted. A local authority might well shy away from creating a so-called "golden" flat which had enforcement rights which other flats still to be sold did not have. On the other hand reallotting to all the retained and tenanted units might bring its own problems when these units came to be sold on a piecemeal basis. Representations were made to the Scottish Executive by local authorities in relation to mixed estates of this type and section 53 was recast.

---

[23] 2000 Act, s.18; and see para.3–03 *et seq.* above.
[24] 2003 Act, s.56; and see para.3–10 above.
[25] 2000 Act, s.18.

The object of the section is to ensure that the unsold units can become related properties for the purposes of section 53 and accordingly all the burdens in respect of properties sold before and after November 28, 2004 will be community burdens with mutual enforcement rights. Section 53 provides therefore that the real burdens can be imposed under a common scheme in a deed registered before the appointed day but that units can be subject to the common scheme whether or not by virtue of a deed registered before the appointed day. What this attempts to do is introduce a factual element into the scenario. The Act does refer in the first place to a deed executed before the appointed day which creates the common scheme. Accordingly if a local authority or other landowner has proceeded by way of individual grants subject to the same burdens as opposed to imposing burdens in a deed of conditions then that landowner can, before the appointed day, grant a deed of conditions over the remaining unsold units containing the same or similar conditions as those contained in the individual feus. That should be enough to make the entire estate, both sold and unsold a community and subject to burdens in a common scheme. In other words it should be enough to make all the units, sold or unsold related properties for the purposes of section 53.

Timing

6–07   Some doubt has been expressed as to whether or not a local authority or other landowner can execute a deed of conditions over residual unsold properties in terms of section 53 after November 28, 2004 with the same effect. Section 53 refers in the first instance to burdens imposed in a deed registered before the appointed day. It then refers to units comprised within a group of related properties subject to a common scheme whether or not by virtue of a deed registered before the appointed day. On one reading of these words (which are in brackets in the section) this might mean that the new deed of conditions can be executed at any time. On the other hand the words in parenthesis do not refer to a deed registered after the appointed day but leave the matter open. It seems to the author that what the words intend is not that the burdens might be imposed after the appointed day but that the property might become a related property after the appointed day even if it is conveyed after the appointed day. Presumably a property cannot be a related property for the purposes of a common scheme until it is conveyed away as a separate entity. Prior to the split-off all the retained properties in the ownership of the local authority or other owner form one related property. Certainly the safer course is to ensure that any separate deed of conditions covering retained properties executed in terms of section 53 is registered prior to November 28, 2004. Professor Reid states[26] that section 53 allows for registration of a deed of conditions at any time even after the appointed day. He points out however that if the deed of conditions is registered after that day the problem then is that the deed would require to comply with the new statutory rules for the creation of real burdens.[27] A deed of conditions executed and registered after the

---

[26] Reid, *The Abolition of Feudal Tenure in Scotland*, para.5.10.
[27] 2003 Act, s.4.

appointed day would require to identify the benefited property having enforcement rights. Presumably it would also specify that the burdens were to be community burdens. One could of course nominate all the remaining unsold units or indeed every unit within the community or area in question.

No pre-emption, redemption or reversion rights implied

The provisions of section 53 do not imply any right of pre-emption, redemption or reversion nor can such a right be a community burden.[28]   6–08

Unrelated properties

Under the existing law of implied third party rights prior to the   6–09
appointed day where there were reciprocal enforcement rights the properties would probably have been "related". However the notion of "related properties" is entirely statutory. No such concept exists in the pre-2004 law. The existing law does however support the notion of a common scheme.[29] Section 52 of the 2003 Act is a virtual re-statement of the existing law. It provides that where real burdens are imposed under a common scheme and the deed by which they are imposed on any particular property refers to that common scheme or is so worded as to imply the existence of a common scheme then any unit subject to the common scheme is to be a benefited property in relation to the burdens. Under existing law a third party enforcement right could either be expressly created in the deed which contains the burdens or could arise by implication because of the existence of a common scheme. Where the third party right arose by implication it could be negatived if there were words in the deed which indicated that only one person, usually a superior, was to have control over the enforceability of the burdens. The most common case was where a superior in a deed creating burdens reserved a right to alter, waive or modify the burdens in respect of any part of the burdened property. It is clear law that such a reserved right is destructive of mutuality and any third party rights unless these are expressly created.[30] The new statutory provision mirrors the existing law in as much as it is provided that there will be no mutual rights of enforcement if there is anything in the deed which expressly or impliedly negatives these enforcement rights.[31] The sub-section goes on to state specifically that a reservation of a right to vary or waive real burdens will negative mutuality.[32] For section 52 to apply there must not only be real burdens imposed under a common scheme but the deed by which they are imposed on any one unit must expressly refer to the common scheme or the existence of the common scheme must be clearly implied. Where the burdens are contained in a deed of conditions then it may be rather obvious that there is a common scheme. It may not be so obvious where burdens are contained in a number of individual

---

28 2003 Act, s.53(3).
29 See *Hislop v MacRitchie's Trs* (1881) 8 R. (HL) 95.
30 *Turner v Hamilton* (1890) 17 R. 494; *Lawrence v Scott*, 1965 S.C. 403.
31 2003 Act, s.52(2).
32 2003 Act, s.52(2).

deeds. In the latter case there has to be a reference to some form of common development plan or scheme.[33] As with section 53 no rights of pre-emption, redemption or reversion are conferred.[34]

The interaction between sections 52 and 53

6–10 In terms of section 52, which sets out the existing common law, a reservation to a superior or some other party to waive or alter title conditions will negative implied third party rights and accordingly in such a situation these burdens could not be community burdens. Section 52 is not in terms stated to be subject to the provisions of section 53. Similarly section 53 does not begin with the words "notwithstanding the provisions of the immediately preceding section". Each section appears to stand independently of the other. The question arises as to the effect of a reserved right to waive or alter burdens where the properties can be said to be related properties within the meaning of section 53. Section 53 does not contain the exception relating to reserved rights to waive or alter which is contained in section 52. One might attempt an argument that section 52 is the first hurdle and that if, because there is a reserved right to waive or modify, there are no mutual enforcement rights then section 53 cannot operate because in effect there cannot be common scheme as referred to in section 53. This of course is to define the term common scheme in terms of the existing common law. The alternative argument is that section 53 will apply where the units or properties subject to the burdens are related properties in terms of the statutory definition contained in that section.[35] On that basis it would not matter that there was any reserved right to waive or modify and the burdens would be community burdens and be enforceable by the owners of all the units as against themselves. If this argument is correct then burdens may fail to be community burdens where there is a reserved right in terms of section 52 but achieve the status of community burdens if the properties on which the burdens are imposed are related properties within the statutory definition of that term contained in section 53. This latter interpretation would appear to be the most likely interpretation of the two sections taken together. Clearly this is a significant alteration in the enforcement rights of parties who own related properties in circumstances where there is a reserved right to waive or modify. Effectively for related properties in terms of section 53 the law is changed.

Abolition of other implied rights

6–11 The new statutory rules in relation to implied rights of enforcement contained in section 52 and 53 of the 2003 Act take over completely from the old rules which are expressly abolished.[36]

---

[33] *Hislop v MacRitchie's Trs* (1881) 8 R. (HL) 95.
[34] 2003 Act, s.53(3).
[35] 2003 Act, s.53(2).
[36] 2003 Act, s.49(1).

Excluded community burdens

Certain burdens which might otherwise be regarded as community **6–12** burdens under the new provisions are expressly excluded. It has already been noted that neither section 52 nor section 53 have the effect of creating any pre-emption, redemption or reversion rights.[37] It is possible that a right of pre-emption, redemption or reversion may have been created in favour of a superior in a deed which also creates community burdens either under section 52 or under section 53. Such a right in favour of the superior may be capable of preservation either as a real-loted burden[38] or as a personal real burden.[39] This type of right however does not transmit to owners of individual units which are part of either a common scheme or are to regarded as related properties. Another and perhaps more obvious exclusion relates to obligations to construct, maintain or renew facilities and services which have been specifically taken over by a local or some other statutory authority. The most obvious example here would be a community burden which related to the maintenance of a road or the maintenance and renewal of pipes, drains, sewers, cables and other conductors. Where responsibility for maintenance has been assumed by a local or other public authority or successor body to any such authority then the burden will not be enforceable either as a facility burden or as a community burden.[40] It should also be noted that the new provisions relating to implied rights of enforcement and community burdens will not breathe life into a burden which was unenforceable before the coming into effect of the legislation.[41] A right to enforce may have been waived or lost through acquiescence or in some other manner prior to the appointed day. If that is the case the burden will not revive through the operation of the new provisions. Sections 28(1)(a) and (d) and 31 do not apply to a community in any period during which a development management scheme applies.[41a]

Existing burdens with no benefited property

Some burdens do not appear to pertain to a benefited property. These **6–13** could only be non-feudal burdens because the superiority title is the benefited property in the latter case. The 2003 Act makes it clear however that even burdens of this type can become community burdens if they are part of a common scheme.[42] However the new statutory provisions cannot be used to confer a right of enforcement in respect of an act or omission in contravention of a real burden before November 28, 2004.[43] Accordingly although new enforcement rights are created they cannot be used in respect of pre-appointed day breaches.

---

[37] 2003 Act, ss.52(3) and 53(3).
[38] 2000 Act, s.18.
[39] 2000 Act, s.18A.
[40] 2003 Act, s.122(2).
[41] 2003 Act, s.57(1).
[41a] 2003 Act, s.31A (introduced by the Tenements (Scotland) Bill, s.22.)
[42] 2003 Act, s.57(2).
[43] 2003 Act, s.57(3).

Sheltered and retirement housing

6–14 The 2003 Act makes special provision in relation to community burdens which apply to sheltered or retirement housing complexes. A sheltered or retirement housing development is defined in the Act as a group of dwellinghouses which, in regard to their design, size and other features are particularly suitable for occupation by elderly people (or by people who are disabled or infirm or in some other way vulnerable) and which for the purposes of such occupation are provided with facilities substantially different from those of ordinary dwellinghouses.[44] The tenure structure of most sheltered and retirement home developments has been feudal. Certain developers tend to specialise in this type of housing and the practice has been to feu the individual units subject to a great many conditions some of which relate to use and others to management. The idea was that the developers would retain control over the management of the property for the benefit of the owner occupiers. In some ways of course this might have been thought of as a misuse of the feudal system and presumably there would be some doubt as to whether or not the intensely personal burdens relating to the occupation of the units by a certain class of people could be real burdens.[45] Not all units within such developments will be designed as sheltered or retirement units. There may be a warden's or caretaker's flat or a guest flat with accommodation for visiting relatives. Such special units will not necessarily be subject to the community burdens which apply to the actual sheltered or retirement housing units. On feudal abolition taking effect the original developers will lose the rights to enforce the real burdens and conditions (to the extent that they are enforceable) but the burdens themselves may not apply to those parts of the development such as a warden's or caretaker's or guest flat. In terms of section 54 each unit shall nevertheless be a benefited property in relation to the burdens notwithstanding the fact that some of the units which are used in some special way are not subject to the burdens provided there is a common scheme.[46] Accordingly the burdens will become community burdens enforceable by the owners of each unit and the original developers if they still own those parts of the development such as a warden's or caretaker's flat which are not subject to the burdens. Real burdens which regulate the use, maintenance, re-instatement or management of a facility or a service which make the development particularly suitable for occupation by a special group of people referred to in the statutory definition of sheltered housing are core burdens.[47] The main provisions relating to community burdens will apply with modifications to sheltered or retirement housing. In particular section 28 of the 2003 Act which contains the power of the majority to appoint a manager and confer powers on that manager is modified. In the case of sheltered or retirement housing a two-thirds majority is required.[48] It will not be competent under section 28 to confer on a manager in a sheltered or retirement housing complex the power to discharge burdens where

---

[44] 2003 Act, s.54(3).
[45] See Rennie, "The Reality of Real Burdens", 1998 S.L.T. (News) 149.
[46] 2003 Act, s.54(1).
[47] 2003 Act, s.54(4).
[48] 2003 Act, s.54(5)(a)(i).

these burdens are core burdens.[49] Similarly it will not be possible to extinguish core burdens using the fall back provisions in section 33 as a required majority for core burdens in a sheltered housing development burden will be two thirds.[50] There is a blanket prohibition of varying or discharging a real burden relating to an age restriction which means that such a burden must now be regarded as valid and enforceable. As with the other provisions in relation to common schemes and community burdens no right of pre-emption, redemption or reversion is conferred.[51] Where a burden of maintenance or renewal is taken over by local authority or other body then the obligation will cease to be a community burden for the purposes of the sheltered or retirement housing complex.[52] Where it is proposed to vary or discharge a community burden relating to sheltered or retirement housing there are special provisions requiring a community consultation notice to be given to the owner of the units in the community.[53]

Community burdens created prior to November 28, 2004

Where a burden has been created in a pre-2004 deed or in a deed regis- **6–15** tered prior to the appointed day and becomes a community burden by virtue of either section 52 or 53 of the 2003 Act there is no need for any owner of a benefited unit to serve any preservation type notice on any of the other burdened proprietors. If the burden comes within section 52 because there are reciprocal enforcement rights or section 53 whether there are reciprocal enforcement rights or not then it will automatically become a community burden. Initially of course there will be no entry in the Land Register or Register of Sasines indicating the change in status of the burden. Under the existing law where there was a third party right to enforce a real burden that does not necessarily appear in any register either especially if the right was by implication as opposed to express provision.

Community burdens—registration requirements

The thrust of the legislation is that the identity of the burdened and ben- **6–16** efited properties should always be apparent from the Register. Unfortunately this will not always be the case where the community burdens arise by virtue of section 52 or 53. The 2003 Act provides that during the period of 10 years from the appointed day the Keeper may where he is satisfied that a real burden subsists by virtue of any of the sections 52 to 56 of the 2003 Act enter on the title sheet of the burdened property a statement that the real burden subsists by virtue of the section in question. Moreover where there is sufficient information to enable the Keeper to describe the benefited property the Keeper may also enter on the title sheet a description of that property. In such a case the Keeper may also enter that statement on the title sheet of the benefited property

---

[49] 2003 Act, s.54(5)(a)(ii).
[50] 2003 Act, s.54(5)(b)(i).
[51] 2003 Act, s.54(6).
[52] 2003 Act, s.54(2).
[53] 2003 Act, s.55.

with a description of the burdened property. For the 10-year period the
provision is not mandatory. However after the expiry of the 10-year
period the Keeper must make these entries in the Register where he is
satisfied that a real burden subsists by virtue of any of these sections. The
same applies to maritime burdens in respect of feudal writs in terms of
section 60 of the 2000 Act. It is clear that there will be practical difficulties for the Keeper in relation to burdens under section 53.

Community burdens created after the appointed day

6–17   Community burdens created after the appointed day will of course
require to conform in all respects to the rules for the constitution of real
burdens set out the 2003 Act.[54] In particular there will be a requirement
to state that the burdens are real burdens and there will be a requirement
to identify the benefited and burdened property.[55] Instead of stating that
the burdens are to be real burdens the deed which creates the burdens,
known as the constitutive deed, may state that the burden is a community burden instead.[56] In such a case however the constitutive deed must
also nominate and identify the community.[57] A community burden is
however relieved of the necessity to be wholly praedial in that it may be
for the benefit of a community as entity or a part of that community as
opposed to for the benefit of identified property.[58] Good examples of
this type of burden are age restrictions in sheltered housing and management schemes. The community burden must however comply with
the definition of community burden contained in section 25.[59] The lati-
tude which may be allowed in respect of existing pre-appointed day
burdens in terms of sections 52 and 53 of the 2003 Act will not apply to
community burdens which are created after the appointed day. These
burdens will require to be imposed under a common scheme on four or
more units. Each of these units must be both a benefited and a burdened
property.[60]

Effect of a declaration that burdens are community burdens

6–18   Community burdens are intended to replace the third party rights
loosely based on the law of *ius quaesitum tertio*. In some deeds of condition there was an express provision to the effect that the burdens could
be enforced by all proprietors within the flat, block or development. The
2003 Act contains a similar provision.[61] It provides that where in relation to any real burdens the constitutive deed states that the burdens are
to be community burdens each unit shall in relation to those burdens be
both a benefited property and a burdened property.

---

[54] See Ch.5 above.
[55] 2003 Act, s.4.
[56] 2003 Act, s.4(3).
[57] 2003 Act, s.4(4).
[58] 2003 Act, s.3(4).
[59] See para.6–03 above.
[60] 2003 Act, s.25(1).
[61] 2003 Act, s.27.

Content of community burdens

The concept of community burdens in the sense of a uniform set of pro-   **6–19**
visions and conditions designed to regulate individual properties
within a development or a block or tenement of flats is not a new one.
However it has in the past been the practice to insert all sorts of provisions and conditions without regard to whether or not these conditions
satisfied the rules for the creation of real burdens.[62] That is not to say
that various provisions relating to the convening of meetings, the
powers of property managers and factors are undesirable. The 2003 Act
removes any doubts or questions as to the validity of such provisions as
real burdens, by providing that community burdens may make provision as respects certain matters.[63] This is without prejudice to the
requirement in the Act[64] that a real burden must either be an obligation
to do something, to refrain from doing something or ancillary to either
type of burden. For the purposes of the 2003 Act a community means
the units subject to the community burdens and in the case of a sheltered
or retirement housing development also a unit which is used in a special
way such as a warden's flat or guest accommodation.[65] A community
burden may make provision in respect of any of the following matters:

(a) The appointment by the owners of units in the community of a
    manager.
(b) The dismissal by the owners of a manager.
(c) The powers and duties of a manager.
(d) The nomination of a person to be the first manager.
(e) The procedures to be followed by owners in making decisions
    about matters affecting the community.
(f) The matters on which such decisions may be made.
(g) The resolution of disputes relating to community burdens.

The list is neither mandatory nor exclusive but permissive and the succeeding provisions of the 2003 Act in relation to the management of the
community contain fall back provisions setting out in greater detail how
the property in the community is to be managed. These provisions only
apply where the titles to the property are silent.

Power of majority to appoint manager—powers of manager

A manager is defined in the 2003 Act[66] in relation to related properties as   **6–20**
any person (including an owner of one of those properties or a firm) who
is authorised by virtue of the Act or otherwise to act generally or for such
purposes as may be applicable in relation to a particular authorisation, in
respect of those properties. Subject to certain special provisions in relation
to sheltered and retirement housing and to any community burdens in the
titles the owners of a majority of the units in the community may appoint
a person to be the manager of the community on such terms as they may

---

[62] See Rennie, "The Reality of Real Burdens", 1998 S.L.T. (News) 149.
[63] 2003 Act, s.26.
[64] 2003 Act, s.2.
[65] 2003 Act, ss.26(2) and 54(1).
[66] 2003 Act, s.122(1).

specify.[67] The majority may also confer on any such manager the right to exercise such powers of the owners as they may specify. The majority may also revoke or vary the right to exercise such powers and more importantly may in most cases dismiss any manager.[68] In the case of sheltered or retirement housing however the majority required to confer powers on a manager and the power to revoke or vary the right to exercise these powers is a two-thirds majority.[69] Similarly where a power is a manager burden[70] any person who is by virtue of that burden a manager cannot be dismissed as long as that manager burden is in operation. The overriding power of dismissal[71] will not apply except in the case of manager burdens imposed on a sale by virtue of the right to buy legislation.[72] A manager burden is a provision conferring on a person specified in the burden the power to act as manager of related properties or the power to appoint some other person to be such manager and the power to dismiss such other person as manager.[73] Accordingly a manager burden is different from the power of a majority to appoint a manager in as much as the person or the right to appoint must be specified in the burden itself.[74] So far as conferring the right to exercise powers on any manager the Act specifies without prejudice to the generality of that statement that these powers may include the power to carry out maintenance, the power to enforce community burdens and the power to vary or discharge such burdens.[75] While a power to carry out maintenance might be regarded as one of the normal duties of a factor or property manager the power to enforce community burdens and the power to vary or discharge such burdens could be regarded as well beyond the normal factorial remit. Such a power would allow the factor or manager to take up a position akin to that of a former superior and there are obvious advantages in having a single person who has the right to enforce, waive or vary community burdens. There are no restrictions on who can be appointed a manager in terms of the power of the majority of owners to make that appointment. That is not the case with a manager burden where the appointment or the right to appoint is created in the community burden itself. In such a case the appointment or right to appoint and dismiss will vest in a person who is the owner of one of the related properties.[76] This will usually be the developer. It should be borne in mind of course that the majority cannot confer on the manager powers which the owners of the units in the community do not have. The Act states that the majority can confer on the manager the right to exercise such of "their" powers as they may specify. Presumably therefore the powers must already exist in terms of the community burdens or at least must be a power specified in the section.[77] It should be noted so far as repairs and renewals are concerned that the statutory power is to carry out maintenance. The commu-

---

[67] 2003 Act, s.28(1)(a).
[68] 2003 Act, s.28(1)(a), (b), (c) and (d).
[69] 2003 Act, s.54(5)(a).
[70] 2003 Act, s.63; and see para.6–26 below.
[71] Contained in 2003 Act, s.64.
[72] 2003 Act, s.63(6).
[73] 2003 Act, s.63(1).
[74] Manager burdens are considered in greater detail at para.6–26 below.
[75] 2003 Act, s.28(2).
[76] 2003 Act, s.63(2).
[77] 2003 Act, s.28(2).

nity burdens may of course grant greater powers. Maintenance is defined in the 2003 Act[78] as including repair or replacement and such demolition, alteration or improvement as is reasonably incidental to maintenance. Where a unit in a community is owned by two or more persons in common ownership then for the purposes of voting on any proposal the vote allocated in respect of that unit shall only be counted if the vote is the agreed vote of those common owners who together own more than a half share of the unit. What this means in the normal case of common owner-ship and equal shares is that if the two owners of the unit cannot agree then no vote can be counted. In the more unusual case of common own-ership being split in an unequal manner then the vote of the party owning the majority share of the unit will prevail.[79] It should be noted that in the case of sheltered or retirement housing the power to discharge or vary a community burden can only be delegated to a manager if the burden in question is not a core burden.[80] So far as the delegation to a manager of the right to exercise a majorities powers and the right of a majority who revoke, vary or exercise these powers or dismiss the manager are con-cerned these powers may be exercised by the majority (or qualified major-ity in sheltered or residential housing) even where the manager was not actually appointed by the majority in terms of section 28 of the 2003 Act.[81] The manager may have been appointed in terms of the constitutive deed[82] or in terms of a manager burden.[83] It should be noted that the power to appoint a manager under section 28 does not apply to tenements which will be governed by the Tenements (Scotland) Bill 2004.[84]

Power of majority to instruct common maintenance

Where community burdens impose an obligation on the owners of all or some of the units to maintain or contribute towards the cost of maintain-ing particular property and the obligation accounts for the entire liabil-ity for the maintenance the 2003 Act sets out useful provisions in relation to the instruction of that maintenance and the collection of the propor-tions of the cost of the maintenance from the owners of individual units.[85] In some cases the existing burdens may contain a bare obligation to maintain common property but no actual framework relating to the appointment of managers or indeed any mechanism for the instruction of repairs and recovery of the cost. Section 29 of the 2003 Act provides a fallback mechanism which allows the owners of a majority of units to instruct maintenance. Again the provisions of the Act are subject to any express provision made in the community burdens.[86] For these fallback provisions to work however the community burdens must impose an obligation which accounts for the entire liability. Accordingly if there is some problem with the existing burdens so that one flat for some reason

6–21

---

[78] 2003 Act, s.122(1).
[79] 2003 Act, s.28(3).
[80] 2003 Act, ss.54(4) and (5)(a)(ii).
[81] 2003 Act, s.28(4).
[82] 2003 Act, s.26(1)(d).
[83] 2003 Act, s.63.
[84] 2003 Act, s.31A as prospectively amended; and see Ch.14 below.
[85] 2003 Act, s.29.
[86] 2003 Act, s.29(2).

does not have the obligation and the remaining five flats only have an obligation to contribute a one-sixth share then the statutory provision cannot apply. If the provision does apply the owners of a majority of the units subject to the obligation may decide that maintenance is to be carried out.[87] Moreover the majority can require each owner to deposit a sum with such person as they may nominate for the purpose of carrying out the maintenance.[88] The notice specifies a date not less than 28 days after the requirement is made by which the amount must be paid. The notice may also specify the amount required. The amount however must not exceed the individual owner's apportioned share in terms of the community burdens or a reasonable estimate of the cost of the maintenance.[89] If the sum required exceeds £100, or if less of the aggregate of that sum taken together with any other sum or sums under £100, required in the preceding 12 months, exceeds £200, the sum must be deposited in a maintenance account. In such a case the owners may authorize persons to operate the account.[89a] A majority may also give an authority to operate the maintenance account to certain persons on behalf of the community.[90] The majority may also instruct or carry out the maintenance.[91] They may modify or revoke anything which they have decided.[92] As has already been noted maintenance is defined in the 2003 Act[93] as including repair or replacement and such demolition, alteration or improvement as is reasonably incidental to maintenance. Accordingly the statutory power relating to maintenance would not apply to what might be regarded as pure improvement or upgrading unless that is allied to maintenance or repair work as such. Presumably therefore a majority could decide in the context of a re-roofing repair that an improved type of slate be used rather than a replacement slate. Similarly if a repair to lead piping was required the majority could instruct that the lead piping be replaced with copper piping or some other modern material. At the other end of the scale the majority would not be able to commission an artist to decorate the outside of a block of flats with a mural on the basis that this improvement might increase the amenity value of all the units in the community. Difficulties of interpretation will arise in cases which fall between the two extremes and where there may be a genuine difference of opinion. Where the community burdens in the existing titles are silent the fallback power contained in section 29 of the 2003 Act only relates to maintenance as defined in the statute. There will be obvious cases where reputable tradesmen or a surveyor or other property professional is prepared to indicate that continued repair would not be worthwhile and indeed in the long run would be less economic than replacement. It should be borne in mind that the statutory definition of maintenance includes renewal and would allow demolition, alteration or improvement which is reasonably incidental. So far as a majority is concerned where a unit is owned in common a vote

---

[87] 2003 Act, s.29(2)(a).
[88] 2003 Act, s.29(2).
[89] 2003 Act, s.29(2)(b)(ii).
[89a] 2003 Act, s.29(3A) and (3B), as prospectively amended by the Tenements (Scotland) Bill 2004, s.22.
[90] 2003 Act, s.29(2)(c) and (4)(h).
[91] 2003 Act, s.29(2)(d).
[92] 2003 Act, s.29(2)(e).
[93] 2003 Act, s.122(1).

will only be counted if it is the agreed vote of those who own more than half of the unit.[94] It should be noted that the power to instruct maintenance under section 29 does not apply to tenements which will be governed by the Tenements (Scotland) Bill 2004.[95]

Content of notice requiring deposit to maintenance account

The notice requiring owners of units in the community to deposit a sum to a maintenance account must contain or have attached to it a separate note which sets out a summary of the nature and extent of the maintenance to be carried out.[96] The note must also detail the estimated cost of carrying out the maintenance and why the estimate is considered to be reasonable.[97] Presumably an estimate would be considered reasonable if it was the lowest of say three estimates and it came from a reputable tradesmen. Cost would not necessarily be a deciding factor in every case however. The note must also indicate how the sum required from the individual owner has been calculated and how the remainder being collected has been apportioned among other owners.[98] In the interests of transparency the attached note must also indicate the date on which the decision of the majority to carry out the maintenance was taken and the names of those by whom it was taken.[99] The timetable for carrying out the maintenance must be given[1] and the owners of the units must be advised in the notice of the identity of the bank or building society which will hold the maintenance account. The number of the account must be given as well as the names and addresses of those authorised to operate the account.[2] The account must be interest bearing and the authority of at least two persons or a manager who has the right to give authority must be required before any payment can be made from the account.[3] If the maintenance programme is modified or revoked and this affects or alters the information which is contained in the original notice then amended information must be sent to the owners forthwith.[4] These provisions will not apply to tenements which will be governed by the Tenements (Scotland)Bill 2004.[5]

6–22

Rights of individual owners

Anyone who has been involved in a dispute among flat owners in a tenement regarding the need for repairs or maintenance will know that some proprietors are keener to take control of situations than others. The powers conveyed on the majority could of course be abused. Accordingly the 2003 Act provides that any owner of a unit in the community shall be entitled to inspect at any reasonable time any tender received in connection with the maintenance work.[6] Moreover if the

6–23

---

[94] 2003 Act, s.29(3).
[95] 2003 Act, s.31A as prospectively amended; and see Ch.14 below.
[96] 2003 Act, s.29(4).
[97] 2003 Act, s.29(4)(a) and (b).
[98] 2003 Act, s.29(4)(c) and (d).
[99] 2003 Act, s.29(4)(e).
[1] 2003 Act, s.29(4)(f).
[2] 2003 Act, s.29(4)(g) and (h).
[3] 2003 Act, s.29(5).
[4] 2003 Act, s.29(6).
[5] 2003 Act, s.31A as prospectively amended; and see Ch.14 below.
[6] 2003 Act, s.29(7)(a).

maintenance work is not commenced within 28 days or such other refund date as may be specified in the notice after the date for commencement specified in the notice then an owner can demand repayment with interest of any sum deposited by that owner from the persons authorised to operate the maintenance account. They will be required to make repayment unless the notice comes after the maintenance work has actually been commenced.[7] The 2003 Act makes it clear that any sums held in a maintenance account are held in trust not just for the majority who instructed the work but for all those who made a deposit for the purpose of being used purely to make payment for the maintenance.[8] In the unlikely event of there being a surplus in the maintenance account after the cost of the work has been paid any balance is to be shared among the owners with accrued interest in proportion. What will be repaid will be the sum which each individual owner deposited less that party's share of the actual cost of the maintenance although it is open to depositors to agree some other division.[9] Notwithstanding the rights of individual owners majority rule is central to the statutory provisions. Anything done including any decision made by the owners in accordance with a provision in the community burdens themselves or by majority in accordance with sections 28 and 29 of the 2003 Act is binding on all the owners and their successors as owners.[10]

Remuneration of manager

6–24   In many cases the community burdens in the titles to all the units will specify that the remuneration of any factor or manager is to be shared among the owners in the same proportion as the cost of common repairs. However where the community burdens themselves are silent on this point liability for the remuneration of a manager (no matter how that manager has been appointed) is to be shared equally among the units in the community except where two or more persons have common ownership of a unit where liability shall be joint and several.[11] As between or among themselves common owners are of course liable in the proportions in which they own the particular unit.[12] These provisions will not apply to tenements which will be governed by the Tenements (Scotland) Bill 2004.[13]

Real burdens of a combined type

6–25   An obligation may be created both as named real burden such as a community burden and as a real burden which is not of that type. Thus a prohibition on the use of a flat for trade, business or profession could be a negative burden enforceable by one flat owner against another and also a community burden enforceable by and against all owners of units within the community. Where the burden is a community burden then the owner of the benefited property which is a unit in the community is

---

[7] 2003 Act, s.29(7)(b).
[8] 2003 Act, s.29(8).
[9] 2003 Act, s.29(9).
[10] 2003 Act, s.30.
[11] 2003 Act, s.31.
[12] 2003 Act, s.31(b).
[13] 2003 Act, s.31A as prospectively amended; and see Ch.14 below.

not entitled to enforce that obligation other than as a community burden.[14] There may be some burdens which are both community burdens enforceable by the owners of units within the community and also positive or negative burdens which happen to be enforceable by parties outside the community. Where this is the case then the burden will be treated as two distinct burdens.[15]

MANAGER BURDENS

Creation of manager burdens

Manager burdens are not the same as the power in a community burden **6–26** vest in all the owners or a majority of owners to appoint a manager. A manager burden is a burden which either appoints a particular party as a manager of related properties or vests in such party the power to appoint another person to be such manager and dismiss that manager. Accordingly a manager burden is an appointment or a power of appointment and dismissal vest in one party.[16] The provisions relating to manager burdens apply to existing burdens of this type and burdens created after the legislation comes into force.[17] The appointment or power of appointment or dismissal is exercisable only if the person appointed or on whom the power is conferred is the owner of a unit.[18] Although no one specific property need be specified and typically such a power of appointment might rest with a developer so long as the developer retained any ownership interest, the new provisions make it clear that the developer will require to exercise any power of appointment before selling the last property or being relieved of the last heritable interest in the community. The holder of the manager burden can assign or transfer the right and the assignation or transfer takes effect on sending written intimation to the owners of the related properties.[19] Presumably the assignee or transferee would have to own one of the other related properties so as to qualify for the appointment.[20] If the party was not the owner of one of the related properties then the burden would then be extinguished after the expiry of a 90-day continuous period throughout which the assignee or transferee was not an owner of a related property.[21]

Extinction of manager burdens

Manager burdens can be a good or a bad thing depending on one's point **6–27** of view and experience. On the one hand it can be extremely useful for a developer to retain control over the management of units in a development while the development is still ongoing. This may also have benefits for the purchasers in relation to ongoing maintenance. On the other hand a perpetual appointment or right of appointment is in effect a

---

[14] 2003 Act, s.62(2).
[15] 2003 Act, s.62(1).
[16] 2003 Act, s.63(1).
[17] This section came into force the day after Royal Assent.
[18] 2003 Act, s.63(2).
[19] 2003 Act, s.63(3).
[20] 2003 Act, s.63(2).
[21] 2003 Act, s.63(4)(c).

monopoly of control and can mean that owner occupiers have little or
no control over the management of common property. The problem
arose quite sharply in the case of sheltered housing where a specialised
developer of this type of housing also retained the management function after all the units were sold. In some cases owner occupiers in sheltered housing complexes were of the view that the situation was or was
capable of being abused. Accordingly the 2003 Act imposes time limits
on this particular monopoly. A manager burden is extinguished either
on the expiry of a period specified in the manager burden[22] or on a relevant date.[23] It has already been noted that the burden is also extinguished on the expiry of a 90-day continuous period during which a
manager burden cannot be exercised because the holder of the burden
does not own any of the related properties.[24] A manager burden is also
extinguished if the manager is dismissed in terms of the overriding
power of dismissal contained in the 2003 Act[25] in which case the date of
extinction of the burden will be the date of dismissal.[26] It should be
noted however that the overriding power to dismiss and appoint a
manager appointed under a manager burden only applies during the
statutory periods where the manager burden is imposed in a sale to a
sitting tenant under the right to buy legislation.[27] In other cases it is
suspended during the period. Where the date of extinguishment is the
relevant date in terms of the 2003 Act that date would normally be five
years after the day on which the constitutive deed setting out the
manager burden is registered. In cases where there is no deed of conditions and the manager burden is contained in each individual title of the
related properties then on the day the first title is registered.[28] Where
however the manager burden is imposed under a common scheme of
any unit of a sheltered or retirement housing development then the
period is three years from registration of the deed or the first deed in
which the manager burden is constituted.[29] Where the manager burden
is imposed on the sale to a sitting tenant by virtue of the right to buy legislation then the period is 30 years from the date of first registration of
the deed or deeds containing the manager burden.[30] To a certain extent
these provisions operate retrospectively in as much as the periods of
five, three and 30 years do not run from the coming into effect of the statutory provisions but from the registration date or first registration date
of the constitutive deed or deeds creating the manager burden. In many
cases therefore the periods will already have run out. That does not
mean that the appointment of a particular manager or factor automatically terminates. The burden which created the monopoly is terminated
but it would then be up to the proprietors of the units to decide simply
as a matter of contract whether or not they wish to continue with the
existing manager or factor.

---

[22] 2003 Act, s.63(4)(a).
[23] 2003 Act, s.63(4)(b).
[24] 2003 Act, s.63(4)(c).
[25] 2003 Act, s.64.
[26] 2003 Act, s.63(4)(d).
[27] Housing (Scotland) Act 1987, s.61; 2003 Act, ss.63(6) and 64(1)(b).
[28] 2003 Act, s.63(5)(a) and (c).
[29] 2003 Act, s.63(5)(b).
[30] 2003 Act, s.63(5)(a).

Overriding power to dismiss and appoint manager

The 2003 Act contains an overriding power to dismiss and appoint a **6–28** manager.[31] This arises where a person is manager of related properties. The majority required to dismiss and appoint some other person is two thirds. The majority is calculated on the basis of one vote per unit and where a unit is owned in common then the vote of the party owning more than one half share will count. If the property is owned equally and there is a disagreement the vote will not count at all. This overriding power of dismissal and appointment is suspended in the case of a manager appointed under a manager burden until the statutory time limits have elapsed except in cases where the manager burden is imposed in a right to buy sale to a sitting tenant. In this case the overriding power to dismiss and appoint appears override the 30 year statutory period from the date of constitution of the manager burden.[32]

Definition of related properties

The term "related properties" arises not just in the context of manager **6–29** burdens but in the context of community burdens created in pre-abolition deeds.[33] The definition of related properties for the purposes of establishing a common scheme under section 53 of the 2003 Act is set out in that section.[34] The definition of related properties for the purposes of sections 63–65 is contained in section 66. The two definitions are similar but not identical. For the purposes of manager burdens certain properties are expressly excluded from the definition. For the purposes of manager burdens whether properties are related is to be inferred from all the circumstances. Without prejudice that generality certain factors give rise to the inference.[35] These are not exclusive but would include:

(a) the convenience of managing the properties together because they share a common feature or an obligation for common maintenance of a facility;

(b) it being evident that the properties constitute a group of properties on which real burdens are imposed under a common scheme; or

(c) there being shared ownership of common property.[36]

In general terms for a manager burden to be effective the power conferred by that burden can only be exercised if the person on whom it is conferred is the owner of a related property. The following are not to be regarded as related properties for the ownership qualification:

---

[31] 2003 Act, s.64.
[32] 2003 Act, s.63(8)(b).
[33] 2003 Act, s.53.
[34] 2003 Act, s.53(2).
[35] 2003 Act, s.66.
[36] 2003 Act, s.66(1)(a), (b) and (c).

(a) property in a sheltered or retirement housing development which is used in some special way[37] such as a warden's flat or guest accommodation;

(b) property to which a development management scheme applies[38]; or

(c) any facility which benefits two or more properties such as a private road or a common recreation area.

The point of these exclusions is to prevent someone attempting to hold on to an appointment under a manager burden simply with reference to ownership of property which would not normally be regarded as an ordinary unit within that particular community. Thus, owning a *pro indiviso* share in some common facility without owning a residential unit would not qualify a person to be a manager or to appoint a manager in terms of section 53 (2) of the 2003 Act. Similarly the fact that the original developer of a sheltered housing complex continued to own a warden's flat but none of the other residential units would not qualify that developer to hold or exercise a right of appointment under a manager burden.

Manager burdens in favour of superiors

6–30   In many cases particularly in developments of sheltered and retirement housing the manager burden creating the appointment or giving the right to appoint will be vest in the superiors. In terms of the 2000 Act of course all real burdens which are created wholly in favour of a superior are extinguished on November 28, 2004.[39] There may be cases where a feudal superior would still qualify as an owner of related properties (within the restricted definition) but would lose the right if it appears to be expressly constituted in their favour as superior. Accordingly the 2003 Act makes special provision[40] to the effect that the provision in the 2000 Act extinguishing burdens in favour of superiors will not apply to manager burdens. The superior will still of course require to qualify in terms of the ownership requirement.[41]

Ineffectual manager burdens in existing titles

6–31   There are many burdens relating to factoring and management which may not be valid because in some way they fail to comply with the existing rules relating to the constitution of real burdens. Moreover where the appointment is to a superior who may not qualify as an owner of a related unit the appointment is not automatically terminated and the person is deemed to have been validly appointed. In such a case of course the manager can be replaced in terms of the statutory provisions.[42]

---

[37] As mentioned in the 2003 Act, s.54(1).
[38] Development management schemes are dealt with in Part 6 of the 2003 Act, ss.71–74 and in Ch.10 below.
[39] 2000 Act, s.17(1).
[40] 2003 Act, s.63(9).
[41] 2003 Act, s.63(2).
[42] 2003 Act, s.65.

Manager burdens—practical examples

The statutory provisions in the 2003 Act aim to strike some sort of balance between the rights of individual owners and the need for management and continuity of management. They are however best understood by looking at some practical examples.

6–32

> *Example 1*—A developer specialising in private sheltered housing carried at a development in 1995 and grants a deed of conditions which is registered in the Land Register in 1995 and which contains a manager burden giving the developer authority to appoint whom it likes to be manager in perpetuity while they own any part of the complex. All the individual residential units are sold between 1995 and 1997 but the developer retains exclusive ownership of a warden's flat and guest accommodation. The result is that the manager burden is terminated in 1998 three years after the registration of the deed of conditions. The existing manager continues until replaced.

> *Example 2*—The same developer of sheltered housing completes a development in 2003 and grants a deed of conditions containing the same manager burden. All the residential units are sold by 2005 but the developer retains ownership of a warden's flat and guest accommodation. The result is that the manager burden is still terminated after the lapse of a continuous 90-day period because the developer does not own a related property, ownership of a warden's flat and guest accommodation not being treated as related property for the purposes of manager burdens. Again the appointment continues until terminated.

> *Example 3*—A local authority sells a flat in a high-rise block to a sitting tenant under the right to buy legislation in 1997 having granted a deed of conditions covering the whole high-rise block which contains a manager burden providing that as long as the local authority is owner of any flat in the high-rise block they will be the factors and managers. The result firstly is that the manager burden will continue for a period of 30 years from the date of registration of the deed of conditions but secondly that a two thirds majority will have an overriding power to dismiss the local authority and appoint another person as manager or factor in terms of section 64 of the 2003 Act. While the local authority retains ownership of two thirds of the units in the high-rise block the appointment will be protected for the 30 year period.

> *Example 4*—A firm of builders develop an estate of 200 houses in 2003 granting a deed of conditions covering the whole estate which contains a manager burden giving the builders a power to appoint a factor of their own choosing. In 2004, 150 houses have been sold but the remaining houses are unsold or are still under construction. The result is that the manager burden will continue until five years after the date of registration of the deed of conditions provided that the builders still own one of the houses. If the builders within the five-year period sell off all the houses but retain ownership of small

pockets of land over which owners of the houses have rights such as private roads, facilities and amenity areas the manager burden will terminate within the five-year period after a continuous period of 90 days from the date the last house sold notwithstanding any residual ownership of ground which is a facility benefiting two or more properties in the estate.

CHAPTER 7

PERSONAL REAL BURDENS AFTER FEUDAL ABOLITION

INTRODUCTION

When the proposals for feudal abolition were being drawn up provision **7–01** was made for the preservation of feudal real burdens in certain circumstances by way of re-allotment of the right to enforce the burden to other land owned by the superior.[1] As has already been noted other burdens such as facility and service burdens are automatically preserved although enforcement rights pass from the superior generally to proprietors of other properties who may also benefit from the burden because they utilise the facility or service. This is the case not only with common facility or service burdens[2] but also with existing burdens which become community burdens.[3] In the case of community burdens the right to enforce is with those owning property within the community. In some cases however the superior will not have other land to which the right to enforce the burden can be realloted. In these cases the 2000 Act as amended by the 2003 Act allows the superior to preserve these burdens as personal real burdens.[4] The personal real burdens which can be preserved are personal pre-emption and redemption burdens, economic development burdens, health care burdens, conservation burdens and maritime burdens. Whereas the 2000 Act allows a superior to preserve these burdens as personal real burdens the 2003 Act allows burdens of these types to be created as personal real burdens not attached to any benefited property after the appointed day.[5] The provisions of the 2003 Act in relation to the creation of these burdens after abolition are of course very similar to the re-allotment provisions in sections 18A, 18B and 18C of the 2000 Act. Although it is possible to preserve a right of pre-emption, redemption or reversion as a personal real burden where that burden was created in a feudal deed it is not possible post-abolition of the feudal system to create a new personal pre-emption, redemption or reversion which is a burden which is real so far as the burdened land is concerned. Such arrangements will require to be left to personal contract or option agreement unless they can be created as praedial real burdens.

---

[1] See para.3–03 *et seq.* above.
[2] 2003 Act, s.56; see para.3–09 above.
[3] 2003 Act, ss.52, 53; see para.6–02 *et seq.* above.
[4] 2000 Act, ss.18A, 18B and 18C and see paras 3–11—3–15 above.
[5] 2003 Act, Part 3, ss.38–48.

CONSERVATION BURDENS

Conservation bodies

7–02　Scottish Ministers have by order prescribed those bodies which are to be regarded as conservation bodies. The list is unsurprising. It includes local authorities and other bodies which are to do with the preservation or conservation of property.[6] Part 3 of the 2003 Act which deals with conservation bodies came into force on November 1, 2003 with the exception of section 43.[7] Before a body can be nominated one of its objects or functions must be to preserve or protect for the benefit of the public the characteristics referred to in the definition of the burden.[8] Scottish Ministers may by order remove conservation bodies from the approved list.[9]

Nature of the burden

7–03　A conservation burden must be for the purpose of preserving or protecting for the benefit of the public the architectural or historical characteristics of any land or any other special characteristics of any land including a special characteristic derived from the flora, fauna or general appearance of the land.[10] Land includes heritable property whether corporeal or incorporeal held as a separate tenement and land covered with water.[11] The definition of land would of course also include any buildings on that land but although the preservation of buildings of architectural or historical importance may be the main object of a conservation burden the section is deliberately phrased to include natural attributes of land which ought to be preserved or protected. The provisions in respect of conservation burdens therefore might be regarded as protecting the environment in the widest sense in the public interest. The land or property subject to the burden must have some special attribute or feature. There are many burdens which attempt to prohibit or restrict alteration or conversion of buildings or which restrict the use to which buildings or land may be put to certain specified purposes. Thus it is common in the titles of residential properties to find a prohibition of physical alteration or sub-division. Similarly it is also common to find a prohibition of certain uses such as trade, business or profession. These are all burdens which might be said in some way to preserve the residential character and architectural integrity of the buildings. These burdens, which are for the most part of general application across a housing development, are not conservation burdens within the meaning of section 38 in that they are not specifically directed to a special individual feature of a particular property or area of land. For a burden to be a conservation burden there must be some special architectural or historical characteristic or some other special

---

[6] Title Conditions (Scotland) Act 2003 (Conservation Bodies) Order 2003, SSI 2003/453 as amended.

[7] Title Conditions (Scotland) Act 2003 (commencement No.1) Order 2003, SSI 2003/454.

[8] 2003 Act, s.38(5).

[9] 2003 Act, s.38(7).

[10] 2003 Act, s.38(1).

[11] 2003 Act, s.122(1).

characteristic possibly of an environmental nature which is being pro-tected.[12] A conservation body may acquire and renovate buildings of architectural or historical interest. As part of its own business plan however it may sell off parts of the renovated property. Thus, for example, a conservation body may wish in terms of its business plan to sell off a row of renovated cottages subject to very strict real burdens in relation to alterations, extensions and use. After abolition the body cannot retain enforcement rights as a feudal superior and it may be that it does not own land in the vicinity of the cottages which could be a ben-efited property which could have enforcement rights for the purposes of a real burden. In such circumstances the body may, post-abolition, create in the dispositions of the renovated cottages or by a constitutive deed akin to a deed of conditions conservation burdens which it will be able to enforce by virtue of its status as a conservation body as opposed to its ownership of other land as a benefited property.

Public benefit

For a burden to be created as a conservation burden it must be for the benefit of the public. This is not the same as saying that any member of the public can enforce a conservation burden. The statutory require-ment relates to the content of the burden. It is quite clear that the burden must be in favour of a conservation body or Scottish Ministers. One might take the view, the author supposes, that if a recognised con-servation body (as opposed to a local authority) decides to impose a conservation burden then there must automatically be public benefit. Opinions on what buildings are worth preserving however vary and of course change over time. There is no suggestion in the section that the public benefit is to be construed in a very wide sense. The benefit referred to in the section presumably relates to the special characteris-tic and is not to be brought in as part of a balancing exercise involving a wider interpretation of the public interest. The demolition of a crum-bling landmark which is dangerous may be in the public interest whereas its preservation might be for the benefit of the public in another sense. It is this latter and more restricted type of public benefit which is referred to in the section. While there is nothing in the legisla-tion to suggest that the building or land subject to the burden must be open to the public there must be some public benefit. A local trust might, for example, take over a large derelict mill complex with adjoin-ing workmen's cottages. The mill itself may be converted so as to include exhibition areas, a shop and a tearoom all open to the public. The cottages on the other hand may be sold off subject to conservation burdens but with no public access. In such a case however there would, it is submitted, be public benefit because members of the public visit-ing the mill complex would see the cottages from the outside as part of the original living and working community. Such burdens would therefore qualify.

7–04

---

[12] This is also the view of Professor Reid, see Reid, *The Abolition of Feudal Tenure in Scotland*, para.4.5.

Creation of the burden

7–05 Conservation burdens can be created in favour of Scottish Ministers or in favour of one of the bodies listed in the statutory instrument. These bodies are local authorities and recognised preservation societies. In the normal course of events the burden will be created either in a constitutive deed similar to a deed of conditions or in a conveyance granted by Scottish Ministers or one of the conservation bodies. However it was recognised that in some cases land or property owners who were not conservation bodies might wish to convey property of historical, architectural or environmental interest subject to burdens which protected these special characteristics. Accordingly the 2003 Act allows a conservation burden to be created by someone other than Scottish Ministers or a conservation body in a deed appointing Scottish Ministers or a conservation body as the party entitled to enforce the burden. The consent of Scottish Ministers or the conservation body to the creation of the burden must be obtained before the deed creating the burden is registered.[13]

The parties who can enforce

7–06 The right to enforce a conservation burden is presumably to be regarded as an incorporeal heritable right. There is no benefited property as such so the dual registration requirements for the creation of praedial real burdens cannot apply. However the right to enforce a conservation burden may be assigned.[14] The right to the burden can only be assigned to another conservation body or to Scottish Ministers. The assignation requires to be registered. It is not clear whether this means registration against the title of the burdened property or registration of the incorporeal heritable right to enforce as a separate heritable interest or both. Similarly there does not appear to be any statutory requirement to intimate the assignation of the right to the conservation burden to the party who for the time being owns the burdened land. It would probably be advisable to do this. As a general rule assignations require intimation and an assignation of the personal obligation of debt ordinarily would require intimation. There is no statutory requirement to intimate the assignation of a standard security but it is normally done either formally or informally. What is clear is that a conservation burden is enforceable by the holder of that burden irrespective of whether the holder has a completed title to the burden.[15] Presumably where the conservation body or Scottish Ministers grant the deed which creates the conservation burden that will be their title or if it is not to be regarded as a title then there will be no requirement to hold a title. On an assignation being registered that will complete a title to the burden. Conservation bodies, particularly local authorities are subject to legislative reorganisation from time to time. The view which has traditionally been taken is that a statute transferring assets from one local authority to a successor local authority does not give the successor local authority a completed title to heritable property or heritable rights. Even where there is a vesting or transfer

---

[13] 2003 Act, s.38(2).
[14] 2003 Act, s.39.
[15] 2003 Act, s.40.

of property order the view is that this only gives the successor authority a right to the heritable interest. A successor authority can complete title in the case of a sasine title by recording a notice of title or in the case of a registered title by producing the Act or property vesting order and the land certificate to the Keeper. Accordingly it is provided in the 2003 Act[16] that where the holder of a conservation burden does not have a completed title then title may be completed by the holder registering a notice of title. The notice of title would contain a clause of deduction of title specifying the reorganisation statute and the transfer of property or vesting order. Without completing title the holder of the burden may grant an assignation or a discharge again containing a deduction of title clause. Presumably if the title to the conservation burden is registered in the Land Register no deduction of title will be required and the Keeper will simply update the title sheet on production of the documents linking the new conservation body or local authority to the previous one. A standard security cannot be granted over a conservation burden.

Demise of conservation body

Where a conservation body ceases to be a conservation body as where **7–07** it is removed by Scottish Ministers from the list[17] or where the body is simply wound up then the conservation burden is extinguished. Presumably a conservation body which is in terminal decline may in appropriate circumstances seek to assign the right to enforce the conservation burden to another conservation body or Scottish Ministers. This extinction provision however emphasises that although a conservation burden must be in some way for the benefit of the public the right to enforce is vest in the conservation body or Scottish Ministers alone. The general public will not have any direct enforcement rights and when the conservation body ceases to exist as a conservation body no-one else will have the right to the conservation burden.

RURAL HOUSING BURDENS

Rural housing bodies

While it is not competent to create a personal right of pre-emption as a **7–08** real burden unattached to a benefited property, a special type of pre-emption right can be created for rural housing bodies.[18] Scottish Ministers will by statutory instrument list the bodies who are to be regarded as rural housing bodies. Presumably they will be local authorities or registered social landlords such as housing associations. The purpose of the statutory provision is clear; it is to allow rural housing bodies to reacquire property so as to have some control over the provision of housing in rural areas. One of the many distortions in the current housing market arises because people who do not live in a rural area are able to buy rural properties at inflated prices as holiday homes whereas those who actually live in the area are often priced out of the market. A

---

[16] 2003 Act, s.41.
[17] 2003 Act, s.38(3).
[18] 2003 Act, s.43.

rural housing burden is defined[19] as including a personal pre-emption burden the holder of which is a rural housing body. Accordingly where a rural housing body has in the past granted feudal titles of tenanted properties subject to a right of pre-emption and has then preserved that right of pre-emption as a personal pre-emption on abolition that personal pre-emption will in effect become a rural housing burden. It should be noted however that a notice must be served in terms of the 2000 Act.[20] There is no automatic preservation of the feudal pre-emption as a rural housing burden.

Nature of the burden

7–09   The right is a pre-emption in favour of a rural housing body other than by reference to that body's capacity as owner of any land.[21] It should be noted however that the burden is not to be known as a personal pre-emption burden or indeed a rural pre-emption burden. The burden is to be known as a rural housing burden. Rural land means land other than "excluded land" having the same meaning as in Part 2 of the Land Reform (Scotland) Act 2003. Although a rural housing burden is presumably some form of incorporeal heritable right[22] it is not competent to grant standard security over a rural housing burden.[23] The right to a rural housing burden can be assigned and enforced in terms of the appropriate provisions relating to conservation burdens and title may be completed using the same provisions.[24] If the rural housing body ceases to be a rural housing body then the burden is automatically extinguished.[25] One of the questions which might arise is whether or not a rural housing burden which is in the nature of a pre-emption is affected by the statutory provisions which relate to the exercise of pre-emption rights.[26] It seems fairly clear that rural housing burdens will be subject to these provisions in as much as section 82 of the 2003 Act states that the new pre-emption provisions will apply not only to existing rights of pre-emption constituted as title conditions but also personal pre-emption burdens or rural housing burdens. In such cases the person last registered as having title to the personal pre-emption burden or rural housing burden is deemed to be the holder of the pre-emption right.[27] Accordingly in so far as rural housing burdens created post feudal abolition are concerned they may be lost.[28] Professor Reid has noted a rather odd result where a feudal superior preserves a pre-emption right as a personal pre-emption[29] which right is then on feudal abolition magically

---

[19] 2003 Act, s.122(1).

[20] 2000 Act, s.18A.

[21] 2003 Act, s.43(1).

[22] 2003 Act, ss.39–42 in relation to community burdens are made applicable to rural housing burdens subject to the deletion of the reference to Scottish Ministers, see the 2003 Act, s.43(10).

[23] 2003 Act, s.43(4).

[24] 2003 Act, ss.39, 40 and 41.

[25] 2003 Act, s.42 as applied by s.43(10).

[26] These provisions are to be found in the 2003 Act, Part 8.

[27] 2003 Act, s.82.

[28] The rural housing body will have one chance to exercise the pre-emption in terms of the 2003 Act, ss.83 and 84.

[29] Under the 2000 Act, s.18A.

transformed into a rural housing burden. In Professor Reid's view[30] this type of pre-emption cannot be subject to the one chance only rule which would have applied to it as a feudal right of pre-emption presumably on the argument that the pre-emption may originally have been created in a feudal deed executed prior to September 1, 1974. The argument is that since the feudal system has been abolished and the pre-emption has in effect by virtue of the statutory provision become a rural housing burden it cannot be regarded as a feudal pre-emption and is, in Professor Reid's words, elevated into a right in perpetuity. In the author's view however the words of section 82 negative this approach in that the section specifically states that the re-cast rules in relation to pre-emptions will apply to pre-emptions constituted as a title condition originally created in favour of a feudal superior.[31]

The parties who can enforce

A rural housing body will be such body as may be prescribed by Scottish Ministers who have the power to remove bodies from the list.[32] In the normal course of events the rural housing burden will have been created in a deed granted by the rural housing body. However as with conservation burdens it is possible for the burden to be created in favour of a rural housing body by another party provided the consent of the rural housing body to the creation of the burden is obtained before the deed is registered.[33] Only rural housing bodies may be added to the list. A rural housing body will be a body whose object or function or one of whose principal objects or functions is to provide housing on rural land or to provide rural land for housing.[34] A trust may be a rural housing body.[35] There is one very important exclusion. The most common sale by any housing authority or registered social landlord is a sale to a sitting tenant by virtue of that tenant's statutory right to purchase.[36] It is not competent to insert a rural housing burden containing a pre-emption in favour of a rural housing body on the sale of a property to a tenant exercising his or her right to buy.[37]

7–10

MARITIME BURDENS

Creation of maritime burdens after feudal abolition

In addition to the automatic preservation of maritime burdens in favour of the Crown as feudal superior over the foreshore or seabed[38] the Crown will, after feudal abolition, be able to create a real burden over

7–11

---

[30] Reid, *The Abolition of Feudal Tenure in Scotland,* para.4.25.
[31] 2003 Act, s.82.
[32] 2003 Act, s.43(8).
[33] 2003 Act, s.43(2).
[34] 2003 Act, s.43(6).
[35] 2003 Act, s.43(7).
[36] Housing (Scotland) Act 1997, s.61.
[37] Presumably this type of burden is more likely to be inserted in conveyances of land or commercial properties.
[38] 2000 Act, s.60.

the seabed or foreshore in favour of the Crown for the benefit of the public and such a burden shall be known as a maritime burden.[39] The right of the Crown to this burden cannot be assigned or otherwise transferred.[40] Seabed means the bed of the territorial sea adjacent to Scotland and "territorial sea" includes any tidal waters.[41] It should be noted that the burden must be for the benefit of the public and not just for the benefit of the Crown estates as a commercial matter.

ECONOMIC DEVELOPMENT BURDENS

Definition

7–12   Where an economic development burden has been created in a feudal writ it is capable of preservation as a personal real burden.[42] After abolition it will be possible for a local authority or Scottish Ministers to create an economic development burden in their favour.[43] The burden must have been imposed for the purpose of promoting economic development.[44] Burdens of this type which have been converted from feudal burdens under the 2000 Act will still be economic development burdens after abolition.[45]

Nature of the burden

7–13   The burden is personal and is not attached to any land as a benefited property but is in favour of Scottish Ministers or a local authority as a personal real burden by virtue of their status. The burden may involve some positive obligations such as the development of land for a particular purpose such as a shopping complex or an industrial estate. In the normal course of events the burden is likely to relate to the land which is being conveyed by the local authority or Scottish Ministers. An economic development burden however differs from a conservation burden in that there appears to be no requirement that the burdens specifically relate to economic development or a commercial benefit derived from development on the burdened land.[46] A local authority may impose a burden with a view to raising money for economic development in the area of the land elsewhere or generally. Perhaps one of the most common types of economic development burden will be a clawback burden. A local authority may sell land for development purposes at a price which may simply reflect the current use value on the basis that the purchaser will expend money on development. An economic development burden may comprise an obligation to pay a sum of money to the local authority or Scottish Ministers.[47] The sum need not be an exact sum provided

---

[39] 2003 Act, s.44.
[40] 2003 Act, s.44(2).
[41] 2003 Act, s.44(3) For discussion of the rights of the Crown which remain after abolition see para.2–04 above.
[42] 2000 Act, s.18B and see para.3–12 above.
[43] 2003 Act, s.45(1).
[44] 2003 Act, s.45(1).
[45] 2003 Act, s.122(1).
[46] see Reid, *Abolition of Feudal Tenure*, para.4.12.
[47] 2003 Act, s.45(3).

the method of determining the sum is specified in the deed creating the economic development burden.[48] If, because of a particular planning permission, the developer, taking into account the cost of development, makes a substantial planning gain the economic development burden may provide for a further payment to be made to the local authority based on a formula. The re-allotment provisions which allow a superior to preserve a burden as an economic development burden do not contain any definition and in particular do not contain any statement to the effect that the burden may comprise an obligation to pay a sum of money far less an uncertain sum of money. The general rule in relation to real burdens for payments of money was and is (apart from maintenance obligations) that the sum of money must be specific. Accordingly although an economic development burden created after feudal abolition may comprise a clawback arrangement of the type illustrated above there must be doubt as to whether or not the provisions of the 2000 and 2003 Acts taken together would validate retrospectively a feudal burden created before abolition which has been realloted as a personal economic development burden in terms of the 2000 Act. Although an economic development burden may be an incorporeal heritable right it cannot be the subject of a standard security[49] nor, unlike a conservation burden or rural housing burden can it be assigned.[50] As with conservation burdens and rural housing burdens an economic development burden is enforceable by the holder of the burden whether or not that holder has a completed title and title may be completed by notice of title or a deed may be granted with a deduction of title as appropriate.[51]

The parties who can enforce

Only a local authority or Scottish Ministers can hold an economic devel- **7–14** opment burden. As with conservation burdens and rural housing burdens other parties can create an economic development burden in favour of a local authority or Scottish Ministers provided they obtain the consent of the authority or Ministers prior to registration of the deed containing the burden.[52] A local authority is a council constituted under the relevant legislation.[53]

HEALTHCARE BURDENS

Definition

A healthcare burden is a burden for the purpose of promoting the pro- **7–15** vision of facilities for health care and this definition includes facilities ancillary to health care as for example accommodation for staff employed to provide health care.[54] It is a personal real burden which can

---

[48] 2003 Act, s.45(3).
[49] 2003 Act, s.45(4)(a).
[50] 2003 Act, s.45(4)(b).
[51] 2003 Act, s.45(5), applying sections 40 and 41(a) and (b)(i).
[52] 2003 Act, s.45(2).
[53] Local Government etc (Scotland) Act 1994, s.2.
[54] 2003 Act, s.46(1) and (6).

only be created in favour of a national health service trust or Scottish Ministers. There are equivalent preservation provisions in respect of feudal burdens which are categorised as healthcare burdens.[55]

The nature of the burden

7–16   A national health service trust or Scottish Ministers may sell land to raise funds but wish to restrict the use of that land to medical purposes which would include ancillary purposes such as staff accommodation. As with economic development burdens there does not appear to be any requirement that the burden relates to the land conveyed. All that is required is that the burden is for the purpose of promoting the provision of facilities for health care. In most cases however the burden will directly apply to the subjects conveyed.[56] Where the burden is created after feudal abolition then it can comprise an obligation to pay money of a specific amount or as calculated in accordance with a formula laid down in the constitutive deed.[57] The health care burden is presumably an incorporeal heritable right but it cannot be subject to a standard security[58] nor, unlike a conservation burden, can it be assigned.[59] The provisions in relation to enforcement without a completed title and completion of title which apply to conservation burdens are applied with modification to health care burdens.[60]

The parties who can enforce

7–17   Normally the burden will be created by a national health service trust or Scottish Ministers in a deed but as with conservation burdens and economic development burdens, health care burdens created after feudal abolition a health care burden can be created by a third party in a deed provided the consent of the trust or Scottish Ministers is obtained before the deed is registered.

PERSONAL REAL BURDENS—TITLE, INTEREST AND EXTINCTION

Title and interest to enforce personal real burdens

7–18   The party seeking to enforce a personal real burden must have title to enforce. In the context of a personal real burden title does not mean title to a benefited property but simply title to the personal real burden itself as a heritable incorporeal right. Where the burden is created post-abolition then presumably the title is created on registration of the constitutive deed. There are provisions for a notice of title to be registered where the title to the personal real burden is incomplete and for deductions of title to be granted in assignations where assignations are com-

---

[55] 2000 Act, s.18C.
[56] See the discussion on direct and indirect promotion of facilities for health care in Reid, *Abolition of Feudal Tenure*, para.4.17.
[57] 2003 Act, s.46(3).
[58] 2003 Act, s.46(4)(a).
[59] 2003 Act, s.46(4)(b).
[60] 2003 Act, ss.40 and 41(a) and (b)(ii), as applied by s.46(5).

petent.[61] Personal real burdens are enforceable by the holder of the burden whether or not that holder has a completed title to the burden.[62] There is of course a conceptual difficulty surrounding interest to enforce. In so far as real burdens in general are concerned it has always been the law (and in so far as praedial real burdens are concerned remains the law) that a party must, have title and interest to enforce. The interest must not be personal but praedial or patrimonial.[63] In the case of a personal real burden there can, by definition, be no praedial interest because the right to enforce the burden is not attached to any land but to a party. In the case of conservation burdens, economic development burdens, health care burdens and maritime burdens only certain very restricted categories of people or institutions can hold the personal real burden. Accordingly the 2003 Act provides specifically that the holder of any personal real burden is presumed to have an interest to enforce it.[64]

Discharge of personal real burdens

The extinction of real burdens in general is dealt with elsewhere.[65] A personal real burden can be discharged by a grant of a deed of discharge by or on behalf of the holder of the burden. The personal real burden is then discharged on registration of that discharge against the title of the burdened property.[66] The deed can discharge the burden completely or only to such an extent as is specified in the discharge itself.[67]

7–19

---

[61] 2003 Act, s.41 as applied to conservation and other burdens.
[62] 2003 Act, s.40 as applied to conservation and other burdens.
[63] See *Aberdeen Varieties Ltd v James F. Donald (Aberdeen Cinemas) Ltd*, 1939 S.C. 788; 1940 S.C. (HL) 52.
[64] 2003 Act, s.47.
[65] See Ch.9 below.
[66] 2003 Act, s.48(1).
[67] 2003 Act, s.48(2).

CHAPTER 8

ENFORCEMENT OF REAL BURDENS

INTRODUCTION

One of the great difficulties with the existing law of real burdens is **8–01** identifying the party or parties entitled to enforce. In the context of a practical conveyancing transaction the problem tends to arise in relation to an already completed contravention of a real burden. There are few occasions on which a solicitor is asked by a client to seek out a feudal superior and co-feuars with a view to obtaining consents before a plastic stick-on conservatory is erected in contravention of a real burden. Nevertheless while the feudal system is in existence the superior provides a focal point for enforcement in so far as feudal real burdens are concerned. Although co-feuars may well have had enforcement rights these were largely ignored in conveyancing practice. Purchasers and their solicitors tended to be satisfied with a waiver or a letter of consent from or on behalf of the superior. The reason for this is not just ignorance of the law relating to third party rights. In an estate of two hundred relatively modern houses all with third party enforcement rights one might be looking at a wholly impractical scenario so far as obtaining consent to the erection of the conservatory is concerned. Accordingly the law of third party rights has been largely ignored. After abolition of the feudal system and the coming into effect of the 2003 Act the matter requires to be looked at afresh. For one thing there will be no feudal superiors; for another there are now two distinct types of burden, the ordinary praedial burden enforceable by a person by virtue of that person's ownership of land and a personal real burden enforceable by a person or institution without reference to the ownership of land.

THE REQUIREMENT FOR TITLE AND INTEREST TO ENFORCE

For a party to be able to enforce a real burden that party has always **8–02** required to have both title and interest to enforce the burden. In so far as the superior was concerned the title to enforce the burden was clear; it was the superiority title itself as a separate estate in land. So far as interest to enforce was concerned, although the interest required to be praedial it was presumed in the case of the superior at least in the first instance.[1] That rule of the common law is restated in general terms for all real burdens both praedial and, to a lesser

---

[1] *Earl of Zetland v Hislop* (1882) 9 R. (HL) 40.

extent, personal in the 2003 Act.[2] So far as praedial real burdens are concerned, title to enforce will of course flow from the ownership of the benefited property. So far as personal real burdens are concerned title will be vest in the holder of the burden from time to time. Some personal real burdens can be assigned in which case the assignee will become the holder of the burden with title to enforce. So far as interest is concerned the owner of the benefited property in the case of a praedial real burden will require an interest to enforce. In the case of personal real burdens however interest to enforce is presumed.[3]

TITLE TO ENFORCE

Title to enforce—praedial real burdens

8–03   The party who has the primary title to enforce a praedial real burden is the owner of the benefited property. However the 2003 Act extends the right to enforce a praedial real burden to other parties who have a connection with the benefited property. This was a matter of some debate before the legislation was passed. It is of course of the essence of a praedial real burden that the title to enforce is vest not so much in a person as in the benefited land itself. That is one reason why the burden is real. Accordingly in strict terms enforcement rights should be vest in the owner of the benefited property and no other party. It was however recognised that parties with subordinate rights such as tenants of the benefited property or indeed liferenters or non-entitled spouses might be more affected by a contravention of a real burden on a neighbouring property. For this reason the 2003 Act confers statutory enforcement rights on other parties. The owner of the burdened property is defined in the 2003 Act,[4] as being, in relation to any property, a person who has right to the property whether or not that person has a completed title. Where the property is held in common ownership *pro indiviso* the term owner includes any *pro indiviso* owner. For the purposes of enforcement where a party does not have a completed title the term owner means such person as has most recently acquired the right.[5] Where a heritable creditor is in lawful possession of the benefited property it appears as thought the heritable creditor is to be deemed to be the owner for the purposes of enforcement. This presumably means that the debtor/owner of the benefited property will lose enforcement rights where the heritable creditor is in possession. This will not apply in relation to the creation, variation or discharge of real burdens where the heritable creditor in possession will simply be treated as one of the owners.[6]

[2] 2003 Act, s.8(1).
[3] 2003 Act, s.47.
[4] 2003 Act, s.123.
[5] 2003 Act, s.123(1)(b).
[6] 2003 Act, s.123(2)(a) and (b).

Tenants

A party who has a real right of lease of the benefited property or has a pro indiviso share in such right will be entitled to enforce real burdens. It should be noted here that there is no requirement that the lease be registered. Accordingly it could be a long or a short term lease provided it was created a real right one way or another.[7]

8–04

Proper liferenters

A party who has a proper liferent of the benefited property or a *pro indiviso* share in such a right will have enforcement rights. A proper liferent is rare nowadays. A proper liferent arises where there is a conveyance to one party in liferent and another party in fee. In legal terms this is a special destination in the title. Most liferents which are created in wills are what are known as beneficiary or improper liferents where the testator or testatrix conveys his or her property or an individual piece of property to trustees and they hold that property in trust for the liferenter and divest themselves in favour of the fiar at the end of the liferent. In the former case the life-renter will have statutory enforcement rights but in the latter the liferenter will not.[8]

8–05

Non-entitled spouses

A party who is the non-entitled spouse of the owner or one owner of the benefited property or a non-entitled spouse of a tenant or proper life-renter will also have statutory enforcement rights provided the non-entitled spouse has occupancy rights in the benefited property.[9] It should be noted that for a non-entitled spouse to have a statutory title to enforce a real burden that spouse must also hold occupancy rights in the property at the time. Presumably the time in question is the time of enforcement rather than the time of creation of the burden. While the drafting of the matrimonial homes legislation[10] does not make it clear whether a non-entitled spouse who has held occupancy rights can effectively lose them simply by non-exercise apart from the statutory five year prescription, the rights can be renounced by the non-entitled spouse.[11] The requirement in relation to occupancy rights however is only that the non-entitled spouse should have them. For the purposes of enforcement of a real burden there does not appear to be any requirement that the non-entitled spouse is actually exercising the occupancy rights.

8–06

---

[7] 2003 Act, s.8(2)(a); on the question of a lease as real right in general see Halliday, *op. cit.*, pp.40–49 *et seq.*

[8] 2003 Act, s.8(2)(a); for a general discussion of liferent, see 13 *Stair Memorial Encyclopaedia*, para.1608 *et seq.*

[9] 2003 Act, s.8(2)(b).

[10] Matrimonial Homes (Family Protection) (Scotland) Act 1981 as amended.

[11] For a general discussion of occupancy rights in the conveyancing context see Halliday, *op. cit.*, para.36-25 *et seq.*

Maintenance burdens—shared cost

8–07   It is no objection to the validity of a real burden whenever created that it is in respect of an uncertain amount of money provided the amount is required to defray some cost.[12] The parties who will be entitled to recover that cost after feudal abolition will of course be the other co-proprietors who are the owners of both benefited and burdened properties. In such a case these other co-proprietors will have a statutory title to enforce such a burden as will tenants, proper liferenters and non-entitled spouses who have occupancy rights of or in relation to the benefited properties.[13]

Praedial pre-emptions, redemptions, reversions and options

8–08   The subsidiary enforcement rights extended to tenants, liferenters and the holders of matrimonial occupancy rights do not apply in the case of a praedial real burden which is constituted either as a pre-emption, redemption, reversion or any other type of option to acquire the burdened property. Only the owner of the benefited property has title to enforce that type of real burden.[14] Obviously the owner of a burdened property which is subject to a right of pre-emption can only deal with one party. In any event these rights are very closely attached to ownership of the benefited property. It would be ludicrous, for example, if a tenant of the benefited property could acquire a property burdened with a right of pre-emption in favour of that tenant's landlord. In so far as redemptions, reversions and options to acquire are concerned it should be noted that after November 28, 2004 although a real burden may consist of a right of pre-emption it cannot consist of a right of redemption, reversion or any other type of option to acquire.[15]

Personal real burdens

8–09   It is the holder of the personal real burden who has title to enforce. Since the burden is personal and is not tied to any benefited property there can be no subsidiary rights in favour of tenants, liferenters or the holders of matrimonial occupancy rights. The holder of the personal real burden need not have a completed title.[16] Personal pre-emption and personal redemption burdens may exist where these have been expressly preserved by a superior.[17] The former superior as the holder of the personal pre-emption or redemption burden can assign this to other parties but the assignation requires to be registered.[18] Neither section 40 nor section 41 of the 2003 Act are made applicable to personal pre-emptions and redemptions. Accordingly it must be presumed that

---

[12]   2003 Act, s.5.
[13]   2003 Act, s.8(2)(c) and (3)(b).
[14]   2003 Act, s.8(4).
[15]   2003 Act, s.3(5).
[16]   2003 Act, s.40 in relation to conservation burdens as applied to rural housing burdens by s.43(10), to economic development burdens by s.45(5) and the health care burdens by s.46(5).
[17]   2000 Act, s.18A(5).
[18]   2000 Act, s.18A(7).

an assignee will not be able to enforce a personal pre-emption or redemption until the assignation has been registered. The right to enforce a maritime burden vest in the Crown is not assignable.[19] The title to enforce this burden simply vests in the Crown by virtue of the section in the 2003 Act which provides for the creation for this type burden.[20]

Community burdens

As has already been noted community burdens can arise either in rela-   **8–10**
tion to pre-feudal abolition burdens which can satisfy the provisions of either section 52 (where there are reciprocal rights of enforcement) or 53 of the 2003 Act[21] or alternatively can be expressly created as community burdens post-abolition.[22] So far as title to enforce is concerned the owner of every unit within the community will have title to enforce a community burden against any other unit within the community. Tenants, proper liferenters and entitled spouses with occupancy rights of or in relation to a unit within the community will also have statutory enforcement rights. However as has already been noted the majority in a community can actually delegate the right to enforce the community burdens to a manager.[23] Existing title deeds may also provide for the appointment of a manager as a manager burden subject to the statutory time limits and restrictions.[24] The majority can also delegate the power to enforce community burdens to such a manager notwithstanding the fact he may have been appointed in terms of a manager burden created prior to November 28, 2004.[25]

Title to enforce by implication

In the case of feudal burdens the superior's title to enforce is obvious; it   **8–11**
is the superiority title itself as a separate estate in land. In some cases the deed creating the real burdens expressly conferred third party rights on co-feuars or co-disponees. In other cases however third party rights arose by implication. Such enforcement rights did not just relate to third party rights of co-feuars or co-disponees but could also relate to successors of original disponers where a real burden was created in a disposition of adjoining or neighbouring land and the disposition itself did not state in express terms that the burden was to be enforceable by the granter of the deed and his or her successors in the ownership of identifiable land. In so far as real burdens created after November 28, 2004 are concerned in most cases both the burdened and benefited properties will require to be identified.[26] Similarly the deed will require to be registered against the titles to both benefited burdened properties.[27]

---

[19] 2003 Act, s.44(2).
[20] 2003 Act, s.44(1).
[21] See the discussion in Ch.6 at para.6-04 *et seq.* above.
[22] 2003 Act, ss.25–27 and see para.6-02 *et seq.* above.
[23] 2003 Act, s.28(1)(b) and 2(b) and see para.6-20 above.
[24] 2003 Act, s.63; see para.6-26 above.
[25] 2003 Act, s.28(4).
[26] 2003 Act, s.4(2)(c).
[27] 2003 Act, s.4(5).

Abolition of existing implied rights

8–12   The general thrust of the 2003 Act is to restate the common law and modify or explain it where necessary. A similar approach is taken in relation to implied rights of enforcement in respect of burdens created prior to November 28, 2004. The fact that the existing law is complicated and unclear does not aid a statutory reinterpretation. In general terms however any implied rights of enforcement created prior to November 28, 2004 are expressly abolished subject to certain rights of preservation.[28] An implied right of enforcement arises where the benefited property is not nominated in the deed which creates the burden.[29] However provisions of sections 52 to 57 of the 2003 Act provide a replacement code which will apply in respect of common schemes and related properties.[30] Accordingly in so far as third party rights are concerned which have been created in pre-November 28, 2004 deeds the new statutory provisions will apply and rights of enforcement will be construed accordingly. Reciprocal rights of enforcement will apply as they would with any other community burden.[31]

Preservation of implied rights to enforce—neighbour burdens

8–13   In the case of burdens created in a disposition which are not expressly stated to be in favour of the granter and that party's successors in identified land there are special provisions which allow these burdens to be preserved. An owner of such land which is a benefited property by virtue of any existing rule of law which creates an implied right may within a period of ten years from November 28, 2004 execute and register a preservation notice in the form contained in Schedule 7 to the 2003 Act.[32] If the owner does so the benefited land shall continue to be a benefited property after the expiry of the period. The notice must identify the burdened property, identify the benefited property and set out the terms of the burdens which are to be preserved. If the party registering the notice does not have a completed title to the benefited property then the mid-couples or links in title must be specified. Finally the notice must set out the grounds both factual and legal for describing the identified land as the benefited property.[33] The notice is only effective when duly registered against both the benefited and burdened properties[34] unless the benefited property is outwith Scotland.[35] As with the re-allotment notices in respect of former feudal burdens the person submitting the notice for registration must swear or affirm before a Notary Public to the best of his or her knowledge and belief that all the information contained in the notice is true.[36] Where the person submitting the notice is subject to disability or incapacity a legal representative may swear or

---

[28] 2003 Act, s.49(1).
[29] 2003 Act, s.49(1).
[30] See para.6-04 *et seq.* above.
[31] See para.8-10 above.
[32] 2003 Act, s.50(1).
[33] 2003 Act, s.50(2).
[34] 2003 Act, s.50(3).
[35] 2003 Act, s.116.
[36] 2003 Act, s.50(4).

affirm and where the person is a juristic person then any party authorised to sign documents may swear or affirm. The 2003 Act makes it clear
that the notice of preservation provision does not apply to third party
rights which continue by virtue of section 52 or 53 as community
burdens.[37] Save where it is not reasonably practical to do so the owner
of the benefited property must before registering the notice send a copy
of the notice to the owner of the burdened property with the appropriate explanatory note. The Keeper of the Registers is not required to
determine whether the service provisions have been complied with. If
the owner of the burdened property objects matters will be dealt with
by the Lands Tribunal.[38] There are detailed provisions in relation to
what is meant by "sending" a notice in the 2003 Act.[39] A notice can be
sent to the agent of any person or simply addressed to the owner or proprietor where the precise identity of the person is not known. Sending
is construed as transmission by post, delivery or electronic transmission
and for the purposes of the Act something which has been posted is
taken to be sent on the day of posting and something transmitted by
electronic means is taken to be sent on the day of transmission.[40]

The ten-year period

If no notice is registered within the 10-year period referred to in section   **8–14**
50 of the 2003 Act then any implied right of enforcement which has
arisen in favour of a successor of a granter of a disposition containing a
burden will not be extinguished until after the expiry of the ten-year
period.[41] If the appropriate notice of preservation is served and registered then the burden will continue to be enforceable by the nominated
benefited property after the ten-year period.[42]

Invalid burdens

As with the statutory provisions relating to reallotment[43] the serving   **8–15**
and registration of a notice of preservation in respect of an implied
enforcement right arising from a disposition creating a real burden will
not validate a real burden which is otherwise invalid. Any notice must
be served by the owner of a benefited property. This means that the
property concerned must under the existing law be entitled to enforcement rights. In some cases a burden in a disposition may be construed
simply as a matter of personal contract between the original disponer
and the original disponee. In such a case service of a notice under
Schedule 7 of the 2003 Act will not elevate the status of the obligation to
that of real burden. The burden may be invalid for other reasons as for
example where it is in unreasonable restraint of trade.[44] It must be recognised that it has always been more difficult to create a real burden that

---

[37] 2003 Act, s.50(6).
[38] 2003 Act, s.115.
[39] 2003 Act, s.124.
[40] 2003 Act, s.124(3).
[41] 2003 Act, s.49(2).
[42] 2003 Act, s.50(1).
[43] Contained in the 2000 Act, s.18 as amended.
[44] 2003 Act, s.3(6).

runs with both burdened and benefited property in a disposition than it is to create one in a feudal writ.[45] Professor Halliday appears to have taken the view[46] that a real burden in disposition could only be enforced by a singular successor of the granter if the lands to be benefited by the real burden were identifiable and the disposition creating the real burden expressed the right as being enforceable by successors in the ownership of identified lands. It has been clear however since the decision in *Braidhills Hotel Co. Ltd v Manuels*[47] that for a real burden in a disposition to be enforceable by a singular successor of the granter there is no need for that burden to be expressly assigned by the granter when the benefited property is conveyed. This had been a matter of doubt as a result of the decision in *J A MacTaggart & Co. v Harrower*.[48] Professor Reid and the authors of the *Stair Memorial Encyclopaedia* appear to have taken a more relaxed view than Professor Halliday. Their view is that if either the granter of the disposition creating the burden owns neighbouring lands or if he nominates such land as a benefited property if it is owned by a third party then continuing enforcement rights are created. Professor Reid states that in a "well drawn disposition" the right to enforce on the adjoining land will be clearly expressed by way of nominating that land as the benefited property but he takes the view that even where there is no express nomination there is probably an implied right to enforce arising from the fact that the granter of the disposition still owns adjoining land.[49] The authors view is that there will be cases where it is fairly obvious that adjoining land retained by the granter of a disposition was intended to benefit from enforcement rights. This will be more obvious in the case of neighbour type burdens which relate to the preservation of the amenity of the adjoining land or burdens which relate to the erection and maintenance of division fences and walls.

The duties of the Keeper

8–16   As with feudal real burdens which have been extinguished[50] burdens in favour of a granter of a disposition and his or her successors will be extinguished at the expiry of the ten-year period assuming no notice is registered. However the Keeper is under no duty to cleanse the Registers by removing unenforceable real burdens unless the Keeper is requested to do so in an application for registration or rectification or is ordered to do so by the court or the Lands Tribunal in a rectification dispute.[51] No such request or order shall be competent however during the ten-year period from the appointed day.[52] An enforceable real burden may be treated for registration purposes as subsisting during the ten-year period.[53] The Keeper cannot remove from the Land Register

[45] See Reid, *The Law of Property in Scotland*, para.378.
[46] Halliday, *op. cit.*, paras 4–49 and 34–64.
[47] 1909 S.C. 120.
[48] (1906) 8 F. 1101.
[49] Reid, *The Law of Property in Scotland*, para.387.
[50] Under the 2000 Act, s.17.
[51] 2003 Act, s.51.
[52] 2003 Act, s.51(2).
[53] 2003 Act, s.51(3) and Land Registration (Scotland) Act 1979, s.6(1)(e).

a real burden which is subject to a notice in respect of which an application has been made for a determination by the court or the Lands Tribunal until two months after the final decision has been taken or a day appointed by Scottish Ministers whichever is the earlier.

Persons against whom burdens are enforceable—praedial and personal real burdens

The provisions in relation to the identity of the parties against whom 8–17 burdens are enforceable are equally applicable to praedial real burdens and personal real burdens. In a sense of course a personal real burden might loosely be said to be praedial or real at least so far as the burdened property is concerned. An affirmative burden (one which requires the owner of the burdened property to do something including an obligation to defray or contribute towards some cost) is enforceable against the owner of the burdened property[54] but not any other party. On the other hand a negative burden such as a prohibition of sub-division or alteration of a building or an ancillary burden which provides for management of common property can be enforced not only against the owner of the burdened property but also against any tenant or any other person who has use of the burdened property.[55] In the case of affirmative burdens whether or not the owner of burdened property could force a tenant of that property to comply with a burden which is an obligation to pay or contribute to common charges in respect of common property will depend on the terms of the lease between the owner of the burdened property and that tenant. There will be no direct enforcement rights as between the owner or owners of the benefited property and the tenant of the burdened property. However where the burden is a negative burden or an ancillary burden it is appropriate that there should be direct enforcement rights against a tenant or other occupier such as a liferenter or a non-entitled spouse exercising occupancy rights. The point of a negative burden is to prevent a certain use or operation on the burdened property and the point of an ancillary burden is normally to facilitate management. These are matters which directly affect the occupier perhaps even more than the owner of the burdened property.

Changes in ownership of burdened property

So far as affirmative real burdens are concerned the fact that the owner 8–18 of the burdened property ceases to be owner does not mean that that party will cease to be liable for the performance of an obligation.[56] A continuing obligation of this type would probably be something like an obligation to maintain or an obligation to contribute an appropriate share of common charges. The new owner is however severally liable with the previous owner for compliance with the burden.[57] In terms of section 123 of the 2003 Act the expression "owner" includes those who have not completed title. Presumably one ceases to be an owner for the

---

[54] 2003 Act, s.9(1).
[55] 2003 Act, s.9(2).
[56] 2003 Act, s.10(1).
[57] 2003 Act, s.10(2).

purposes of continuing liability on delivery of a conveyance although this will not of itself remove liability from the old owner. The new owner is entitled to relief from the former owner in respect of any expenditure incurred by the new owner in the performance of the relevant obligation where the liability truly rests with the former owner.[58] It will be necessary in dealing with disputes between former owners and new owners to determine precisely the time at which the obligation under the affirmative burden became enforceable or due for performance. Where the burden is a community burden and a binding decision has been taken by the community to incur the expenditure then the obligation becomes binding when the decision is made.[59] Accordingly for a former owner to incur a liability it would not be necessary for the owners of units in the community or a factor or manager acting on their behalf to have actually instructed a tradesman to carry out work. All that is needed is for the community to have come to a decision in accordance with the rules which apply to community burdens. However a former owner will not incur a liability if there has merely been discussion among owners of the units in the community about the possible need to carry out work in terms of a maintenance obligation which is a community burden. In the case of other affirmative burdens which are not community burdens the obligation in relation to the burden becomes due on such date or on the occurrence of such event as may be stipulated for performance whether in the constitutive deed or otherwise.[60] So far as negative or ancillary burdens are concerned of course the obligation is of a continuing nature. The provisions relating to continuing liability do not apply to tenements[60a].

Division of the benefited property

8–19   After feudal abolition there will be no feudal superior with a title to enforce a burden. A burden may have been realloted by a feudal superior[61] to another benefited property. Alternatively a burden may be created in a disposition registered before abolition or some other constitutive deed akin to a deed of conditions registered after November 28, 2004. Where a part only of the benefited property is split off and conveyed away then the general rule is that on registration of the conveyance that part conveyed away shall cease to be a benefited property unless in the conveyance itself some other provision is made.[62] It will be possible to provide in the conveyance that both the part retained and the part conveyed away are both to constitute benefited properties.[63] It will also be possible to stipulate in the conveyance that it is the retained part which is to cease to be a benefited property.[64] It will be possible to make different provisions in respect of different real burdens on the sub-division taking effect.[65] If special provision is to be made in the split-off deed then

[58] 2003 Act, s.10(3).
[59] 2003 Act, s.10(4)(a).
[60] 2003 Act, s.10(4)(b).
[60a] 2003 Act, s.10(5) as prospectively amended by the Tenements (Scotland) Bill, s.22(3); tenements will be subject to separate providers.
[61] Under 2000 Act, s.18.
[62] 2003 Act, s.12(1).
[63] 2003 Act, s.12(1)(a).
[64] 2003 Act, s.12(1)(b).
[65] 2003 Act, s.12(2).

these provisions must identify the original constitutive deed by which the burden or burdens were created with reference to the place of registration and date of registration of that deed. The special provision must also identify the real burden or burdens concerned.[66] Where the real burden is a right of pre-emption, redemption or reversion or some sort of option to acquire then either the right to enforce must remain with the retained property[67] or must pertain wholly to the property conveyed away.[68] The reason for this is obvious. A pre-emption, redemption, reversion or option can only be exercised by one party.[69] These special provisions in relation to sub-division of the burdened property do not apply in the case of community burdens created after November 28, 2004 or created prior to that date but achieving the status of community burdens by virtue of section 52 or 53 of the 2003 Act.[70] Similarly these provisions do not apply to burdens in a deed of conditions which sets out the terms of the burdens imposed on the part conveyed that part being one of two or more properties in a common scheme. The reason for this is that a deed of conditions contemplates sub-division of the original area into parts which will all be subject to the burdens contained in the common scheme.[71]

Division of the burdened property

The general rule is that where part of burdened property is conveyed whether before or after November 28, 2004 then on registration of the conveyance the part retained and the part conveyed shall separately constitute burdened properties unless the real burden cannot relate to one of the parts in which case that part shall on registration cease to be burdened.[72] Accordingly if land is conveyed subject to a real burden that it is not to be used for the purposes of trade, business or profession that burden will continue to apply notwithstanding the fact that the land is sub-divided. On the other hand if the burden is to the effect that a specified half acre part of the land as shown outlined in red on a plan annexed to the deed creating the burden is not to be used for trade business or profession then on a conveyance of any part of the land apart from the land outlined in red on the plan these sub-divided parts will cease to be burdened. Similarly if there is an obligation to erect or maintain a boundary feature such as a wall or fence on a particular boundary then a conveyance of part of the land which does not include that boundary or is not bounded by that feature will be free of that particular burden.

8–20

There are special rules in relation to division of the burdened property in the case of affirmative burdens.[73] An affirmative burden is a burden which places a positive obligation on the proprietor of the burdened

8–21

---

[66] 2003 Act, s.12(3)(a) and (b).
[67] By virtue of 2003 Act, s.12(1).
[68] By virtue of a provision to that effect in the conveyance in terms of 2003 Act, s.12(1)(b).
[69] 2003 Act, s.12(3)(c).
[70] 2003 Act, s.12(4)(a) and (b).
[71] 2003 Act, s.12(4)(c).
[72] 2003 Act, s.13.
[73] 2003 Act, s.11.

property to do something or to pay or contribute to some cost. If a burdened property is divided and is subject to an affirmative burden whether before or after November 28, 2004 then the owners of the parts are severally liable in respect of the burden to the party who owns the benefited property.[74] As between or among themselves the burdened proprietors are liable in the proportions which the areas of their respective parts bear to the total area of the burdened property.[75] Where however the affirmative burden can only relate to one part of the property then on the conveyance away of other parts of the property these parts will be free of the burden.[76] Accordingly if there is an obligation in terms of a real burden to erect three detached houses on part of the ground shown outlined in red on a plan annexed to the deed creating the burden and a provision to the effect that three blocks of flatted dwellinghouses are to be erected on the remaining parts of the burdened land then on a conveyance away of the detached dwellinghouses they will be free of any burden relating to the erection of flatted properties and vice versa. Where flats are concerned and an apportionment of liability is required[77] then the appropriate proportion will not be surface area but floor area.[78] Floor area is calculated by measuring the total floor area including areas taken up by internal walls or divisions but excluding balconies and lofts or basements only used for storage. It will be possible in the constitutive deed creating the affirmative burdens to provide specifically that the obligation to comply with the affirmative burden will apply only to a particular part of the property. It will also be possible in the constitutive deed to indicate a different method of calculation in so far as liability between or among burdened proprietors is concerned.[79] So far as common owners are concerned as where title is taken in joint names then so far as any affirmative burden is concerned each common owner is severally liable to the party entitled to enforce. As between or among all common owners themselves they are liable in the proportions in which they actually own the burdened property.[80]

Interest to Enforce

The statutory provisions

8–22   Under the existing law a superior's interest to enforce was presumed.[81] Under the 2003 Act however the position is reversed. A person has an interest to enforce a praedial real burden if in the circumstances of any case failure to comply with the real burden is resulting in or will result in material detriment to the value or enjoyment of the benefited proprietor's ownership of, or right in, the benefited property.[82] The definition of interest contained in the 2003 Act will also apply to the interest of a

---

[74] 2003 Act, s.11(1)(a).
[75] 2003 Act, s.11(1)(b).
[76] 2003 Act s.11 (2).
[77] In terms of the 2003 Act, s.11(1)(b).
[78] 2003 Act, s.11(3); 2003 Act, s.11(3A), prospectively introduced by the Tenements (Scotland) Bill 2004, s.22. See Ch.14 in relation to tenements in general.
[79] 2003 Act, s.11(4).
[80] 2003 Act, s.11(5).
[81] *Earl of Zetland v Hislop* (1882) 9 R. (HL) 40.
[82] 2003 Act s.8 (3)(a).

former superior in relation to a realloted burden. A party will also have an interest in the enforcement of a real burden if that burden is an affirmative burden which is created as an obligation to defray or contribute towards some cost where the person seeking to enforce the burden is seeking, and has grounds to seek, payment of that cost. While a statutory definition of interest is welcome it is not clear just how far the definition clarifies the existing law. Certainly one can be sure that there is no such thing as a presumed interest, except in the case of personal real burdens. However cases involving interest even where non-superiors had the title to enforce, have always been fact specific. It is very difficult to deduce any particular principle.[83]

Interest to enforce community burdens

Although interest is presumed in the case of some personal real burdens because there is no benefited property interest is not presumed in the case of all community burdens. Interest will be presumed where the community burden relates to a maintenance charge such as the cost of maintaining a common amenity area[84] but in respect of other community burdens parties wishing to enforce will require to show that they have an interest. An interest will arise[85] where failure to comply with the community burden results in or will result in material detriment to the value or enjoyment of the benefited property. In the context of a practical conveyancing transaction it is important to remember the new statutory definition of interest to enforce. There has been some concern that the new rules relating to implied third party rights and community burdens will result in purchasing solicitors seeking waivers or consents in respect of alterations or additions from everyone who has a title (as opposed to an interest) to enforce the burden. While adjoining proprietors may have an interest (in the legal sense) in what goes on next door the further away a property is the less likely it is going to be that there will be interest to enforce. It is the author's experience that proprietors tend to take objection in respect of certain breaches. The most obvious are:-

8–23

(a) Breach of a prohibition of alterations or additions to buildings as where a new extension is being built which blocks a view or casts a shadow or will contain windows which overlook adjoining property.
(b) Breach of a prohibition of alteration of a common boundary feature such as a wall, hedge or fence as where one party wishes to achieve or maintain privacy by the erection of a high boundary feature and the other does not.
(c) Breach of a prohibition of the carrying on of trade, business or profession as where a party seeks to run a business from home and this causes noise, increased traffic or some other difficulty. The most recent example known to the author arose where the

---

[83] see *Macdonald v Douglas* 1963 SC 374; *Howard De Walden Estates Ltd v Bowmaker* 1965 SC 163; *Co-operative Wholesale Society v Ushers Brewery* 1975 S.L.T. (Lands Tr.) 9; Halliday, *Conveyancing Law and Practice* (2nd ed.) 34–42 *et seq*; Reid, *The Law of Property in Scotland* para.407 *et seq*; Gordon, *Scottish Land Law* (2nd ed.) paras 22–32, 22–66, 23-15.
[84] 2003 Act, s.8 (3) (b).
[85] 2003 Act, s.8 (3) (a).

owner of a large house in a residential area was running a small
nursery for children and there was noise in the garden and
increased traffic as the children were dropped off and picked up.
(d) Breach of a prohibition in relation to pets or animals as where
someone keeps more than one dog and there is continual
barking or where someone seeks to breed animals.
(e) Breach of a prohibition of the parking of commercial vehicles
such as vans either on the ground pertaining to a particular unit
or along the street. In some cases parties also object to other
vehicles such as caravans and boats or trailers. Objections to
breaches of this type of provision are often taken together with
objections to the carrying on of trade, business or profession.

It is obvious that the parties who will have an interest to enforce the
burdens referred to in the foregoing examples will be those who are
closest to the burdened property. By no stretch of the imagination would
someone who lives at the end of a street have any interest to object to
the erection of an extension some six houses away which cannot be seen
from that first party's property. One cannot, however, exclude the possibility that a proposed use might be so dramatic as to have an effect on
the whole estate as where, for example, a developer acquired a whole
street of houses and proposed to demolish them and erect in their stead
a small factory unit thus altering the character of the area. Unless the
estate is particularly small interest to enforce is in general likely to be
restricted to adjoining proprietors.

Practice

8–24   While it is risky to offer guidance the following examples may help.

Example 1. A widow owns a house with a large garden which has
become too much to manage. In 1999 she grants a feu disposition of the
lower part of the garden subject to an affirmative real burden that the
vassal will erect a single storey bungalow and also subject to several
negative burdens which prohibit additions, alterations and trade, business or profession. Being properly advised by her solicitor, the distin-
guished Roderick Reid-Brymer Von Gretton,[86] she successfully reallots
the right to enforce the feudal burden from her superiority title to the
ordinary title to her own house and retained garden. She therefore has
a title to enforce both the affirmative and negative real burdens. In 2005
the bungalow changes hands and the new owner, a brash IT consultant,
tells the widow casually that the days of feudalism have gone and that
he intends to add a further storey to the bungalow thus obscuring the
widow's view. In such a case it seems clear that the widow would have
an interest because there would be material detriment given the proximity of the two properties.

Example 2. A development of 200 residential houses is subject to a deed
of conditions executed in 1998 which provides that none of the houses
are to be altered or added to in any way. The burdens are clearly part of

---

[86] Apologies to Alexander McCall Smith.

a common scheme and accordingly become community burdens in terms of either section 52 or 53 of the 2003 Act. Accordingly in terms of title to enforce all the proprietors within the community have title to enforce the terms of the burden against each other. The owner of a house on the southern perimeter of the estate wishes to erect a kitchen extension. He consults his solicitor Wortley Scott-Rennie[87] and is advised that he should obtain the consent of the two proprietors on either side of his house and the three proprietors who have houses backing on to his house but that it is not necessary to obtain the consent of anyone else. Subsequently however the owner of a house on the northern perimeter of the estate some three streets away with whom our luckless proprietor has had a serious business dispute gets wind of the proposal to build the extension and seeks to object in terms of the real burden. It cannot be the case that the proprietor on the northern perimeter of the estate would have any interest to enforce against the proprietor at the southern end of the estate since there can be no material detriment.

Example 3. A small development of some 15 exclusive detached dwellinghouses in a crescent is subject to a constitutive deed of community burdens executed in 2005. One of the negative burdens is to the effect that none of the houses shall be used for the purposes of any trade, business or profession. The houses in question are all sold at individual prices exceeding £300,000. The proprietor of the first house in the crescent has recently been made redundant and has decided to set up his own business as a courier of parcels and packages. To the consternation of everyone else in the exclusive estate three or four rusty second-hand vans are parked either in his driveway or along the crescent which has been adopted by the local authority. Various workers arrive at five in the morning to drive away these vans slamming doors as they go. Packages are left on the pavement. The owner of the despatch business stays at home taking orders by telephone and communicating with his drivers by radio or mobile phone. Since this activity might be said to affect the amenity of the whole estate, given its size and location, all the proprietors would have an interest to enforce because there would be material detriment to the whole estate.

REMEDIES

Remedies for enforcement

Before feudal abolition the primary remedy of a superior was irritancy. **8–25** Superiors managed to extract payments for waivers and consents mainly because in many instances there was the threat of that remedy. Irritancies in relation to feudal burdens were abolished on June 9, 2000.[88] There has always been some doubt as to whether an irritancy in respect of a non-feudal burden was competent. In any event non-feudal irritancies have now been abolished with effect from April 3, 2003.[89] The most

---

[87] He cannot afford the expensive East coast solicitor mentioned in the previous example.

[88] 2000 Act, s.53.

[89] 2003 Act, s.67.

effective judicial remedy is now likely to be that of interdict. If a neighbour fears that someone is about to contravene a real burden then that threatened act of contravention can be the subject of interdict.[90] An action of specific implement ordaining a party to implement an affirmative burden would also be competent.[91] An action of damages may also be competent if it can be shown that the benefited proprietor has indeed suffered some loss. If a building has been erected in contravention of a burden then although it is possible to ask the court to order demolition courts are unlikely to grant such orders where a building has stood unchallenged for some time. It must be borne in mind that the 2003 Act contains provisions which would prevent a party entitled to enforce from having any remedy if there has been acquiescence.[92] Other real remedies will have gone with the abolition of the feudal system. Where a party who has title to enforce a real burden does not know the precise identity of the owner of the burdened property as where the property has recently changed hands there is a statutory obligation on a previous owner to supply the name and address of the current owner or failing that such other information which that party has which might enable the party entitled to enforce to discover the name and address of the current owner.[93]

---

[90] See for example *Howard De Walden Estates Ltd v Bowmaker*, 1965 S.C. 163.
[91] See *Marshall v Callander & Trossachs Hyrdropathic Co. Ltd* (1896) 23 R. (HL) 55.
[92] 2003 Act, s.16 and see para.9-21 below.
[93] 2003 Act, s.70.

CHAPTER 9

VARIATION AND EXTINCTION OF REAL BURDENS

INTRODUCTION

Discharge, in whole or in part, of a real burden is perhaps more common than variation although one might regard a partial discharge or a limited waiver or consent as in effect a variation of a burden. In so far as discharge is concerned this can be express by virtue of a written formal deed or by operation of law as where, for example, the right to enforce a real burden is lost through acquiescence[1] or negative prescription.[2] Real burdens can also be extinguished where they are terminated under the new provisions of the 2003 Act.[3] Very often the question of extinction arises in the context of a conveyancing transaction where there is a suggestion that the seller or a predecessor in title may be in breach of the real burden thus rendering the title unmarketable.[4] Variation and discharge of real burdens by the Lands Tribunal are dealt with elsewhere.[4a]

9–01

EXPRESS DISCHARGE

Praedial real burdens

Under the existing pre-feudal abolition law a burden would normally be discharged either by a minute of waiver or, where there was to be some variation of a feudal condition a charter of *novodamus*. Minutes of waiver will still be competent post-abolition but obviously a charter of *novodomus* being a feudal grant will not. In terms of the 2003 Act a real burden is discharged as respects the benefited property by registration of an express deed of discharge against the title of the burdened property. This may seem odd in the case of praedial real burdens given the requirement to register the burden against the title of both burdened and benefited properties at the time of its creation. The point of dual registration is that a party looking at the title of either the burdened or benefited property should be able to ascertain who can enforce. A party examining the title of the benefited property in a praedial real burden may form the view that the burden is still enforceable even although a discharge has been registered against the title to the burdened property.

9–02

---

[1] 2003 Act s.16.
[2] 2003 Act s.18.
[3] 2003 Act ss.20–24 and see para.9-14 below.
[4] See for example *McLennan v Warner & Co.*, 1996 S.L.T. 1349 where interference with a servitude right of access was deemed to render the title unmarketable.
[4a] See Ch.13.

The Keeper is given a discretion which will allow him to alter the title sheet of the benefited property so as to take account of any document which varies, discharges, renews, reallots, preserves or imposes a real burden or servitude.[5] The deed of discharge is granted by or behalf of the owner of the benefited property.[6] The discharge can be in whole or in part as where a prohibition of trade, business or profession is discharged only to the extent of a particular profession such as the giving of piano lessons at home.[7] It should be noted that although certain real burdens can be enforced by tenants, liferenters and the holders of matrimonial occupancy rights of or in connection with the benefited property only the owner or a person on behalf of the owner can grant a deed of discharge or variation. Moreover there does not appear to be any statutory requirement to obtain the consent of a tenant, liferenter or holder of occupancy rights to the discharge. It may seem rather odd that a party's rights of enforcement created by statute[8] can, in effect be discharged by another party (the owner of the benefited property). These subordinate rights however are derivative, depending for their existence on the owner's right to enforce and when that right to enforce has been discharged the subordinate rights must fall away. The definition of "owner" includes a person who has right to property but no completed title.[9] A heritable creditor in lawful possession of benefited property would also be an owner for the purposes of the grant of a deed of discharge, variation or waiver.[10] If the benefited property is owned in common then the discharge will require to be granted by all *pro indiviso* proprietors. There is no statutory form of discharge. The normal deed will be a minute of waiver which will be granted expressly in favour of the burdened proprietor. There is however no requirement to specify the identity of any particular grantee in the deed of discharge.[11] Any deed of discharge may be registered by an owner of the burdened property or by any other person against whom the real burden is enforceable.[12] A deed of variation or a deed of discharge in relation to a community burden by majority or by owners of adjacent units[13] may be registered by the granter.[14] The discharge or minute of waiver must of course be registered. There are special rules in relation to deeds of discharge and variation for community burdens and personal real burdens.[15]

Personal real burdens

9–03   A deed of discharge or waiver in respect of a personal real burden will be granted by the holder of that burden. The holder of the burden will normally have some sort of registered title. The title may arise on the

---

[5] 2003 Act, s.105.
[6] 2003 Act, s.15(1).
[7] 2003 Act, s.15(2).
[8] 2003 Act, s.8(2).
[9] 2003 Act, s.123.
[10] 2003 Act, s.123(1).
[11] 2003 Act, s.69(1).
[12] 2003 Act, s.69(2).
[13] 2003 Act, ss.33 and 35.
[14] 2003 Act, s.69(3); this is a complicated procedure involving the Lands Tribunal.
[15] 2003 Act, ss.33, 35 and 48 and see paras 9–03 and 9–04 below.

registration of a notice of preservation, for example, in relation to a pre-served feudal conservation burden or may be by way of registered assignation where the personal burden is one which can be assigned. The holder of a personal real burden can complete a title by registering a notice of title or in the case of a registered title sending the appropriate link to the land register and asking the Keeper to update the title sheet. However a deed of discharge can be granted even where the holder of the personal real burden does not have a completed title in which case a clause of deduction of title will be appropriate in Sasine cases.[16] It should be noted of course that a personal real burden is not a separate estate in land as such. Accordingly registration of the deed of discharge can only be against the title of the burdened property. Oddly the same single registration requirement also applies to a discharge of a praedial real burden. Prior to the coming into effect of the 2003 Act a waiver could only be granted by a party who had a completed title, a waiver not being one of those deeds in which a deduction of title was competent.[17]

Community burdens

One of the areas of property law which has been largely ignored by prac-titioners in the past is that of third party rights to enforce real burdens such as the rights of co-feuars or co-disponees. This area of law has been complicated and the court decisions are both confused and confusing. This may be one reason why, when parties have sought a waiver or a dis-charge of a real burden, they have simply gone to the party who appears to have primary enforcement rights. In most cases this would have been a feudal superior although in some cases parties have sought and indeed accepted minutes of waiver granted by an existing developer who had not feued any of the individual units in a development. Where third party rights existed all those holding these rights would have had a title to enforce the burdens. Whether they would all have had an interest is of course another matter.[18] The other reason for ignoring the law relating to third party rights of enforcement has been purely practical. It is simply not possible to obtain the consent of 199 owner occupiers in a housing estate of 200 houses in the context of an ordinary conveyancing transac-tion relating to the sale of one unit. For one thing the legal expense involved would be enormous. For another not everyone would consent. In any event even if a party wished to consent that party's heritable cred-itor might have to be involved. Some practitioners took the view that few co-proprietors had an interest to enforce anyway. During the reform process it was recognised that if third party rights were to continue as community burdens and if the superior was to be removed as a focal point for enforcement greater emphasis would undoubtedly be placed on the remaining third party rights of enforcement. Accordingly the 2003 Act contains specific provisions relating to the variation and discharge of community burdens.[19]

9–04

---

[16] 2003 Act, s.41.
[17] Conveyancing (Scotland) Act 1924, s.3.
[18] For a general discussion of title and interest to enforce real burdens see para.8–22 *et seq.* above.
[19] 2003 Act, ss.32–37.

Community burdens—majority rule

9–05   Where there is both title and interest to enforce a community burden and it is desired to waive or discharge the same the existing law would require every proprietor of a benefited property to grant the necessary document because all parties who have title and interest have separate rights which are not affected by a waiver or discharge granted by any other benefited proprietor.[20] A community burden may be varied or discharged by the registration against each affected unit of a deed of variation or discharge.[21] An affected unit is a unit in respect of which a community burden is to be varied or discharged.[22] The deed of discharge or variation may be granted by particular parties on behalf of all the owners where there is provision in the constitutive deed to this effect.[23] A manager may also be appointed in terms of a community burden and that manager may be given power to vary or discharge community burdens.[24] Where there is no provision in the constitutive deed then a deed of variation or discharge will be effective if it is granted by or on behalf of the owners of a majority of the units in the community.[25] If however one person owns the majority of the units then the deed must also be granted by at least one other owner.[26] The affected unit in respect of which the variation or discharge is to be granted is counted for the purposes of calculating the majority so in effect the party seeking the waiver, discharge or variation will have a vote.[27] This will apply either in the case of a procedure for voting set out in the constitutive deed or in the case of the statutory procedure for majority rule. If a particular unit is owned by more than one person in common then the vote will only count if it is made by or on behalf of those common owners who own more than a one half share in the unit unless the constitutive deed makes another provision.[28] It should be noted that although burdens relating to sheltered or retirement housing complexes are community burdens a majority can only vary core burdens. The majority cannot discharge them.[29] For sheltered or retirement housing a two-thirds majority would be required in any case and no real burden relating to a restriction as to age may be varied or discharged even by the two-thirds majority.

Community burdens—protection of minority

9–06   Section 33 of the 2003 Act merely deals with the grant of a deed of variation or discharge by a majority. It does not provide for any meeting of proprietors or any voting procedure as such. Accordingly in terms of

---

[20] *Dalrymple v Herdman* (1878) 5 R. 847; *Arnold v Davidson Trust Ltd*, 1987 S.C.L.R. 213.
[21] 2003 Act, s.33(1).
[22] 2003 Act, s.32.
[23] 2003 Act, s.33(1)(a).
[24] 2003 Act, s.28(1)(b), (2)(c) and 33(2)(b).
[25] 2003 Act, s.33(2)(a).
[26] 2003 Act, s.33(2)(a).
[27] 2003 Act, s.33(3).
[28] 2003 Act, s.33(4).
[29] 2003 Act, ss.33(5) and 54(5)(b) and (c) core burdens are burdens which regulate the use, maintenance, reinstatement or management of a facility or service which is one of those which make a sheltered or retirement housing development particularly suitable for occupation by elderly or infirm, disabled or vulnerable people.

that section a majority could get together and grant the discharge without the minority even knowing. The 2003 Act provides[30] that owners of units in the community who have not granted the deed of variation or discharge must receive intimation before the deed is registered.[31] Intimation is given by sending a copy of the deed together with a notice in the form set out in Schedule 4 and the explanatory note attached to the schedule.[32] Notice may be given to the owner of the other unit or units or his or her agent and may be given by posting, personal delivery or in electronic form.[33] The notice must identify the properties which will be affected by the deed of variation. The notice must also set out the terms of the community burden or burdens which are to be varied or discharged and the effect of registration of the deed (presumably variation or discharge). It should be noted that it is possible in such a deed to actually impose new burdens as part of a variation.[34] The notice must also alert the recipient that an application can be made to the Lands Tribunal for preservation of the community burden or burdens affected within a certain time limit which is to be not less than eight weeks after intimation.[35] The recipient of the notice can make application to the Lands Tribunal for Scotland asking them to preserve the burden unvaried or undischarged in so far as that particular party's property is concerned or in respect of all other properties owned by parties who have not granted the deed of variation or discharge.[36] Before the deed of variation or discharge can be registered the Clerk to the Lands Tribunal has to sign a certificate endorsed on the deed which confirms either that no application to preserve has been received or that if one has been received it has been withdrawn or the notice for the application to preserve only relates to some or one of the community burdens but not all of them.[37] In the latter case a deed of variation or discharge can be registered in relation to community burdens which are not the subject of any application to preserve. The community burdens in respect of which application to preserve has been made will remain in force until the Lands Tribunal has dealt with the application.[38] If there are no outstanding applications to preserve and the Clerk to the Lands Tribunal has signed the endorsed certificate then before the deed of variation or discharge is registered the party proposing to register it must swear or affirm that the deed has been granted either in accordance with provisions in the constitutive deed creating the community burdens or in accordance with the statutory provisions for variation or discharge by majority.[39] The oath must also indicate the date on which the statutory period for lodging an application to preserve the community burden expires. Where a deed of variation or discharge is being granted by more than one party then only one need swear or affirm. If an individual is unable by reason of legal disability or incapacity to swear or

---

[30] 2003 Act, s.34.
[31] 2003 Act, s.34(1).
[32] 2003 Act, s.34(2).
[33] 2003 Act s.124
[34] 2003 Act, s.33(1).
[35] 2003 Act, s.34(3) and Sch.4.
[36] 2003 Act, s.34(3).
[37] 2003 Act, s.37(2).
[38] 2003 Act, s.37(3).
[39] 2003 Act, s.37(4).

affirm then a legal representative may do so and where the party is not an individual then any person authorised to sign documents on behalf of the entity may swear or affirm.[40]

Effect of registration

9–07   Once this procedure has been gone through assuming there are no out-standing applications to preserve the community burden the deed of variation and discharge granted by the majority can be registered. The variation or discharge effected then binds all the benefited properties whether or not all the owners of these properties were parties to the deed.

Community burdens—variation and discharge by owners of adjacent units

9–08   Putting aside for the moment any question of interest to enforce a com-munity burden[41] the procedure for discharge by a majority is cumber-some and may be impractical. Accordingly the 2003 Act provides an alternative method of variation and discharge of community burdens where there is no specific provision in the constitutive deed providing for a method of discharge or variation.[42] In this case the deed is granted not by a majority of the units in the community but by or on behalf of all the owners of the affected (burdened) units who wish discharge or variation and by or on behalf of all the owners of so called adjacent units.[43] Adjacent units are defined as being, in relation to an affected or burdened unit, any unit which is at some point within four metres of the burdened unit.[44] For the purposes of the distance calculation measure-ment is made along a horizontal plane disregarding the width of any intervening road if of less than twenty metres and any pertinent of either the affected (burdened) unit or the adjacent unit.[45] So far as flatted properties are concerned all flats in the same block will be treated as having no distance between them on a horizontal plane. The vertical distance will be irrelevant. The exclusion of roads of less than a twenty metre width restates the rule for neighbour notification in planning matters. A pertinent to be disregarded could be something like a common right in a back green attached to a tenement or block of flats. If there was such a tenement then the four metre measurement would start from the wall of the tenement flat and not from the back edge of the common back green.

9–09   It should be noted that this shorthand method of obtaining a variation or a discharge does not apply in two cases:

---

[40] 2003 Act, s.22(2) as applied by s.34(6) and s.37(5).
[41] See para.8-23 above.
[42] 2003 Act, s.35.
[43] 2003 Act, s.35(1).
[44] 2003 Act, s.32.
[45] 2003 Act, s.125.

a) where the community burden is a facility or a service burden[46] or where the units constitute a sheltered or retirement housing development[47]; and

b) where the constitutive deed creating the community burdens expressly disapplies this particular method of waiver or discharge.[48]

Where an affected (burdened) unit is owned in common then any deed of discharge or variation must be granted by the party who owns the majority share unless the constitutive deed creating a community burden specifies otherwise.[49]

Community burdens—variation and discharge—affected and adjacent units—intimation

The 2003 Act contains fairly stringent intimation requirements where the shorthand method of discharge by affected and adjacent units is used. Clearly in such a case not even the majority of owners of units within a community may know of the grant of the deed. Accordingly a proposal to register a deed of discharge or variation under section 35 of the 2003 Act must be intimated to any owners of any units in the community who have not granted the deed.[50] Intimation may be given by sending a copy of the deed (presumably once it has been signed by the owners of affected (burdened) and adjacent units).[51] The copy deed must be sent together with a notice in the form of Schedule 5 and an explanatory note set out in that schedule.[52] As an alternative to actual intimation by post, hand delivery or electronic means intimation may be made by affixing to each affected unit and to a lamppost or lampposts a conspicuous notice in the form set out in Schedule 6 to the 2003 Act.[53] Where there exists only one lamppost within 100 metres of the affected (burdened) units then that is the lamppost to which the notice must be affixed. Where there is more than one lamppost within 100 metres then the notice must be affixed on each of at least two such lampposts. The 2003 Act does not define the term "conspicuous" in relation to the notices to be affixed to the affected (burdened) units and the lamppost or lampposts. Presumably the notice would require to be roughly at eye level to be conspicuous. There are specific provisions in the 2003 Act which relate to the affixing of notices to lampposts.[54] A party is entitled to affix a notice to a lamppost regardless of who owns the lamppost but must take all reasonable care not to damage the lamppost and remove the notice no later than one week after the date specified in the Schedule 6 notice by which an application for preservation of the community burden must be made to the Lands Tribunal for Scotland. The period is

9–10

---

[46] As defined in the 2003 Act, s.56.

[47] 2003 Act, s.35(1)(a).

[48] 2003 Act, s.35(1)(b).

[49] 2003 Act, s.33(4) as applied by s.35(2).

[50] 2003 Act, s.36(1).

[51] 2003 Act, s.36(2)(a).

[52] Sending is defined in the 2003 Act, s.124 which allows transmission by post, hand delivery or through electronic mail.

[53] 2003 Act, s.36(b).

[54] 2003 Act, s.21(6) as applied by s.36(5).

eight weeks from the latest date on which intimation of the proposal to register the deed of variation or discharge is given. The party who affixes the notice must, until the day immediately following the expiry of the time limit, take all reasonable steps to ensure the notice continues to be displayed and remains conspicuous and readily legible.[55] No planning permission is required for the affixation of any notice.[56]

Intimation by advertisement

9–11   There may be cases where there are no lampposts within the appropriate 100 metre radius. In such a case as an alternative to postal, hand or electronic delivery and affixation of a notice, intimation may be given by advertisement in a newspaper circulating in the area of the affected unit.[57] The advertisement must identify the land which is the affected (burdened) unit and set out the terms of the community burden either in full or by reference to the constitutive deed where the burden is created. The advertisement must also specify the name and address of the person who proposes to register the deed of variation or discharge and state that a copy of the deed may obtained either from that person or some other person whose name and address are supplied in the advertisement. The advertisement must also state that any owner of any unit who has not granted the deed of variation or discharge may apply to the Lands Tribunal for Scotland for the community burden to be preserved. The advertisement must go on to state that if no such application is received by the expiry of the eight-week period, the consequence may be that the community burden will be varied or discharged in relation to the affected unit or units.[58] The party who proposes to register the deed of variation or discharge must provide any other person with a copy of the deed if requested.[59] If the intimation procedure is properly carried out then the deed of variation or discharge must be endorsed with a certificate signed by the Clerk to the Lands Tribunal to the effect that no applications to preserve have been received or if they have they have been withdrawn or that they only relate to some of the burdens. Thereafter an oath or affidavit must be sworn and the deed can then be registered.[60] Any deed of variation or discharge granted does not vary or discharge a burden which is still the subject of a preservation application in so far as any unit whose owners have made application to preserve are concerned.[61]

Variation and discharge of community burdens—practice

9–12   The provisions of sections 32 to 37 of the 2003 Act are designed to make variation and discharge of community burdens easier than under the existing law. Despite this because of the need to balance the interests of

---

[55] 2003 Act, s.21(6)(b) as applied by s.36(5).
[56] 2003 Act, s.21(7) as applied by s.36(5).
[57] 2003 Act, s.36(2)(c).
[58] 2003 Act, s.36(3).
[59] 2003 Act, s.36(4).
[60] If application to preserve is made then the matter will be decided by the Lands Tribunal.
[61] 2003 Act, s.37(3).

the majority with the interests of the minority and at the same time take account of the obvious fact that in most cases only adjacent proprietors require much of a say in the variation and discharge of community burdens the provisions might be regarded as somewhat cumbersome. The author offers the following practical suggestions:

(a) *Interest to enforce required.* It should be borne in mind that a party who seeks to enforce a praedial burden including a community burden must generally have an interest to enforce that burden. Where the burden relates to an obligation to pay the cost or a proportion of the cost of maintenance then that interest is presumed but in other cases the party seeking to enforce will have to satisfy the material detriment test.[62]

(b) *Acquiescence.* Where there has been a completed contravention of a community burden a waiver or a discharge by a majority of the benefited proprietors or all of the adjacent proprietors may not be required if the statutory provisions in relation to acquiescence apply.[63]

(c) *Prescription.* Where there has been a completed contravention of a community burden the right of benefited proprietors in the community to enforce that burden in respect of that particular breach may have been lost through the operation of the new five year statutory prescription.[64]

Letters of consent

Many real burdens in existing titles are not absolute prohibitions as such. Typically a feudal writ or a deed of conditions may provide that the owner of a unit in a community will not sub-divide or otherwise alter or add to the property without the consent of the superior. Under the existing law no third party right would be created in favour of co-feuars even though they might be regarded as owning properties subject to a common scheme. On abolition of the feudal system of course there will be no superior to consent and the status of these burdens may be elevated to community burdens enforceable by all the benefited proprietors.[65] Most people have in the past ignored the law relating to third party rights in any event and simply obtained a letter of consent by or on behalf of the superior or the original developer. After feudal abolition a burden which prohibits a use without consent of a superior may be extinguished in total if the superior alone has a right to enforce.[66] However there is a further provision in the 2000 Act[67] to the effect that where a burden refers to a superior then after abolition that term is to be deemed to apply to a party who is entitled to enforce the burden by virtue of the reallotment provisions[68] or in the case of facility and service burdens by those entitled to enforce by virtue of the provisions in the

9–13

---

[62] See para.8–22 *et seq.* above.
[63] 2003 Act, s.16 and see para.9–22 below.
[64] 2003 Act, s.18 and see para.9–24 below.
[65] 2003 Act, s.53.
[66] 2000 Act, s.17(1)(a).
[67] 2000 Act, s.73(2A).
[68] 2000 Act, ss.18, 18A, 18B, 18C, 19, 20, 28, 28A and 60.

2003 Act.[69] There does not appear however to be a provision to the effect that parties who become the owners of benefited units under the new implied rights of enforcement provisions[70] will automatically have the right to consent. However the 2000 Act goes on to provide[71] that any clause which provides in relation to a right enforceable after November 28, 2004 that a person other than the person entitled to enforce the burden may waive compliance or vary the burden is to be disregarded. Presumably what that means is that if a burden provides that there is to be no sub-division, alteration or addition without the consent of a named superior then if that superior reallots the burden[72] then he will be the party entitled to grant that consent. If however there is no real-lotment by the superior who loses the right to enforce on November 28, 2004 but the burden survives as a community burden[73] then the burden is to be construed as a simple prohibition without the words requiring consent tacked on. That is not to say that all these proprietors would have interest to enforce.[74]

STATUTORY TERMINATION

The sunset rule

9–14   There was at one time a proposal to the effect that the enforceability of all real burdens should be limited in point of time. What was proposed was a "bonfire" of burdens in respect of burdens which were more than a hundred years old. The 2003 Act makes some provision towards limiting the existence of real burdens.[75] These are perfectly sensible provisions. There are many real burdens which are assiduously repeated in the burdens section of title sheets transaction after transaction which have absolutely no application in the present day. However some of these burdens contain general words which might be interpreted as prohibiting some reasonable modern use. A prohibition of so called nauseous or noxious trades is sometimes coupled with a general prohibition of trade, business or profession or a prohibition of nuisance.[76] No doubt the framers of such real burdens will have had in mind obvious uses such as a shop open to the public or an iron foundry. There will however be instances where those who wish to object to a particular use of a property in the vicinity of their own property may attempt to use anachronistic burdens of this type for their own purposes. In *Meriton Ltd v Winning*[77] there was a real burden in a feudal deed of 1897 which imposed a condition that the subjects should not be used to carry on any business, process or operation of any description which the granters or their foresaids might deem objectionable. The burden went on to provide that the buildings were not to be employed for any purpose

---

[69] 2003 Act, s.56.
[70] 2003 Act, ss.52 and 53.
[71] 2000 Act, s.73(2A).
[72] In terms of the 2000 Act s.18.
[73] In terms of either s.52 or 53.
[74] See para.8–22 *et seq.* above.
[75] 2003 Act, ss.20–24.
[76] See *Meriton Ltd v Winning*, 1995 S.L.T. 76.
[77] 1995 S.L.T. 76.

whatsoever other than as private dwellinghouses and offices thereto. A minute of waiver was granted in 1987 which allowed the property to be converted into a residential nursing home but otherwise confirmed that the burdens of 1897 would remain in force. The pursuers (who were the current superiors) averred that the defenders (who owned the *dominium utile*) had been using the property since 1991 as a drug rehabilitation and detoxification centre and that this was a breach of the real burdens contained in the 1897 feu as varied by the minute of waiver. The defenders admitted that the subjects were being used for the care of persons suffering from drug abuse. The defenders argued that the prohibition of anything which the superiors might deem to be objectionable was insufficiently precise and also that the pursuers had not offered to prove that the use was non-residential. Lord Coulsfield held that the word "objectionable" was not so indefinite as to be incapable of enforcement but that any objection must be based on real and substantial effects arising directly from the use of the premises. His Lordship also held that there were no relevant averments to infer any breach, nor any averments to support the contention that the current use of the subjects did not qualify as a residential nursing home. He dismissed the action. However he did hold that a general word such as "objectionable" was not too imprecise. Presumably therefore if the pursuers had been more specific in their averments relating to use the result might have been different. The case is an example of an old burden causing difficulty in a more modern age.

Notice of termination—eligible burdens

If at least one hundred years have elapsed since the date of registration   **9–15**
of the deed in which the burden is created then an owner of the burdened property or any other person against whom the burden is enforceable may, having given the appropriate intimation, execute and register a notice of termination in the form contained in Schedule 2 to the 2003 Act.[78] it does not matter that the burden in question has been varied or renewed within the hundred year period. The 100-year period starts from the registration of the constitutive deed. The notice of termination procedure does not apply to a conservation burden, a maritime burden, a facility burden, a service burden or any real burden listed in Schedule 11 to the 2003 Act.[79] The title conditions listed in Schedule 11 to the 2003 Act are those title conditions which are not subject to discharge or variation by the Lands Tribunal. They are obligations relating to the right to work minerals, title conditions enforceable by the Crown for naval, military or airforce purposes, title conditions enforceable by the Crown or any public or international authority for civil aviation purposes or in connection with the use of land as an aerodrome and obligations in relation to a lease of an agricultural holding, a holding within the meaning of the Small Landholders (Scotland) Act 1886 to 1931 or a croft. The notice of termination procedure applies to community burdens as well as other praedial burdens.

---

[78] 2003 Act, s.20(1).
[79] 2003 Act, s.20(3).

Who may give notice—the terminator

9–16　The party who can register a notice of termination is the owner of the burdened property or any other person against whom the burden is enforceable. Presumably notice can be registered by one *pro indiviso* owner without the consent of another because the words used in the section are "an owner". It must also be presumed that notice can be given by a tenant of the burdened property because the burden is enforceable against that tenant.[80] The notice can be executed and registered by a successor in title of any person who has given the appropriate intimation.[81] The party who executes, serves and registers the notice is known quaintly as "the terminator".[82]

Notice of termination—content

9–17　The notice of termination must identify the burdened land and describe the terminator's connection with the property by identifying the terminator as the owner or tenant. The notice must set out the terms of the real burden and specify the extent to which it is to be terminated. The notice must also specify the date on or before which an application to renew or vary the burden must be made to the Lands Tribunal and it must also specify the date on which appropriate intimation has been made to those who are entitled to intimation.[83] The statutory form of notice of termination is set out in Schedule 2 to the 2003 Act. It will be possible to retain parts of a burden. There does not appear to be a requirement to specify the benefited property or properties but the notice must list those to whom intimation has been sent. The renewal date by which applications to vary or renew the burden must not be less than eight weeks after the date of the last intimation. An application for renewal can only be made after the renewal date with the consent of the terminator.[84] Even where an application is made for renewal after the expiry of time limit but with the consent of the terminator it must still be made before the Lands Tribunal have actually endorsed a certificate on the notice[85] to the effect that no application for renewal or variation has been made.[86] Where intimation is given by affixing a notice the period runs from the date on which the notice is first affixed. Where a property is subject to two or more real burdens it is competent to execute and register a single notice of termination in respect of both or all of the burdens.[87]

Notice of termination—intimation

9–18　Before the notice can be registered it must be intimated to the owner of each benefited property or in the case of a personal real burden to the holder of that burden. It must also be intimated to the owner (or if the

---

[80] 2003 Act, s.9(2).
[81] 2003 Act, s.20(2).
[82] 2003 Act, s.20(2); presumably the procedure will be known as "Serving an Arnold".
[83] 2003 Act, s.21.
[84] 2003 Act, s.90(4)(a).
[85] In terms of the 2003 Act, s.23.
[86] 2003 Act, s.90(4)(b).
[87] 2003 Act, s.20(6).

terminator is an owner to any other owner) of the burdened property.[88] However the definition of an owner of a benefited property is restricted to a property which is at some point within four metres measured along a horizontal plane of the burdened property.[89] The notice in terms of Schedule 2 must be sent with the appropriate explanatory note. Normally intimation will be by post where the benefited proprietors are within the four metre radius. Otherwise it is sufficient to fix a notice on the burdened property and on an appropriate lamppost or lampposts. If there is no lamppost within one hundred metres of the burdened property or if the burdened property comprises minerals or salmon fishings intimation in respect of parties with enforcement rights who are outwith the four metre radius may be made by advertisement in a local newspaper giving the appropriate details including the right to apply to the Lands Tribunal to have the burden renewed within the eight-week period.[90] The terminator must provide any person with a copy of the proposed notice of termination and with any explanatory note if requested.[91] There is a statutory authority for affixing the notice to the lamppost regardless of who owns the lamppost and obligation to take reasonable steps to ensure the notice continues to be displayed. Presumably the notice would require to be laminated or waterproofed so that it remained legible.[92] No planning permission is required for the affixation of a notice.[93]

Oath or affirmation

Before submitting the notice of termination for registration the termina-   **9–19** tor must swear or affirm before a notary public that the best of his or her knowledge and belief all the information contained in the notice is true and that the intimation procedures have been carried out.[94] Where the terminator is unable by reason of incapacity or disability to swear or affirm then a legal representative may do so. Where the party is not an individual but is a juristic person then any person authorised to sign documents may swear or affirm.[95]

Notice of termination—certificate by the Lands Tribunal

Before the notice can be registered there must be endorsed on it a certif-   **9–20** icate issued by a member of the Lands Tribunal or by their clerk dated after the renewal date has expired stating that no application to renew the burden has been received or alternatively that any such application has been withdrawn. The certificate may also state that an application has been received in relation to some but not all of the burdens in which case the notice may be registered in relation to the burdens which are

---

[88] 2003 Act, s.21(1).
[89] 2003 Act, s.21(3)(a).
[90] 2003 Act, s.21(2)(c).
[91] 2003 Act, s.21(5).
[92] 2003 Act, s.21(6).
[93] 2003 Act, s.21(7).
[94] 2003 Act, s.22(1).
[95] 2003 Act, s.22(2).

not subject to the application for renewal.[96] A notice of termination may be withdrawn at any time before the certificate is endorsed by the Lands Tribunal.[97]

Notice of termination—effect of registration

9–21   When all the procedure has been gone through the notice of termination may be registered against the title of the burdened property.[98] When this happens the real burden is extinguished wholly or to such extent as may be described in the notice.[99] Where there has been an application for renewal which relates only to some of the benefited properties or some of the burdens then registration of the notice of termination only extinguishes the real burden or burdens so far as not subject to any application for renewal.[1] However a further certificate may be endorsed on the notice if the benefited proprietor or holder of a personal real burden later withdraws an application for renewal. If the application for renewal has not been withdrawn but the Lands Tribunal have refused the application and discharged the burden then it is the order of the Lands Tribunal which should be registered.[2]

EXTINCTION BY OTHER MEANS

Extinction as a result of acquiescence

9–22   One of the unfortunate features of any land tenure system which includes real burdens or land covenants is that it affords an opportunity to warring neighbours to pursue unjustified vendettas against each other. Neighbours may fall out for a variety of reasons some or most of which may have nothing to do with property rights. However the law of property does provide a neighbour holding a grudge which may relate to the playing of loud music or the barking of a dog with an opportunity to get back at an adjoining proprietor. A typical example relates to an ordinary extension to a dwellinghouse in a residential estate. Proprietor A may have erected the extension in 1998 and then fallen out with proprietor B because Stuart, proprietor A's Alsatian, ate Roddy the hamster belonging to proprietor B's four year old son, George. The families will never have spoken to each since that fateful meal. Eventually proprietor A decides to sell after abolition of the feudal system and a solicitor for a purchaser objects to the title because there is no consent from the adjoining proprietor to the erection of the extension. If the burden is a community burden in terms of section 28 or either section 52 or 53 of the 2003 Act then the neighbour may have title and interest to enforce. In such circumstances the sale may be held up indefinitely or the neighbour with the grudge who requires to consent may demand an outrageous sum of money. In such a case under the existing

---

[96] 2003 Act, s.23(1)(a) and (b).
[97] 2003 Act, s.23(2).
[98] 2003 Act, s.24(1).
[99] 2003 Act, s.24(1).
[1] 2003 Act, s.24(2).
[2] 2003 Act, s.104(2).

law an argument may be put forward to the effect that the party entitled to enforce the burden has acquiesced in its breach. Acquiescence is a branch of the law of personal bar.[3] As the law stands at the moment however the onus of proving acquiescence rests firmly on the party who challenges the enforceability of the burden.[4] Moreover acquiescence has always been more readily inferred against a superior who may be a remote figure or entity than a co-feuar who is likely to be a neighbour.[5] The difficulty with the law relating to acquiescence at the moment is that it is case specific and solicitors acting for prospective purchasers tend to take the safety first position by insisting on some sort of waiver, discharge or letter of consent. The 2003 Act makes specific provision which clarifies the law in this regard.[6] It is provided that where a real burden has been breached in any way so that material expenditure has been incurred and any benefit arising from the expenditure would be substantially lost were the burden to be enforced then acquiescence may apply. The doctrine does not apply to conservation burdens, economic development burdens or healthcare burdens.[7] If the party having an interest to enforce the burden in respect of the breach consents to the carrying on of the activity, is aware that the carrying on of the activity or ought to be aware of it he or she will be personally barred from enforcing the burden. For the personal bar to operate the party or parties entitled to enforce must have stood back and watched the breach which results in the material expenditure. If that party has not objected by the expiry of such period as is in all the circumstances reasonable but in any event does not exceed 12 weeks beginning with the date by which the activity resulting in the expenditure has been substantially completed then the burden is extinguished to the extent of the breach.[8] In the case of a conservation burden, economic development burden or healthcare burden the person by whom the burden is enforceable must actually consent to the carrying out of the activity.[9] There is no statutory definition of the words "substantially completed". It is to be hoped that this does not prove to be an awkward provision. It does suggest that an adjoining proprietor with a title and interest to enforce could take objection when an extension was three quarters complete having waited several months while his luckless neighbour incurred expense. It might be held that this would not be a reasonable period for the purposes of the statutory provision. It should be noted that where an express consent is obtained this must come not just from the owner of the benefited property but all others entitled to enforce such as tenants, liferenters and spouses holding occupancy rights. The same appears to apply to the implied consent by virtue of the statutory acquiescence. It would appear therefore that if a spouse with occupancy rights objected that would be sufficient to prevent extinguishment of the burden by acquiescence even if the owner of the benefited property consented or acquiesced. The

---

[3] See Halliday, *Conveyancing Law and Practice* (2nd ed.) para.34–53 *et seq.*; see E. Reid, "Personal Bar: Case-Law in Search of Principle" (2003) 7 *Edinburgh Law Review* 340.

[4] *Earl of Zetland v Hislop* (1892) 9R. (HL) 40; *Scottish Co-operative Wholesale Society v Finnie*, 1937 S.C. 835.

[5] *MacTaggart & Co. v Roemmele*, 1907 S.C. 1318.

[6] 2003 Act, s.16.

[7] 2003 Act, s.16(1)(c)(i).

[8] 2003 Act, s.16(1)(c)(i).

[9] 2003 Act, s.16(1)(c)(ii).

provisions here are different from those relating to a voluntary discharge in writing in terms of section 15 which only requires the signature of the owner of the benefited property.[10] Where the period of 12 weeks has expired then it shall be presumed unless the contrary is shown that the person by whom the real burden was enforceable was or ought to have been aware of the carrying on of the activity and did not object.[11] Establishing acquiescence under the common law is difficult mainly because knowledge has to be proved. Accordingly after the expiry of the 12-week period following substantial completion of the activity knowledge will be presumed as will the lack of objection.

No party having interest to enforce

9–23 If a real burden has been breached but at the time of the breach no person has an interest to enforce in respect of the breach the burden is extinguished to the extent of that breach.[12] This might arise post-feudal abolition where in the absence of a feudal superior there does not appear to be any party who has any interest.

Negative prescription

9–24 The general view has been that the long negative prescription of 20 years applied to breaches of real burdens.[13] The position is now clarified.[14] If a real burden is breached to any extent and during the period of five years beginning with the breach no relevant claim is made by the party or parties entitled to enforce and no relevant acknowledgement is made of the breach by the burdened proprietor then the burden is extinguished to the extent of the breach on the expiry of that five year period.[15] The five-year period will run from the date of the breach unless the breach occurred before November 28, 2004 in which case the five years will run from that day.[16] Alternatively for very old breaches they will prescribe after the expiry of a period of 20 years beginning with the breach.[17] Where the real burdens consists of the right of pre-emption, redemption or reversion or any other type of option to acquire and the owner of the burdened property fails to comply with an obligation to offer in terms of the pre-emption or convey back in terms of the redemption or reversion then the burden is extinguished on the expiry of five years from the failure. In some cases a pre-emption has been missed or ignored and a disposition granted in favour of a third party purchaser without reference to the party entitled to the pre-emption. Strictly speaking the deed is subject to reduction but the holder of the pre-emption right will lose the right to make any sort of claim or bring any sort of action on the expiry of five years from the granting of the deed.

---

[10] 2003 Act, s.15 and see para.9–02 above.
[11] 2003 Act, s.16(2).
[12] 2003 Act, s.17.
[13] See Reid, *The Law of Property in Scotland*, para.431; Gordon, *Scottish Land Law* (2nd ed.), para.22–82; Reid, *The Abolition of Feudal Tenure in Scotland*, para.7.25
[14] 2003 Act, s.18.
[15] 2003 Act, s.18(1).
[16] 2003 Act, s.18(5).
[17] 2003 Act, s.18(7).

Where the prescription applies to a real burden the real burden is only extinguished to the extent of the breach. If therefore there is a real burden to the effect that property is not to be sub-divided, altered or extended and an extension has been erected in breach of that prohibition in 1998 no action can be taken in respect of that breach. However that does not mean that the proprietor of the burdened property can go ahead and make further alterations or additions. The burden still remains in force for the future; it is the right to take action in relation to the particular breach which has gone. In the case of a pre-emption, reversion, redemption or option however the situation may be slightly different. It is interesting to note that the words "to the extent of the breach" are not included in the sub-section dealing with these particular types of real burden. This could mean therefore that if a breach occurs in relation to a pre-emption contained in a non-feudal deed executed prior to September 1, 1974 then the pre-emption is extinguished forever although that is not the implication to be taken from the provisions in the 2003 Act which deal with pre-emptions.[18] Section 82 specifically preserves a distinction among pre-emptions in feudal deeds, pre-emptions in other deeds executed before September 1, 1974 and pre-emptions contained in deeds executed after September 1, 1974. The implication however of the negative prescription provision in relation to pre-emptions is that the pre-emption will have gone forever because the sub-section states that the burden shall be extinguished in relation to the property on the expiry of the period. Various provisions of the Prescription and Limitation (Scotland) Act 1973 are made applicable to the new five-year prescription with the appropriate modifications. A burdened proprietor will be regarded as having acknowledged that the burden is still in force if he or she has given an acknowledgement in writing to this effect or has acted in some way as to actually implement the terms of the burden.[19]

Confusio not to extinguish a real burden

For a real burden to be enforceable there must be separate benefited 9–25 and burdened properties. The 2003 Act makes it clear that the fact that both properties happen to be in the same ownership will not extinguish the burden.[20] This may have some significance under the 2003 Act given that burdens can now be enforced against tenants. Effectively therefore a landlord who becomes the owner of the benefited property may be able to enforce the burden as against his own tenant in the burdened property. The same will apply in connection with personal real burdens such as conservation burdens, manager burdens and the like except that there will of course be no benefited property.[21] The section will operate where the party in whose favour the conservation or other personal real burden is constituted becomes owner of the burdened property.

---

[18] 2003 Act, ss.82–85.
[19] 2003 Act, s.18(3) and (4).
[20] 2003 Act, s.19.
[21] 2003 Act, s.19(b).

Extinction of real burden on compulsory purchase

9–26 There has always a view that the statutory vesting of heritable property in a local authority by virtue of compulsory purchase legislation extinguished feudal relationships and indeed real burdens and even servitudes. Difficulty arises from the appalling drafting of various sections the Lands Clauses Consolidation (Scotland) Act 1845.[22] The 2003 Act clarifies matters by providing that after November 28, 2004 all real burdens and servitudes will be extinguished on the registration of a conveyance which follows a compulsory purchase order except in so far as the order or conveyance provide otherwise.[23] The order or conveyance may provide for the preservation or variation of real burdens or servitudes and may also provide that only certain real burdens or servitudes are to be extinguished as regards the whole or any part of the property. There may also be provisions in respect of the enforcement rights of the owners of certain of the benefited properties. Where there are exceptions of this type the conveyance in implement of the acquisition cannot be registered unless the owners of benefited properties consent, or in the case of a development management scheme[24] the owners' association consents. In the case of the holder of any personal real burden the holder would have to consent if the terms of the disposition do not conform to the exceptions or variations of the real burdens contained in the compulsory purchase order. Compensation is payable to the holders of personal real burdens thus extinguished. In some cases an authority acquires by voluntary agreement rather than compulsory purchase. Where the heritable interest could have been acquired by compulsory purchase then burdens and servitudes are also extinguished.[25] However in this case the acquiring authority must notify the owner of the benefited property or the holder of a personal real burden or the owners' association where a development management scheme is involved so that they are afforded the chance to make application to the Lands Tribunal to renew the burdens. Not less than 21 days' notice must be given and any conveyance in implement of such a voluntary agreement must contain a certificate from the Lands Tribunal to the effect that no objection has been received or that all objections have been withdrawn or that the objections relate only to particular burdens. Such a conveyance in terms of the agreement can be registered without a certificate. A conveyance would be valid but the real burdens or servitudes would not be extinguished. Where the certificate is not obtained until after registration of the conveyance the conveyance can be re-registered with the certificate. New rules have been promulgated in relation to applications to the Tribunal.[26]

Variation and discharge by the Lands Tribunal

9–27 The Lands Tribunal for Scotland retains jurisdiction to vary or discharge real burdens.[27]

---

[22] See *Town Council of Oban v Callander and Oban Railway* (1892) 19 R. 912.
[23] 2003 Act, s.106.
[24] Under the 2003 Act, s.71–74.
[25] 2003 Act, s.107.
[26] Land Tribunal for Scotland Rules 2003 (SSI 2003/452).
[27] 2003 Act, s.90–104 and see Ch.13 below.

CHAPTER 10

DEVELOPMENT MANAGEMENT SCHEMES

INTRODUCTION

Part 6 of the 2003 Act introduces the concept of development manage-   **10–01**
ment schemes which may be applied to any land by the registration of
a deed of application. The deed of application must include a specification of matters which the scheme requires along with certain specific
definitions. At the time of writing the order setting out the terms of the
scheme is awaited. The order will set out a scheme of rules for the management of land[1] and the order may contain a general scheme or be in
relation to a particular development. The scheme will contain rules
rather than real burdens but the rules for the management of the land
will have effect as if they were community burdens.[2]

APPLICATION OF THE SCHEME

For the development management scheme to apply to any land a deed of   **10–02**
application must be registered against that land. The land is known as
"the development".[3] The deed of application is granted by or on behalf of
the owner of the land. If the statutory instrument setting out the development management scheme allows then the scheme may be applied with
variations as specified in the deed of application. The scheme takes effect
in relation to the development on the date of registration or on such later
fixed date as may be specified or on the date of registration of another
deed.[4] A scheme cannot take effect on the occurrence of an event.[5] The
deed of application must include a specification or description of all the
matters which the scheme requires.[6] The deed of application must include
a definition section in which the terms "the development", "scheme property" and "unit" are defined in relation to the particular land. The definition section must also include the name by which any owners association
established by the scheme is to be known. The name must end with the
words "Owners Association" or it must begin with those words preceded
by the definite article.[7] The deed of application must also state the name
and address of the first manager of any owners association established.[8]

---

[1] 2003 Act, s.71(3).
[2] 2003 Act, s.72.
[3] 2003 Act, s.71(1).
[4] 2003 Act, s.71(1)(a) and (b).
[5] 2003 Act, s.71(1)(a).
[6] 2003 Act, s.71(2).
[7] 2003 Act, s.71(2)(b).
[8] 2003 Act, s.71(2)(c).

APPLICATION OF THE 2003 ACT TO THE SCHEME

10–03   While the Act does not indicate in express terms that the rules of the scheme are to be real burdens most of the provisions of the Act relating to real burdens will apply to the rules of the scheme.[9] However section 1 of the 2003 Act does not apply. That section defines a real burden. Effectively therefore the rules of the scheme are probably best regarded as statutory obligations having the nature of community burdens. Section 2 of the 2003 Act does apply and that section states that a real burden can only be created as an affirmative, negative or ancillary burden. Accordingly the rules must take on many of the characteristics of real burdens. Section 4 of the 2003 Act does not apply because it lays down rules in relation to constitutive deeds and a scheme is not a constitutive deed as such although a deed of application is. Section 5 of the 2003 Act in relation to payments of uncertain amounts in respect of costs does apply. Sections 7, 8 and 9 do not apply. Section 10 does apply with the exception of subsection (4) (a). Sections 11, 13, 14, 16, 18, 34–61, 67–70, 98, 100, 104 and 105 apply. All of these sections apply as they apply to community burdens. Where these sections do apply then references to the owner of a benefited property shall be construed as references to the manager of any owners association established by the scheme. This places the manager in a very important position in relation to enforcement. The benefited property is construed as any unit of the development so far as advantaged by the rules and the burdened property as one which is constrained by the rules. A community will be construed as the development and the constitutive deed is construed as the deed of application.

DISAPPLICATION OF THE SCHEME

10–04   A development management scheme may be disapplied to the development as a whole or any part of the development by an owners association established by the scheme.[10] The owners association have to register a deed of disapplication in accordance with the rules of the scheme. Disapplication will take effect on the date of registration or such later date as is specified in the deed of disapplication which could be a fixed date but cannot be by reference to the occurrence of an event. The deed of disapplication may create real burdens which provide for the future management and regulation of the whole development or of any part of the development or that particular part in respect of which the deed of disapplication is being registered. The deed of disapplication in such a case will be a constitutive deed for the purposes of the creation of a new real burden.[11]

---

[9] 2003 Act, s.72.
[10] 2003 Act, s.73.
[11] 2003 Act, s.73(2) applying s.4.

PROCEDURE AND INTIMATION FOR DISAPPLICATION

Deed of disapplication

Where a deed of disapplication is granted any proposal to register that **10–05** deed must be intimated by the owners association to every person who is the owner of a unit in the development.[12] The intimation is given by sending a copy of the deed of disapplication together with an explanatory notice outlining the effect of the registration of the deed and stating that an owner who does not agree to the granting and registration of the deed and who wishes to apply to the Lands Tribunal for preservation of the development management scheme must do so by a date specified in the notice.[13] Any person who wishes to object to disapplication has a period of eight weeks from intimation to apply to the Lands Tribunal.[14] For a deed of disapplication to take effect on registration either in relation to disapplication of the scheme or in relation to the imposition of new real burdens a certificate must be endorsed on the deed or on an annexation executed by a member of the Lands Tribunal or their Clerk to the effect that no application for preservation of the scheme has been received or that any such application has been withdrawn.[15] Before submitting a deed of disapplication for registration a person authorised to sign documents on behalf of the owners association must swear or affirm that proper intimation has been made.[16]

Jurisdiction of Lands Tribunal

The Lands Tribunal will have jurisdiction in relation to any application **10–06** to vary or discharge rules of a development management scheme.[17] The jurisdiction extends to determining any question as to the validity of the rule or its applicability, enforceability or how it is to be construed. The Tribunal of course also have specific jurisdiction in relation to preservation of schemes where there is a proposal to register a deed of disapplication.[18] Where there is an unopposed application for preservation of a development management scheme then the application to preserve shall be granted as of right.[19] The application will be unopposed if as at the date, on which the application falls to be determined no representations opposing the application to preserve have been made[20] by the owners association or any person proposing to register a conveyance to an acquiring authority.[21] If the application is contested then the Lands Tribunal can only grant the application to preserve if they are satisfied that disapplication of the development management scheme is not in the best interests of the owners of the units of the development or is

---

[12] 2003 Act, s.74(1).
[13] 2003 Act, s.74(2).
[14] 2003 Act, s.74(3).
[15] 2003 Act, s.73(3).
[16] 2003 Act, s.73(4).
[17] 2003 Act, s.90(1)(ii).
[18] 2003 Act, s.90(1)(d) and (e).
[19] 2003 Act, s.99(1).
[20] 2003 Act, s.96.
[21] 2003 Act, s.99(2).

unfairly prejudicial to one or more of those owners.[22] In the case of a conveyance to an acquiring authority the Tribunal can only grant the application to preserve if, having regard to the purpose for which land is being acquired, it is reasonable to grant the application.[23]

DEVELOPMENT MANAGEMENT SCHEMES—PRACTICE

10–07   It is difficult to know just how to define a development management scheme. On the one hand it has the appearance of a deed of conditions creating community burdens. On the other hand it also has the appearance of a planning agreement under section 75 of the Town and County Planning (Scotland) Act 1997 or the statutory management scheme set out in the Tenements (Scotland) Bill 2004. The owners association occupies a key position in relation to the scheme. In so far as interpretation of the rules of the scheme is concerned section 14 of the 2003 Act applies which provides that real burdens are to be construed in the same manner as other provisions of deeds which relate to land and are intended for registration.[24] Oddly perhaps the provisions relating to acquiescence also apply to the rules of the scheme[25] as does the five year negative prescription.[26] One might have thought that the owner of a unit would be bound by the rules of the scheme no matter what but if an owner of a unit breaches one of the rules incurring material expenditure and the 12-week acquiescence period expires then that owner cannot be challenged. An owner of a benefited unit does not require a title or interest to enforce since section 8 of the 2003 Act does not apply. Although the rules have the nature of community burdens the complicated provisions in relation to the management of a community and the variation and discharge of community burdens do not apply. However sections 54–61 of the 2003 Act do apply which means that a development management scheme could be made applicable to a sheltered or retirement housing complex. The rules of the scheme can be facility or service burdens.[27]

---

[22] 2003 Act, s.99(4)(a).
[23] 2003 Act, s.99(4)(b).
[24] See para.5–27 above.
[25] 2003 Act, s.16.
[26] 2003 Act, s.18.
[27] As defined in the 2003 Act, s.56.

CHAPTER 11

SERVITUDES

INTRODUCTION

Under the existing law, servitudes may be created in a variety of **11–01** ways:

(a) By express grant in a written deed which need not necessarily be recorded or registered.

(b) By express reservation in a written deed which need not necessarily be recorded or registered.

(c) By implied grant on the severance of land where the servitude existed *de facto* before the severance and is reasonably necessary for the comfortable enjoyment of the dominant or benefited tenement.

(d) By implied reservation on the severance of land where the servitude has existed *de facto* and is more than reasonably necessary for the use of the dominant or benefited tenement.

(e) Sometimes by acquiescence, fact and circumstances, *rebus ipsis et factis*.

(f) By prescription where the servitude has been exercised as of right for a period of twenty years in terms of section 3 of the Prescription and Limitation (Scotland) Act 1973.

It has also been held in certain circumstances that there may be a natural right of access as a necessary implication of ownership where land is effectively landlocked.[1] It is beyond the scope of this text to examine the law of servitudes in any detail.[2] The 2003 Act however makes certain important changes in relation to the law of servitudes.[3] The 2003 Act alters the rules in relation to a discharge of a positive servitude by formal deed. The 2003 Act prohibits the creation of other negative servitudes and effectively converts them into real burdens. Perhaps the most significant change is the relaxation of the principle (if indeed there is such a principle) that for a right to be a servitude it must be of a known type.

---

[1] *Bowers v Kennedy*, 2000 S.C. 555.

[2] For an exhaustive treatise on the law of servitudes see Cusine and Paisley, *Servitudes and Rights of Way*.

[3] 2003 Act, Part 7, ss.75–81; and see Connolly, "The Title Conditions (Scotland) Act 2003 and Servitudes" (2003) 8 S.L.P.Q. 217.

CREATION OF POSITIVE SERVITUDES BY DEED

11–02   As the law stands at the moment a servitude can be created in a written deed which is not recorded or registered.[4] The deed must of course comply with the rules for execution relating to heritable property.[5] The 2003 Act changes these rules by providing that a deed is not effective to create a positive servitude by express grant unless that deed is registered against both the benefited property and the burdened property.[6] This provision however relates only to the creation of servitudes by express grant or reservation in a deed. The other methods of creation of a positive servitude remain perfectly competent and in particular a servitude can be created by prescription either on the strength of an *a non domino* deed or simply by possession and the exercise of the servitude for the 20-year period.[7] However if the proprietor of the dominant or benefited tenement wishes the servitude to be shown in the property section of a title sheet and land certificate relating to the dominant or benefited tenement the servitude will normally require to have been created in a written deed unless there is a declarator of servitude.[8] The requirement that the written deed be recorded or registered does not apply to positive servitudes created in writing for the leading of pipes, cables, wires or other services.[9]

RELAXATION OF THE RULE REQUIRING SEPARATE TENEMENTS

11–03   Under the existing law it has always been a requirement that there be a dominant and servient tenement in separate ownership.[10] The maxim was *nemini res sua servit*. Notwithstanding this rule it has been quite common for developers to grant a deed of conditions while owning the whole development in which mutual servitude rights of access are purportedly created in favour of all the plots or units in the development against each other. The common cross servitude of this type is one in respect of pipes, cables, sewers, drains and other services which pass through various plots. In such a case a plot or a unit can be a dominant tenement in so far as that plot uses the service and a servient tenement in so far as the service passes through the plot and serves others.[11] If the rule requiring the dominant and servient tenement to be in separate ownership was applied strictly then there would obviously be doubt as to the competency of the creation of servitude rights of this type in a deed of conditions. The counter-argument of course would be that the servitudes lie dormant until such time as the developer conveys away the individual plots thus creating the separate ownerships. There is specific provision in the 2003 Act which confirms this approach. It is pro-

---

[4] Provided the existence of the servitude is evidenced by possession.
[5] Requirements of Writing (Scotland) Act 1995, s.2 (1)(a).
[6] 2003 Act, s.75(1).
[7] Prescription and Limitation (Scotland) Act 1973, s.3.
[8] The policy of the Keeper was set out in an article, Davis, *Positive Servitudes in the Land Register* (1999) 4 S.L.P.Q. 64
[9] 2003 Act, s.75(3)(b) and 77(1).
[10] Cusine and Paisley, *Servitudes and Rights of Way*, para.2.04 *et seq.*; Gordon, *Scottish Land Law* (2nd ed.), para.24-09.
[11] See *North British Railway v Park Yard Co. Ltd* (1898) 25 R. (HL) 47.

vided that it shall be no objection to the validity of a positive servitude that at the time when the deed is registered against both the benefited and burdened property the same person owns both interests.[12] However the servitude lies dormant and is not actually created until there is a separation of ownership.[13]

SPECIAL PROVISIONS FOR SERVICES

There are in existence countless agreements (generally known as way-leave agreements) with statutory undertakers or providers or former statutory undertakers or providers which relate to pipes, drains, cables, sewers, media services and other conductors. There has always been a doubt as to whether or not these were properly constituted servitudes. There is no doubt that a servitude for a water pipe or a drain is a servitude which is known to the law. The difficulty has always been in identifying the dominant and servient tenement because the pipes, cables and others provide a service which is in many cases generated by or provided from some sort of central source such as a power station, substation, reservoir or waterworks. In so far as drainage is concerned it is the ultimate outfall which may essentially provide the service as would be the case with a sewage works. In reality the concept of a dominant and servient tenement does not apply in such cases.[14] In one unfortunate sheriff court case it was even held that a servitude in respect of overhanging cables was not a recognised servitude in the law of Scotland and accordingly could not be enforced.[15] This decision has been doubted.[16] The 2003 Act moves to a certain extent to alleviate this difficulty by providing[17] that a right to lead a pipe, cable, wire or other enclosed unit over or under land for any purpose may be constituted as a positive servitude. Moreover this provision is retrospective in that it shall be deemed always to have been competent to constitute such a servitude.[18] However the Act does not remove the requirement for there to be a dominant and a servient tenement. Servitudes for services although they will require to be constituted in a written deed will not require to be recorded or registered and this provision is also retrospective.[19]

11–04

THE LIST—CLOSED OR OPEN?

The view of most academic writers has been that a servitude must be known to the law or at least must be a reasonable extension of a servitude known to the law. Difficulties have arisen over such things as servitudes of parking.[20] Such a servitude has recently been upheld in the

11–05

---

[12] 2003 Act, s.75(2).
[13] 2003 Act, s.75(2).
[14] See *North British Railway Co. Ltd v Park Yard Co. Ltd* (1898) 25 R. (HL) 47.
[15] *Neill v Scobbie*, 1993 G.W.D. 8–572.
[16] Cusine and Paisley, *Servitudes and Rights of Way*, para.3.44.
[17] 2003 Act, s.77.
[18] 2003 Act, s.77(2).
[19] 2003 Act, s.75(3)(b).
[20] See *Murrayfield Ice Rink Ltd v Scottish Rugby Union*, 1973 S.L.T. 99.

sheriff court.[21] Cusine and Paisley list some doubtful servitudes.[22] There is a relaxation of the closed list rule in the 2003 Act. It is provided that any rule of law that requires that a positive servitude be of a type known to the law shall not apply where the servitude is created in a written deed which is duly registered against the titles of both the burdened and benefited properties.[23] There are certain qualifications to this relaxation. In the first place it only applies where the servitude is created in a written deed which is registered. The relaxation therefore will not apply to purported servitudes which are created, for example, by implied grant, implied reservation or prescription. The reason for this is clear. It might not be obvious to an owner of land that someone who fished in a river belonging to that owner was attempting to assert some sort of servitude right there being no recognised servitude of fishing at the present time. In the second place the 2003 Act will not permit the creation of any servitude which can be regarded as being repugnant with ownership of the servient tenement.[24] This presumably means that a servitude right cannot be so extensive as to actually remove all the normal benefits of ownership. There has always been a doubt as to whether or not there was such a thing as a servitude of the exclusive use of land.[25] While there can be no argument that a servitude of way over a road would not allow the owner of the road to build on the road in such a way as to obstruct the servitude, it is unlikely that the opening of the list in terms of the 2003 Act would allow a servitude of exclusive use over an area of land where that servitude effectively prohibited the owner of the servient tenement from doing anything on that land. Such a servitude would presumably be repugnant with ownership. There is an analogy here with the law relating to real burdens. The 2003 Act also provides that a real burden must not be contrary to public policy, illegal nor repugnant with ownership.[26] The radical Lord Young stated[27] that one cannot make a man proprietor of land and yet prohibit him from exercising the rights of proprietorship. Indeed, in *Earl of Zetland v Hislop*,[28] the same judge took the view that a prohibition of the sale of alcohol was repugnant with the right of ownership. The House of Lords took a different view. Professor Reid's view is[29] that in order to be real a burden must be a natural incident of the grant in which it is contained. Professor Reid draws a distinction between positive obligations to do something and prohibitions of specific uses. These distinctions are easier to draw in relation to real burdens. Servitudes almost always involve some sort of restriction on the servient proprietor while conferring a positive benefit on the dominant proprietor. The servient proprietor need not do anything. It is perhaps risky to draw too much of an analogy where servi-

---

[21] *Moncrieff v Jamieson*, Lerwick Sheriff Court, Sheriff Principal D. J. Risk Q.C., June 23, 1999; G.W.D. 26–1222.

[22] *Servitudes and Rights of Way*, Ch.3.

[23] 2003 Act, s.76(1).

[24] 2003 Act, s.76(2).

[25] *Moffat v Milne*, 1993 G.W.D. 8–572; Cusine & Paisley, *Servitudes and Rights of Way*, para.3.77.

[26] 2003 Act, s.3(6).

[27] In *Moir's Trustees v McEwan* (1880) 7 R. 1141 at 1145.

[28] (1881) 8 R. 675 at 681.

[29] Reid, *The Law of Property in Scotland*, para.391.

tudes are concerned.[30] It has, for example, been held that an exclusive right to shoot is incompetent.[31] Unfortunately the new provisions in relation to the preservation of sporting rights as a separate tenement in favour of a former superior do nothing to help the discussion.[32] One would have to agree with Professor Reid's view that some of the older cases in relation to real burdens have arisen purely because of the difficulty of creating servitudes outwith the recognised list.

It does not appear that the provisions of the 2003 Act in relation to ser-   **11–06** vitudes are retrospective except in relation to servitudes for leading pipes and other services. Although for the most part the provisions relating to real burdens apply to real burdens created whether before or after November 28, 2004[33] that provision would not apply to servitudes. Accordingly if, for example, a deed of servitude has been granted in 2003 which gives the proprietor of a ground floor pub the right to hang a sign on the exterior wall of a first floor flat that will not necessarily be a valid servitude even after November 28, 2004.[34] An interesting question may arise if in such a case the sign remains in place for a period of 20 years following on the grant of the 2003 deed. The opening of the closed list only applies to servitudes created in a registered deed but that provision appears only to apply to deeds which are executed and registered after November 28, 2004. If the servitude were to be created *a non domino* by written provision in a registered deed after November 28, 2004 then presumably prescription could run.

DISCHARGE OF POSITIVE SERVITUDE

Where a positive servitude has been registered against the burdened   **11–07** property or is noted in the title sheet of that property it can only be discharged by a deed which is also registered.[35] There is no requirement to register the discharge against the title to the benefited property. In terms of the 2003 Act however[36] the Keeper could alter the title sheet of the benefited property by removing the servitude even where the discharge is recorded in the sasine register. A registered discharge will be required even in cases where a servitude is noted in the title sheet in circumstances where it was constituted by prescription or implied grant as opposed to in a registered deed. This section however does not apply to discharges which have been executed before the appointed day,[37] nor does it prevent a servitude from being extinguished in any other way such as by non-exercise for the period of long negative prescription, acquiescence or destruction of one or more of the properties. The section is concerned purely with formal discharge of a positive servitude in a written document.

---

[30] Reid, *The Law of Property in Scotland*, para.391.
[31] *Beckett v Bisset*, 1921 2 S.L.T. 33.
[32] See para.3–15 above.
[33] 2003 Act, s.119(10).
[34] *Mendelssohn v The Wee Pub Co. Ltd*, 1991 G.W.D. 26–1518.
[35] 2003 Act, s.78.
[36] 2003 Act, s.105.
[37] 2003 Act, s.119(8).

PROHIBITION OF NEGATIVE SERVITUDES

11–08   Negative servitudes exist principally for the protection of amenity. The most common are servitudes which prohibit the obstruction of light or prospect or building above a certain height. The same effect can of course be achieved by the imposition of a real burden which prohibits building. There has always been considerable doubt as to whether or not a negative servitude could be constituted by any means other than by written provision.[38] There is a certain irresistible logic in this view. The owner of vacant ground over which an adjoining proprietor has had a view for 20 years could hardly be expected to realise that that adjoining proprietor was attempting to obtain a servitude of light and prospect by prescription. The Act goes further and prohibits the creation of any negative servitude by any means on or after November 28, 2004.[39] After that date restrictions on building of this type will require to be created as negative real burdens.[40]

EXISTING NEGATIVE SERVITUDES—TRANSITIONAL PROVISIONS

11–09   Existing negative servitudes will cease to be servitudes on the appointed day and forthwith become real burdens known as "converted servitudes".[41] However such converted servitudes will have a limited life of 10 years from the appointed day unless they are preserved.[42] A negative servitude which was registered against the burdened property as a servitude or was noted in or otherwise appeared in the title sheet of the burdened property is not extinguished on the expiry of the 10 year period.[43] Where the negative servitude has not been registered or noted then the holder may preserve the servitude by executing and registering against the title of the burdened property a notice in the form of Schedule 9.[44] The notice must identify the burdened property, the benefited property and the converted servitude itself but the person registering the notice does not require to have a completed title provided the notice sets out the links in title.[45] In a case where the negative servitude has been constituted in a deed but has not been registered[46] then the notice must include as an annexation any constitutive deed or a copy of that deed.[47] If the land identified as the benefited property in the notice is not specifically nominated in a constitutive deed then the notice must set out the grounds both factual and legal for describing that land as the benefited property.[48] The notice must be registered against both benefited

---

[38] *Dundas v Blair* (1886) 13 R. 759; Rankine, *Land Ownership*, p.440; see the discussion in Gordon, *Scottish Land Law* (2nd ed.), pp.24–28; Cusine & Paisley, *op. cit.*, para.9.02 *et seq.*
[39] 2003 Act, s.79.
[40] In terms of the 2003 Act, s.2(1)(b).
[41] 2003 Act, s.80(1).
[42] 2003 Act, s.80(2).
[43] 2003 Act, s.80(3).
[44] 2003 Act, s.80(4).
[45] 2003 Act, s.80(5).
[46] So as to take the benefit of the 2003 Act, s.80(3).
[47] 2003 Act, s.80(5)(b).
[48] 2003 Act, s.80(5)(f).

and burdened properties.[49] As with other preservation notices the party registering the notice must swear or affirm that what the notice contains is accurate.[50] Moreover the party registering the notice must also send a copy of the notice to the owner of the burdened property with the appropriate statutory note where it is reasonably practicable to do so and the provisions of section 115 apply to such intimation.[51] The party registering the notice must state in the notice that a copy has been sent to the burdened proprietor or that it was not reasonably practicable to do so.[52] The Keeper is not required to determine whether the person submitting a notice for registration has complied with the intimation provisions.[53] If for some reason the notice is rejected by the Keeper but a court or the Lands Tribunal determines that the notice is registerable then the notice may be registered within two months of the date of determination by the court or the Tribunal but must be registered before a date fixed by Scottish Ministers.[54] The Lands Tribunal has specific jurisdiction to deal with disputes in relation to notices of converted servitude.[55] There are no time limits for challenging a notice of converted servitude but obviously a challenge to the Lands Tribunal would require to be mounted before the expiry of the 10-year period.

CONVERSION OF CERTAIN REAL BURDENS TO POSITIVE SERVITUDES

Many real burdens confer rights to enter or make use of the burdened property. It is quite common in deeds of condition for residential developments or blocks of flats to provide that each owner will have a right of access over adjoining property for the purposes of carrying out maintenance and repair. Although there is no particular reason why such a right should not be a real burden these rights are obviously in the nature of positive servitudes. The type of burden envisaged is a right to use which has been held to be a real burden in at least one case.[56] Accordingly just as it is sensible to convert negative servitudes to negative real burdens so too it is sensible to convert positive real burdens giving rights of access to positive servitudes. The 2003 Act provides[57] that a real burden consisting of a right to enter, or otherwise make use of burdened property shall on the appointed day cease to exist but shall forthwith become a positive servitude. There is no requirement for intimation or registration of any notice. The provision however does not apply in such a way as to preserve a burden in favour of a superior which has been extinguished by feudal abolition.[58] Where the burden is an ancillary burden[59] it is not

11–10

---

[49] 2003 Act, s.80(6).
[50] 2003 Act, s.80(7).
[51] 2003 Act, s.80(8).
[52] 2003 Act, s.115(3).
[53] 2003 Act, s.115(5).
[54] 2003 Act, s.115(6).
[55] 2003 Act, s.102(1).
[56] *B & C Group Management v Haren*, December 4, 1992, unreported (OH) and see the discussion in Reid, *The Law of Property in Scotland*, para.291.
[57] 2003 Act, s.81.
[58] 2003 Act, s.81(2)(a).
[59] In terms of the 2003 Act, s.2(3)(a).

converted into a positive servitude but remains as an ancillary burden because the 2003 Act contains specific provision in relation to that type of burden.[60]

---

[60] 2003 Act, s.81(2)(b).

CHAPTER 12

PRE-EMPTIONS AND REVERSIONS

INTRODUCTION

Pre-emptions and redemptions can be real burdens. In the past, pre-emptions and reversions have mainly been created in favour of feudal superiors. After November 28, 2004 it will not be competent to create any reversion or redemption or any type of option to acquire burdened property as a real burden.[1] After the appointed day superiors will lose all existing rights of pre-emption, redemption and reversion. Pre-emptions and redemptions can be realloted to other land as real burdens[2] or preserved as personal burdens.[3]

12–01

PRE-EMPTIONS[4]

Application of new provisions

The 2003 Act contains new provisions in relation to pre-emptions.[5] It should be borne in mind that these provisions will apply to existing rights of pre-emption constituted as real burdens in favour of an original feudal superior and realloted as a real burden or preserved as a personal real burden. The new provisions will also apply to pre-emptions created as real burdens in non-feudal deeds executed after September 1, 1974. The new provisions have no application to pre-emptions created in non-feudal deeds executed prior to September 1, 1974.[6] The existing law relating to pre-emptions was originally contained in section 9 of the Conveyancing Amendment (Scotland) Act 1938 as amended by section 46 of the Conveyancing and Feudal Reform (Scotland) Act 1970 and section 13 of the Land Tenure Reform (Scotland) Act 1974. The basic requirement under the previous law was for the party whose land was subject to the right of pre-emption to make an offer to sell to the party entitled to the pre-emption on whatever terms were provided in the pre-emption. In the normal case the pre-emption would require the owner of the burdened property to sell back at whatever price was being offered on the open market by a third party although that need not be the case. What the 1938 Act provisions

12–02

---

[1] 2003 Act, s.3(5).
[2] Under the 2000 Act, s.18.
[3] Under the 2000 Act, s.18A.
[4] For a general discussion of pre-2004 law see Halliday, *op. cit.*, para.32–69 *et seq.*
[5] 2003 Act, ss.82–85.
[6] 2003 Act, s.82.

contemplated therefore was a formal offer to sell to the holder of the pre-emption in writing. In practice however solicitors acting for a seller of property burdened with a pre-emption simply adopted the practice of asking the holder of the pre-emption whether he or she wished to exercise the right. A letter of declinature by or on behalf of the holder of the pre-emption was then simply exhibited to the solicitor acting for the purchaser of the property and this was taken as sufficient evidence of non-exercise. In the case of a pre-emption in a feudal writ or in a non-feudal writ executed after September 1, 1974 this meant, so far as the purchaser was concerned, that the pre-emption had been lost forever. There was however no statutory warrant for this informal procedure. In land registration cases the Keeper accepted letters of declinature from the holders of pre-emption rights as sufficient evidence that the pre-emption no longer existed and was prepared to remove the pre-emption from the title sheet of the burdened property. Presumably the legal basis for this was that the superior or other party holding the pre-emption would be personally barred from exercising it. The 2003 Act now provides two methods by which pre-emptions covered by the Act can be extinguished. A pre-emption to which the provisions apply may be extinguished if the holder of the pre-emption grants a pre-sale undertaking not to exercise the right or if the party whose land is burdened with the pre-emption makes a formal offer to the holder of the pre-emption and this is refused.

Extinction following pre-sale undertaking

12–03   Under the new provisions[7] the owner of the burdened property which is subject to the pre-emption may obtain an undertaking from the holder of the pre-emption that the pre-emption will not be exercised for a specific period. This undertaking may be given by the holder of the pre-emption subject to conditions. There is a statutory form of undertaking set out in schedule 10 to the 2003 Act. If the conveyance in implement of a sale of a burdened property is then registered before the end of the period specified in the undertaking and if any other conditions attached to the undertaking are met then the pre-emption is extinguished on registration of the conveyance.[8] If for some reason the sale falls through during the period of the undertaking then the pre-emption revives at the expiry of the period. It should be noted that the pre-emption is only extinguished if there is a conveyance in implement of the sale and this is registered with the period. The new provision appears to apply only where there is a sale. There will be some pre-emptions which specifically cover conveyances by way of gift as opposed to sale.[9] The term "sale" is not defined in the 2003 Act as including any other form of disposal such as a gift. Any undertaking given by the holder of the pre-emption is binding not only on the holder but may also become binding on any successor of the holder provided the undertaking is registered against the title of the burdened property before the successor com-

---

[7] 2003 Act, s.83.
[8] 2003 Act, s.83(1).
[9] See Halliday, para.32–73; Cusine ed., *The Conveyancing Opinions of J. M. Halliday, Conveyancing Law and Practice* (2nd ed.), No.108.

pletes title.[10] It should be noted that there is no requirement to register the notice unless it is desired to preserve rights against the successor of the holder of the pre-emption. In so far as any conditions attached to the undertaking are concerned these will really be a matter for the holder of the pre-emption. It is possible however that the holder might wish to exercise the pre-emption depending on the price. Thus the holder of the pre-emption might wish to insert a condition to the effect that the pre-emption would not be exercised if the price to a third party on the open market exceeds a certain figure.

Extinction following offer to sell

The 2003 Act preserves the existing statutory procedure whereby the **12–04** owner of the burdened property may make an offer to sell the property to the holder of the pre-emption.[11] If the pre-emption covers not just the whole property but any part of it then the offer may be in respect of the part to be sold. The offer requires to be in writing and in conformity with the provisions of section 2 of the Requirements of Writing (Scotland) Act 1995.[12] The offer is open for acceptance during the period of 21 days, or, in the case of a rural housing burden, 42 days or alternatively such lesser number of days as may be specified in the deed constituting the pre-emption.[13] One of the difficulties of course is deciding whether or not to incorporate standard clauses in any offer to sell. The Act offers a little help here by providing[14] that an offer is to be made in such terms as may be set out or provided for in the constitutive deed. Where no such terms are set out an offer is to be made on such terms as are reasonable in the circumstances. If the holder of the pre-emption right objects to the terms of the offer then that party must inform the other party of the nature of the objection within the statutory time limits of 21 or 42 days. If no objection is made then the terms of the offer are deemed reasonable.[15] The Act does not provide what is to happen if the holder of the pre-emption makes an objection to the terms of the offer within the statutory period. Presumably the hope is that the parties will then negotiate terms. One would have to assume that the holder of a pre-emption right would not make objection to the terms unless serious about reacquiring the property. If the holder of the pre-emption right cannot by reasonable enquiry be identified or found an offer may be sent to the Extractor of the Court of Session.[16]

Pre-emptions excluded from the new provisions

The new provisions do not apply to pre-emptions created in non-feudal **12–05** deeds which have been executed prior to September 1, 1974.[17] These pre-emptions will require to be interpreted in accordance with their

---

[10] 2003 Act, s.83(2).
[11] 2003 Act, s.84.
[12] 2003 Act, s.84(2).
[13] 2003 Act, s.84(3).
[14] 2003 Act, s.84(4).
[15] 2003 Act, s.84(5).
[16] 2003 Act, s.84(6).
[17] 2003 Act, s.82(b).

own terms. In effect there are no statutory provisions. In particular if the holder of a pre-emption created in a non-feudal pre-September 1, 1974 deed declines to exercise a pre-emption on any one occasion the pre-emption is not extinguished for the future and will arise on every other occasion stipulated in the pre-emption clause. Where the pre-emption is a rural housing burden[18] then although the new provisions relating to pre-sale undertakings and offers to sell apply the pre-emption is not extinguished for all time if the holder declines to exercise it. A pre-emption contained in a rural housing burden will continue to apply for the future and the holder of the pre-emption will require to be contacted each time circumstances giving rise to the pre-emption occur.[19] The provisions relating to a pre-sale undertaking appear only to apply where the pre-emption is triggered by a sale as opposed to a gift.

Extinction of pre-emptions in respect of churches

12–06   Local authorities had a right of pre-emption in respect of certain churches where the churches were to be sold.[20] These rights of pre-emption are now extinguished.[21]

Reversions and Redemptions

12–07   It is often difficult to decide whether a clause is a reversion or a redemption or simply a real burden prohibiting certain acts subject to an irritancy. Many practitioners are genuinely frightened when they hear or read the words "reversion" or "redemption". Most practitioners understand a pre-emption but it is rather difficult to grasp a legal concept which gives a party an unfettered right to take back property. A right of redemption or reversion can be created as a real right as the law stands at the moment.[22] An reversion or redemption right created as a real burden after September 1, 1974 must be exercised within a 20-year period.[23] This provision has little practical effect because most rights of redemption or reversion tend to be in ancient deeds. Irritancies in both feudal and non-feudal deeds have now been extinguished.[24] Where a right of reversion or redemption exists as a real burden it appears as though the owner of the burdened property must actually grant some sort of re-conveyance. There is no automatic vesting of the property in the holder of the reversion or redemption simply because of the occurrence of the event which triggers the right.[25] The position in relation to rights of reversion and redemption which are constituted as real burdens by virtue of the provision in deeds now is as follows:-

---

[18] In terms of the 2003 Act, s.43.

[19] 2003 Act, ss.83(1) and 84(1).

[20] Under a scheme framed in terms of s.22 (1) of the Church of Scotland (Property and Endowments) Act 1925 (schemes for the ownership, maintenance and administration of churches, etc).

[21] 2003 Act, s.85 and Sch.14.

[22] Reversion Act 1469.

[23] Land Tenure Reform (Scotland) Act 1974, s.12.

[24] 2000 Act, s.53; 2003 Act, s.67.

[25] See the excellent and concise discussion of reversions and redemptions in Reid, *The Abolition of Feudal Tenure in Scotland*, para.1.23.

(a) A reversion or redemption constituted in a deed executed and registered prior to September 1, 1974 will remain valid in accordance with its terms.

(b) A right of redemption or reversion created in a deed executed and registered between September 1, 1974 and November 28, 2004 will be valid and enforceable according to its terms but will be extinguished if it is not exercised within a period of 20 years from the date of its creation.

(c) It will not be competent to create a right of redemption or reversion in any deed executed and registered after November 28, 2004.[26]

Statutory reversions under the School Sites Act 1841

In the nineteenth century landowners were encouraged to provide sites **12–08** for schools, playgrounds and schoolhouses. In some cases local landowners simply made the sites available without actually conveying land to the appropriate parish school board. In other cases conveyances were granted either for a consideration or by way of gift. The School Sites Act 1841 contained a provision whereby a site could be provided by a landowner for the purpose of a school, playground or school masters house and in the event that the property in question ceased to be used for these educational purposes the property was stated to revert to the estate from which it had been conveyed. The 1841 Act did provide a style of conveyance but unfortunately did not state in terms that the style was mandatory. In some cases the conveyance made specific reference to the Act and in these cases there was little doubt that the statutory reversion would apply. In other cases there was simply a conveyance in ordinary form which made no reference to the Act. In these cases it appeared to be a matter of doubt as to whether or not the statutory reversion applied. Unfortunately the policy of the Keeper in land registration cases was to treat conveyances by landowners to parish education boards and similar authorities as being conveyances under the School Sites Act 1841 whether or not the Act was mentioned. Accordingly unless there was a discharge of the reversionary right indemnity was excluded. In some cases conveyances were taken by an education authority which was stated to be set up under the Education (Scotland) Act 1872 or later Educations Acts. In such a case it was generally accepted by the Keeper that the School Sites Act 1841 could not apply because the 1872 Act gave the education authorities a statutory power of acquisition. Nevertheless where the reversion did apply it was upheld.[27] As often happens certain parties appeared to take advantage of the provisions of the Act. So called title raiders acquired the rump of old estates hoping that there might be pockets of land still within the title or reversionary rights outstanding under the School Sites Act 1841. Although the Act itself was repealed by the Education (Scotland) Act 1945.[28] The repeal was not retrospective and any reversions which had been incurred still applied.

---

[26] 2003 Act, ss.3(5) and 89 which repeals the Reversion Act 1469.
[27] See *Hamilton v Grampian Regional Council*, 995 GWD 8–443; 1996 GWD 5–227.
[28] Education (Scotland) Act 1945, s.88, Sch.5.

Extinction of the reversionary right

12–09　The 2003 Act provides that in a case where any person entitled to a reversion under the 1841 Act has not completed title to the property prior to April 4, 2003 then certain provisions apply. If the property has ceased prior to April 4, 2003 to be used for educational purposes and a contract of sale has been concluded by or on behalf of an education authority in respect of the property to a third party then the authority must pay to the party entitled to the statutory reversion an amount equal to the open market value of the land as at the day the provision comes into force.[29] If however the property ceases to be used for educational purposes after April 4, 2003 then the amount to be paid to the holder of the reversionary right is the open market value of the land as at the date of cessation of the educational use less any improvement value as at that date.[30] If the education authority has not sold the property then the holder of the reversion has certain options. The holder may ask the authority to convey the property to him or her in terms of the statutory reversion or to pay compensation. If the holder of the reversion asks for a conveyance in terms of the reversion rather than compensation the local authority can opt to retain the land and pay compensation. The local authority must indicate which option they are to exercise within three months of the request for a conveyance.[31] This provision will apply where the property has ceased to be used for educational purposes but remains unsold. Where there has been no sale, if the cessation of the educational purpose occurs before April 4, 2003, then the land is to be conveyed to the holder of the reversion or compensation paid based on current open market value without deduction of improvement value. If however the cessation of educational use occurs after April 4, 2003 improvement value is deducted either by reducing the amount of compensation or by requiring the holder of the reversion to pay an amount equal to the improvement value at the time that holder obtains a conveyance.[32] "Improvement value" is defined as such part of the value of the land as is attributable to any building or other structure other than any building erected by or at the expense of the party who originally conveyed the land under the 1841 Act or any predecessor as owner.[33] Effectively what this means is that the value of any building such as a school, or schoolhouse erected by an education authority or board will be deducted from the amount of compensation.[34] Any dispute in relation to the assessment of value may be referred to and determined by the Lands Tribunal.[35] The compensation and re-conveyance provisions do not apply where the person entitled to the reversion has, before April 4, 2003, accepted an offer of compensation in respect of the land or concluded a contract for or accepted a conveyance of the land in terms of the reversion.[36] Where any proceedings have been commenced to enforce the reversion the provisions

---

[29]　2003 Act, s.86(2)(a).
[30]　2003 Act, s.86(2)(a).
[31]　2003 Act, s.86(3).
[32]　2003 Act, s.86(4).
[33]　2003 Act, s.86(6).
[34]　2003 Act, s.86(6).
[35]　2003 Act, s.86(5).
[36]　2003 Act, s.86(9).

relating to the abolition of irritancy rights[37] will apply to the proceedings to enforce the reversion.[38] Effectively proceedings commenced are deemed to be abandoned without further process and without the requirement to pay judicial expenses except in a case where final decree, not subject to appeal, has been granted prior to the coming into force of the section.

Practical effect of section 86

The practical effect of the reform is to remove any problems relating to the reversion from the title. Many of the difficulties which were caused by the operation of the reversion were caused not to local authorities but to third parties who had acquired former schools or schoolhouses from these authorities. The title of these parties was often challenged by someone claiming to hold the reversion. In other cases the Keeper excluded indemnity in respect of the reversion which made the title unmarketable. In terms of the new statutory provisions even if a party claims a reversion the title of someone to whom the property has been sold and conveyed will not be challengeable although the party holding the reversion may have some sort of claim for compensation against the local authority.

12–10

Petitions under section 7 of the Entail Sites Act 1840

The 2000 Act automatically disentails any remaining entailed land on the appointed day. In terms of section 7 of the Entails Sites Act 1840 certain restricted areas of land could be conveyed out of entailed estates for public spirited purposes. The heir of entail and possession could reclaim that land if it was not used for these public spirited purposes. This right to reclaim will go when the 2000 Act automatically disentails remaining entailed land. If these parties would have had a right to demand a reversion of the site but for the compulsory disentailment then they will have a right to claim compensation in the same manner as is set out in respect of statutory reversions under the School Sites Act 1841.[39] The scope is wider here because conveyances under the Entail Sites Act 1840 were not just to educational bodies. In many cases the property will have been conveyed to a trust for public trust purposes. The 2003 Act expressly provides that the land need no longer be held for the purposes for which the land in question was originally feued or leased under the 1840 Act.[40]

12–11

Prescriptive period for claims

The five-year negative prescription will apply to any obligation arising in relation to rights of reversion under the School Sites Act 1841 or rights to petition for forfeiture under the Entail Sites Act 1840. Any time which occurs before these provisions came into effect will not count. If the right

12–12

---

[37] 2003 Act, s.67(1)(b) and (2).
[38] 2003 Act, s.86(10).
[39] 2003 Act, s.87.
[40] 2003 Act, s.87(3).

is not claimed for five years after the event which led to its becoming due (for example a school ceasing to be used as a school) no claim can be made.[41]

---

[41] 2003 Act, s.88 amending Sch.1 to the Prescription and Limitation (Scotland) Act 1973.

CHAPTER 13

THE ROLE OF THE LANDS TRIBUNAL

INTRODUCTION

On November 28, 2004 the jurisdiction of the Lands Tribunal will be **13–01** expanded. In so far as real burdens and other land obligations are concerned the jurisdiction has related to the variation or discharge of land obligations with a power, used sparingly, to award compensation where a land obligation has been varied or discharged.[1] The definition of land obligations was wide enough to cover not only real burdens but servitudes,[2] obligations in a long lease which was either registered or at least capable of being registered[3] and rights of pre-emption if these were tied to a benefited property.[4] On the other hand an irritancy was not capable of being varied or discharged because it was a remedy rather than a land obligation.[5] Although the jurisdiction of the Tribunal extended to the addition or substitution of land obligations where an original one was varied or discharged,[6] it was held that apart from substitution there was no jurisdiction to enlarge an existing right.[7] Certain specific land obligations were expressly excluded.[8] Although the definition of land obligations appears to have been reasonably wide it did not include a right to vary or discharge land obligations which were expressly constituted by statute.[9] It has always been the view that the obligations contained in a planning agreement[10] although binding singular successors of the owner of the land are not land obligations capable of being varied or discharged by the Tribunal.[11] The jurisdiction of the Tribunal however only extended to land obligations which were enforceable as such. The Tribunal had no jurisdiction to decide that a real burden, for example, was unenforceable either because it failed to comply with the rules of constitution for real burdens or because the wording used was too imprecise.[12] In one case the applicant had to accept that the land obligation in question was a

---

[1] For a general discussion on variation and discharge of land obligations see C. Agnew of Lochnaw, *Variation and Discharge of Land Obligations*; Halliday, *Conveyancing Law and Practice* (2nd ed.), paras 34–66 to 34–97; Gordon, *Scottish Land Law* (2nd ed.), Ch.25.

[2] *Devlin v Conn* 1972 S.L.T. (Lands Tr.) 11.

[3] *McQuiban v Eagle Star Insurance Co.*, 1972 S.L.T. (Lands Tr.) 39.

[4] *Banff and Buchan District Council v Earl of Seafield's Estate*, 1988 S.L.T. (Lands Tr.) 21.

[5] *Highland Regional Council v MacDonald-Buchanan*, 1977 S.L.T. (Lands Tr.) 37.

[6] Conveyancing and Feudal Reform (Scotland) Act 1970, s.1 (4).

[7] *George T Fraser Ltd v Aberdeen Harbour Board*, 1985 S.L.T. 384.

[8] Conveyancing and Feudal Reform (Scotland) Act 1970, Sch.1, paras 1–5.

[9] *MacDonald*, 1973 S.L.T. (Lands Tr.) 26.

[10] Under s.75 of the Town and Country Planning (Scotland) Act, 1997.

[11] Rowan-Robinson, *Scottish Planning Law and Procedure*, 10.83.

[12] *Solway Ceder v Hendry*, 1972 S.L.T. (Lands Tr.) 42; *McCarthy & Stone (Developments) Ltd v Smith*, 1995 S.L.T. (Lands Tr.) 19.

validly created real burden before the application to vary or discharge could proceed.[13] The Tribunal did however come close to taking a decision on the enforceability or otherwise of a real burden in a case where it appeared to hold that a burden restricting use of retail units in a very small development could be praedial and was not necessarily in restraint of trade.[14]

THE NEW JURISDICTION

13–02　The original provisions in the Conveyancing and Feudal Reform (Scotland) 1970 relating to the variation and discharge of land obligations are repealed in their entirety.[15] After November 28, 2004 the Lands Tribunal may, by order following an application by an owner of burdened property or any other person against whom a title condition is enforceable, discharge or vary it in relation to that property.[16] If the title condition is a real burden or a rule of a development management scheme the jurisdiction extends to determining any question as to the validity, applicability or enforceability of the title condition or real burden or rule and its interpretation.[17]

The obligations covered—title conditions

13–03　The jurisdiction applies to title conditions or purported title conditions which are enforceable or bear to be enforceable.[18] A title condition is defined[19] generally as a real burden or a servitude. The statutory definition however also includes an affirmative obligation imposed in a servitude on the proprietor of the dominant tenement such as an obligation to maintain or pay a share of the costs of maintaining a road. Conditions in registerable leases which relate to the land are also included in the definition but not conditions which impose obligations to pay rent or obligations of relief relating to payment of rent. The definition also covers conditions or stipulations in assignations of recorded or registered leases which are themselves registered. Conditions in agreements entered into under section 7 of the National Trust for Scotland Order Confirmation Act 1938 are also covered. Other conditions relating to land may be brought within the definition by Scottish Ministers by order. The new definition of title conditions does not appear to include obligations in recorded or registered planning agreements under section 75 of the Town and Country Planning (Scotland) Act 1997. These planning agreements are, where recorded or registered, enforceable by the local planning authority against the owner of the land and that party's successors as owner of the land but they do not depend for their enforceability against singular successors on the local planning authority owning any adjoining or neighbouring land. They are very much of

---

[13] *Rowan Property Investments Ltd v Jack*, 1996 G.W.D. 16–948.
[14] *Co-operative Wholesale Society v Ushers Brewery*, 1975 S.L.T. (Lands Tr.) 9.
[15] 2003 Act, s.128 and Sch. 15.
[16] 2003 Act, s.90 (1)(a)(i).
[17] 2003 Act, s.90 (1)(a)(ii).
[18] 2003 Act, s.90 (1)(a).
[19] 2003 Act, s.122 (1).

the character of personal real burdens such as conservation burdens or economic development burdens but they are essentially statutory obligations and fall outwith the jurisdiction of the Tribunal. It must be borne in mind that although real burdens are included within the jurisdiction a real burden will have a statutory definition which restricts the category of real burden to obligations which are enforceable by a person by virtue of owning land.[20]

Title conditions specifically excluded

As before certain obligations are expressly excluded from the definition.[21] The excluded title conditions are: **13–04**

(a) Obligations however constituted relating to the right to work minerals or to any ancillary rights in relation to minerals, the definition of "minerals" and "ancillary rights" having the same meanings as in the Mines (Working Facilities and Support) Act 1966.

(b) Obligations enforceable by the Crown which are created or imposed for naval, military or airforce purposes or for civil aviation purposes or in connection with the use of land as an aerodrome.

(c) An obligation created and imposed in or in relation to an agricultural holding (as defined in section 1 (1) of the Agricultural Holdings (Scotland) Act 1991 or a holding within the meaning of the Small Landholders (Scotland) Act 1886 to 1939 or a croft within the meaning of the Crofters (Scotland) Act 1993.

There is no exclusion in relation to payments of feuduty ground annual or other ground burdens because these are abolished as real burdens on the land on the appointed day.[22]

THE EXTENDED JURISDICTION

Preservation and renewal notices

The Tribunal can also consider applications by the owner of a benefited property to renew or vary a title condition in favour of the benefited property where that title condition is a real burden in respect of which the owner of the burdened property has executed and registered a notice of termination under the sunset rule.[23] The Tribunal can also consider an application by the owner of a benefited property to renew or vary a real burden or servitude which is going to be extinguished on the registration of a conveyance to a local authority where land has been acquired by agreement in circumstances where it could have been acquired by compulsory purchase.[24] The Tribunal can also deal with an application **13–05**

---

[20] 2003 Act, s.1 (1).
[21] 2003 Act, s.90 (3) and Sch.11.
[22] 2000 Act, s.7.
[23] 2003 Act, ss.21 and 90(1)(b) (i).
[24] 2003 Act, ss.107 (4) and 90(1)(b)(ii).

by the owner of a unit in a community to preserve a community burden in respect of which intimation of a proposal to register a deed of variation or discharge has been given.[25] The owner of a unit of a development which is subject to a development management scheme in respect of which intimation of a proposal to register a deed of disapplication of the scheme has been made may also make application to preserve the scheme.[26] Where the Lands Tribunal refuses an application to preserve or renew a burden either where notice of termination has been executed and registered or where there is a proposal to vary or discharge a community burden the Tribunal must discharge the title condition in relation to the benefited property wholly or partly as the case may be. In the case of community burdens where not all owners have granted the deed, variation or discharge the Tribunal shall vary or discharge the community burden accordingly. Where the Tribunal refuses an application by the owner of a unit in a development to which a development management scheme applies then the development management scheme must be disapplied. Where it is a personal real burden that is the subject of the application to renew or vary then the same provisions will apply except there will be no reference to property or benefited property.[27] It is not competent to make an application for variation or renewal after the appropriate renewal dates except with the consent of the party who seeks to terminate, vary or discharge the title condition.[28] Similarly it is not possible to lodge an application for preservation or variation where the appropriate certificate to the effect that no application to preserve has been endorsed by the Tribunal.[29] The Tribunal also has jurisdiction to consider any dispute arising in relation to a notice registered under section 50 (notices of preservation) and 80 (conversion of negative servitudes to real burdens) of the 2003 Act.[30] In determining the dispute the Tribunal may make such order as it thinks fit discharging or to such an extent as may be specified in the order, restricting the notice question. The burden of proving any disputed question of fact in relation to a section 50 or section 80 notice is on the party relying on the notice.[31] An extract of any order made in relation to a dispute under sections 50 or 80 may be registered and the order shall take effect *quoad* third parties on registration.[32]

Substituted obligations

13–06 The Tribunal has in certain circumstances the power to impose a new obligation or to vary an obligation which might result in property becoming a benefited property. This is not competent in relation to ordinary applications for discharge or variation without the consent of the owner of the burdened property.[33] Where the application is by the owner of a

---

[25] 2003 Act, ss.34(1), 34(3), 36(1), 37(1) and 90(1)(c).
[26] Under 2003 Act, ss.71 and 90(1)(d).
[27] 2003 Act, s.90(2).
[28] 2003 Act, s.90(4)(a).
[29] 2003 Act, s.90(4)(b).
[30] 2003 Act, s.102(1).
[31] 2003 Act, s.102(2).
[32] 2003 Act, s.102(3).
[33] 2003 Act, s.90(5)(a).

benefited property to preserve, renew or vary a title condition then the Tribunal is entitled to impose a new obligation which would result in the property becoming a benefited property without the consent of the owner of the burdened property.[34] Under the previous legislation[35] the Tribunal had power to add or substitute any condition if it appeared to the Tribunal to be reasonable as a result of variation or discharge. The Tribunal has taken the view this power does not allow a simple substitution of one burden for a different burden.[36] The Tribunal's view was that the substituted provision must in some way relate to the title condition to be varied or discharged. The previous provisions also required the consent of the applicant. Presumably, as before, if the applicant refuses to accept the substituted or varied provision the Tribunal will still require to decide whether to discharge or vary the original title condition.[37] Where the application is one to preserve, or renew a burden which someone else seeks to terminate, discharge or vary then the Tribunal's power to impose a substitute condition does not require the consent of the burdened owner. Presumably the Tribunal will use this power as it has in the past to soften the impact of a discharge of what might be regarded as an amenity or neighbour burden. Thus if a burden prohibiting use of a site for retain purposes is discharged the Tribunal may impose a new burden relating to landscaping, tree screening and the like.[38] The Tribunal may impose a new title condition on a burdened property or vary a title condition at the time any order is made.[39] This is different from the power of the Tribunal to impose a new obligation resulting in other property becoming a benefited property.[40] The Tribunal can only do this however where the owner of the burdened property consents.[41]

Compensation

Where the Tribunal grants an order discharging, renewing or varying a title condition it may direct that the applicant pays compensation. Compensation may also be awarded where a real burden or a rule of a development management scheme is declared invalid, inapplicable or unenforceable or is interpreted in a particular way. The compensation would be payable to any person who in relation to the particular title condition was an owner of the benefited property. Where the title condition is a personal real burden and there is therefore no benefited property the compensation will be payable to the holder of the title condition. Where an application is made to preserve or renew a real burden which is under threat of termination or where there is an attempt to vary a community burden then any compensation will be payable to the terminator or the person proposing to vary as the case may be. Compensation can be awarded under one of two heads but not under both. The heads are:

13–07

---

[34] 2003 Act, s.90 (5)(b).
[35] Conveyancing and Feudal Reform (Scotland) Act 1970, s.1(5).
[36] *Strathclyde Regional Council v MacTaggart & Mickel Ltd*, 1984 S.L.T. (Lands Tr.) 33.
[37] *Strathclyde Regional Council v MacTaggart & Mickel Ltd*, 1984 S.L.T. (Lands Tr.) 33.
[38] See Gordon, *Scottish Land Law* (2nd ed.), paras 25–29.
[39] 2003 Act, s.90(8).
[40] Under the 2003 Act, s.90(5).
[41] 2003 Act, s.90 (11).

    (a) A sum to compensate for any substantial loss or disadvantage suffered by, as the case may be—

        (i) the owner, as owner of the benefited property; or

        (ii) the holder of the title condition;

    in consequence of the discharge.

    (b) A sum to make up for any effect which the title condition produced, at the time when it was created, in reducing the consideration then paid or made payable for the burdened property.

These provisions are roughly the same as those which were contained in the previous legislation.[42] Presumably the Tribunal will take the same view as it has in the past and make awards sparingly. Compensation has been given for patrimonial loss relating to the property.[43] Loss of trade can however have an effect on the value of property and accordingly may result in a patrimonial loss.[44] Applications under the second head where the burdened proprietor argues that the original consideration was reduced because of the impositions of the burden have been few and far between. The feudal superior does have the alternative of attempting to preserve the right to compensation in relation to a development value burden.[45] A direction by the Tribunal to a party to pay compensation can only be made if the party directed consents.[46] Presumably this provision would allow an applicant to withdraw the application rather than pay compensation. Where there is an application to preserve a real burden or servitude which is going to be extinguished following on a conveyance in favour of the local authority after a voluntary acquisition[47] and that application is refused so that the burden or servitude is extinguished no compensation is payable unless the burden is a personal real burden.[48] The reason for this is presumably that personal real burdens do not attach to other land but are in favour of particular parties possibly by virtue of the status of the party or its function. The Tribunal can decide to decline jurisdiction where the application is simply to determine that a title condition is invalid, inapplicable or unenforceable or how it is to be interpreted. The reason for this is that the courts have a concurrent jurisdiction.[49]

Variation and discharge of community burdens

13–08   There are special provisions in relation to community burdens because of the number of people who are both benefited and burdened proprietors. Owners of 25 per cent of the units in a community may apply to the Lands Tribunal for a variation or discharge of a community burden and the Tribunal may vary or discharge the community burden either in relation to all of the community or part of the community.[50] Where

---

   [42] Conveyancing and Feudal Reform (Scotland) Act 1970, s.1(4); the new provisions are in the 2003 Act, s.90(6).

   [43] *Bolton v Aberdeen Corporation*, 1972 S.L.T. (Lands Tr.) 26.

   [44] *Co-operative Wholesale Society v Ushers Brewery*, 1975 S.L.T. (Lands Tr.) 9.

   [45] 2000 Act, ss.33 to 40.

   [46] 2003 Act, s.90(9).

   [47] Under the 2003 Act, s.107 (4).

   [48] 2003 Act, s.90 (10).

   [49] 2003 Act, s.90 (12).

   [50] 2003 Act, s.91 (1).

the application is made by only some of the owners in the community it does not matter that the burdens which they seek to have discharged or varied affect other units as compensation can be awarded in accordance with the compensation provisions.[51] It should be noted that this provision is quite separate from the rights of owners of units in a community to execute and register a deed of variation. The provisions here allow owners of units in a community to make a direct application to the Lands Tribunal. The application would of course require to be intimated in the usual way.

PROCEDURE

Early applications for discharge

In terms of the earlier legislation[52] an application could not be brought **13–09** to the Tribunal for a variation or discharge if it related to an obligation which was less than two years old. The new provisions in the 2003 Act[53] are to the effect that the constitutive deed creating the title condition may provide that there can be no application for variation or discharge for a fixed period not more than five years after the creation of the condition. If there is no such provision in the constitutive deed then presumably applications can be made at any time although the Tribunal will still be wary of granting discharges in respect of recently created burdens.[54]

Notification of application

Where the application is to discharge or vary a title condition or declare **13–10** a real burden or a rule of a development management scheme invalid or unenforceable or to interpret any such burden or rule or where there is an application by the owners of at least 25% of the units in a community[55] then the Tribunal must give notice of the application to certain persons. These persons are any owner of the burdened property, any owner of any benefited property and the holder of any title condition in the case of a personal real burden.[56] Where the application is for preservation, renewal or variation as where someone opposes a notice of termination of a burden then the Tribunal must give notice to the terminator and the owner of the burdened property.[57] Where the application is to preserve a real burden or servitude which is going to be extinguished on the registration of a conveyance in favour of the local authority following a voluntary agreement to acquire then notification must be made to the person proposing to register that conveyance.[58]

---

[51] 2003 Act, s.91(2) and (3).
[52] Conveyancing and Feudal Reform (Scotland) Act 1970, s.2(5).
[53] 2003 Act, s.92.
[54] See *Murrayfield Ice Rink v Scottish Rugby Union*, 1972 S.L.T. (Lands Tr.) 20; 1973 S.L.T. 99; *Solway Cedar Limited v Hendry*, 1972 S.L.T. (Lands Tr.) 42; *James Miller and Partners Limited v Hunt*, 1971 S.L.T. (Lands Tr.) 9.
[55] Under s. 91(1).
[56] 2003 Act s.93 (1)(a).
[57] 2003 Act s.93 (1)(b)(i) and (ii).
[58] 2003 Act s.93 (1)(b)(iii).

Where the application is by the owner of a unit in a community to pre-serve community burdens then the Tribunal must give notice to the person proposing to register the deed of variation or discharge. Where the application relates to a development management scheme in respect of which intimation to register a deed of application has been made notification must be made by the Tribunal to the owners associ-ation. Where there is a proposal to register a conveyance in favour of a local authority following on an acquisition by agreement and the sub-jects are affected by a development management scheme then the Tribunal must give notification to the person proposing to register the conveyance.[59] Intimation is made by sending the notice. Sending is defined in the Act.[60] Intimation can be made to the agent of the person concerned or to an owner of property if only the property is known and not the name of the owner. Similarly the notice can be addressed to "the proprietor". Where an intimation is sent by post then it is sent on the day of posting. Where it is transmitted by electronic means then it is sent on the day of transmission. As an alternative to these more usual methods of intimation however the Tribunal is empowered to give notice by advertisement or by such other method as the Lands Tribunal thinks fit in certain circumstances.[61] These alternative methods can be used if the person to whom intimation is to be made cannot by reason-able enquiry be identified or found or in a case where so many people require to be given notice that in the opinion of the Tribunal it is not rea-sonably practicable to send notices. In a case where the application is to determine the question of validity, applicability or enforceability of a real burden or rule of a development management scheme or how that burden or rule is to be construed or interpreted notice may be given by advertisement or by such other method as the Lands Tribunal thinks fit if the person to whom it is given does not appear to the Tribunal to have any interest to enforce the title condition.[62] The Tribunal however retain a discretion in relation to parties to whom inti-mation is to be made. The Tribunal can give notification to such other people as it thinks fit.[63]

Content of notice

13–11   Where intimation is given by the Lands Tribunal of an application either to discharge, vary or to preserve then the Tribunal must in any notice give certain basic information.[64] The notice must summarise or repro-duce the application which has been made. It must also set a date no earlier than 21 days after notice is given by which representations may be made to the Tribunal in relation to the application. The Tribunal must also indicate the fee which must accompany any representation. Where the application is for the discharge, renewal or variation of a real burden or for the preservation of a real burden or development management scheme the notice must state that if the application is not opposed then

---

[59] 2003 Act, s.93(1)(e).
[60] 2003 Act, s.124.
[61] 2003 Act, s.93(2).
[62] 2003 Act, s.93(2)(c).
[63] 2003 Act, s.93(3).
[64] 2003 Act, s.94 .

it may be granted without any further enquiry. In any notice given other than by advertisement in respect of an application to vary or discharge a title condition or to vary or discharge a community burden notice must also set out the name and address of every person to whom the notice is being sent.

Representations to the Tribunal

The 2003 Act sets out the persons who are entitled to make representa- **13–12** tions in relation to applications either to vary or discharge or to preserve or renew.[65] These persons are:

(a) any person who has title to enforce the title condition;
(b) any person against whom the title condition is enforceable;
(c) in a case where a local authority or other acquiring authority seek to register a conveyance after a voluntary agreement to acquire and that conveyance will extinguish real burdens or servitudes the person proposing to register the conveyance;
(d) in the case where there is a proposal to register a deed of dis-application of a development management scheme the owners association and the owner of any unit of the development.

In general terms those who are entitled to make representations are persons with a title to enforce the title condition or those against whom the title condition can be enforced. This could include tenants, liferent-ers, heritable creditors in possession and non-entitled spouses. The holder of a personal real burden will have title to enforce. Representations must be in writing and must comprise a statement of the facts and contentions upon which the person proposes to rely.[66] Representations are made when they are received by the Lands Tribunal with the requisite fee.[67] The party sending in such representations to the Tribunal must forthwith send a copy of them to the applicant. Despite the time limits for making representations[68] the Lands Tribunal may if it thinks fit accept representations made late.[69] Scottish Ministers may make rules regulating any application to the Tribunal and may in par-ticular make provision as to the evidence which may be required for such an application.[70] Presumably rules will be promulgated dealing with hearings and evidence. Under the previous provisions benefited or burdened proprietors were entitled to speak at a hearing. This has meant that submissions in writing had to be spoken to in evidence so that they could be the subject of cross examination.[71] Presumably parties will be entitled to be heard in an opposed application.

---

[65] 2003 Act, s.95.
[66] 2003 Act, s.96(1).
[67] 2003 Act, s.96(2).
[68] 2003 Act, s.94(a)(ii).
[69] 2003 Act, s.96(3).
[70] 2003 Act, s.101.
[71] Conveyancing and Feudal Reform (Scotland) Act 1970, s.2(2); *Scott v Wilson*, 1998 S.L.T. (Lands Tr.) 51. The current rules are the Lands Tribunal for Scotland Rules (SI 1971/218) as amended by Lands Tribunal for Scotland (Amendment) Rules (SI 1985/581).

Unopposed applications

13–13   One of the difficulties with the existing provisions for variation and discharge has been that the Tribunal has had to consider the merits of each application even in cases where the application is unopposed. Difficulties have arisen in two distinct types of case. In the first place there may be a real burden in a title in favour of a superior or some other party but it has been impossible to trace the superior or other party. In many cases superiority titles were never transmitted to heirs executors or beneficiaries on the death of the original superior and effectively the superiority has "died out". In such a case however the only way to clear the register of the offending burden was to make application to the Lands Tribunal. Even where it became obvious that no-one was going to oppose the burden the Tribunal had to go through the procedure of considering the case on the merits. In the second case the superior or other party may be very much to the fore. It may be clear that there is some doubt as to the enforceability of the burden but the party who may be entitled to enforce refuses to grant a waiver except in return for an exorbitant sum. The obvious course in such a case is to threaten that party with an application to the Tribunal. The response however often is that although the superior or other party may not wish to incur the expense of disputed application they will hang back and allow the Tribunal to take the proper time. Where the burden is holding up development time is money and in such cases money often changes hands in respect of dubious burdens where either there may be doubt as to enforceability or there is little doubt that the Tribunal would grant the variation or discharge required. The 2003 Act makes provision for unopposed applications.[72] These provisions apply to applications for discharge or renewal of real burdens. It should be noted that the provisions do not appear to apply to all title conditions but only to real burdens. This will of course include personal real burdens. The unopposed application procedure applies to discharge or variation, renewal or variation or preservation of a real burden and the general provision is to the effect that where the application is unopposed it must be granted as of right.[73] Where the application is unopposed and is granted as of right there is no question of compensation nor of substituting any other real burden. The unopposed procedure will not apply in the case of an application for discharge or variation of a facility or a service burden or in the case of an application for discharge or variation of a community burden imposed on a unit in a sheltered or retirement housing development.[74] An application is unopposed in the case of an application to vary or discharge a real burden or to have it declared invalid or unenforceable or to interpret the same where no representations opposing the application have been made either by the owner of a benefited property or by the holder of a personal real burden.[75] Where the application is one to preserve a burden as where it is subject to a notice of termination or there is a conveyance to be registered in favour of the local authority which will extinguish a burden

---

[72] 2003 Act, s.97.
[73] 2003 Act, s.97(1).
[74] 2003 Act, s.97(2).
[75] 2003 Act, s.97(3)(a).

or servitude then the application to preserve will be unopposed if no representations have been made by the terminator (the party seeking to extinguish the burden) or the person proposing to register the conveyance following on the voluntary acquisition.[76] Where the application is to preserve a burden where there is an application to register a deed of variation or discharge as might be the case in relation to community burdens then the application to preserve is unopposed where no representations opposing the application have been made by the persons proposing to register the deed of variation or discharge.[77] Similarly an application can be treated as unopposed where a representation has been made but has been withdrawn.[78] Presumably the lodging of an incompetent representation will not mean that an application is to be treated as opposed. For example in the case of a notice to preserve a burden under threat of termination only representations by the terminator will be treated as proper opposition. If the Tribunal accepts representations late as it is empowered to do[79] then a previously unopposed application will become an opposed application. If these representations are subsequently withdrawn then the application could then proceed unopposed.

Development management schemes

An unopposed application for preservation of a development manage-   **13–14**
ment scheme will also be granted as a right.[80] An application is unopposed where no representations have been made by the owners association or by the person proposing to register the conveyance in the case of a conveyance in favour of a local authority.[81] An application for preservation of a development management scheme shall, unless it falls to be granted as a right as an unopposed application, only be granted if the Tribunal is satisfied that the disapplication of the scheme is not in the best interests of the owners of the units in the development or is unfairly prejudicial to one or more of these owners. Alternatively in the case of the acquisition of the land or part of the land affected by the scheme by an acquiring authority the Tribunal shall not grant the application to preserve unless they are satisfied that having regard to the purpose for which the land is being acquired it is reasonable to grant the application.[82]

Expenses

The Lands Tribunal may, in determining any application, make such   **13–15**
order as to expenses as it thinks fit and shall have regard in particular to the extent to which the application or any opposition to the application is successful.[83] There are special provisions however in relation to

---

[76] 2003 Act, s.97(3)(b).
[77] 2003 Act, s.97(3)(c).
[78] 2003 Act, s.97(3).
[79] 2003 Act, s.96(3).
[80] 2003 Act, s.99(1).
[81] 2003 Act, s.99(2).
[82] 2003 Act, s.99(4).
[83] 2003 Act, s.103(1).

certain types of application. Where application has been made for the renewal or variation of a burden in circumstances where a notice of termination has been registered or a deed of variation or discharge or conveyance has been registered then the Tribunal may order the terminator or the party who executed the deed of variation, discharge or conveyance or any successor of these parties to pay the applicant for preservation or renewal a specific sum in respect of the expenses incurred by the applicant or such proportion of these expenses as the Tribunal may think fit. This would apply where the party in question (terminator or opposer) does not oppose an application for renewal or preservation. The reason for this is that that party's actions have necessitated the application being made by the benefited proprietor to preserve that benefited proprietor's interests. Where there is an unopposed application for preservation of a development management scheme in a case where there is an acquisition by a body such as a local authority under a voluntary agreement which would extinguish the scheme the Tribunal may order the owners association or the party registering the conveyance to pay the applicant a specific sum in respect of expenses. The applicant in this case would be the acquiring authority who proposed to register the conveyance.[84]

OPPOSED APPLICATIONS—FACTORS TO BE TAKEN INTO ACCOUNT

13–16   Where an application for variation, discharge, renewal or preservation of a title condition is opposed so that it cannot be granted as a right the Tribunal must in general terms act reasonably and take into account a number of factors which are set out in the Act.[85] In the cases of applications to preserve community burdens where a deed of variation or discharge has been executed either by majority[86] or by the owners of adjacent units[87] the Tribunal must not grant the variation or discharge if it is not in the best interests of the owners of all the units in the community or is unfairly prejudicial to one or more of those owners.[88]

The factors to be taken into account

13–17   In terms of the earlier legislation there were three grounds for variation and discharge of land obligations.[89] These grounds were:

(a) That the obligation was unreasonable or inappropriate by reason of changes in the character of the land affected by the obligation or of the neighbourhood or other circumstances which the Tribunal might deem material.

(b) That the obligation had become unduly burdensome compared with any benefit resulting or which would result from its performance.

---

[84] 2003 Act, s.99(3).
[85] 2003 Act, s.98; the factors are set out in the 2003 Act s.100.
[86] 2003 Act, ss.33 and 34.
[87] 2003 Act, ss.35 and 36.
[88] 2003 Act, s.98(b).
[89] Conveyancing and Feudal Reform (Scotland) Act 1970, s.1(3).

(c) That the existence of the obligation impeded some reasonable use of the land.[90]

The 2003 Act lists no fewer than ten factors which the Tribunal may take into account in determining applications. It should be noted that these factors do not just apply in the case of an application for variation and discharge of a real burden. They apply in relation to any application which comes before the Tribunal. This may be, for example, an application to renew a burden which is threatened with termination or it may be an application to preserve a community burden which is threatened with discharge or variation. The factors are the same although it is clear that some of the factors are more likely to weigh with the Tribunal than others depending on the nature of the application before them. It is convenient to look at the factors individually.

Factor (a)—Change in circumstances

The first factor which the Tribunal may take into account[91] is any change in circumstances since the title condition was created including without prejudice to that generality any change in the character of the benefited property, of the burdened property or of the neighbourhood of the properties. This factor is very similar to the original ground for variation and discharge that the obligation has become unreasonable or inappropriate by reason of a change in the character of the land or the neighbourhood or other circumstances. The new factor however focuses more on change of circumstances. In the past the Tribunal has considered changes in the character of the land affected and the neighbourhood.[92] **13–18**

Factor (b)—Benefit to other property

The second factor which the Tribunal may take into account is the extent to which the title condition confers benefit on the benefited property or where there is no benefited property confers benefit on the public.[93] This factor is similar to the original ground that the obligation has become unduly burdensome compared with the benefit it conferred. However this factor focuses on the benefit to the benefited property rather than the unreasonableness of the burden so far as the burdened property is concerned. This factor will be of most relevance in relation to applications to discharge neighbour burdens designed to protect amenity. The widow, mentioned in various examples throughout this book, may have conveyed one half of her garden as a building plot subject to very strict conditions about the number of buildings to be erected, the height of the **13–19**

---

[90] For a general discussion of these grounds, see Gordon, *Scottish Land Law* (2nd ed.) 25–13 to 25–26; Crispin Agnew of Lochnaw, *Variation and Discharge of Land Obligations*, Ch.6.

[91] 2003 Act, s.100(a).

[92] See *MacDonald*, 1973 S.L.T. (Lands Tr.) 26; *Bolton v Aberdeen Corporation*, 1972 (Lands Tr.) 26; *Manz v Butter's Trustees*, 1973 S.L.T. (Lands Tr.) 2; *Main v Lord Doune*, 1972 S.L.T. (Lands Tr.) 14; see Gordon, *Scottish Land Law* (2nd ed.), paras 25–14 *et seq*, Crispin Agnew of Lochnaw, *Variation and Discharge of Land Obligations*, paras 6–02 *et seq*.

[93] 2003 Act, s.100(b).

buildings, the use to which the land is be put and the maintenance of mutual boundary walls. Quite clearly these are burdens which have a direct benefit to the property retained by the widow as owner of the remaining land to which the enforcement rights attach. Although the factors to be taken into account are set out separately in a list that does not mean that the Tribunal will not consider one or more of the factors taken together. For example the Tribunal will consider the extent to which the condition confers benefit on the benefited property at the same time as considering the extent to which the condition might impede enjoyment of the burdened property. In many cases a balance will require to be struck. Loss of amenity will be the crucial factor here.[94] The widow is likely to be successful in opposing the application where her amenity is threatened.

Factor (c)—Enjoyment of the burdened property

13–20   The third factor which the Tribunal could consider is the extent to which the condition impedes enjoyment of the burdened property. Again this factor is very similar to the third ground under the Conveyancing and Feudal Reform (Scotland) Act 1970 namely that the existence of the obligation impedes a reasonable use of the land. However the factor here does not refer to use but "enjoyment" of the burdened property. This suggests that the Tribunal will not necessarily consider under this head a proposed development but is more likely to focus on how the burden might impede a normal use as opposed to a development use. The Tribunal is likely to consider this particular factor together with the preceding factor in relation to benefit to the benefited property. The third ground under the 1970 Act was always the widest ground. It was the ground which allowed the Tribunal to look forwards as opposed backwards in relation to a burden.[95]

Factor (d)—Impracticable or costly performance

13–21   The fourth factor which the Tribunal may consider is how practicable or costly it is for the owner of the burdened property to comply with the obligation. This is a new factor but the Tribunal could consider this factor together with the extent to which the condition might confer benefit on the benefited property. The best example would be an obligation to maintain a building in a proper state of repair. If the building on the burdened property has become ruinous but the owner has received a reasonable offer from a party who is prepared to acquire the site and demolish the building then the Tribunal may consider that it is impracticable and too costly to actually implement the burden. Similarly in such a situation the Tribunal may consider that the burden does not confer a great deal of benefit on the benefited property.

---

[94] See *Bachoo v George Wimpey & Co. Ltd*, 1977 S.L.T. (Lands Tr.) 2.
[95] See *Main v Lord Doune*, 1972 S.L.T. (Lands Tr.) 14; *West Lothian Co-op Society v Ashdale Land & Property Co. Ltd*, 1972 S.L.T. (Lands Tr.) 30; *Mercer v MacLeod*, 1977 S.L.T. (Lands Tr.) 14.

Factor (e)—Age of title condition

The fifth factor which the Tribunal can take into account is the length **13–22** of time which has elapsed since the condition was created. At the time when cities like Glasgow and Edinburgh were being developed real burdens were created with a view to ensuring orderly development. In many ways the law of real burdens at that time was an elementary but very successful private system of town planning. However a great many burdens are obsolete in a modern age. There are obvious examples such as burdens which relate to the formation of roads, footpaths, sewers and drains. In most cases of urban property these services will have been taken over by the appropriate authority. In such a case there is usually little difficulty. There are however older burdens which can cause difficulty even although they have little practical significance. A nineteenth century burden may provide that a property is to be used for residential purposes only. In many cities terraces of townhouses have been converted into offices. In some cases waivers will have been granted. In other cases the law of acquiescence will have been relied on. However there will be cases where it is appropriate or necessary to clear the register of the burden. An application to the Lands Tribunal would be appropriate and the Lands Tribunal could consider the age of the burden as one of the factors. Of course this is a factor which could cut both ways. The Tribunal may be reluctant to vary or discharge a recently created burden especially where the party seeking to discharge or vary the burden was one of the original contracting parties.[96]

Factor (f)—The purpose of the title condition

In some cases it will be obvious that the title condition was created to **13–23** achieve a certain end or purpose. It may also be obvious particularly in relation to older burdens that the purpose for which the real burden was created is no longer relevant. This is a factor which could be taken together with other factors such as factors (c) and (e). There may be a title condition to the effect that land is to be used for the erection of a village school or village hall. However with the passage of time the school or the hall may be too small or otherwise inappropriate. A new and larger school in a more densely populated area may have been erected by the education authority or a new community centre with halls, a theatre and a swimming pool may have constructed elsewhere. In such a case the Tribunal may consider that the original purpose of the title condition, however laudable, is no longer relevant.

Factor (g)—Planning consent and other licences or permissions

The Tribunal may consider whether in relation to the burdened prop- **13–24** erty there is a consent or a deemed consent of a planning authority or the consent of some other regulatory authority for a use which the title

---

[96] See *Murrayfield Ice Rink v Scottish Rugby Union*, 1972 S.L.T. (Lands Tr.) 20; 1973 S.L.T. 79; *Solway Cedar Ltd v Hendry*, 1972 S.L.T. (Land Tr.) 42; *James Miller and Partners Ltd v Hunt*, 1971 S.L.T. (Lands Tr.) 9.

condition prevents. The Lands Tribunal has always been able to take account of planning permissions or licences in respect of a proposed use.[97] The view which has been taken by the Tribunal in the past has been that the existence of a permission or licence is only a factor in assessing whether a burden impedes a reasonable use of the land. The Tribunal has drawn a distinction between permissions and licences which are granted or refused in the context of the pubic interest and title conditions such as real burdens which are essentially matters of private right and obligation. It should be noted that a refusal (as opposed to a grant) of planning permission or a licence will also be a factor which the Tribunal can take into account. This particular factor would presumably be taken together with other factors such as factor (a)—change in circumstances, factor (b)—lack of benefit to benefited property, and factor (c)—extent to which the condition impedes enjoyment of the burdened property.

Factor (h)—Offer of compensation

13–25 The Tribunal will be entitled to take on board any commercial offer which the owner of the burdened property has made to the owner of the benefited property by way of compensation for a waiver or a discharge of a title condition. There will be cases where there are genuine issues of amenity and the applicant has offered a reasonable amount of compensation to obtain a waiver or a discharge from the benefited proprietor. This does not mean of course that the Tribunal would be entitled to waive or discharge a title condition which the benefited proprietor did not wish to give up no matter what compensation was offered. The deliberations of the Tribunal are not meant to be price sensitive in this sense. This factor however would allow the Tribunal to assess the overall reasonableness of the situation and to deal with matters where it was apparent that the party opposing the application was simply exploiting a situation for unreasonable monetary gain as opposed to attempting to protect a genuine amenity interest.

Factor (i)—Compulsory acquisition

13–26 Where an application is made to preserve a real burden or servitude which is to be extinguished on the registration of a conveyance in implement of a voluntary agreement to acquire land which could have been acquired compulsorily then the Tribunal is entitled to take into account the purpose for which the land is being acquired. There may be circumstances where the purpose of the acquisition might not be hampered or impeded in any way if the burden was preserved. On the other hand there may well be cases where the whole purpose of the acquisition would be frustrated if the burden was preserved.

---

[97] *Main v Lord Doune*, 1972 S.L.T. (Lands Tr.) 14; *Mercer v MacLeod*, 1977 S.L.T. (Lands Tr.) 14; *Co-operative Wholesale Society v Ushers Brewery*, 1975 S.L.T. (Lands Tr.) 9.

Factor (j)—Other factors considered material

The Tribunal has an overall discretion to consider any other factor   **13–27**
which it deems to be material to the application. This factor echoes the
ground under the 1970 Act which allowed the Tribunal to discharge a
title condition which had become unreasonable or inappropriate having
in regard to changes in the character of the burdened land or the neighbourhood or other circumstances which the Tribunal deemed material.
These were alternatives and Professor Gordon took the view that the
consideration of other material circumstances opened a very wide
gate.[98] However as Professor Gordon notes the Tribunal has applied the
ejusdem generis rule and still looks for some change in the character of
the burdened land or neighbourhood.[99] Essentially what the Tribunal
has looked for are demographic or social changes in the area as opposed
to the personal circumstances of the applicant.[1] It must be borne in mind
however that the provisions in the 1970 Act in relation to other material
circumstances were tied to the ground which required the Tribunal to
find that the obligation had become unreasonable or inappropriate. The
discretion afforded by factor (j) sits on its own and accordingly could
not be subject to the *ejusdem generis* rule. One assumes however that the
Tribunal is likely to be cautious in its approach. One could not see the
Tribunal granting any application on this ground alone. It would of
course be quite appropriate for the Tribunal to assess a number of
factors and then take the view that the balance was tipped in favour
of an application by some other factor which was considered material.

EFFECTIVE DATE OF ORDERS

In general terms orders of the Tribunal will come into effect when they   **13–28**
are registered and at that point the title condition will be discharged,
varied, renewed or preserved. This provision however does not apply
to orders declaring a burden to be invalid or unenforceable or interpre-
tive orders.[2] This may seem an odd exclusion particularly when a
burden appears in the burdens section of a title sheet. Presumably if the
Lands Tribunal declares a burden to be invalid or unenforceable the burdened proprietor will wish the burden removed from the title sheet. The
Keeper does of course have a discretion to note things on the title sheet
and no doubt the order could be noted as opposed to registered.
Alternatively where an order indicates that a burden is wholly invalid
the Keeper may accept the order as evidence of this and delete the
burden. The reason for this specific exclusion is that contractual enforceability is unaffected by any order of the Tribunal.[3] The Tribunal might
declare a burden to be unenforceable because it was not praedial in its
nature. This might not affect its status as a contractual obligation
between the original parties although in one case a burden was deemed

---

[98] Gordon, *Scottish Land Law* (2nd ed.), para.25–20.
[99] See *James Miller & Partners Ltd v Hunt*, 1974 S.L.T. (Lands Tr.) 9.
[1] See *United Auctions (Scotland) Ltd v British Railways Board*, 1991 S.L.T. (Lands Tr.) 71;
Miller Group Ltd v Gardner's Exrs, 1992 S.L.T. (Lands Tr.) 53.
[2] In terms of the 2003 Act, s.90 (1)(a)(ii).
[3] 2003 Act, s.104(4).

to be so unreasonably in restraint of trade that it was not even enforceable as a personal obligation.[4] Scottish Ministers are, after consultation with the Scottish Committee of the Council on Tribunals, entitled to make rules as to when orders of the Lands Tribunal will take effect.[5] Apart from the exclusions already mentioned other orders may be registered against the burdened property by any person who was a party to the application or was entitled to make representations and on the order being so registered the title condition to which it relates is discharged, renewed, imposed, preserved or varied according to the terms of the order.[6] An order which disapplies a development management scheme or preserves such a scheme and which has taken effect in accordance with any rules made by Scottish Ministers may also be registered against the units of the development by the owners association or as the case may be by an owner of a unit of the development.[7] Where there is a conveyance on a voluntary acquisition by an acquiring authority which affects the scheme then the order can also be registered by any person proposing to register the conveyance. On the order being so registered the scheme will be disapplied or preserved as the case may be depending on the decision of the Tribunal.

---

[4] *Phillips v Lavery*, 1962 S.L.T. (Sh. Ct.) 57.
[5] 2003 Act, s.104(1).
[6] 2003 Act, s.104(2).
[7] 2003 Act, s.104 3).

CHAPTER 14

THE LAW OF THE TENEMENT

THE EXISTING LAW

Introduction

In his book, *The Tenement; A Way of Life,* Frank Worsdall points out that **14–01** tenements or blocks of flats, were used in Scotland as early as the six-teenth century.[1] However, very little was written about the law in this area and there are very few reported cases prior to 1800. It is not clear what the reason for that is, but it may be that few legal issues arose, or that matters were resolved more or less amicably by the occupants. In the past, a failure by proprietors to agree on repairs has given rise to problems, the most extreme example being one which resulted in a con-tract being taken out on the life of one proprietor who would not agree to a scheme for repairs![2]

The physical tenement

As a physical matter a tenement consists of two or more units which are **14–02** under the same roof and enclosed by the same outer walls. In many instances, the units are all residential, but it not uncommon to find that the units on the ground floor are shops with the dwellings above. In some instances, there may be small commercial units in the upper floors with the rest of the units being dwellinghouses.

Different ownership regimes

Because there are at least two and often a number of units all under the **14–03** one roof, matters of ownership and maintenance obviously differ from what pertains in relation to many other dwellinghouses. Owners of semi-detached houses share a wall, as do the owners of terraced hoses, but the roof and other walls are probably not owned in common with any other proprietor. In the case of a tenement, an individual unit owner owns certain things exclusively, most of them being within the unit. When the unit owner is the sole owner, it follows that the owner has the sole responsibility for maintenance. Other items may be owned in common with one other proprietor. For example, the joists above one unit form part of the ceiling of that unit, but also form part of the floor of the unit above, and walls separating flats may be owned in common

---

[1] p.3.
[2] *Baxter v HMA*, 1998 S.L.T. 414; 1997 S.C.C.R. 437.

by the two proprietors on either side. In other instances, there are items which may be owned in common by all of the proprietors, and the roof and the *solum*, or ground on which the tenement is built, are frequently in this position. It is obvious that there may be different ownership regimes close to each other. For example, the chimney head or stack may be owned in common by all of the proprietors, but the chimney pots will usually be owned by the individual proprietors whose units they serve. The obligations in relation to maintenance are usually a mirror image of the ownership regime. Where they differ there are difficulties.

Deeds of condition

14–04　In many instances, a deed of conditions will regulate the ownership and maintenance regimes. Such deeds are common in Glasgow where they have been in use for a considerable period. They are also common in new flatted developments where there may be several blocks of flats all within the one development. In such a case, there may be items, for example, the unbuilt on part of the development which are owned by and have to be maintained by all of the proprietors.

The unworkable common law

14–05　If a deed of conditions or similar regulatory deed does not exist, or is silent on a particular matter, the common law comes into play. At common law, the roof is owned by the upper proprietor(s) and the maintenance obligations reflect that.[3] Thus, if the roof needs repair, or worse, replacing, it is the sole responsibility of the upper proprietors. This will involve erecting scaffolding and health and safety considerations are also relevant. The upper proprietors may not be able to afford to repair the roof, far less replace it and if the necessary works are not carried out the other proprietors may suffer. Even if the failure to repair the roof does not cause physical damage to their units, these units may be unsaleable because of the condition of the roof. If the upper proprietor in such a case does not accept that the roof needs to be repaired, or cannot afford to carry the repairs out, the remaining proprietors have a right of common interest which permits them to instruct the repairs and then to recover from the proprietor of the upper flat. It is, of course, unlikely that recovery would be possible in every case.

14–06　The roof is not the only problem with the common law. For example, if the parts which are owned in common by two or more of the proprietors need repair, the consent of the other proprietors concerned would normally be needed, and so if one objects, or cannot be found, or is legally incapable of giving consent, the repairs might not go ahead, unless they can be said to be necessary to protect the common property.[4]

14–07　Because of the difficulties which arise from the uncertainties of the common law, deeds of conditions often exist which contain detailed information about the ownership and maintenance regimes. One

---

[3] *Taylor v Dunlop* (1872) 117 25; *Sanderson's Trustees v Yule* (1897) 25R. 211.
[4] *Bell Prin.* S.1075; see *Rafique v Amin*, 1997 S.L.T. 1385.

feature of these is usually that the common law position regarding the ownership and maintenance of the roof and the *solum* is changed and these are owned by all of the proprietors who are also obliged to maintain them. In many instances, the deed of conditions will have a mechanism for appointing a factor whose responsibilities include instructing repairs and replacements. However, not all deeds do deal with all matters, and not every tenement is governed by such a deed. The Scottish Law Commission published a discussion paper and that was followed in 1998 by a report.[5] In March 2003, the Scottish Executive published a Consultation Paper on the law of the tenement. Responses were sought by July and in September, these were published. On January 30, 2004 a Bill from the Scottish Executive was presented to the Scottish Parliament. It is anticipated that it will be passed without difficulty and come into force on November 28, 2004.

THE NEW LAW

The tenement legally defined

The Tenements (Scotland) Bill defines a tenement[6] as: **14–08**

> "a building or a part of a building which comprises two related flats which, or more than two such flats at least two of which:
>
> (a) are, or are designed to be, in separate ownership; and
> (b) are divided from each other horizontally;
>
> and, except where the context otherwise requires, includes the *solum* and any other land pertaining to that building or as the case may be, part of the building; and the expression 'tenement building' shall be construed accordingly."

In determining whether flats comprised in a building or part of a building are related for the purposes of the statutory definition regard shall be had among other things to the title of the tenement and any tenement burdens which treat the building or part thereof for that purpose as if it were a tenement.[7] A flat is defined[8] as including any premises whether or not used or intended to be used for residential purposes and whether or not on the one floor. It should always be borne in mind that the Bill covers commercial properties. A tenement burden is defined[9] as any real burden within the meaning of the 2003 Act which affects the tenement or any sector in the tenement. A sector is defined[10] as a flat, any close or lift or any other three-dimensional space not comprehended by a flat, close or lift. The tenement building is taken to be entirely divided into sectors. *Solum* is defined[11] as the ground on which a building is erected. The

---

[5] Scot Law Com. No. 162.
[6] Tenements (Scotland) Bill, s.23 (hereinafter the 2004 Bill).
[7] 2004 Bill, s.23(2).
[8] 2004 Bill, s.25(1); this definition is the amended definition at Stage 2.
[9] 2004 Bill, s.25(1).
[10] 2004 Bill, s.25(1).
[11] 2004 Bill, s.25(1).

definition is wide enough to cover Victorian tenements of dwelling-houses or shops and dwellinghouses, modern blocks of flats and conversions of former self contained dwellinghouses into two or more flats. There could be a situation where part of a building is a tenement but another part is not. For a building to be a tenement it must comprise related flats. Accordingly if one half of a large semi-detached building were to be converted into two or more flats that would be a tenement but the other part of the building namely the other unconverted semi-detached dwellinghouse would not be part of that tenement. Similarly a terrace of tenemental properties with mutual gables will not be a single tenement but a series of independent tenements each governed by their own tenemental burdens and conditions and a tenement management scheme.[12] Apart from these special considerations the physical structure of any building comprising more than one unit will also be relevant in coming to a view as to whether or not a building is a tenement within the meaning of the Bill. If the title deeds of the various units in the building create common rights and impose burdens of maintenance on common property these will be relevant factors in deciding whether a building fulfils the statutory requirements.

The scope of the 2004 Bill—human rights

14–09   The two main purposes of the legislative proposals are (i) to enact provisions dealing with the law of the tenement which will replace the existing common law and clarify the doubts which exist there, and (ii) to provide a statutory scheme for maintenance for tenements. The existing law of the tenement is based on the law of common interest. It favours exclusive ownership of part of the tenement slice by slice and floor by floor with a common interest in those parts of the tenement which are part of a particular slice but which provide either support or shelter for the whole building. Most other jurisdictions have a statutory code for tenements, flatted properties or condominiums. This is what the 2004 Bill intends to produce although it is in much modified form in comparison with the detailed codes which apply elsewhere. One of the difficulties which faces the framers of legislation of this type is to decide whether or not it will apply across the board no matter what the existing titles say or whether it will only apply where the existing titles are silent. Another difficulty which presents itself is whether or not the new statutory code should apply to existing tenement properties no matter when they were built or whether it should only apply to tenements and blocks of flats erected after the coming into effect of thelegislation. Altering a person's rights of property or ownership is a matter of some difficulty because of Article 1 of Protocol 1 to the European Convention on Human Rights which is now part of Scots Law. In general terms Article 1 of Protocol 1 provides that the state cannot interfere with the property rights of individuals except in the general public interest. It is the author's view that the abolition of feudal tenure does not contravene Article 1 of Protocol 1 even although it abolishes without compensation a property right, namely the estate of superiority. However altering ordinary property rights, even to the extent of creating common rights

---

[12] 2004 Bill, s.4 and Schedule in so far as applicable.

is another matter. For this reason the approach of the Bill is to leave property rights very much as they are while imposing statutory obligations of maintenance no matter who actually owns the part of the tenement which is in need of repair.[13]

OWNERSHIP

Retention of the common law

The Scottish Law Commission, while accepting that the common law is uncertain in relation to some matters, recommended that it be retained, and that approach is followed in the 2004 Bill. The Commission did consider the possibility of a radical approach which would have made all parts of a tenement used in common, common property. Where the titles did not alter the common law that would have resulted in a substantial re-distribution of ownership within the tenement. For some that would have meant a loss of property rights and for others the acquisition of property rights. Those affected persons would have purchased their properties against the background of the old property regime within the tenement. Where the titles are silent upper flats may be significantly less expensive because they carry an obligation to maintain the roof and lower flats in the same tenement consequently more expensive. Furthermore, the loss of property rights ought to sound in compensation which would be difficult to assess. All of these matters gave rise to concerns that any legislative re-distribution of property rights within a tenement might fall foul of Article 1 of Protocol 1 of the of the European Convention on Human Rights. The Commission also took also took on board that deeds of conditions had been drafted with the existing common law in mind and if there was a radical overhaul of property rights these deeds might have to be interpreted differently. **14–10**

Application to all tenements

The Scottish Law Commission recommended that the new law as set out in the Tenements (Scotland) Act should apply not only to tenements constructed after it comes into force, but also to tenements existing at that time. They also recommended that it should be permissible to make other or different provisions in the titles themselves. That matter was put out for discussion by the Scottish Executive and three-quarters of the respondents agreed. That said, the Commission recognised that it would not be practical to apply the new law to all tenements without exception and so they proposed a Tenement Management Scheme which would allow the owners to take decisions about maintenance of the property within the Scheme. **14–11**

---

[13] For a general discussion on human rights issues in relation to land tenure reform, see Ch.16 below.

The new rules of ownership

14–12   Sections 1 to 3 of the 2004 Bill effectively restate the common law rules of ownership with some clarification. Taking the Bill as a whole however the difference in approach is quite radical in as much as maintenance obligations are no longer tied to ownership. There would be little point in a Tenements (Scotland) Bill which did not change the law relating to maintenance and management. Thus, although where the titles are silent, the roof will still pertain to the upper flat, the roof will be scheme property for the purposes of maintenance.

BOUNDARIES AND PERTINENTS

Title to rule

14–13   Sections 1 to 3 of the 2004 Bill deal with the boundaries and pertinents of the various sectors in the tenement. The legislation assumes that a sector which is a self-contained flat will be adequately described in the deeds or title sheet of that flat. Section 1 provides however that so far as ownership, boundaries and pertinents are concerned the existing title deeds will rule. It is provided[14] that except in so far as any different boundaries or pertinents are constituted by virtue of the title to the tenement or any enactment the boundaries and pertinents of sectors shall be determined in accordance with sections 2 and 3. A title to the tenement means any conveyance or reservation of property which affects the tenement or any sector in the tenement or the title sheet of any interest in the tenement or any such sector.[15]

Boundaries of flats

14–14   The boundary between any two contiguous flats (described as sectors for the purposes of the legislation) is the middle line of the structure that separates them.[16] However where the boundary is an external part of the building such as an exterior wall or foundations and *solum* then the whole wall or *solum* adjacent or subjacent to that flat or sector will be within the ownership of that flat or sector.[17] Accordingly where the titles are silent a top flat extends to and includes the roof over that flat[18] and a bottom flat extends to and includes the *solum* under that flat.[19] Where the structure separates two contiguous sectors such as a flat and a close but wholly or mainly serves only one of these sectors that thing is in its entire thickness owned with the sector which it serves.[20] The obvious example here would be a door or a window in a wall. In terms of the legislation the boundary between the flat and the common close would

---

14 2004 Bill, s.1(1).
15 2004 Bill, s.1(2).
16 2004 Bill, s.2(1).
17 2004 Bill, s.2(1)(b).
18 2004 Bill, s.2(3).
19 2004 Bill, s.2(4).
20 2004 Bill, s.2(2).

be the middle line of the wall. It would not however be the middle line of a door or window which served a particular flat. These are owned exclusively with the flat.

Roof, roof void and dormers

Where the titles are silent the top flat extends to and includes the roof **14–15** over that flat.[21] The words "extends to" necessarily imply that where the titles are silent any attic or roof space will also pertain to the top flat. Where the roof of the tenement building slopes a sector such as a top flat which includes the roof or any part of the roof also includes the triangle of air space above the slope of the roof up to the highest point of the roof which is normally the ridge in a pitched roof.[22] The point of the special provision is that it would allow the owner of a top flat who owns the roof or that part of the roof above the flat to throw out a dormer into the triangle of air space. This statutory provision might be said to alter the common law rules of ownership in relation to the air space as they exist at the moment. The existing common law would imply that ownership of the air space vests in the owners of the *solum*.[23] It should be noted of course that if the titles provide that the roof is common then although the rood void or attic space may be in the ownership of the top flat the rules of common property will apply to the roof and the owner of the top flat cannot throw out a dormer or otherwise interfere with the roof without the consent of all the other common owners. For one thing that would be an interference with a common roof. For another if the *solum* is common or owned by the owner of the ground flat then the incursion into the air space may be objected to by the owner or owners of the *solum*. The special provision relating to the triangle of air space formed by the ridge and pitch of the roof would only apply in a case where the roof was in the owner-ship of the top flat. It follows that if the roof is common the triangle of air space is also common. So far as velux windows are concerned these also are an interference with the roof and if it is common it is thought that the owners of the roof could prevent the top flat proprietor from inserting these windows. However the law of common property does allow a common owner to make normal uses of the common property and it could be argued, for example, that if there are existing skylights in the common roof and they have been there since the building was erected or have been in position and tolerated for a considerable period of time, a velux window is a similar use to which objection could not be taken. The velux window would have to be properly installed so that the shelter of the roof is maintained. There is no pro-vision in the Bill which deals with dormers which have been thrown out of a common roof in the past. These dormers do cause difficulties from time to time when the top flat is sold. It should always be borne in mind however that positive prescription can sometimes cure any title defect provided that the description of the top flat in a deed more than 10 years old is *habile* to include the dormer. Thus a general

---

[21] 2004 Bill, s.2(3).
[22] 2004 Bill, s.2(7).
[23] *Watt v Burgess' Trustees* (1891) 18 R. 766.

description of a top flat as the topmost flat or dwellinghouse which at the time the deed was granted did include a dormer bedroom followed by ten years possession of the flat with the dormer should suffice provided there has been no challenge during the ten year period.[24] The law of encroachment and personal bar should also be borne in mind. Where an encroachment such as a dormer window has been in position for a considerable time and the owners of the roof or air space above have made no objection or where previous owners have actually consented courts are very reluctant to order removal of the offending structure[25] although in some cases they may.[26] Acquiescence or personal bar has been held to transmit to singular successors in cases of encroachment on heritable property.[27] As an alternative to ordering removal of an offending structure which is an encroachment a court can award damages but these damages are likely to be minimal in relation to an encroachment which has been in position for a number of years without objection.

Air space

14–16   Apart from the triangle of air space up to the ridge of the roof already referred to ownership of the air space above the tenement goes with ownership of the *solum* or part of the *solum* if it is in diverse ownership. If the *solum* is common to all proprietors in the tenement then the air space above the ridge of the roof will similarly be common.[28] If the roof is common then the triangle of air space to the ridge of the roof will also be common because it pertains to the roof.[29]

Close

14–17   "Close" is defined as a connected passage, stairs and landings within a tenement building which together constitute a common access to two or more of the flats.[30] Close, as defined, extends to and includes the roof over and the *solum* under the close.[31] This definition of course only applies if the titles are silent although few titles go to the lengths of defining the boundaries of the close as such. A close is a sector of the tenement as is a lift. Accordingly where a flat wall bounds with a close and the close is common the boundary will be the middle line. If the titles are silent concerning ownership of the close then it will become a common pertinent.[32]

---

[24]   Prescription and Limitation (Scotland) Act 1973, s.1.
[25]   *Anderson v Brattisanni's*, 1978 S.L.T. (Notes) 42.
[26]   See *Property Selection and Investment Trusts Ltd v United Friendly Insurance plc*, 1998 S.C.L.R. 314.
[27]   *Duke of Buccleuch v Magistrates of Edinburgh* (1865) 3 M. 528.
[28]   2004 Bill, s.2(6).
[29]   2004 Bill, s.2(7).
[30]   2004 Bill, s.25(1).
[31]   2004 Bill, s.2(5).
[32]   2004 Bill, s.3(1).

Pertinents

Where the titles are silent as to ownership the Bill provides that certain **14–18**
pertinents will attach to each of the flats. The law of pertinents has of
course been described as both confused and confusing.[33] Nevertheless
the law of pertinents has saved the day in many cases where some
common part or other of a tenement has been omitted by mistake in a
conveyance. Section 3 of the 2004 Bill clarifies the law of pertinents so
far as tenements are concerned by identifying what are pertinents and
by making them common property.

The service test

While the common law provides for ownership in common of the close **14–19**
or common passage and the stairway, it is not clear whether it is ownership in common by all of the proprietors, or whether the ownership
in common is limited to those parts of the building which are served, for
example, by the stairway.[34] If it were the latter, the owners of the ground
floor flats would not have any rights of ownership in the stairway, and
would have a right of ownership in the passage only if the flat had a
door which opened on to that passage. That is usually the case, but not
always. The Scottish Law Commission recommended that ownership
should be based on the benefit or service to the flat. Adopting that test
the Commission proposed that each flat would have an equal share in
all the parts serving that flat. This would mean that not only the
common passage and stairs, but also pipes and cables for gas, water, and
electricity services would be common.

Common services

In relation to pipes, rhones, flues, conduits, cables, tanks, chimney stacks, **14–20**
fire escapes and other common services, the Bill provides[35] that where the
titles are silent and a pipe etc. serves more than one flat, then each flat
served by the pipe should have a right of common ownership share in that
pertinent. That differs from the position originally taken by the Executive,
but reflects what was suggested by the consultees. What is specifically
provided is that if a tenement includes any part such as a path, outside
stair, fire escape, rhone pipe, flue, conduit, cable, tank or chimney stack or
indeed any other part not already dealt with as a pertinent then if that part
wholly serves one flat it attaches as a pertinent to that flat alone. Where
however such a part serves two or more flats then it attaches to each of the
flats served as a pertinent as a right of common property in the whole of
that part. In relation to the chimney stacks, the Bill provides[36] that the
share allocated to each flat will be determined by the number of flues in
each flat. Thus if there are eight owners each with one flue, they will each
have an eighth share, but if there are nine flues and one flat has two flues,
there will be nine shares, and that flat will have two-ninths.

---

[33] Halliday, *Conveyancing Law and Practice* (2nd ed.), paras 33–38.
[34] See 18 *Stair Memorial Encyclopaedia*, para. 231 and authorities referred to therein.
[35] 2004 Bill, s.3(4).
[36] 2004 Bill, s.3(5).

Gardens and attached ground

14–21   Specific recommendations relate to the garden and other ground attached to the tenement. The Scottish Law Commission recommended that the common law position relating to the garden ground should prevail and so it will be owned by the ground floor flat or flats. Any land other than the *solum* of the tenement building which pertains to the tenement attaches as a pertinent to the bottom flat most nearly adjacent to the land or part of the land where the titles are silent as to owner-ship.[37] This provision however does not apply to any part of the ground which constitutes a path, outside stair or any other way of affording access to any sector other than that flat. Such paths or stairs are governed by the service test.[38]

Closes, passages and lifts

14–22   In general terms each flat has a right of common property as a pertinent in any close or any lift by means of which access can be obtained to more than one of the flats.[39] The definition of a close as including stairs and land-ings should be borne in mind. If the close or lift does not afford a means of access to a flat then that flat shall not have the benefit of this common right or pertinent.[40] It should be borne in mind that this statutory provision will only apply where the titles are silent. In many cases passages, stairs, land-ings and lifts are made the common property of all flats in a tenement or block. This can sometimes cause difficulty where a ground floor proprie-tor is aggrieved at having to pay a share of the cost of maintenance of a lift which he or she never uses. The statutory provision caters for this even-tuality but it will only apply where the titles are silent.

Share of common property pertinents

14–23   Where the statutory provisions apply and a pertinent attaches to a par-ticular flat as a right of common property then the shares of the common property applying to each flat shall be equal shares.[41] The only excep-tion to this is where the common property is a chimney stack in which case the share allocated to a flat is determined in accordance with the ratio which the number of flues serving that flat in the stack bears to the total number of flues in the stack.

MAINTENANCE AND MANAGEMENT

The common law

14–24   Where the title deeds are completely silent in relation to maintenance and management of common parts in a tenement then under the exist-ing law the obligations will depend on whether or not any parts of the

---

[37] 2004 Bill, s.3(3).
[38] 2004 Bill, s.3(4).
[39] 2004 Bill, s.3(1).
[40] 2004 Bill, s.3(2).
[41] 2004 Bill, s.3(5).

tenement have been made common. If they have been made common but there are no provisions for maintenance or management then only essential repairs can be insisted upon because of the rule that every common owner is entitled to a say in the management of the common property. If the deeds are silent as to common ownership then the improperly understood law of common interest will apply. In terms of that law the owner of the roof must maintain the roof but only so as to provide shelter for the floors below. Similarly the owner of the ground flat cannot interfere with the *solum* or the foundations so as to endanger the structural stability of the tenement. Apart from this there are few clear rules. The major drawback of the common law is that it does not provide adequately for a system of maintenance and decision-making. If an item is owned in common by all of the proprietors, they would be obliged to maintain it, but it follows from that that the consent of all would be required for any routine repairs unless absolutely necessary. If there is a security over the flat, the conditions of that may also provide that the consent of any heritable creditor is required. In practice, it may be impossible to obtain all of the consents required, and in such a case, it may be that a repair or other work is not done, or the remaining proprietors instruct the work, in the knowledge that they will not be able to recover the share from any proprietor who cannot give, or refuses to give consent.

The statutory Tenement Management Scheme

The Scottish Law Commission recommended that the norm should be that a majority can make decisions, and the mechanism through which that would be achieved would be the Tenement Management Scheme. The Commission thought that this scheme should apply only to existing buildings, and that future buildings should be governed either by the Development Management Scheme or by a scheme drawn up by the developers. The Tenement Management Scheme is applied to all tenements,[42] except those to which the Development Management Scheme applies.[43] The Executive justifies that approach on its simplicity, and a significant majority of these who responded to the Consultation Paper favoured the proposal that the Tenement Management Scheme should apply to all buildings and not just existing ones. **14–25**

The Scheme which contains eight rules providing for a system of maintenance and management did not prove to be controversial. Essentially it is a fall back Scheme. The Scheme cannot apply while a development Scheme[44] is in force.[45] The provisions of rule 1 of the Scheme apply if it is relevant for the purpose of interpreting any other provision of this Scheme.[46] Rule 1 sets out the scope of the Scheme, the meaning of a Scheme decision and other definitions. For a proper understanding of the Scheme it is necessary to take section 4 of the Bill and the Scheme together. **14–26**

---

[42] 2004 Bill, s.4.
[43] 2003 Act, ss.71–74; and see Ch.10 above.
[44] In terms of the 2003 Act, s.71.
[45] 2004 Bill, s.4(2).
[46] 2004 Bill, s.4(3).

Relationship with Title Conditions (Scotland) Act 2003

14–27   The 2003 Act contains detailed provisions relating to community burdens and these burdens can provide for managers, meetings and maintenance. In the case of tenements however the 2004 Bill will apply and sections 28(1)(a) and (d) and (2)(a), 29 and 31 of the 2003 Act will not apply where the community consists of one tenement.[47]

Rule 1—scope and interpretation—definition of maintenance

14–28   The Scheme provides for the management and maintenance of scheme property of a tenement.[48] Scheme property is defined as any part of a tenement which is common property of two or more owners or any part of a tenement not being common property which is by virtue of a tenement burden maintainable by two or more owners.[49] This definition will be adequate where the titles provide for the usual common parts. However if the deeds are wholly or partially silent the following parts of a tenement are also scheme property[50]:

>   (i)   the ground in which it is built;
> (ii)   its foundations;
> (iii)   its external walls;
> (iv)   its roof (including any rafter or other structure supporting the roof);
>   (v)   if it is separated from another building by a gable wall that part of the gable which is part of the tenement building;
> (vi)   any wall (not being a common gable) beam or column that is load bearing.

Certain parts are specifically excluded from Scheme property. These are any extension which forms part of one flat or any door, window, skylight, vent or other opening which serves only one flat. Thus the roof of an extension will not be Scheme property. Any chimney stack or chimney flue is also excluded.[51] A Scheme decision is a decision which is made either in accordance with a tenement burden or burdens providing a procedure for making decisions or where there is no such burden in accordance with rule 2 of the Tenement Management Scheme. There has been much difficulty in the past over what might be regarded as normal maintenance or repair.[52] In many cases flat owners, factors and property managers have had great difficulty in carrying through upgrading schemes which include not only repair and maintenance but improvement. Even where the main parts of the building are common property difficulties arise because of the unanimity rule. Maintenance is defined in the Bill[53] as including repairs and replacement, cleaning, painting and other routine works, gardening and day to day running of

---

[47]   2004 Bill, s.223(5) adding s.31A to the 2003 Act.
[48]   rule 1.1.
[49]   rule 1.2 (a) and (b).
[50]   rule 1.2 (c).
[51]   rule 1.3.
[52]   See *Rafique v Amin*, 1997 S.L.T. 1385.
[53]   rule 1.5.

a tenement and the reinstatement of a part (but not most) of the tenement building, but not including demolition, alteration or improvement unless reasonably incidental to the maintenance. The author suspects that this is as good a definition as one can get keeping, as it does, the fine balance between a sensible improvement and an unnecessary upgrading. If a tenement were to be serviced by lead pipes and these pipes were in need of repair the statutory definition of maintenance would allow for their replacement by copper pipes or some other modern material. At the other end of the scale of course a repainting scheme which provided for an expensive mural on an end gable would not fall within the definition of maintenance. Unfortunately there are likely to be many cases in between. One would, for example, think that it was sensible to replace old rotten window frames with new double glazed units. Clearly there could be an argument that replacing a single glazed unit with a double glazed unit was a clear case of improvement which was not incidental to ordinary maintenance or repair. In such a case an argument might however be based on cost. It is conceivable that there might not be a great difference in cost between single glazing and double glazing given that double glazing units tend to come ready made. So far as roofs are concerned they can be repaired and re-patched from time to time but ultimately the time will come when piecemeal repair is uneconomic and complete reroofing is dictated. In such a case replacement of the roof would be incidental to maintenance. Rule 1 also contains other definitions. A manger is a person appointed either in terms of the title deeds or by virtue of rule 3.1 (c) (i) to manage the tenement. Scheme costs are defined in rule 4.1. Where a flat is owned by two or more persons then either of them or any one of them may do anything that the owner is entitled to do by virtue of the scheme.[54]

Rule 2—procedure for making scheme decisions—majority rule

Rule 2 does not apply where a tenement burden provides procedures for the making of decisions by owners and, more importantly perhaps, the same procedures apply to each flat.[55] There has been doubt expressed over whether or not well thought out procedures for meetings and decisions could be real burdens. There is now no doubt that they can be ancillary burdens or may be manager burdens in terms of the 2003 Act. Where the deeds provide comprehensive procedures then these will apply and rule 2 will not apply. However there are many tenements where the individual titles to each flat are inconsistent. In some cases the burdens will contain provisions for meetings of proprietors, the appointment of factors and other matters. In other titles of properties in the same tenement these provisions may be omitted in whole or in part. In such cases rule 2 will apply as in other cases where there is no decision-making procedure at all laid down. In terms of rule 2 any decision to be made by the owners is made by vote and one vote is allocated as respects each flat and is exercisable by the owner of the flat or someone nominated by that owner.[56] If however a scheme decision

14–29

---

[54] rule 1.6.
[55] 2004 Bill, s.4(4).
[56] rule 2.2.

relates to maintenance of scheme property and the owner of a particular flat is not liable in accordance with the scheme for maintenance of the property concerned then that owner will have no vote.[57] If a flat is owned by two or more persons the vote may be exercised by either or any of them. If however the common owners of the flat disagree as to how the vote is to be cast then the vote is not counted unless one of the persons owns more than a half share in the flat in which case that person's vote will count. Similarly if two or more common owners of a flat own more than a half share together then their vote (if agreed) will count.[58] In most cases a scheme decision will be made by a simple majority vote of all the votes allocated.[59] However if the number of votes allocated does not exceed three then a scheme decision must be unanimous.[60] This provision will affect flatted conversions of single villas. If any owner wishes to call a meeting of the owners with a view to making a scheme decision at that meeting that owner must give the other owners at least 48 hours' notice of the date and time of the meeting, its purpose and the place where it is to be held.[61] There may be circumstances where an owner wishes to propose that a scheme decision is made but does not wish to call a meeting for the purpose. In such a case that owner must instead, unless it is impracticable to do so whether because of absence of any owner or for other good reason, consult on the proposal with each of the other owners of flats who have a vote and then count the votes cast by them.[62] The requirement to consult each owner is satisfied as respects any flat which is owned by more than one person if one of those persons is consulted.[63] These provisions are designed to overcome the difficulty which clearly exists in getting flat owners to come to meetings. For whatever reason owners of flatted properties in Scotland seem reluctant to come together to discuss matters of common concern. Presumably there is an inbuilt fear that a meeting will only result in a bill for repairs somewhere down the line. Where a scheme decision is made at a meeting it must be notified as soon as practicable to all the owners who were not present when the decision was made by such person as may be nominated for this purpose by the persons who made the decision.[64] In other cases where there has been informal consultation as opposed to a meeting the decision of the majority must be made known to each of the other owners by the owner who proposed that the decision be made.[65] Any owner or owners who did not vote in favour of a scheme decision to carry out or authorise maintenance to scheme property and who would be liable for not less than 75% of the scheme costs arising from that decision may within, a certain time limit, annul that decision by sending a notice stating that the decision is annulled to each of the other owners.[66] The time limit within which an annulment notice must be sent is 21 days

---

[57] rule 2.3.
[58] rule 2.4.
[59] rule 2.5.
[60] rule 2.6 (Stage 1).
[61] rule 2.7.
[62] rule 2.8.
[63] rule 2.9.
[64] rule 2.10(a).
[65] rule 2.10(b).
[66] rule 2.11.

after the date of a meeting at which the decision was taken or 21 days after the date on which notification of the making of a decision by consultation was sent.[67]

Rule 3—matters on which scheme decisions may be made

The provisions of rule 3 apply to the extent that there is no tenement burden in the titles enabling the owners to make scheme decisions in any matter on which a scheme decision may be made under rule 3. The title deeds of tenemental properties may contain general obligations of maintenance and repair but may not specify in detail what type of decisions may be taken. Rule 3 will fill this gap. A basic scheme decision is a decision on any of the following matters:[68]

14–30

(a) to carry out maintenance to scheme property.
(b) to arrange for an inspection of scheme property to determine whether or to what extent it is necessary to carry out maintenance to the property.
(c) except where there is a power conferred by a manager burden in terms of the 2003 Act to appoint a party to manage the tenement and to dismiss any such manager.
(d) to delegate to a manager power to decide that maintenance costing no more than a specific amount needs to be carried out to scheme property and to instruct it and to arrange for an inspection to be carried out.
(e) to arrange a common policy of insurance complying with section 15 of the Bill against such other risks as the owners may determine and to determine on an equitable basis the liability of each owner to contribute to the premium.
(f) to determine that an owner is not required to pay a share or some part of a share of scheme costs as may be specified.
(g) to authorise any maintenance of scheme property already carried out by an owner.
(h) to modify or revoke any scheme decision.

If the scheme owners decide under rule 3.1 (a) to carry out maintenance to scheme property or if a manager decides by virtue of a scheme decision under rule 3.1 (d) that maintenance is to be carried out on a scheme property the owners may make a scheme decision on certain matters. These matters are:

(a) to appoint on such terms as they may determine a person (who may be an owner or a firm) to manage the carrying out of the maintenance.
(b) to instruct or arrange for the carrying out of the maintenance.
(c) subject to rule 3.3 to require each owner to deposit a sum of money being a sum not exceeding that owner's apportioned share of a reasonable estimate of the cost of maintenance and

---

[67] rule 2.12.
[68] rule 3.1.

that by a certain date not less than 28 days after the requirement is made.

(d) to take such other steps as are necessary to ensure that the maintenance is carried out to a satisfactory standard and completed in good time.

Where a scheme decision is taken requiring each owner to deposit a sum of money then the decision will nominate a person as the holder of the deposits. A scheme decision which requires a deposit exceeding £100 or £100 or less where the aggregate of that sum and other sums required in the preceding 12 months exceeds £200 must be made by written notice to each owner. In such a case the sum must be deposited into an account known as a maintenance account as the owners may nominate for the purpose.[69] These financial limits may be altered by Scottish Ministers by order.[70] In so far as the maintenance account is concerned the owners may make a scheme decision which authorises certain persons to operate the account on behalf of all the owners.[71] Where notice is given under rule 3.3 requiring a deposit there must be an accompanying note which summarises the nature and extent of the maintenance to be carried out together with the following information:

(i) the estimated cost of carrying out that maintenance.
(ii) why the estimate is considered a reasonable estimate.
(iii) how the sum required from the owner in question and the apportionment among the owners have been arrived at.
(iv) what the apportioned shares of the other owners are.
(v) the date on which the decision to carry out the maintenance was made and the names of those by whom it was made.
(vi) a timetable for carrying out the maintenance including the dates by which it is proposed the maintenance will be commenced and completed.
(vii) the location and number of the maintenance account.
(viii) the names and addresses of the person who will be authorised to operate the account on behalf of the owners.

The maintenance account must be located with a bank or building society which is interest bearing and the authority of at least two persons or of a manager on whom the right to give authority has been conferred must be required before any payment is made from it.[72] If a basic scheme decision is modified or revoked[73] and this affects the information which is contained in the note to rule 3.4 (b) then fresh information, duly modified, must be sent again to the owners.[74] Any owner is entitled to inspect at any reasonable time any tender received in connection with the maintenance.[75] If the maintenance is not commenced by a specified refund date or the twenty-eighth day after the proposed date

---

[69] rule 3.3.
[70] 2004 Bill, s.4 (11).
[71] rule 3.4.
[72] rule 3.4(c).
[73] in terms of 3.1(h).
[74] rule 3.4(d).
[75] rule 3.4(e).

for its commencement as specified in the original notice under rule 3.4
(b) owners have certain rights in relation to the deposits. Any owner can
then demand by written notice from the persons who are authorised to
deal with the account repayment with accrued interest of the deposit
made.[76] If however the maintenance is actually commenced (even late)
before receipt of the notice requiring repayment then there is no obligation to make repayment. Sums held in the maintenance account are held
in trust for all the depositors and the trust purpose is payment of the
maintenance.[77] If there is any surplus left in the maintenance account
after payment of the costs of maintenance this is shared among the
owners by repaying each depositor with accrued interest the sum which
that person deposited less their actual share of the cost of maintenance
although it is open to the depositors to agree some other apportionment
of the surplus in writing.[78]

Rule 4—scheme costs: liability and apportionment

Apart from the special conditions set out in rule 5 liability is appor-   **14–31**
tioned in terms of rule 4. Scheme costs are defined[79] as:

(a) any costs arising from any maintenance or inspection of
scheme property where the maintenance or inspection is in
pursuance of, or authorised by, a scheme decision.

(b) any remuneration payable to a person appointed to manage
the carrying out of maintenance in terms of rule 3.2 (a).

(c) running costs relating to any scheme property (other than costs
incurred solely for the benefit of one flat).

(d) any costs recoverable by a local authority in respect of work
relating to any scheme property carried out by them by virtue
of any enactment.

(e) any remuneration payable to a manager.

(f) the cost of any common insurance to cover the tenement
arranged by virtue of rule 3.1 (e).

(g) any costs relating to the calculations of floor area made to
determine the appropriate share of maintenance costs.

(h) any other costs relating to the management of scheme property.

Where scheme costs relate to scheme property which is owned in
common in terms of the title then these costs are shared among the
owners in the proportions in which they share ownership of that common
property.[80] If the scheme costs relate to scheme property which is not
owned in common but must be maintained in terms of the title deeds by
two or more owners or is scheme property within the meaning of rule 1.2
(c) then the scheme costs are shared among the owners. The basis of
sharing will depend on whether or not the various flats or other units are
roughly of equal size. The rules provide for situation where some flats or
units are much bigger than others. In any case where the floor area of the

---

[76] rule 3.4(f).
[77] rule 3.4(g).
[78] rule 3.4(h).
[79] rule 4.1.
[80] rule 4.2(a).

largest or larger flat or unit is more than one and half times that of the smallest or smaller flat or unit each owner is liable to contribute towards these costs in the proportion which the floor area of that owner's flat bears to the total floor area of all (or both) flats or units. Where this is not the case then the scheme costs are simply shared equally among the flats and each owner is liable accordingly.[81] It should be borne in mind that the definition of "flat" includes not just a dwellinghouse but any other premises in a tenement building.[82] In some cases a part of a tenement may be scheme property because it is common property[83] and also scheme property.[84] If that is the case then unless there is a real burden in the title in relation to maintenance of this item[85] then it will be treated as common property for the purposes of sharing the scheme costs in terms of rule 4.2 in which case of course the costs are shared in proportion to the shares of common ownership.[86] Where the part in question is the roof over the close and that is common property by virtue of being a pertinent,[87] it will be treated for the purposes of the apportionment of the scheme costs[88] as scheme property[89] in which case the scheme costs will be apportioned either by floor area or equally in terms of rule 4.2 (b).[90] There is a special provision in relation to remuneration of a manager. Scheme costs which relate to this are shared equally among the flats or units and are not apportioned in any other way.[91] Insurance premiums are shared among flats or units in such proportions as may be determined by the owners.[92] If this is a common insurance arranged by virtue of a title condition then the premium is shared equally. Management costs[93] are also shared equally among flats or units. These special provisions in relation to remuneration of managers, insurance premiums, management and general management costs reflect the view that all of these items are of equal importance to flat or unit owners notwithstanding the size of the flats or units they own. The Bill provides that each owner is liable for scheme costs from the date when the scheme decision to incur these costs is made.[94] That date is the date of a meeting where the decision is made at a meeting or in any other case the date at which notification of the making of the decision is sent to each owner.[95] There are special cases however. Liability for the cost of any emergency work arises as soon as the work is instructed.[96] Liability for scheme costs which relate to the implementation of a statutory notice by a local authority[97] arises at the date of the statutory notice to which the costs relate.[98] Liability for accumulating scheme

---

[81] rule 4.2(b).
[82] 2004 Bill, s.25(1).
[83] In terms of rule 1.2(a).
[84] By virtue of rule 1.2(c).
[85] Under rule 1.2(b).
[86] rule 4.2(a).
[87] In terms of 2004 Bill, s.3(1)(a).
[88] In terms of rule 4.2.
[89] In terms of rule 1.2(c).
[90] rule 4.3(b).
[91] rule 4.4.
[92] In terms of rule 4.5.
[93] In terms of rule 4.1(g) or (h).
[94] 2004 Bill, s.10A(1).
[95] 2004 Bill, s.10A(2).
[96] 2004 Bill, s.10A(3).
[97] In terms of rule 4.1(d).
[98] 2004 Bill, s.10A(4).

costs such as insurance premiums accrue on a daily basis.[99] The provisions of rule 4 apply in relation to scheme costs unless a burden in the title provides that the full amount of these scheme costs is to be met by one or more of the owners in so far as that amount is not met by someone else.[1] Accordingly the rule will apply in cases where the title or the titles of all flats and other units in the tenement taken together do not contain provisions which provide for the full amount of scheme costs to be paid. There are titles where the shares of maintenance costs simply do not add up. In these cases rule 4 will apply.

Rule 5—scheme costs: special cases

Where two or more persons are owners of a flat or other unit in a tenement they are severally liable for the share of scheme costs applicable to the flat but as between themselves they are liable in proportion to the shares of ownership.[2] There may be cases where a share of scheme costs cannot for one reason or another be recovered from an owner. A scheme decision may have been made[3] determining a share or a part of a share will not be paid by a particular owner. The more likely case is where a share simply cannot be recovered from an owner because such owner has been sequestrated or simply vanished. In all of such cases the irrecoverable share must be paid by the other owners as if it were a scheme cost for which they are liable.[4] If the missing owner turns up and is solvent the owners who have paid his or her share have a right of recovery. In cases of procedural irregularity in relation to scheme decisions the rules provide that an owner who was not aware that scheme costs were being incurred or on becoming aware immediately objected to the incurring of these costs is not liable for any costs whether incurred before or after the date of objection.[5] The other proprietors must bear his or her share. The provisions of rule 5 are supplementary to the provisions of rule 4 and since they deal with special cases involving liability or lack of liability for scheme costs they are subject to anything that is in the title.[6] These provisions which saddle the remaining owner with other owners' bills have proved controversial.

14–32

Rule 6—emergency work

No procedures need be put in place either by way of meetings or consultations or scheme decisions if emergency work requires to be carried out. Emergency work is defined as work which, before a scheme decision can be obtained, requires to be carried out to scheme property to prevent damage to any part of the tenement or in the interest of health or safety.[7] Any owner may instruct or carry out emergency work without calling any meeting or engaging in any consultation.[8] Owners are liable for the

14–33

---

[99] 2004 Bill, s.10A(5).
[1] 2004 Bill, s.4(6).
[2] rule 5.1.
[3] Under rule 3.1(f).
[4] rule 5.2.
[5] rule 5.3.
[6] 2004 Bill, s.4(7) and (10).
[7] rule 6.3.
[8] rule 6.1.

cost of emergency work instructed or carried out as if the costs of that work were ordinary scheme costs arising from maintenance or inspection of scheme property.[9] The provisions of rule 6 relating to emergency work only apply to the extent there is no real burden in the titles which deals with emergency work as defined in the rule. For the provisions of the title to displace rule 6 however the work defined as emergency work in the title must be the same as the work defined as emergency work in rule 6.3.[9a]

Rule 7—enforcement

14–34   As between or among owners the Tenement Management Scheme is binding on all.[10] Any scheme decision is binding not only on all the owners but also on their successors as owners.[11] This has proved to be controversial but it only mirrors the existing law of real burdens. Any obligation which is imposed by the scheme or arising from a scheme decision may be enforced by any owner.[12] An owner may give written authorisation to any other person to enforce an obligation in terms of the scheme or a scheme decision and any person so authorised may bring any claim or action in their own name.[13] Presumably therefore an owner or the owners could authorise a manager to enforce the scheme or scheme decisions.

Rule 8—general

14–35   Procedural irregularities do not affect the validity of a decision.[14] Presumably however this is subject to the rule which states[15] that any owner who is directly affected by a procedural irregularity will have no liability for scheme costs. In so far as notices are concerned any notice may be given in writing by sending the notice to an owner or the owner's agent.[16] Notice is sent if it is posted, delivered or transmitted by electronic means.[17] Where an owner's name is not known then any notice may be addressed to "The Owner" or some other similar designation such as "The Proprietor".[18] A notice which is posted is taken to be given on the day of posting and a notice transmitted by electronic means is taken to be given on the day of transmission. Presumably a notice which is hand delivered is treated as having been given on delivery.[19] Since the provisions of this rule are general they are subject to any different provisions in any burden in the titles.

---

[9] rule 6.2.
[9a] 2004 Bill, s.4(8).
[10] rule 7.1.
[11] rule 7.2.
[12] rule 7.3.
[13] rule 7.4.
[14] rule 8.1.
[15] rule 5.3.
[16] rule 8.2.
[17] rule 8.3.
[18] rule 8.4.
[19] rule 8.5.

Inadequate title provision

In some cases the title deeds will make limited provision for manage- **14–36**
ment and maintenance. There may however be gaps which render
enforcement of these provisions difficult. In such cases the scheme will
apply where there are these gaps and references in the 2004 Bill or in the
scheme itself shall be read as references only to those provisions of the
scheme which apply.[20]

RESOLUTION OF DISPUTES

Social and psychological factors

It would be foolish to assume, the author supposes, that the fact that the **14–37**
Scottish Parliament has taken the trouble to pass a Tenements (Scotland)
Bill with a perfectly sensible management scheme will mean that all will
be sweetness and light up the close in the future. Human nature dictates
that some people will be more dominant or indeed aggressive than
others in relation to their so called rights. There will no doubt be those
owners who carry the Tenement Management Scheme with them on a
daily basis in much the same way as French citizens after the French
Revolution carried copies of the Code Napoleon. Some more timid flat
owners will be happy to sit back and let others take responsibility for
calling meetings, pushing through scheme decisions and instructing
maintenance. However these timid persons may themselves become
aggressive when asked to pay some money especially if they live in a
ground flat and the maintenance relates to the roof or top landing which
they have never seen. Accordingly the framers of the Bill, being realis-
tic people, have made provision for the resolution of disputes by application to the sheriff.[21] It should be noted that the provisions for
resolution of disputes apply where a management scheme other than a
development management scheme[22] applies in relation to the management of the tenement and a decision has been made by the owners in
accordance with the scheme.[23] Accordingly the statutory provisions do
not apply where the dispute relates to the interpretation or implementation of a tenement burden in a title. The statutory provisions provide
for an application to the sheriff for annulment of certain scheme decisions and also to applications to the sheriff for an order to resolve certain
disputes.

Application for annulment of scheme decisions

If a decision is made by a majority under the Tenement Management **14–38**
Scheme and an owner is not in favour of it he or she may, by summary
application, apply to the sheriff to have the decision set aside.[24] In such
a case the defenders are all the other owners and presumably therefore

---

[20] 2004 Bill, s.4(12).
[21] 2004 Bill, s.5.
[22] Under the 2003 Act, ss.71–74.
[23] rule 5.1.
[24] 2004 Bill, s.5 (1).

not just the majority who voted in favour of the decision.[25] Where the decision was made at a meeting the application to annul the decision must be made not later than 28 days after the date of the meeting.[26] In other cases where a decision is made after the consultation process the application to the sheriff must be made not later than 28 days after the date on which notice of the making of the decision was sent to the owner who wishes to make the application for annulment.[27] The sheriff must consider the age of the property, its condition, the cost involved and the reasonableness of that cost where the application is made in relation to the decision to carry out maintenance, improvements or alterations.[28] If the sheriff decides that the decision is either not in the best interests of all the owners affected, or is unfairly prejudicial to one or more of the owners he or she may order that the decision be annulled in whole or in part.[29] The sheriff may make consequential orders following on an annulment order in relation to the liability of owners for costs already incurred.[30] A right of appeal against an annulment order or a refusal to grant such an order lies to the Court of Session but only on a point of law[31] and the decision of the Court of Session on such an appeal is final.[32] A party wishing to appeal must do so within 14 days of the annulment order or the interlocutor dismissing the application. Where a scheme decision has been taken it appears as though no step can be taken to implement that decision until such time as the 28 day period for making application to the sheriff for annulment of the decision has expired.[33] Where an application to annul has been made and notified no step can be taken to implement the scheme decision until the application has been disposed of and the 14 day period for lodging an appeal to the Court of Session on a point of law has expired. Where an appeal to the Court of Session is lodged then no steps can be taken to implement the scheme decision until the appeal has been disposed of.[34] Where an application has been made to the sheriff but has been abandoned then the scheme decision can be implemented.[35] The provisions in relation to non-implementation of scheme decisions pending applications or appeals do not apply to a decision relating to work which requires to be carried out urgently.[36]

Applications to resolve disputes

14–39   An application may also be made to the sheriff to resolve certain disputes relating to the operation of the Tenement Management Scheme or the Act.[37] What information must be presented to the court is not made

---

[25] 2004 Bill, s.5(2).
[26] 2004 Bill, s.5(3)(a).
[27] 2004 Bill, s.5(3)(b).
[28] 2004 Bill, s.5(5).
[29] 2004 Bill, s.5(4).
[30] 2004 Bill, s.5(6).
[31] 2004 Bill, s.5(7).
[32] 2004 Bill, s.5(8).
[33] 2004 Bill, s.5(9)(a).
[34] 2004 Bill, s.5(9)(b)(i).
[35] 2004 Bill, s.5(9) (b) (i).
[36] 2004 Bill, s.5(10).
[37] 2004 Bill, s.6(1).

clear but the sheriff can make any order which is considered necessary or expedient or the sheriff may simply grant the order craved.[38] Once again there is an appeal to the Court of Session but only on a point of law[39] and the decision of the Court of Session is final.[40] Where the development management scheme applies[41] no application is competent under the 2004 Bill.[42]

COMMON INTEREST—SUPPORT AND SHELTER

Abolition of common interest

The previous law of the tenement relied on the principles of common   **14–40**
interest. Although the top most proprietor owned the roof void and roof his or her right of ownership was limited by the common interest of the other proprietors in the tenement. Accordingly the top most proprietor had to maintain the roof so as to provide shelter. Similarly the owner of the ground flat could do nothing to the foundations or the *solum* which might affect the structural integrity of the whole building because his or her right of ownership in the *solum* and foundations was limited by the common interest of all the other proprietors in the tenement. The law of common interest is particularly difficult to understand and the extent of the obligations which it imposes are far from clear.[43] In some cases the terminology in titles leaves room for doubt as to whether or not rights of common ownership or rights of common interest are being created.[44] The statutory provisions in the Bill and of the Tenements Management Scheme replace the existing rules of common interest as they apply to tenements.[45] Common interest may continue to apply however in relation to questions affecting a tenement and another building or former building such as an adjoining tenement or relating to any land which does not actually pertain to the tenement.

New duties of support and shelter

At common law common interest entitled an owner within a tenement   **14–41**
to rights of support, shelter, light and the right to use the chimney vents. These are not rights of property but real rights in the property of other parties which entitled one owner to carry out works on the property of another. Sections 8 and 9 of the Bill deal with the duty to provide support and shelter and introduce a prohibition against interfering with these. Section 14 deals with access for maintenance

---

[38] 2004 Bill, s.6(2).
[39] 2004 Bill, s.6(3).
[40] 2004 Bill, s.6(4).
[41] Under the 2003 Act, ss.71–74.
[42] 2004 Bill, s.6(1)(a).
[43] Cusine, *Common Interest Revisited*, 1998 E.L.R. 315.
[44] See *Barclay v McEwan* (1880) 7 R. 792; *WVS Office Premises Ltd v Currie* 1969 S.C. 170; Gordon, *Scottish Land Law* (2nd ed.), para.15–31 *et seq*; Reid, *The Law of Property in Scotland*, para.354 *et seq*; Reid, "Common Interest" (1983) 28 J.L.S. 428.
[45] 2004 Bill, s.7.

purposes. The right to use flues is dealt with in section 3 which provides that flues are pertinents of the various flats which they serve. The
statutory provision in relation to support and shelter is to the effect
that the owner of any part of a tenement building which provides or
is intended to provide support or shelter to any other parts must maintain the supporting or sheltering part so as to ensure that it provides
the support or shelter required.[46] However an owner is not obliged to
maintain any part of a tenement building if it would not be reasonable
to do so having regard to all the circumstances including in particular
the age of the tenement building, its condition and the likely cost of
maintenance.[47] Presumably therefore where a ruinous tenement property has been abandoned by all the owners bar one recalcitrant owner
that remaining owner cannot insist on the upper floor proprietors carrying out expensive repairs to provide shelter. This at least is the position in relation to the statutory provisions which are designed to
replace the law of common interest. There may of course be provisions
in the title. It should be borne in mind that the statutory provisions
replace the common interest provisions. They do not necessarily
supersede the obligation in the title. The duty which is imposed to
provide support and shelter is to be a statutory duty and may be
enforced by any other owner who is or would be directly affected by
any breach of that duty. Presumably therefore these statutory duties
are in the nature of statutorily created servitudes for shelter and
support.[48]

Prohibition and interference with support, shelter and light

14–42   No owner or occupier of any part of a tenement is entitled to do anything
in relation to that part which would or would be reasonably likely to
impair to a material extent the support or shelter provided to any other
part of the tenement building or the natural light enjoyed by any other
part of the tenement building.[49] It should be noted that this statutory prohibition applies not just to owners but also to occupiers of any part of a
tenement. The prohibition may be enforced by any such other owner who
is or would be directly affected by any breach of the prohibition. It should
be noted that the right to enforce is only vest in owners. Presumably
tenants of owners who are affected by a breach of the prohibition have no
direct rights against the party in breach.[50] The appropriate remedy would
be interdict if there is a threatened breach or continuing breach or
damages where loss has already occurred as a result of a breach of the
statutory duty. If an owner by virtue of the statutory obligations relating
to support and shelter carries out maintenance to any part of a tenement
and incurs costs and the management scheme provides for maintenance
of that particular part then the owner, despite the fact that the work has
been carried out by him or her in furtherance of his or her statutory obligation is entitled to recover from any other owner any share of the cost of
that maintenance for which that other owner would have been liable had

---

[46] 2004 Bill, s.8(1).
[47] 2004 Bill, s.8(2).
[48] 2004 Bill, s.8(3).
[49] 2004 Bill, s.9(1).
[50] 2004 Bill, s.9(2).

the maintenance been carried out by virtue of the management scheme in question.[51] Accordingly if maintenance work is carried out to the foundations in terms of the obligation of support as opposed to as a result of an ordinary scheme decision for maintenance the ground flat proprietor who has had to carry out this work will still be entitled to recover the share where the management scheme is in operation. If the management scheme is not in operation then there will of course be other title provisions which would allow recovery.

RIGHTS OF ACCESS

Access for maintenance purposes

Statutory rights of access will apply where an owner requires access for the following purposes:[52]

14–43

    (a) carrying out maintenance by virtue of the management scheme which applies in respect of the tenement.

    (b) carrying out maintenance to any part of the tenement owned (whether solely or in common) by the person requiring access.

    (c) carrying out an inspection to determine whether it is necessary to carry out maintenance.

    (d) determining whether the owner of the part is fulfilling his or her duties of support and shelter.[53]

    (e) determining whether the owner or occupier of the part is complying with the prohibitions of interference with support and shelter or natural light.[54]

    (f) where the floor area is relevant for the purposes of determining any liability of owners, measuring the floor are.

To exercise these rights of access the owner must give reasonable notice to the owner or occupier of the part to which access is to be taken.[55] If a development management scheme applies notice may be given by the manager of any owners' association to the owner or occupier of the part of the tenement over which access is required.[56] The notice must be reasonable unless access is required in respect of urgent maintenance.[57] An owner occupier may refuse to allow access or to restrict access to a particular time if having regard to all circumstances it is reasonable to refuse access.[58] It might be reasonable to refuse access if in fact the requirement to take access is unreasonable in itself. Where access has been allowed in terms of the statutory provision for any purpose the right may be exercised by owner or the manager who gave notice that access was required or any person authorised in writing.[59] Presumably therefore a tradesman

---

[51] 2004 Bill, s.10.
[52] 2004 Bill, s. 14(3).
[53] In terms of 2004 Bill, s.8(1).
[54] In terms of 2004 Bill, s.9(1).
[55] 2004 Bill, s.14(1).
[56] 2004 Bill, s.14(2).
[57] 2004 Bill, s.14(4).
[58] 2004 Bill, s.14(5).
[59] 2004 Bill, s.14(6).

with a written authorisation or a factor or surveyor would be entitled to access. Where an authorised person is liable for damage caused to any part of the tenement then although as a matter of the law of delict it may be the authorised person who is liable the owner who authorised that person or if the person was authorised by a manager in a development management scheme, the owners' association concerned are severally liable with the authorised person for the cost of remedying the damage.[60] In the normal way of course an owner or an owners' association who has to make payment in relation to the cost of such damage will have a right of relief against the authorised person who caused the damage. Where access is allowed, the party taking access must insure so far as reasonably practicable that the part of the tenement over which access is taken is left substantially in no worse condition.[60a] If this provision is not complied with, the owner who allowed access can carry out remedial work and recover the cost from the accessing owner.[60b]

INSURANCE

14-44   Quite apart from an obligation in the title to maintain a common insurance or indeed a scheme decision to maintain a common insurance there is an obligation on each owner to effect and keep in force a contract of insurance against prescribed risks for the reinstatement value of that owner's flat or any part of the tenement attaching to that flat as a pertinent.[61] It should be borne in mind that the definition of flat includes not just a dwellinghouse but any other premises in a tenement building.[62] Where a tenement burden requires each flat or unit to be insured by way of common policy then the duty of insurance is satisfied if a common policy is in existence.[63] In such a case the insurance must be a common policy. In so far as the prescribed risks are concerned these are to be set out in an order by Scottish Ministers.[64] There may be cases where it is difficult to obtain insurance against a particular risk. Where this occurs or where such insurance can only be obtained at an unreasonably high cost there is no duty to insure against that particular risk.[65] Owners are entitled to see evidence of insurance and payment of premiums in respect of other flats or units not later than 14 days after giving notice to any other owner.[66] The duty to insure may be enforced by any owner against another owner.[67]

LIABILITY FOR REPAIRS COSTS

14-45   Liability for costs pertains to the owner who does not cease to be liable by virtue only of ceasing to be an owner.[68] Where a person becomes a

---

[60]   2004 Bill, s.14(7).
[60a] 2004 Bill, s.14(8).
[61b] 2004 Bill, s.14(9).
[61]   2004 Bill, s.15(1).
[62]   2004 Bill, s.25(1).
[63]   2004 Bill, s.15(2).
[64]   2004 Bill, s.15(3).
[65]   2004 Bill, s.15(4).
[66]   2004 Bill, s.15(5).
[67]   2004 Bill, s.15(6).
[68]   2004 Bill, s.11(1).

new owner that person is severally liable with the former owner for relevant costs.[69] Accordingly anyone purchasing a flat or other unit in a
tenement will want to know that there are no outstanding charges. As
between new owner and old owner the new owner may recover any
amount which was properly due by the old owner.[70] These provisions
have caused some controversy. The costs for which owners are liable are
stated to be "relevant costs" which mean as respects any flat or unit in
a tenement any share of any costs for which the owner is liable by virtue
of the Tenement Management Scheme, by virtue of a real burden in the
title or by virtue of the Act.[71] The section applies to costs for which an
owner becomes liable after the day on which the Bill comes in to force
which will presumably be November 28, 2004. A successor owner who
has a right of relief against a previous owner for a share of costs does
not lose that right of relief simply because he or she has sold on again.[71a]
The five-year prescriptive period[72] will apply to any obligation to pay
money by way of costs under section 11 of the 2004 Bill.[73] In the same
way that the principles of common interest are abolished so far as tenement properties are concerned the rules which enable owners of
common property to recover the cost of necessary maintenance from
other owners of property will not apply in relation to common property
in a tenement where the maintenance of that property is provided for in
the management scheme which applies to the tenement.[74] The point of
this provision is to prevent owners carrying out routine (as opposed to
emergency) work then using the common law of common property to
recover costs without going through the decision-making procedures
which are set out in the management scheme.

DEMOLITION AND ABANDONMENT OF TENEMENT BUILDING

Ownership rights

One of the difficulties often encountered in relation to older tenemental   **14–46**
property which is beyond repair is obtaining the consent of all the
owners to demolition. In some cases the local authority in the exercise of
statutory powers may demolish in which case the problem then relates
to ownership of the *solum* of the site. The site may itself be available for
development but unless all those who own the *solum* or may have a
right of common interest in it can be traced the site may be sterilised or
a potential developer/purchaser may be faced with accepting a title
which is partially *a non domino*. There are provisions in the 2004 Bill in
relation to demolition and use of and disposal of the site. In the first place
demolition of a tenement will not of itself effect any change as respects
any right of ownership in the *solum* or the air space nor any right over
the land as a pursuit of any feat or sector.[75] Demolition is defined[76] as

---

[69]   2004 Bill, s.11(2).
[70]   2004 Bill, s.11(3).
[71]   2004 Bill, s.11(4).
[71a] 2004 Bill, s.11A.
[72]   In schedule 1 to the Prescription and Limitation (Scotland) Act, 1973.
[73]   2004 Bill, s.12.
[74]   2004 Bill, s.13.
[75]   2004 Bill, s.16.
[76]   2004 Bill, s.25(1).

including destruction and cognate expressions and demolition may occur on one occasion or over any period of time. Accordingly if each flat or unit owner owns their own flat or unit and has a right in common to the *solum* then on demolition taking place each flat or unit owner will have a common right of property in the vacant site, an exclusive right of property in the air space that was taken up by the flat or unit and a common right of property in the air space above the roof.

Cost of demolition

14–47   The provisions in relation to the apportionment of cost apply not only to total demolition of the tenement building but also to partial demolition.[77] The statutory provisions also apply to flats or units which were in the tenement before its demolition.[78] The titles may unusually make provision for the cost of demolition but if they are silent the cost is shared equally among the flats or units in the tenement except where one flat or unit has a very large floor area.[79] It should be borne in mind that the definition of flat would include other premises as well as a dwellinghouse. Where however the floor area of the largest or larger flat or unit in the tenement is more than one and half times that of the smallest or smaller flat or unit in the tenement the owner of each flat or unit is liable to contribute towards the cost of demolition in the proportion which the floor area of the flat or unit bears to the total floor area of all or both of the flats or units.[80] These provisions are designed to regulate liability among the owners themselves. They do not affect liability to third parties. Accordingly the provisions in relation to the cost of demolition are subject to section 123 of the Housing (Scotland) Act 1987 which makes provision in respect of the demolition of buildings in pursuance of local authority demolition orders and the recovery of expenses by local authorities. A local authority which has carried out demolition under that section can recover from the owners in such proportions as the owners may agree or failing agreement as is determined by arbitration.[81] Liability arises from the date of the agreement of an owner to the proposal that the tenement building is demolished.[82] Where there has been no agreement then liability arises from the date on which the carrying out of the demolition is instructed.[83] Where there is partial demolition only the owners of flats or units in the demolished part of the tenement will be liable for the costs.[84]

Use and disposal of site after demolition

14–48   Special provisions apply in a case where a tenement building has been demolished where two or more flats or units were in separate ownership. Accordingly the provisions will not apply where a single person

---

[77] 2004 Bill, s.17(4).
[78] 2004 Bill, s.17(5).
[79] 2004 Bill, s.17(1).
[80] 2004 Bill, s.17(2).
[81] 2004 Bill, s.17(6).
[82] 2004 Bill, s.17(3)(a).
[83] 2004 Bill, s.17(3)(b).
[84] 2004 Bill, s.17(4).

owned every flat or unit in the demolished tenement.[85] Unless the owners of all or both of the former flats or units agree or unless there is a requirement imposed by a tenement burden or otherwise to erect a building on the site or rebuild the tenement no owner may build on or otherwise develop the site.[86] This provision reflects the normal rule of common property which is to the effect that no one common owner can carry out any unusual operation without the consent of the others. Except where the owners have agreed or are required to build or develop the site then any owner of a former flat is entitled to apply for power to sell in accordance with the provision of Schedule 2 to the 2004 Bill.[87] Where a former flat or unit or unit has been owned *pro indiviso* by two or more people then any of the *pro indiviso* owners has the right to require that the site be sold.[88] This right is quite close to the right of a common owner to demand a division and sale. So far as the sharing of the proceeds of sale is concerned the normal division will be an equal sharing unless the titles provide otherwise.[89] However where the floor area of the largest or larger former flat or unit was more than one and half times that of the smallest or smaller former flat or unit then the proceeds of sale are to be shared among or between the flats or units in the proportion which the floor area of each flat or unit bore to the total floor area of all or both flats or units if evidence of floor area is readily available.[90] It should borne in mind that the definition of a flat or unit includes a business or other premises in the tenement. References to the site are a reference not just to the *solum* of the tenement building but also to all the air space which is directly above the *solum* and any land pertaining to the tenement as a means of access prior to demolition.[91] The prohibition of voluntary sale[92] may be enforced by any owner.[93] The provision is to the effect that any owner of a former flat or unit is entitled to apply for power to sell. Specific procedure is contained in Schedule 2 to the 2004 Bill.

Procedure on sale

The procedure is set out in Schedule 2 to the 2004 Bill. The procedure applies in relation to the sale of a vacant site and the sale of an abandoned tenement.[94] In either case, application is to the sheriff by summary application. The owner applying for the power of sale must give notice to the other owners. The sheriff must grant the power of sale unless satisfied that to do so would not be in the best interests of all the owners taken as a group or be unfairly prejudicial to one or more of the owners.[95] If there has been a previous unimplemented power of sale order the sheriff must revoke this.[96] A power of sale order must contain

14–49

---

[85] 2004 Bill, s.18(1).
[86] 2004 Bill, s.18(2).
[87] 2004 Bill, s.18(3).
[88] 2004 Bill, s.24(4).
[89] 2004 Bill, s.18(4).
[90] 2004 Bill, s.18(5).
[91] 2004 Bill, s.18(7).
[92] In terms of the 2004 Bill, s.18(2).
[93] 2004 Bill, s.18(6).
[94] In terms of the 2004 Act, s.20(1).
[95] 2004 Bill, Sch.2, para.1(4).
[96] 2004 Bill, Sch.2, para.1(4)(b).

the name and address of the owner in whose favour it is granted, the postal address of each flat or former flat and a sufficient conveyancing description of each flat or former flat.[97] Where title to a flat is registered the description must be the title number and in other cases must be by reference to a deed recorded in the Register of Sasines.[98] The application must state whether the sharing of the proceeds is to be equal or in accordance with floor area.[99] If floor area is to be the basis of the split the floor areas and proportions of proceeds must be stated.[1] A power of sale order has no effect until registered in the Land Register or recorded in the Register of Sasines and must be so recorded or registered within fourteen days of the date of making of order.[2] The owner who has obtained the power of sale order may sell by private bargain or public auction but must advertise and take all reasonable steps to ensure that the price at which the sale subjects are sold is the best that can be reasonably obtained.[3] Presumably the power of sale will allow the owner who has applied to sign a disposition under the power in the same way a heritable creditor executes a disposition under a power of sale. When the sale is settled the selling owner must, within seven days of settlement, calculate each owner's share and then apply it in the following order:[4]

> (a) by repaying any heritable creditor holding a security affecting the particular owner's flat;
> (b) by defraying expenses incurred in repaying the heritable creditor;
> (c) finally by paying the particular flat owner the remainder of his or her share of the proceeds.

If there is more than one heritable security they are to be repaid according to their ranking in order.[5] If any flat owner cannot be found by reasonable enquiry the selling owner may consign the net share in the sheriff court.[6] The selling owner must give the other owners a written statement showing the calculation and expenses.[7] The general expenses of the sale will of course be deducted before any flat owner's gross share is arrived at.[8]

Undischarged securities

14–50 Where the tenement building or the site is sold but there exists a heritable security over any flat or unit which was formerly part of the tenement and that security has not been discharged then on registration or recording of the disposition by the owner holding the power of sale order, all heritable securities affecting the sale subjects shall be discharged.[9]

---

[97] 2004 Bill, Sch.2, para.1(5).
[98] 2004 Bill, Sch.2, para.1(6).
[99] 2004 Bill, Sch.2, para.1(7).
[1] 2004 Bill, Sch.2, para.1(7)(b).
[2] 2004 Bill, Sch.2, para.2.
[3] 2004 Bill, Sch.2, para.3.
[4] 2004 Bill, Sch.2, para.4(1) and (2).
[5] 2004 Bill, Sch.2, para.4(3)
[6] 2004 Bill, Sch.2, para.4(4).
[7] 2004 Bill, Sch.2, para.4(5).
[8] 2004 Act, s.18(6A).
[9] 2004 Bill, Sch.2, para.5.

Sale of abandoned tenement building

Difficulties arise not just in relation to demolished tenements but also in relation to unoccupied tenements in a derelict condition. Where a tenement building has been entirely unoccupied by any owner or person authorised by an owner for a period of more than six months and it is unlikely that any such owner or other occupier will return then any one owner is entitled to apply for power to sell in accordance with the provision of Schedule 2 to the 2004 Bill.[10]

14–51

LIABILITY FOR CERTAIN COSTS

Liability to non-owners

Where any part of the tenement is damaged as the result of the fault of any person and the management scheme makes provision for maintenance of that part any other owner of a flat in the tenement who is required to contribute to the cost of maintenance of the damaged part but who at the time when the damage was done was not an owner of the damaged part will be deemed to be an owner for the purposes of determining liability between the owner damaging the part and the other owner.[11] Fault means any wrongful act, breach of duty or negligent act or omission which gives rise to liability and damages.[12] This provision covers the case where there is an obligation to maintain without ownership. Where there is damage owners of a tenement who are liable to pay for maintenance but who do not have ownership rights so that the injured party cannot recover the cost of repairs under the general law have a statutory liability to pay.

14–52

MISCELLANEOUS AND GENERAL

Amendments of 2003 Act

The 2004 Bill contains certain minor amendments of the 2003 Act.[13] Section 10 of the 2003 Act provides a continuing liability of former owners for the implementation of affirmative burdens. This provision will not apply where the special provisions in relation to the liability of owners and successors in the 2004 Bill apply.[14] Section 29 of the 2003 Act which deals with the power of majority to instruct common maintenance in a community is amended by the insertion of a new sub clause (3A) which provides for deposits for maintenance for sums exceeding £100 or £100 or less where the aggregate taken together with any other sums required in the preceding 12 months exceeds £200 in a maintenance account.[15] A new section 31A is inserted in to the 2003 Act which disapplies sections 78, 29 and 31 of the 2003 Act where the community consists of a tenement.[16]

14–53

---

[10] 2004 Bill, s.20.
[11] 2004 Bill, s.21(1).
[12] 2004 Bill, s.21(2).
[13] 2004 Bill, s.22(2).
[14] 2004 Bill, s.11 and 22(3).
[15] 2004 Bill, s.22(4).
[16] 2004 Bill, s.22(5).

Meaning of owner

14–54   The term owner is used throughout the 2004 Bill. An owner is a person who has right to a flat, whether or not that person has a completed title. If more than one person comes within the description of owner then owner means such person as has most recently acquired the right.[17] Where a heritable security has been granted over a flat and the heritable creditor has entered into lawful possession the term owner will include the heritable creditor in possession.[18] It should be noted that a heritable creditor who calls up, evicts and then exercises a power of sale is not deemed to be in possession even although they may have a set of keys. If two or more people own a flat in common then the term "owner" applies to all of these parties.[19] However in relation to certain rights conferred on owners[20] a *pro indiviso* owner can exercise the rights without consulting his or her fellow common owners.[21] In so far as obligations are concerned where two or more people own a flat then they are jointly and severally liable for any costs.[22] As between or among themselves they are liable in the proportions in which they own the flat.[23]

Floor areas

14–55   Certain calculations may be dependent on floor areas. The floor area of a flat is calculated for the purposes of the 2004 Bill by measuring the total floor area within the flats boundaries taking no account of any of the pertinents or a balcony or a loft or a basement used simply for storage.[24] A loft or basement which is used for purposes other than storage would require to be taken into account for the purposes of the calculation of floor area.

Notices and intimations

14-56   Any notice which is to be given to an owner other than under the Tenement Management scheme may be given by sending it to the owner or an agent.[25] "Sending" means posting, delivery or electronic transmission.[26] Where the name of the owner is not known, a notice may be addressed to the owner or the proprietor.[27] A notice posted is given on the day of posting and a notice electronically transmitted on the day of transmission.[28]

---

[17] 2004 Bill, s.24(1).
[18] 2004 Bill, s.24(2).
[19] 2004 Bill, s.24(3).
[20] in 2004 Bill, ss.5(1), 5(3), 6(1), 8(3), 9, 10, 14(1), 14(6), 14(7), 15(5), 15(6), 18, 20 and 21.
[21] 2004 Bill, s.24(4).
[22] 2004 Bill, s.24(5)(a).
[23] 2004 Bill, s.24(5)(b).
[24] 2004 Bill, s.25.
[25] 2004 Bill, s.25(A).
[26] 2004 Bill, s.25A(2).
[27] 2004 Bill, s.25A(3).
[28] 2004 Bill, s.25A(4).

CHAPTER 15

SPECIAL RIGHTS—LAND REFORM ACT 2003

INTRODUCTION

This chapter seeks to examine the statutory rights created in the Land **15–01**
Reform (Scotland) Act 2003.[1] It might be said that the 2000 Act, the 2003
Act and the 2004 Bill[2] are all measures which deal with matters of land
tenure as opposed to matters of land use although the law relating to real
burdens and servitudes does of course have a bearing on how land and
buildings can be used. There has always been a view that too much land
in Scotland is concentrated in too few hands and that ownership is often
vest in absentee landlords who may have little or no interest in the local
community guarding their ownership rights with unnecessary vigilance.
The Land Reform (Scotland) Act 2003 received Royal Assent on February
25, 2003. Sections 95 and 97 which contain anti-avoidance provisions and
provisions relating to the Scottish Land Court came into force on Royal
Assent. Other sections came into force on September 30, 2003 and June
14, 2004. The Act is in four parts. Part 1 creates statutory access rights in
favour of the public which rights are to be exercised reasonably and
responsibly. Part 2 creates a right in favour of a community to buy certain
land with which that community has a connection. The right is exercised
by a body representing a rural community. Part 3 gives a right to buy to
bodies representing crofting communities in respect of certain land. Part
4 contains general and supplementary provisions. The Act contains 100
sections and 2 Schedules.

STATUTORY ACCESS RIGHTS

The Nature of the Access Rights

There is no doubt that this part of the 2003 Reform Act aroused consid- **15–02**
erable feeling on both sides of the argument. It proved to be more controversial than the measures contained in other parts of the Act. There
has always been an argument to the effect that there is no such thing as
a law of trespass in Scotland. On the other hand it has always been the
case that anyone who is on another's land will be liable for any damage
caused and may be interdicted from causing damage. The opening

---

[1] Hereinafter referred to as the 2003 Reform Act; for a more detailed treatment see the
excellent annotations by Malcolm Strang Steel, Alisdair G. Fox and Keith Graham published in *Current Law Statutes.*
[2] Abolition of Feudal Tenure etc. (Scotland) Act 2000; Title Conditions (Scotland) Act
2003; Tenements (Scotland) Bill 2004.

section of the 2003 Reform Act provides that everyone has the statutory rights established by the Act.[3] The right of access is the right to be on land for certain specified purposes and the right to cross that land.[4] The specified purposes are recreational purposes, educational activity purposes and, more controversially, commercial or profit-making activities which the person could carry on otherwise than commercially or for profit.[5] There is no suggestion in the Act that any existing legal rights at common law such as servitudes or public rights of way have been replaced although presumably those exercising rights of access may wish to exercise the statutory rights rather than rely on the vagueness of the common law especially where the servitude or right of way has been constituted by prescription. Educational activity is defined as an activity which is carried on by a person for the purposes of furthering that person's understanding of natural or cultural heritage or for the purposes of enabling or assisting another person to further their understanding of natural or cultural heritage.[6] Oddly, although there is a definition of educational activity, there is no definition of recreational activity nor commercial or for profit activity. So far as commercial activity is concerned it must be activity which is capable of being carried on on a non profit basis. A mountain guide could work commercially or for nothing. Only a restricted number of commercial activities cannot be carried on gratuitously. Sale of goods is an obvious example but most services could be provided on a not for profit basis. There are certain activities which are excluded from access rights.[7] These are listed as certain types of conduct as follows:

(a) Being on or crossing land in breach of an interdict or other order of a court;
(b) Being on or crossing land for the purposes of doing anything which is an offence or a breach of an interdict or order of a court;
(c) Hunting, shooting or fishing;
(d) Being on or crossing land while responsible for a dog or other animal which is not under proper control;
(e) Being on or crossing land for the purpose of taking away, for commercial purposes or for profit, anything in or on the land;
(f) Being on or crossing land in or with a motorised vehicle or vessel (other than a vehicle or vessel which has been constructed or adapted for use by a person who has a disability and which is being used by such a person);
(g) Being, for any of the purposes set out in section 1(3), on land which is a golf course.

The access rights are exercisable above and below as well as on the surface of the land.[8] Presumably a recreational activity such as paragliding or potholing is therefore permissible. A person exercising these

---

[3] 2003 Reform Act, s.1(1).
[4] 2003 Reform Act, s.1(2).
[5] 2003 Reform Act, s.1(3).
[6] 2003 Reform Act, s.1(5).
[7] 2003 Reform Act, s.9.
[8] 2003 Reform Act s.1(6).

rights must exercise them responsibly.[9] A person will be treated as exercising the rights responsibly if the rights are exercised so as not to cause unreasonable interference with any of the rights of another person.[10] These other rights may themselves be access rights but are more likely to be ordinary rights of ownership. Moreover references to the responsible exercise of rights are references to the exercise of these rights in a way which is lawful and reasonable and takes proper account of the interests of others and of the features of the land in respect of which the rights are exercised.[11] Where a person engages in excluded conduct,[12] contrary to any bye-law,[13] or does anything which undoes anything done by Scottish Natural Heritage[14] that person will be taken as not exercising access rights responsibly.[15] Further in determining whether or not a person is exercising rights responsibly regard will be had to the Access Code[16] and whether or not the party has disregarded any request included or which might reasonably be implied in anything done by Scottish Natural Heritage.[17] The exercise of access rights will not of themselves amount to trespass.[18] It would be easy to take the view that access rights are some form of servitude or public right of way created by statute. Professor Gordon took the view that a servitude could be constituted by an Act of Parliament in which it case it was to be regarded according to Rankine as a servitude constituted by express grant.[19] Cusine and Paisley do not categorise statutory rights as servitudes as such but treat these rights as rights which resemble servitudes.[20] It seems clear that the statutory access rights cannot be servitudes in as much as there is no dominant tenement. They are of course quite close to public rights of way but the statute treats them as different in as much as access rights do not diminish or displace existing rights of access to land or public rights in relation to the foreshore.[21] Moreover the exercise of statutory access rights over the prescriptive period of 20 years cannot be used to claim a public right of way or servitude or any public right of navigation.[22] This raises a difficult problem for those attempting to set up a public right of way by possession. The possession may be ascribed to the exercise of the statutory right of access rather than an assertion of a public right of way. Land over which access rights are exercisable is not a road for the purposes of the Roads (Scotland) Act 1984.[23] It is probably best to regard the access rights as simply a species of statutory public right. Despite the legal distinction certain of the statutory provisions are made applicable to public rights of way. The provisions of sections 14 (Prohibition of

---

[9] 2003 Reform Act, s.2(1).
[10] 2003 Reform Act, s.2(2).
[11] 2003 Reform Act, s.2(3).
[12] Within the meaning of the 2003 Reform Act, s.9.
[13] Made under the 2003 Reform Act, s.12(1)(a)(i).
[14] Under the 2003 Reform Act, s.29.
[15] 2003 Reform Act, s.2(2)(a).
[16] Under the 2003 Reform Act, s.10.
[17] Under the 2003 Reform Act, s.29.
[18] Land Reform Act 2003, s.59(1).
[19] Gordon, *Scottish Land Law* (2nd ed.), paras 24–27.
[20] Cusine and Paisley, *Servitude and Rights of Way*, Ch.26.
[21] 2003 Reform Act, s.5(3) and (4).
[22] 2003 Reform Act, s.5(5).
[23] 2003 Reform Act, s.5(6).

Signs, Obstructions and Dangerous Implements) and 15 (Measures for Safety, Protection and Guidance and Assistance) apply not only to statutory access rights but also to public rights of way.[24] The party who is subject to the access rights is of course the owner of the land but owner is defined[25] as the owner of the land and where the owner is not in natural possession the person who is entitled to such natural possession. This would include a party such as an agricultural tenant or someone with a grazing let.

The owner's common law remedies

15–03 One of the difficulties in framing legislation of this type is that it seeks to maintain a balance between the rights of the general public and the rights of individual land owner. This dilemma is brought into sharp focus when one tries to provide an adequate and yet reasonable remedy for a landowner who feels that someone is not exercising access rights in a responsible manner. Obviously the remedy of interdict would be available but for practical purposes it is hardly a useful remedy given the fact that the owner would have to know the identity of the party exercising the access rights irresponsibly. Moreover by the time the owner went to court the offending member of the public will have left the land. It seems to the author therefore that the most that a landowner can do is simply to point out to the offending member of the public the irresponsible nature of that person's behaviour and ask them to leave the land. The scope for breaches of the peace in such circumstances appears to be limitless. So far as the remedy of interdict is concerned one wonders just how far the courts will want to be involved. A contested interdict action is likely to arise in circumstances where a particular member of the public or group has strong views on land ownership and land use issues and the landowner has equally strong views in the opposite direction. What seems to be responsible conduct to one party will be wholly irresponsible to the other. The 2003 Reform Act does provide for summary applications to the sheriff.[26]

The definition of land

15–04 Land is defined[27] as including bridges and other structures built on or over land, inland waters, canals and the foreshore. This definition covers most rural features. At first glance the definition would include gardens and ordinary suburban property. However there is a list of specific subjects over which access rights are not exercisable.[28] The exclusions would not preclude the exercise of a properly constituted servitude of way or a public right of way nor, more importantly, do the exclusions apply to a core path. The exclusions are:[29]

---

[24] 2003 Reform Act, s.122.
[25] 2003 Reform Act, s.32.
[26] 2003 Reform Act, s.28 and see para.15–16 below.
[27] 2003 Reform Act, s.32.
[28] 2003 Reform Act, s.6.
[29] 2003 Reform Act, s.6.

(a) Land on which there is erected a building or other structure or works, plant or fixed machinery.

(b) Land on which there is erected a caravan, tent or other place affording a person privacy or shelter.

(c) Land which forms the curtilage of a building which is not a house or of a group of buildings none of which is a house.

(d) Land which forms a compound or other enclosure containing any such structure, works, plant or fixed machinery as has already been referred to in (a) above.

(e) Land which is contiguous to and used for the purposes of a school.

(f) Land which comprises in relation to a house or any of the places mentioned in (c) above sufficient adjacent land to enable persons living there to have a reasonable measure of privacy in that house or place and to ensure that their enjoyment is not unreasonably disturbed.

(g) Land which is owned in common and used by two or more persons as a private garden.

(h) Land to which public access is prohibited, excluded or restricted under an enactment.

(i) Land which has been developed or set out as a sports or playing field or for a particular recreation purpose.

(j) Land to which for not fewer than 90 days in the year ending on January 31, 2001 members of the public were permitted only on payment and after that date for not fewer than 90 days in each year beginning on February 1, 2001 members of the public are or are to be so admitted.

(k) Land on which building, civil engineering or demolition works or other works are being carried out.

(l) Land on which works are being carried out by a statutory undertaker for the purposes of the undertaking.

(m) Land which is used for the working of minerals by surface workings including quarrying.

(n) Land on which crops have been sown or are growing.

(o) Land which has been specified in an order under section 11 of the 2003 Reform Act (exemption of land from access rights) or bye-laws under section 12 as land in respect of which access rights are not exercisable.

For the purposes of excluded land a bridge, tunnel, causeway, launching site, groyne, weir, boulder weir, embankment of a canalised waterway, fence, wall or anything designed to facilitate passage is not to be regarded as a structure and accordingly access can be exercised over these facilities. It remains to be seen whether there will be any difficulty concerning the exclusion of what might be regarded as garden ground pertaining to a dwellinghouse. There are large gardens and small gardens. The exclusion only appears to apply to "sufficient adjacent land" to enable persons living in the house to have a reasonable measure of privacy and to ensure that their enjoyment is not unreasonably disturbed. These words are suitably vague and may yet cause difficulty. The Act contains further clarification[30] in that it provides that

---

[30] 2003 Reform Act, s.7(5).

location and other characteristics of the house are factors to be taken
into account in determining the amount of excluded land to go with that
house. Presumably what has historically been regarded as the garden
area of a house will be relevant. It seems obvious that the bigger the
house the larger the garden will be. Ministers may modify the exclusion
provisions.[31] Where a planning permission would bring land within one
of the exclusions that land will not be deemed to be excluded if planning permission has either not been granted or is subject to a condition
which has not been complied with.[32]

Obligations of owners

15–05   One might have thought that the role of the owner in relation to statutory access rights was purely passive. Nevertheless the Act does
place[33] a duty on every owner in respect of land over which access rights
are exercisable to use and manage the land and otherwise conduct ownership of it in a way which, as respects the access rights, is responsible.
Responsible ownership for the purposes of access rights is ownership
which does not cause unreasonable interference with the access rights
of any person exercising or seeking to exercise them. Regard will be had
as to whether or not any act or omission of an owner contravenes the
Access Code. Local authorities may make bye-laws in relation to land
over which access rights are exercisable.[34] An owner who contravenes a
bye-law is almost bound to be deemed to be acting irresponsibly.
Similarly if an owner contravenes a prohibition of signs, obstructions
and dangerous impediments[35] the owner is almost bound to be treated
as acting irresponsibly.

The Scottish Outdoor Access Code

15–06   Scottish Natural Heritage were given the duty of drawing up and
issuing the Scottish Outdoor Access Code.[36] The Code contains guidance as to the circumstances in which those exercising rights are to be
regarded as doing so responsibly. It also sets out guidance for owners
who are carrying out activities on the land affecting access rights. The
Code also gives guidance as to circumstances in which owners of land
are to be regarded as using or managing or otherwise conducting ownership in a responsible manner. The same would apply to land not
subject to access rights which is contiguous to land subject to these
rights. The statutory notion of acting responsibly or reasonably is suitably general. Presumably the function of the Access Code is to put some
flesh on these bones by way of example.[37]

---

[31] 2003 Reform Act, s.8.
[32] 2003 Reform Act, s.7(2).
[33] 2003 Reform Act, s.3.
[34] 2003 Reform Act, s.12.
[35] 2003 Reform Act, s.14.
[36] 2003 Reform Act, s.10.
[37] At time of press the Executive were considering a draft access code. For more details
on this see the Scottish Natural Heritage website, *http://www.snh.org.uk.*

LOCAL AUTHORITY POWERS

General powers

The local authority[38] whose area includes the land[39] may by order   **15–07**
exempt it for a particular purpose from the access rights which would
otherwise be exercisable. There are detailed provisions in relation to the
making of such an order.[40] Similarly a local authority may, in relation to
land in respect of which access rights are exercised, make bye-laws in
relation to responsible exercise of access rights and responsible use, management and conduct of ownership of land. The bye-laws may provide
for preservation of public order and safety, prevention of damage, prevention of nuisance or danger and conservation or enhancement of
natural or cultural heritage.[41] Apart from this there is a statutory duty on
a local authority to assert, protect and keep open and free from obstruction or encroachment, any route, waterway or other means by which
access rights may reasonably be exercised.[42] The local authority may, for
these purposes, institute and defend legal proceedings and take such
steps as they think expedient.[43] However a local authority is not required
to do anything in pursuance of the duty which would be inconsistent
with its other functions.[44]

Threatening notices and obstructions

One of the difficulties which those wishing to exercise rights to walk   **15–08**
or ramble have faced in the past have been threatening notices and
obstructions put up by landowners. The owner of land over which
access rights are exercisable is prohibited from putting up any sign,
notice, fence or wall or planting, growing or permitting to grow any
hedge, tree or other vegetation. There is also a prohibition of position-
ing or leaving at large any animal or carrying out agricultural or other
operations on land or taking or failing to take any other action. These
prohibitions only apply where the sign, notice, fence etc. or other
action has as its main purpose the preventing or deterring of the exercise of access rights.[45] Where the local authority consider that anything
has been done in contravention of these prohibitions they may, by
written notice to the owner, require remedial action within such reasonable time as is specified.[46] If the owner fails to comply with a notice
the local authority may remove any sign or notice or take any other
remedial action as is specified in the notice and recover the costs.[47] The
owner has a right of appeal by summary application to the sheriff.[48]

---

[38] This may be a National Park Authority.
[39] 2003 Reform Act, s.32.
[40] 2003 Reform Act, s.11.
[41] 2003 Reform Act, s.12(1)(c).
[42] 2003 Reform Act, s.13(1).
[43] 2003 Reform Act, s.13(3).
[44] 2003 Reform Act, s.13(2).
[45] 2003 Reform Act, s.14(1).
[46] 2003 Reform Act, s.14(2).
[47] 2003 Reform Act, s.14(3).
[48] 2003 Reform Act, s.14(4) and (5).

Safety, protection, guidance and assistance

15–09 The local authority may also take measures for safety, protection, guidance and assistance and these steps may include the putting up and maintenance of notices and fences.[49] These powers include the power to instal and maintain gates, styles, moorings and other facilities. The local authority may acquire land to enable or facilitate the exercise of access rights.[50]

Core paths

15–10 A statutory duty is placed on local authorities to draw up not later than three years after the coming into force of the provision a plan for a system of paths to be known as core paths sufficient for the purpose of giving the public reasonable access throughout their local authority area.[51] Access rights are exercisable in respect of all core paths.[52] The statutory provision gives examples of paths or routes which may be included in the system of core paths. These include existing rights of way by foot, horseback, pedal, cycle or any other combination of these which have already been established whether under an enactment[53] or at common law. A core path may also be a path delineated by a path agreement or set up under a path order.[54] Generally core paths may be across other routes, waterways or other means by which persons cross land. In drawing up a core path plan a local authority must have regard to various factors.[55] These factors are:

(a) The likelihood that persons exercising rights of way and access rights will do so by using core paths;

(b) the desirability of encouraging such persons to use core paths, and

(c) The need to balance the exercise of those rights and the interests of the owner of the land in respect of which those rights are exercisable.

A core path plan may consist of and include maps showing core paths and where it does not must refer to maps.[56] Presumably the hope is that eventually where people are exercising their access rights they will do so using a network of core paths. It should however be borne in mind that the access rights created are not restricted to paths, core or otherwise, although in coming to a view as to whether or not access rights are being exercised responsibly regard would presumably be had as to whether or not the rights were being exercised over core paths or in a more indiscriminate manner where core paths exist.

---

[49] 2003 Reform Act, s.15.
[50] 2003 Reform Act, s.16.
[51] 2003 Reform Act, s.17(1).
[52] 2003 Reform Act, s.7(1).
[53] Such as the Countryside (Scotland) Act 1967.
[54] 2003 Reform Act, ss.21 and 22.
[55] 2003 Reform Act, s.17(3).
[56] 2003 Reform Act, s.17(4).

Procedures are set out providing for the local authority to give public notice of a core paths plan and to consult the local access forum and other representatives such as Scottish Natural Heritage.[57] The local authority may do anything which it may consider appropriate for the purposes of maintaining a core path, keeping the same free from obstruction or encroachment and providing the public with an indication of the extent of a core path.[58] A core path plan may be amended.[59] Local authorities may enter a path agreement with a person having the necessary power for delineation and maintenance, or delineation, creation and maintenance of a path within land in respect of which access rights are exercisable.[60] A path agreement may be on such terms and conditions as to payment or otherwise as may be specified in it.[61] The Act also gives power to local authorities to make path orders.[62] The local authority will exercise these powers where, in the circumstances, it appears to be impracticable to delineate a path by means of a path agreement. A path order may be made where it appears to the local authority that, having regard to the rights and interests of the landowner and the rights and interests of those exercising access rights, it is expedient to delineate a path. Where a path order is made the local authority will have a duty to maintain or create and maintain the path.[63] A path order must contain a map showing the delineation of the path[64] and may be revoked.[65] There may be existing paths in terms of agreements of orders under the Countryside (Scotland) Act 1967. Where access rights become exercisable over such a path by virtue of the coming into effect of the 2003 Reform Act then the original agreement or order[66] which created the path shall be treated as a path agreement or as the case may by a path order in terms of the 2003 Reform Act.[67] The procedures for making a path order are set out in Schedule 1.[68] Where access rights are exercised by virtue of a path order they will be an overriding interest for the purposes of land registration.[69] A core path may be constructed on lanes which would otherwise be excluded from the general right of access such as garden gravel.[69a]

Core paths—agricultural operations

There is statutory provision which allows an owner to plough or other-   **15–11**
wise disturb land in accordance with good husbandry even where that land incorporates a core path or indeed a right of way.[70] However the owner who carries out this work must reinstate the path or right of

---

[57] 2003 Reform Act, s.18.
[58] 2003 Reform Act, s.19.
[59] 2003 Reform Act, s.20.
[60] 2003 Reform Act, s.21(1).
[61] 2003 Reform Act, s.21(2).
[62] 2003 Reform Act, s.22.
[63] 2003 Reform Act, s.22(3).
[64] 2003 Reform Act, s.22(6).
[65] 2003 Reform Act, s.22(5).
[66] Made under ss.38 to 36 of the Countryside (Scotland) Act 1967.
[67] 2003 Reform Act, s.22(7).
[68] 2003 Reform Act, s.22(8).
[69] 2003 Reform Act, s.22(9).
[69a] 2003 Reform Act, s.7(1).
[70] 2003 Reform Act, s.23(1).

way within 14 days of disturbance or such longer period as the local authority may allow.[71] Failure to do so is an offence and the local authority may on giving a further 14 days' notice take all necessary steps to reinstate the path at the owner's expense.[72]

Rangers

15–12 Local authorities have power to appoint rangers in relation to land over which access rights are exercisable for certain purposes.[73] The purposes are to advise and assist the owner of land and other members of the public as to any matter relating to the exercise of access rights in respect of the land and to perform such other duties in relation to the exercise of these rights as the local authority may determine. A ranger so appointed may enter any land in respect of which access rights are exercisable to exercise any of these functions[74] Presumably a local authority is not likely to appoint a ranger unless there is a fairly extensive network of core paths or where access rights are otherwise likely to be exercised of a regular basis. It is to be hoped that the ranger is not left in the position of holding the jackets for the landowner and rambler on too many occasions.

Local Access Forums

15–13 Local authorities must establish for their areas at least one body known as a Local Access Forum to carry out certain statutory functions.[75] More than one Forum may be established for the local authority area.[76] So far as the composition of the Forum is concerned although there is a discretion given to the local authority[77] the local authority must ensure that there is a reasonable representation of persons and bodies representing the interests of persons with an interest in public access and the interests of landowners.[78] The idea is to ensure some sort of reasonable balance of interests. The local authority may appoint one or more of its own members to such a forum.[79]

Power of entry

15–14 A local authority may authorise any person to enter land for a purpose connected with the exercise or proposed exercise of any of the local authority's functions in relation to access rights.[80] Such an authorised person however must only enter the land at a reasonable time and on giving reasonable notice to the owner except in the case of emergency or for the purpose of warning the public of, and protecting the public

---

[71] 2003 Reform Act, s.23(2).
[72] 2003 Reform Act, s.23(3) and (4).
[73] 2003 Reform Act, s.24(1) and (2).
[74] 2003 Reform Act, s.24(3).
[75] 2003 Reform Act, s.25(1).
[76] 2003 Reform Act, s.25(6).
[77] 2003 Reform Act, s.25(3).
[78] 2003 Reform Act, s.25(4).
[79] 2003 Reform Act, s.25(5).
[80] Land Reform Act, s.26(1).

from, danger and taking measures to facilitate the exercise of access rights or fulfilling duties in relation to core paths.[81] Those authorised persons may take machinery or other equipment or materials on to the land if required for the purpose for which they are entering the land.[82]

Guidance

Scottish ministers may give guidance to local authorities in general or to a particular local authority in relation to the performance of local authority functions in respect of access rights. Before giving guidance ministers must consult with the local authority or authorities concerned and the draft of the guidance has to be laid before the Scottish Parliament. The guidance cannot be given until 40 days after the date of laying and during this time the Parliament may direct that the guidance be not be given.[83]

15–15

JUDICIAL AND SUPPLEMENTARY POWERS

Determinations

The Role of the Courts

Where there is a core path agreement or a core path order then it will presumably be obvious that there are access rights and that these access rights are to be exercised on a certain line. In other cases however it may not be so obvious that access rights exist. The 2003 Reform Act contains provisions for the judicial determination of the existence and extent of access rights and ordinary rights of way.[84] These provisions apply not just to statutory access rights but to public rights of way.[85] The procedure is by way of summary application to the sheriff and the sheriff may determine whether or not access rights are exercisable over particular land, whether persons exercising those rights are doing so responsibly, and whether the owners of the land are using, managing or conducting ownership in a responsible way.[86] An application may be made to the sheriff for a determination as to whether or not any path or other means of land is or is not a right of way by foot, horseback, cycle or any combination of these.[87] The remedy sought is a declarator[88] and, except where the person seeking the declarator is the owner of land, the application must be served on the local authority who are entitled to be a party to proceedings.[89] Where the person seeking the declarator is not the owner then the application must be served on the owner.[90] Rules of

15–16

---

[81] 2003 Reform Act, s.26(2) and (3).
[82] 2003 Reform Act, s.26(4).
[83] 2003 Reform Act, s.27.
[84] 2003 Reform Act s.28; as to common law remedies see 15-03 above.
[85] 2003 Reform Act, s.28(2).
[86] 2003 Reform Act, s.28(1).
[87] 2003 Reform Act, s.28(2).
[88] 2003 Reform Act, s.28(3).
[89] 2003 Reform Act, s.28(4)(5) and (6).
[90] 2003 Reform Act, s.28(7).

court will be promulgated to govern proceedings.[91] The purpose of these provisions is to provide a simple method of determining day to day disputes in relation to access rights. However the ordinary remedies available to protect rights are not abrogated.[92] Presumably therefore the owner of land who feels that a particular party is not exercising access rights responsibly may bring an action of interdict. Similarly a party who seeks to exercise access rights responsibly but feels that the owner of land is not acting reasonably (as would be the case where obstructions are being laid down) may also bring an action of interdict or for declarator and removal of the obstructions.

Supplementary powers—natural and cultural heritage

15–17 Scottish Natural Heritage and Scottish Ministers may put up and maintain notices for the purposes of protecting the natural heritage of land in respect of which access rights are exercisable.[93] Any notice may warn persons of any adverse affect that their presence on the land or any activities they might conduct there might have on the natural or cultural heritage which is to be protected.[94] Natural heritage is defined as including the flora and fauna of land, its geological and physiographical features and its natural beauty and amenity. Cultural heritage includes structures and other remains resulting from human activity of all periods, traditions, ways of life and the historic, artistic and literary associations of people, place and landscapes.[95]

Existing bye-laws

15–18 Many local authorities in the past have promulgated bye-laws providing for public access to land. These bye-laws may or may not be appropriate after the coming into being of statutory access rights. All such bye-laws relating to public access to land must be viewed by the body that made them within two years of the coming into force of the access rights and if necessary modified to ensure consistency with the provisions of the Act.[96]

COMMUNITY RIGHT TO BUY

Registration of Interest

Introduction

15–19 Much of the criticism, justified or not, of the pattern of land ownership in Scotland has been directed against large estates owned by persons who, on one view, have little interest in the local community. Part 2 of the 2003 Reform Act[97] confers a pre-emptive right to buy on rural com-

---

[91] 2003 Reform Act, s.28(8).
[92] 2003 Reform Act, s.28(9).
[93] 2003 Reform Act, s.29(1) and (2).
[94] 2003 Reform Act, s.29(3).
[95] 2003 Reform Act, s.32.
[96] 2003 Reform Act, s.30.
[97] ss.33–67.

munities in circumstances where an interest has first been registered. The pre-emptive right to buy applies not just to land but to salmon fishings and mineral rights associated with the land. The community must show that they have a connection with the land. The provisions are set out in chapters. Chapter 1 defines registrable land capable being the subject of a pre-emptive purchase. Chapter 2 sets out procedures for late applications for registration of an interest, the effect of registration, anti avoidance provisions and other matters. Chapter 3 deals with the exercise of the right to buy itself and the procedures relative to the transfer. Chapter 4 contains further procedures which apply when the right to buy has been activated. These provisions deal with ballots of the community and the consent of Ministers. Chapter 5 deals with the assessment of the value of the land and contains the procedure for valuation. Chapter 6 deals with appeals including appeals to the Lands Tribunal in respect of valuation and compensation matters. Chapter 7 deals with general and miscellaneous provisions including the effect of the right to buy on other rights. The community right to buy is essentially a right vest in a community body which will have to be a company limited by guarantee. The initial right is to register an interest in appropriate land. It is only when the owner of that land in which an interest has been registered decides to sell that the pre-emptive right to buy is activated.

Registrable land—excluded land

Land in which a community interest may be registered is simply **15–20** defined as any land other than excluded land.[98] Excluded land is defined as land described in an order made by Ministers.[99] [As at the date of writing no such order has been promulgated]. However in determining what land is to be excluded Ministers may have regard to factors relating to population and such other factors associated with or characteristic of the land as they think fit.[1] Moreover Ministers must secure that registrable land is land which appears to be rural.[2] A draft of any order excluding land must be approved by resolution of the Scottish Parliament.[3] In some cases of course it will not be obvious whether land is to be regarded as rural or urban. There may, for example, be difficulties in relation to small villages in the middle of rural areas. It was originally suggested that settlements having a population of over 3,000 would be excluded.[4] An order excluding land must either include a map showing the boundary of the land excluded or refer to a map which shows these boundaries. If the order simply contains a reference to another map Ministers are required to make copies of the map available for public inspection.[5] Registrable land includes land which consists of salmon fishings or mineral rights which are owned separately from land in respect of which they are exigible but does not include any such fishings or mineral rights which are exigible in respect of excluded land.[6]

---

[98] 2003 Reform Act, s.33.
[99] 2003 Reform Act, s.33(2).
[1] 2003 Reform Act, s.33(3)(a).
[2] 2003 Reform Act, s.33(3)(b).
[3] 2003 Reform Act, s.98(5).
[4] Policy Memorandum November 23, 2001, para.14.
[5] 2003 Reform Act, s.33(4) and (5).
[6] 2003 Reform Act, s.33(6).

However the minerals which are reserved to the Crown or government and quasi government bodies are excluded from the definition of registrable land. These are oil, coal, gas, gold and silver.[7]

Community bodies—general

15–21 The notion that a community should be able to buy land related to that community is all very well in theory. In law a community is not a legal entity and a scheme which allowed individual members of a community to exercise a right to buy piecemeal would be unworkable. Accordingly the pre-emptive right to register an interest and then buy is restricted to community bodies. A community body must be a company which is limited by guarantee the memorandum and articles of association of which include the following:[8]

(a) A definition of the community to which the company relates.

(b) A provision enabling the company to exercise the right to buy land under the 2003 Reform Act.

(c) A provision that the company must have no fewer than twenty members.

(d) A provision that the majority of the members of the company must consist of members of the community.

(e) A provision whereby the members of the company who consist of members of the community have control of the company.

(f) A provision ensuring proper arrangements for the financial management of the company and the auditing of its accounts.

(g) A provision that any surplus funds or assets of the company are to be applied for the benefit of the community, and

(h) A provision that on the winding up of the company and after satisfaction of its liabilities its property (including any land acquired by it under the pre-emptive right to buy) will pass either to such other community body or crofting community body as may be approved by Ministers or if no such body is so approved to Ministers or to such charity as Ministers may direct. It will be possible however for property to pass to another party only if that party is a charity.[9] A charity is a body entitled to describe itself as a Scottish Charity within the meaning of the relevant Charities legislation.[10]

A community body which has registered a community interest or bought land cannot modify its Memorandum or Articles of Association without Ministers' consent so long as the interest remains registered or the land remains in that body's ownership.[11] The interest is registered with the Keeper of the Registers of Scotland and if Ministers are satisfied that a body which has registered an interest is

---

[7] 2003 Reform Act, s.33(7) and see Rennie, *Minerals and the Law of Scotland*, para.3.1 *et seq.*
[8] 2003 Reform Act, s.34(1)(a)–(h).
[9] 2003 Reform Act, s.34(7).
[10] Law Reform (Miscellaneous Provisions) (Scotland) Act 1990, s.1(7).
[11] 2003 Reform Act, s.35(1).

no longer a community body they may direct the Keeper to delete the interest from the Register.[12] In circumstances where the body has actually acquired land and then is no longer a community body Ministers may acquire the land compulsorily from the body.[13] It was recognised however that some communities were smaller than others and accordingly in appropriate circumstances Ministers may reduce the minimum number of 20 members if Ministers think it is in the public interest to do so.[14]

Sustainable development

A community body cannot be recognised as such until Ministers have **15–22** given written confirmation that they are satisfied that the main purpose of the body is consistent with furthering the achievement of sustainable development.[15] Unfortunately the term "sustainable development" is not defined in the Act nor is any guidance given in the explanatory notes issued by Scottish Ministers with the Act. The Executive had difficulty in finding an appropriate definition which balanced economic progress, social justice and environmental benefits. It may be that when guidance is issued to communities in relation to applications for the registration of interests and the exercise of the right to buy the definition of "sustainable development" will be revisited. However what does appear to be clear is that a community body will not be recognised as such if its only purpose is to take land from a local landowner and hold it for behoof of the community. Presumably there must be some sort of plan for development. Development is of course defined in planning legislation.[16] There development is defined as the carrying out of building, engineering, mining or other operations in, on, over or under land, or the making of any material change in the use of any buildings or other land. Just how much development would be required is not clear. Presumably it could be development over a lengthy period of time provided the development was sustainable.

The community

The community is defined by reference to a postcode unit or postcode **15–23** units.[17] A postcode unit is an area in relation to which a single postcode is used to facilitate the identification of postal service delivery points within the area.[18] A community comprises therefore the persons from time to time who are resident in that postcode unit or in one of those postcode units and are entitled to vote at a local government election in a polling district which includes that postcode unit or those postcode units or part of it or them.[19]

---

[12] 2003 Reform Act, s.35(2).
[13] 2003 Reform Act, s.35(3).
[14] 2003 Reform Act, s.34(2).
[15] 2003 Reform Act, s.34(4).
[16] Town and Country Planning (Scotland) Act 1997, s.26(1).
[17] 2003 Reform Act, s.34(5)(a).
[18] 2003 Reform Act, s.34(6).
[19] 2003 Reform Act, s.34(5)(b).

Register of community interests in land

15–24 The 2003 Reform Act requires the Keeper of the Registers of Scotland to set up and keep a Register to be known as the Register of Community Interest in Land.[20] Ministers may appoint persons other than the Keeper to carry out this function.[21] Different persons may actually be appointed for different purposes relating to the Register.[22] The Register will be a public register and must contain the following information and documents relating to each community interest registered in it[23]:

(a) The name and address of the registered office of the company which constitutes the community body which has registered the interest.

(b) A copy of the application for registration.[24]

(c) A copy of any notice of prohibition.[25]

(d) A copy of the notice of Ministers' decision that the interest is to be entered in the Register.[26]

(e) The date of registration.

(f) A description of the land, including maps, plans or other drawings prepared to such specifications as may be prescribed.

(g) The date when the registration will cease to have effect.[27] The life of a registered interest is five years from the date of registration subject to renewal on the application of the community body.

(h) The date of any deletion of the interest.[28] If there is a change in circumstances Ministers, after consultation with the community body and the owner of the land, may be require deletion of a community interest from the Register.[29] Ministers are required to direct the Keeper to delete the community interest if the community body does not exercise its right to buy or the right is extinguished by the seller withdrawing from negotiations for the sale to the community body.[30]

(i) A copy of any notification[31] relative to a proposed transfer. There is a requirement on the owner of the land or a heritable creditor with a security over the land in respect of which a community interest has been registered to notify the community body and Ministers of any proposal to transfer the land or part of the land other than by way of an exempt transfer.

(j) A copy of any notice[32] sent by Ministers to the community body holding the registered interest asking the community body to

---

[20] 2003 Reform Act, s.36(1).
[21] 2003 Reform Act, s.36(9).
[22] 2003 Reform Act, s.36(10).
[23] 2003 Reform Act, s.36(2)(a)(p).
[24] Under the 2003 Reform Act, s.37.
[25] Under the 2003 Reform Act, s.37(5)(e).
[26] Under the 2003 Reform Act, s.37(17).
[27] Under the 2003 Reform Act, s.44.
[28] Under the 2003 Reform Act, ss.45 or 54.
[29] Under the 2003 Reform Act, s.45.
[30] Under the 2003 Reform Act, s.54.
[31] Under the 2003 Reform Act, s.48.
[32] Under the 2003 Reform Act, s.49.

confirm whether it is to exercise its right to buy the land where Ministers have received notification of a transfer proposal.[33] A copy of the notice to the owner of the land that Ministers have complied with their obligation to serve the requisite notice to the community body[34] must also be registered.

(k) A copy of any confirmation received by Ministers from the community body in response to their notice of a proposed transfer that the body intends to exercise its right to buy the land. If no such confirmation is received Ministers are deemed to have received notice from the community body that it will not be proceeding to exercise its right to buy.

(l) A copy of any notice[35] by the Lands Tribunal. If an owner or heritable creditor attempts to transfer land or takes action to transfer any part of it which is subject to a registered community interest the Lands Tribunal can activate the right of the community body to buy the land. Ministers must give notice to the Keeper of the Tribunal's determination to each community body which has registered or has applied to register.

(m) A copy of any decision as to consent.[36] Ministers will normally be required to consent to the acquisition of the land by a community body with a registered interest if they are satisfied on certain matters. Ministers will then be required to send a notice of their decision to consent in writing to the community body, the owner of the land and to direct the Keeper who will register that decision.

(n) A copy of any notice of declinature.[37] A community body must give notice to the owner or heritable creditor where it declines to exercise its right to buy or where the owner or heritable creditor extinguishes the right to buy by withdrawing land from the market.

(o) A note of the date of the original document where copies are registered.

(p) Such other information as Ministers consider appropriate.

Although the Register of Community Interests in Land is a public register a community body can ask that information or documents which relate to the arrangements for raising or spending money to enable the land to be put to a particular use is withheld from the public register and kept simply by or on behalf of Ministers separately.[38] This does not mean however that the community body has an obligation to give Ministers such information in relation to the raising of finance although it may wish to do so by way of indicating to Ministers that any development is viable.[39] Ministers have power to modify the information and documents which are to be registered and also the provisions relating to financial information.[40] Any such order would require to be approved

---

[33] Under the 2003 Reform Act, s.48.
[34] Under the 2003 Reform Act, s.49(2).
[35] Under the 2003 Reform Act, s.50(3).
[36] Under the 2003 Reform Act, s.51.
[37] Under the 2003 Reform Act, s.54.
[38] Under the 2003 Reform Act, s.36(3) and (4).
[39] Under the 2003 Reform Act, s.36(5).
[40] Under the 2003 Reform Act, s.36(6).

by resolution of the Scottish Parliament.[41] The public have the right to inspect the Register free of charge and must be given copying facilities. However charges are payable for copies of entries and official extracts of entries.[42] An extract certified by the Keeper is sufficient evidence of the original.[43]

Applications to Ministers for registration of an interest in land

15–25 A community body cannot simply proceed to register an interest directly into the Register. A community interest can only be registered after an application has been made by the community body to Ministers in the prescribed form and accompanied by the prescribed information including information about the location and boundaries of land by reference to maps or drawings.[44] "Prescribed" means prescribed in regulations made by Ministers.[45] If there is a standard security in favour of a heritable creditor which relates to the land or a heritable interest to which the application relates the community body must provide Ministers with notice of that fact in the prescribed form.[46] There may be cases where the owner or a heritable creditor is unknown or simply cannot be found. In such a case Ministers are relieved of their various statutory duties of intimation where the community body has given public notice of the proposed application by advertisement and the affixing of a conspicuous notice to a part of the land.[47] Where however an owner or heritable creditor can be traced Ministers have a statutory duty on receipt of any application from a community body to send a copy of the application and the accompanying information to the owner of the land and to any heritable creditor.[48] Ministers must then invite the owner of the land to send them not later than twenty one days after the sending of the invitation views in writing on the application. It should be noted here that what are requested are not objections but "views".[49] Where there is a heritable creditor holding a standard security Ministers must also invite that creditor to notify the community body and Ministers within 21 days if a calling up notice or notice of default has not been complied with.[50] Heritable creditors will also provide Ministers with their views in relation to the application. In the case of a notice of default a heritable creditor must advise whether objection has been taken by the debtor[51] and if so whether the court has upheld or varied the notice of default.[52] A heritable creditor must also advise Ministers if a court has granted a warrant to exercise remedies in respect of the standard security.[53] Scottish Ministers must also send a copy of any invitation for the views of the owner and heritable creditor to the

---

[41] Under the 2003 Reform Act, s.98(5).
[42] Under the 2003 Reform Act, s.36(7).
[43] Under the 2003 Reform Act, s.36(8).
[44] Under the 2003 Reform Act, s.37(1).
[45] Under the 2003 Reform Act, s.98(1).
[46] Under the 2003 Reform Act, s.37(2).
[47] Under the 2003 Reform Act, s.37(3) and (4).
[48] 2003 Reform Act, s.37(5)(a).
[49] 2003 Reform Act, s.37(5)(b).
[50] 2003 Reform Act, s.37(5)(c) and (6).
[51] In terms of the Conveyancing and Feudal Reform (Scotland) Act 1970, s.22.
[52] In terms of the Conveyancing and Feudal Reform (Scotland) Act 1970, s.22(2).
[53] In terms of the Conveyancing and Feudal Reform (Scotland) Act 1970, s.24.

community body.[54] Most importantly Ministers must send a notice to the owner and any heritable creditor which prevents the owner and that creditor from taking any action which would be prohibited.[55] Effectively this prohibits the owner and heritable creditor from transferring or taking any action to transfer the land whilst Ministers are determining the application. Any transfer made in the teeth of that prohibition is of no effect.[56] Ministers must send copies of any application made by a community body with the accompanying information and the prohibition notice to the Keeper.[57] Where Ministers receive a response to any invitation for the views of the owner or heritable creditor within the appropriate time limit they must send a copy or copies to the community body and invite them to comment on these views within a further period of twenty one days.[58] Ministers have a statutory duty to take into account any views sent to them.[59] There is no suggestion that this will be a judicial or quasi-judicial process involving the parties appearing before someone appointed by Ministers akin to a reporter in a planning appeal. Ministers must decline to consider any application which does not comply with the statutory requirements, is incomplete, discloses that any land is not registerable land or otherwise indicates that it is an application which Ministers would be bound to reject.[60] Where an application is declined this is regarded as a decision not to enter the community interest in the Register.[61] More than one community interest may be registered in respect of the same land and a community body may register an interest in more than one holding of land but cannot register more than one interest in the same land.[62] Within 63 days of receiving an application Ministers must send a notice of their decision with a statement of their reasons to the applicant community body, the owner of the land and any heritable creditor who has responded to the invitation to give views.[63] Where Ministers decide that a community interest is to be entered in the Register they will direct the Keeper to enter the interest with effect from the date on which the Ministers made the decision.[64] This is an interesting provision. In most cases of registration it is the applicant who registers. In this case it is Ministers. A decision notice to the applicant, owner and heritable creditor must contain information detailing the effect of registration of the community interest or of a decision not to allow registration as the case may be and also rights of appeal.[65] It appears that registration can still be effected even if Ministers fail to issue their decision within the 63-day time limit.[66] The parties are not to be prejudiced by a procedural failure on the part of Ministers.

---

[54] 2003 Reform Act, s.37(5)(d).
[55] Under 2003 Reform Act, s.40(1).
[56] 2003 Reform Act, s.37(8).
[57] 2003 Reform Act, s.37(7).
[58] 2003 Reform Act, s.37(9).
[59] 2003 Reform Act, s.37(10).
[60] 2003 Reform Act, s.37(11).
[61] 2003 Reform Act, s.37(12).
[62] 2003 Reform Act, s.37(13), (14) and (15).
[63] 2003 Reform Act, s.37(17).
[64] 2003 Reform Act, s.37(20).
[65] 2003 Reform Act, s.37(18).
[66] 2003 Reform Act, s.37(19).

Criteria for registration

15–26 Before Ministers can decide that a community interest is to be registered they must be satisfied on various matters.[67] Obviously they must be satisfied that the land is registerable land and not excluded land. They must also be satisfied that a significant number of members of the community have a substantial connection with the land or that the land in question is sufficiently near to land with which those members of the community have a substantial connection so that its acquisition by the community is compatible with furthering the achievement of sustainable development.[68] In common with the general approach there is no statutory definition of "significant number" or "substantial connection". As has already been noted there is no definition of "sustainable development". The view of the Executive appears to have been that to provide statutory definitions might have resulted in owners trying to frustrate a community body who wished to register an interest by putting forward technical reasons based on a failure to comply with the precise wording in a statutory definition. Whether or not this approach will result in more or less litigation remains to be seen. Similar difficulty may surround the phrase "sufficiently near to" which is used in relation to adjoining land. In coming to a decision therefore Ministers presumably have a discretion as to how to interpret these terms. Where the land is salmon fishings or mineral rights Ministers cannot decide to register a community interest unless the community body has already registered or is registering an interest in, or has acquired or is acquiring, other land containing or contiguous to the waters in which the salmon fishings exist or the land in which those mineral rights are exigible.[69] Presumably it does not matter that the owner of the salmon fishings or minerals is a different party from the owner of the contiguous or containing land. Ministers must also be satisfied that there is within the community a level of support sufficient to justify registration of the interest and that registration is in the public interest.[70] One tenth or more of members of the community appears to be the bench mark for a sufficient level of support although Ministers may regard an indication of approval of less than one tenth as enough.[71] Unlike the provisions in relation to the actual exercise of the right to buy there is no requirement for any ballot of members of the community before the interest is registered.

Late applications

15–27 Detailed procedure is set out in relation to applications which have been made late. This may arise where an application is made after the owner of the land or a heritable creditor has taken some action to transfer the land but before the missives have been concluded or an option to acquire is granted in pursuance of that action. The provisions will also apply to a situation where another community body with a registered interest has been notified of an intended sale.[72] In the latter case a late application is

---

[67] 2003 Reform Act, s.38(1).
[68] As defined in the 2003 Reform Act, s.34(1)(a).
[69] 2003 Reform Act, s.38(1)(c).
[70] 2003 Reform Act, s.38(1)(d) and (e).
[71] 2003 Reform Act, s.38(2).
[72] 2003 Reform Act, s.39(1).

only competent before Ministers have consented to the transfer to the first community body.[73] In such a case the owner or heritable creditor to which the late application relates must notify Ministers in which case the period for Ministers to make a decision is shortened to thirty days. Ministers would require to be satisfied there were good reasons why the community body did not submit an application before the owner or heritable creditor took action to transfer or notify the other community body of the proposed transfer. Ministers would also require to be satisfied that the level of support within the community is significantly greater than would otherwise be required and that the factors bearing on whether the application is in the public interest are strongly indicative that it is.[74] If Ministers decide to register a community interest in respect of a late application then the community body's right to buy is to be treated as having been activated immediately[75] and the community body will be treated as having already confirmed its intention to proceed to buy the land.[76] Where missives have been concluded by an owner or heritable creditor with a third party purchaser or where an option to acquire has been legally conferred Ministers must decline a late application.[77]

Effect of registration of interest—permitted transfers

While the community interest in land remains registered the owner of the land and any heritable creditor with a right to sell the land is prohibited from transferring the land or any part of the land or taking any action with a view to transfer of that land or any part of the land.[78] Any transfer of land in breach of this prohibition is ineffective. The Keeper will have a duty to refuse an application for registration of a transfer where he has not been provided with sufficient evidence to confirm that the application for registration does not relate to a prohibited transfer.[79] This prohibition will apply not just to transfers or dispositions of land in respect of which an interest has been registered but also transfers and dispositions of larger areas part of which are subject to a registered interest.[80] Presumably this provision is to avoid complications which might arise in relation to the partial ineffectiveness of a disposition of the larger area. There are certain transfers in relation to land over which there is a registered interest which are not subject to the statutory prohibition. These are[81]:

    (a) A transfer otherwise than for value such as a gift.
    (b) A transfer in implement or pursuance of a court order (other than an order allowing a heritable creditor simply to exercise remedies) or a decree in an action of division and sale.
    (c) A transfer between spouses in pursuance of an arrangement entered into between them after they have ceased living together. It should be noted that this exclusion is only likely to

15–28

---

[73] 2003 Reform Act, s.39(1)(b).
[74] 2003 Reform Act, s.39(3).
[75] Under the 2003 Reform Act, s.47.
[76] 2003 Reform Act, s.39(4).
[77] 2003 Reform Act, s.39(5).
[78] 2003 Reform Act, s.40(1).
[79] 2003 Reform Act, ss.40(2) and 66.
[80] 2003 Reform Act, s.40(3).
[81] 2003 Reform Act, s.40(4).

arise where there is a separation agreement or an obvious physical separation. There is no general exclusion of transfers
between family members although gratuitous transfers are
permitted under (a) above.

(d) A transfer of croft land to the crofting tenant.

(e) An inter company transfer between companies in the same
group.

(f) A transfer to a statutory undertaker for the purpose of carrying
out its undertaking. Statutory undertaker is construed in accordance with Section 214 of the Town and Country Planning
(Scotland) Act 1997.[82]

(g) A transfer:

    (i) implementing the compulsory acquisition of the land
under an enactment.

    (ii) by agreement, of land which could have been acquired
compulsorily under an enactment.

    (iii) implementing any right to buy by a community body
or crofting community body.[83]

    (iv) implementing missives for the sale and purchase of
land concluded, or an option to acquire land which
existed on a date on which the Register did not contain
a note of community interest or an application to register a community interest in the land.

    (v) conveying a house to a person who has purchased it
under the tenant's right to buy legislation.[84]

    (vi) which requires or, but for the provisions of section 14
of the Housing (Scotland) Act 1987 would require the
consent of Ministers under sub-section (5) or (7) of
section 12 of the Housing (Scotland) Act 1987. This
provision relates to the sale of common or open space
or allotments or of any house to which the housing
revenue account relates which sales can only be made
with the consent of Ministers.

    (vii) under section 65 of the Housing (Scotland) Act 2001.
This would be a transfer by a registered social landlord.

    (viii) vesting the land in a person for the purposes of
any enactment relating to sequestration, bankruptcy,
winding up or incapacity or for the purposes for
which judicial factors may be appointed.

(h) A transfer of land in consequence of the assumption, resigna-
tion or death of one or more partners in a firm or one or more
trustees of a trust.

The 2003 Reform Act defines "action taken with a view to transfer of
land" as advertisement or exposure for sale, the entering of negotiations
with a view to transfer or proceeding with a transfer initiated prior to
the date on which interest was registered.[85] Presumably a transfer of

---

[82] 2003 Reform Act, s.40(7).
[83] In terms of the 2003 Reform Act, Part 3.
[84] Under Part III of the Housing (Scotland) Act 1987.
[85] 2003 Reform Act, s.40(5).

land must be a transfer of actual ownership as opposed to the grant of some sort of subsidiary right such as a lease or a servitude. The anti-avoidance provisions[86] relate to transfers which form part of a scheme or series of transactions.

Anti-avoidance provisions

A transfer will not be permitted if it forms part of a scheme or arrange-   **15–29** ment or is one of a series of transfers one of the main purposes or effects of which is the avoidance of the requirements or consequence of the community right to buy.[87] The heritable creditor's power of sale[88] is subject to the prohibition even although the right of sale is in exercise of a statutory remedy.[89] It may be that the Scottish Executive feel there will be difficulties over permitted transfers and what constitutes action with a view to transfer. Accordingly Ministers have power to modify the provisions.[90] Where land subject to a registered interest is being transferred by way of an excluded transfer to a party other than a community body the transferor must incorporate in the disposition a declaration specifying which category of exclusion[91] applies.[92] Where the transfer is a gift, an inter company transfer or a transfer following changes in the identity of partners or trustees the declaration must also state that the transfer does not form part of a scheme or arrangement and is not one of a series.[93]

Duration, renewal and deletion of registered interests

A registered community interest has a life of five years from the date of   **15–30** registration[94] but can be renewed if the community body applies again for registration at any time within six months before the expiry of the five year period.[95] The application would of course have to follow the same original procedure.[96] When such an application is made Ministers will have to have regard to the original criteria for considering applications.[97] If they are satisfied however they may direct the Keeper to re-enter the interest in the Register.[98] When the interest has been re-registered it will have effect for a further period of five years from the date the original period of five years expires.[99] A registered interest will affect land notwithstanding a permitted transfer by way of say a gift or on separation.[1] In such a case the right to buy would arise on a transfer or proposed transfer by the transferee. If Ministers are satisfied that

---

[86] 2003 Reform Act, s.43.
[87] 2003 Reform Act, s.43(1).
[88] Under the Conveyancing and Feudal Reform (Scotland) Act 1970, s.25.
[89] Under the Conveyancing and Feudal Reform (Scotland) Act 1970, s.25; 2003 Reform Act s.40(6).
[90] 2003 Reform Act, ss.42 and 98(5).
[91] In terms of the 2003 Reform Act, s.40(4).
[92] 2003 Reform Act, s.43(2)(a).
[93] 2003 Reform Act, s.43(2)(b).
[94] 2003 Reform Act, s.44(1).
[95] 2003 Reform Act, s.44(2).
[96] Under the 2003 Reform Act, s.37.
[97] Under the 2003 Reform Act, s.38.
[98] 2003 Reform Act, s.44(3).
[99] 2003 Reform Act, s.44(4).
[1] 2003 Reform Act s.44(5).

there has been, since the date on which they decided to register the community interest, a change in any circumstances which would have had a bearing on their final decision to register they may direct the Keeper to delete the interest.[2] If an interest has been lost either through lapse of time or deletion from the Register there is nothing to prevent a community body from applying again to register an interest in land.[3]

COMMUNITY RIGHT TO BUY

Exercise of the right

The three stage process

15–31   The legislation draws a distinction between the activation of the right to buy and the actual exercise of the right to buy. Essentially there is a three stage process. In the first place a community body must register an interest.[4] In the second place circumstances must arise, such as a decision of the owner or heritable creditor to sell, which activate the right to buy. In the third place the community body must decide to exercise the right to buy. The right to buy will only arise where an interest has been registered and may be exercised when the owner of the land or heritable creditor gives or is deemed to have given notice that a transfer is proposed.[5] The right to buy is specific to particular holdings of land and cannot simply be general.[6] A "holding" is defined as land in the ownership of one person or in common or joint ownership.[7] Where the owner or creditor proposes to transfer land and the transfer is not a permitted transfer notice must be given to the community body or bodies in respect of which the interest is registered and to Ministers in accordance with the prescribed form.[8] The same notification requirement will apply in the case of a transfer which relates partly to land for which there is no registered community interest and partly to land for which there is.[9] On receipt of notification from an owner or heritable creditor Ministers must direct the Keeper to enter the particulars of notification in the Register.[10] Ministers must also, not later than seven days after receipt of the notification, send to the community body with the registered interest a note in the prescribed form seeking confirmation that the body will exercise its right to buy.[11] Ministers must also send a notice in the prescribed form to the owner of the land indicating that they have sent this notification to the community body.[12] The notice to the community body must indicate that the body has 30 days within which to confirm to

---

[2] 2003 Reform Act, s.45(1).
[3] 2003 Reform Act, s.46.
[4] Under the 2003 Reform Act, ss.37–40 and see para.15-25 above.
[5] 2003 Reform Act, s.47(1).
[6] 2003 Reform Act, s.47(2).
[7] 2003 Reform Act, ss.37(14), (15) and 47(4).
[8] 2003 Reform Act, s.48(1) and (2).
[9] 2003 Reform Act, s.48(3).
[10] 2003 Reform Act, s.49(1).
[11] 2003 Reform Act, s.49(2)(a).
[12] 2003 Reform Act, s.49 (2)(b).

Ministers that it intends to exercise the right to buy.[13] If the community body does not indicate within the 30-day period that it does intend to exercise the right to buy then Ministers are deemed to have received written notice that it will not exercise that right.[14] Ministers must send a copy of the notice to the community body and any confirmation of the exercise of the right to buy from that community body to the Keeper.[15] If Ministers fail to comply with the seven day time limit[16] it will not affect the validity of the right to buy procedure.[17] There are detailed provisions which would allow a community body to apply to the Lands Tribunal to determine that a prohibition of transfer or action to transfer land in respect of which a notice has been registered has been breached and that the applicant has, since the transfer or action, had a registered interest in the land in relation to which the breach occurred.[18] These provisions could have a serious effect on a singular successor who has in good faith accepted a transfer of land believing it to be a permitted transfer. Theoretically the Lands Tribunal could decide that despite declarations *in gremio* of the disposition[19] the transfer is not a permitted transfer. If the Keeper has registered the title presumably there cannot be rectification[20] because the singular successor will be a proprietor in possession and presumably not guilty of fraud. The question of carelessness however might arise in a question with the Keeper. The effect of the statutory provisions however is only to keep the interest alive and activate the community body's right to buy the land from the singular successor.

Community approval—ballot and Ministers' approval

Assuming the community body has indicated to Scottish Ministers that **15–32** it wishes to exercise the right to buy within the appropriate statutory time limit the next step is for that community body to obtain approval of the community which it represents and the consent of Ministers.[21] Community approval will be taken to be given if a majority of members of the community vote in a ballot in favour of the proposition provided that at least half of those eligible to vote do so or where less than half vote a sufficient number to justify the community purchase do so.[22] Ministers would have to be satisfied that these conditions have been met before giving their own approval. Ministers must also be satisfied that the land is registrable and that the community body continues to comply with the provisions of section 34. They must also be satisfied that what the community body proposes to do with the land is compatible with the furthering of sustainable development and that the proposed purchase of land is in the public interest. There must not have been, since the registration of interest, a change in any matter to the

---

[13] 2003 Reform Act, s.49(3) and (4).
[14] 2003 Reform Act, s.49(4).
[15] 2003 Reform Act, s.49(5).
[16] In terms of the 2003 Reform Act, s.49(2).
[17] 2003 Reform Act, s.49(6).
[18] 2003 Reform Act, s.50.
[19] In terms of the 2003 Reform Act, s.43.
[20] In terms of the Land Registration (Scotland) Act 1979, s.9.
[21] 2003 Reform Act, s.51(1).
[22] 2003 Reform Act, s.51(2).

extent that if the application to register the interest were made afresh it would be refused.[23] Community bodies may require confidentiality in respect of financial information.[24] Within 21 days of the last ballot by a community body Scottish Ministers require to notify that body and the owner of the land of their decision whether or not to give consent and they must direct that that decision is registered in the Register.[25] A failure on the part of Ministers to comply with the time limit however will not affect the validity of anything done nor the right to buy.[26] The ballot must be conducted in accordance with prescribed regulations. If it is not so conducted the right to buy is extinguished.[27] The community body must give information in relation to the ballot to Ministers.[28] This information must be given within 28 days beginning with the date when the valuer notifies the community body of the assessed value of the land or the price is determined by appeal.[29] Where the land in which the interest has been registered is salmon fishings or mineral rights Ministers cannot consent to the exercise of the right to buy unless they are in addition satisfied that the fishings are in waters which are within or contiguous to land which the community body is at the same time exercising its right to buy or already owns. Where minerals are involved and are in separate ownership from the land Ministers have to be satisfied where the minerals that the mineral rights are exercisable within the land.[30]

Declinature or extinction of right to buy

15–33   A community body holding a registered interest may give up the right to buy at any time whether or not the owner or heritable creditor has indicated an intention to transfer.[31] If the right to buy has been activated before declinature then the right to buy is extinguished together with the registered interest.[32] Ministers must give this information to the Keeper for registration.[33] Declinature does not prevent a community body from registering a community interest in the same land for a second or subsequent time.[34] The owner of land may also withdraw from a sale to a community body at any time prior to the conclusion of missives with that community body.[35] The owner must in that case give notice to Ministers and each community body which has registered an interest and Ministers must then send a copy of that notice to the Keeper.[36] Where the owner gives this notice the right to buy the land is extinguished but the interest will still remain as a registered interest.[37]

---

[23] 2003 Reform Act, s.51(3).
[24] 2003 Reform Act, s.51(4).
[25] 2003 Reform Act, s.51(5) and (6).
[26] 2003 Reform Act, s.51(7).
[27] 2003 Reform Act, s.52(1) and (2).
[28] 2003 Reform Act, s.52(3).
[29] 2003 Reform Act, s.52(4).
[30] 2003 Reform Act, s.53.
[31] 2003 Reform Act, s.54(1).
[32] 2003 Reform Act, s.54(3).
[33] 2003 Reform Act, s.54(2).
[34] 2003 Reform Act, s.54(4).
[35] 2003 Reform Act, s.54(5).
[36] 2003 Reform Act, s.54(5) and (6).
[37] 2003 Reform Act, s.54(9).

An owner cannot extinguish a right to buy by withdrawing before missives are concluded where the right to buy has arisen following a determination of the Lands Tribunal[38] that there has been a breach of prohibitions relating to transfer of land.

Competitions among community bodies

It is possible that more than one community body will have registered an interest in the same land. In such a case only one community body may exercise the right to buy.[39] It will be up to Ministers to decide between competing community bodies.[40] When the decision is made the unsuccessful community body's right to buy land is extinguished and the Keeper must be directed to delete that interest. Ministers must also notify the owner of the land and the community body of the decision. Ministers will also have to decide between community bodies and crofting community bodies.[41]

15–34

Conclusion of missives

The 2003 Reform Act provides that the actual acquisition shall proceed by way of offer and acceptance in the normal way. It is for the community body to make the offer to buy.[42] The price is to be a figure agreed between the community body and the owner of the land or where no such agreement can be reached a figure equal to the value assessed by an appointed valuer or determined on an appeal from such a valuation.[43] The offer must specify the date of entry and date of payment of the price. Where the price has been agreed between the community body and the owner of the land then the date of entry and the date of payment is to be a date not later than six months from the date when the community body sent confirmation that they were to exercise their right to buy to Ministers.[44] Where the price has been assessed by the appointed valuer and is the subject of an appeal other provisions apply. If the appeal has not, within the period of four months after the date when the community body sent the confirmation to Ministers been determined or abandoned by agreement then the date of payment and entry is a date not later than two months after the appeal is determined or abandoned.[45] The landowner and community body can always agree a later date of entry.[46] The offer may include such other reasonable conditions as are necessary or expedient to ensure efficient progress on completion of the transfer.[47] Presumably such conditions would be the standard conditions which would appear in any offer for rural land. Obvious provisions would be an obligation to deliver a valid disposition and exhibit a valid and marketable title or a land certificate with no exclusion of indemnity. It should be borne in mind that what might be regarded as standard

15–35

---

[38] Under the 2003 Reform Act, s.50.
[39] 2003 Reform Act, s.55(1).
[40] 2003 Reform Act, s.55(2).
[41] 2003 Reform Act, s.55(4) and (5).
[42] 2003 Reform Act, s.56(1).
[43] 2003 Reform Act, s.56(2).
[44] 2003 Reform Act, s.56(3)(a).
[45] 2003 Reform Act, s.56(3)(b).
[46] 2003 Reform Act, s.56(3)(c).
[47] 2003 Reform Act, s.56(4).

conditions in an offer for a semi-detached suburban dwellinghouse would not necessarily be standard conditions in respect of a large rural estate. For example a rural estate would normally be sold subject to any servitudes or wayleaves or rights of access which might exist whether constituted in a formal deed or not. There may also require to be special conditions in relation to sewage, drainage and water supply.

Failure to conclude missives

15–36 In some cases it may, for whatever reason, prove difficult to conclude missives irrespective of questions of price or value. Obviously in such a case the land in question cannot remain subject to a registered interest indefinitely. The legislation provides that if the community body has not, within the period fixed or agreed,[48] done any of the things required by the Act then the community body's right to buy the land is extinguished and Ministers must direct the Keeper to delete the interest from the Register and notify the owner and/or heritable creditor of that fact.[49] To prevent extinguishment the things which the community body must do[50] are either to conclude missives with the owner of the land or heritable creditor or where missives have not been concluded take all steps which in the opinion of the Lands Tribunal it could reasonably have taken in the time available towards concluding missives short of applying to the Lands Tribunal for an order.[51] Where missives have not been concluded and all reasonable steps have been taken in the time available to conclude missives and there has in the opinion of the Lands Tribunal been reasonably sufficient time to apply to the Lands Tribunal for an order then the community body must apply to the Lands Tribunal accordingly.[52] The power of the Lands Tribunal to make an order in the event of failure or delay to conclude missives is exercisable on an application to the Tribunal either by the owner of the land or the community body.[53] The terminology however in section 56 seems to suggest that it is more likely to be the owner who delays. Where either party applies to the Tribunal and the Tribunal is satisfied that either the owner/heritable creditor or the community body has unreasonably delayed the progress of transferring title the Tribunal may order either party to take such remedial action as is specified in the order and to do so within a specified time.[54] If a community body is at fault and fails to comply with the order within whatever time limit is specified and has not given notice to Ministers that it no longer wishes to exercise its right to buy the land then the Lands Tribunal may make an order extinguishing the right to buy and where such an order is made the Tribunal must send a copy of the order to Ministers and the owner of the land.[55] In such a case Ministers must direct the Keeper to delete the community body's interest from the Register and notify the owner of the land of that fact.[56] If

---

[48] In terms of the 2003 Reform Act, s.56(3).
[49] 2003 Reform Act, s.56(5).
[50] 2003 Reform Act, s.56(6).
[51] 2003 Reform Act, s.56(6).
[52] 2003 Reform Act, s.56(6)(c).
[53] 2003 Reform Act, s.57(1).
[54] 2003 Reform Act, s.57(1).
[55] 2003 Reform Act, s.57(2).
[56] 2003 Reform Act, s.57(3).

the owner of the land (which term includes the heritable creditor) fails to comply with an order of the Tribunal and has not given notice to Ministers and the community body that he, she or it no longer wishes to proceed with the transfer of the land then the Lands Tribunal may make an order authorising the community body to acquire the land subject to such terms and conditions as may be specified in the order and requiring the owner of the land to transfer the land to the community body in accordance with such terms and conditions.[57] If the owner refuses or fails to effect a transfer of the land in pursuance of an order the Lands Tribunal may authorise its principal clerk to adjust, execute and deliver such deeds or other documents as are necessary to complete the transfer to the like, force and effect as if the owner had acted in the manner required by the order.[58] This provision avoids the need to go to court to enforce any order of the Tribunal.

Procedure under section 50(3)

The procedure is different where the right to buy has been activated by notice under section 50(3). Such a notice would be served by Ministers where an owner or heritable creditor transferred or had taken steps to transfer land in breach of the right to buy provisions of the Act.[59] In such a case it might be supposed that the transferee will be unwilling to co-operate. The statutory provisions therefore make it clear that it is up to the community body to secure the expeditious exercise of their right to buy and to prepare all documents necessary to effect the transfer.[60] The price to be paid in such a case will be assessed by the appointed valuer or determined by an appeal.[61] There is no question therefore of the community body being able to buy the land for the same price that a transferee may have paid to the original owner who transferred in breach of the statutory provisions. The owner/transferee of the land must make available to the community body such deeds and other documents as are sufficient to enable the body to complete its title to the land and transfer the land accordingly.[62] If the owner of the land refuses or fails to make those deeds and other documents available or cannot be found then the Lands Tribunal may, on the application of the community body, order the owner or such other person appearing to the Tribunal to have those deed or documents to produce them.[63] If the owner/transferee of the land refuses or fails to effect the transfer the Lands Tribunal may on the application of the community body authorise its principal clerk to adjust, execute or deliver such deeds or other documents as will complete the transfer to the like, force and effect as if done by the owner.[64]

15–37

---

[57] 2003 Reform Act, s.57(4).
[58] 2003 Reform Act, s.57(5).
[59] 2003 Reform Act, s.58.
[60] 2003 Reform Act, s.58(2).
[61] 2003 Reform Act, s.58(3).
[62] 2003 Reform Act, s.58(4).
[63] 2003 Reform Act, s.58(5).
[64] 2003 Reform Act, s.58(6).

COMMUNITY RIGHT TO BUY

Valuation

Valuation—General

15–38   In some cases the price may be agreed between the community body and the owner or heritable creditor. Whether or not the price is agreed there is a statutory obligation on Ministers to appoint a valuer within seven days of receipt by Ministers of confirmation[65] of the community body's wish to exercise its right to buy.[66] The valuer must be suitable qualified, independent and have knowledge and experience of valuing land of a kind which is similar to the land being bought. Finding an independent valuer may be more difficult than at first sight it appears. In many cases the most suitable valuer will be a local valuer who has experience of local properties. However such a valuer may have acted in the past for the owner or possibly members of the community who now are members of the community body. Statutory valuers such as the district valuer will presumably not be regarded as independent because Ministers instruct the valuer and, indeed, pay the valuer's expenses.[67] Moreover there is a specific provision to the effect that the valuer does not act on behalf of the owner of the land or heritable creditor or the community body.[68] The valuer is to act as an expert and not as an arbiter.[69] The task of the valuer as expert is to ascertain the market value of the land as at the date on which the owner or heritable creditor notified Ministers[70] of his or her intention to sell the land or in the case where the community body's interest was registered in pursuance of a late application for registration[71] the date upon which Ministers received the community body's application.[72] Where the land includes salmon fishings or mineral rights the value of the fishings or mineral rights must be separately assessed.[73] Market value is defined[74] as the aggregate of:

    (a) The value on the open market as between a willing seller and a buyer, and

    (b) Where the right to buy is being exercised in relation to a part of the land in respect of which the owner has been given notice of proposed transfer the amount of any diminution in the value of the other part of the land which is attributable to severance.

This second factor in the valuation is similar to the injurious affection factor in the negotiation of compulsory purchase compensation. Where the whole of the land is being acquired account may be taken in so far as a willing seller or buyer would do so of any factor attributable to the

---

[65] Under the 2003 Reform Act, s.49(2)(a).
[66] 2003 Reform Act, s.59(1).
[67] 2003 Reform Act, s.59(10).
[68] 2003 Reform Act, s.59(3)(a).
[69] 2003 Reform Act, s.59(3)(b).
[70] Under the 2003 Reform Act, s.48(1).
[71] Under the 2003 Reform Act, s.39.
[72] 2003 Reform Act, s.59(4).
[73] 2003 Reform Act, s.59(5).
[74] 2003 Reform Act, s.59(6).

known existence of a third party who would be willing to buy the land at a price higher than other parties because of a characteristic of the land which relates peculiarly to that third party's interest in buying it.[75] This rather complicated provision must be taken together with the previous provision in relation to injurious affection on severance. Both of these provisions are designed to be as fair as is possible to the owner of the land. In addition to taking account of a reduction in the value of any remaining land where the right to buy is not in respect of the whole land proposed to be transferred the valuer must take into account the existence of a higher offer by a third party who may be prepared to pay a premium price for the land because, for example, it would be convenient to join that land on to other land owned by the third party. This type of added value is known as "marriage value".

Valuation—disregards

The statutory provisions contain certain matters which are to be disregarded in any valuation. These disregards are: **15–39**

(a) The registration of an interest in or the exercise of the right to buy the land by the community body. The valuation is not to be affected by the fact that the transaction is not entirely voluntary but under statutory provisions.

(b) The absence of the period of time which the land would, on the open market, be likely to be advertised and exposed for sale. Rises and falls in the market or projected rises and falls in the market after the valuation date will not be taken into account. The valuation date is the date of notification.[76]

(c) Any depreciation in the value of any other land owned by the seller. A distinction must be drawn between a case where an owner or heritable creditor indicates an intention to transfer land and the interest registered by the community body only applies to part of that land and the case where all of the land proposed to be transferred is to be bought by the community body but there is still some other land retained by the owner or heritable creditor. In the first case the severance is as a result of the action of the community body in only exercising the right to buy in respect of part of the land; in the second case the owner had already decided on the severance before giving notice of intention to sell and accordingly must be held to have taken the risk of a reduction in the value of the retained land on severance.

(d) The expenses of the valuation or otherwise related to the sale and purchase of the land.

Valuation—moveables

Where moveable property is being sold with the land the valuer must   **15–40**
include a valuation of that moveable property but that valuation must be separate from the valuation of the land. The principles on which the

---

[75] 2003 Reform Act, s.59(7)(a).
[76] Under the 2003 Reform Act, s.48(1).

valuation of the land is made to apply so far as appropriate to the valuation of the moveables.[77] There is no suggestion that a different valuer (such as an auctioneer) will be involved in the valuation of moveables and each moveable item has to be valued separately. Presumably an inventory will be drawn up. However the moveables to be valued must, in terms of the statutory provision, be moveables "used in connection" with the land being sold.

Valuation—procedure

15–41 As with other provisions relating to the obligations of the Ministers a failure to appoint a valuer within the seven day period will not affect the validity of the valuation or anything done in the valuation process.[78] The statutory procedure for carrying out the valuation provides that the valuer must invite the owner of the land or heritable creditor and the community body exercising the right to buy to make written representations as to the value of the land and any moveable property being bought with the land and must consider these representations accordingly.[79] There is no provision for any hearing or meeting, formal or informal, to be held at which the parties or agents on their behalf can make oral representations. The valuer must within a period of six weeks beginning with the date of appointment or such longer period as may be fixed by Ministers on the application of the valuer notify Ministers, the owner of the land and the community body of the assessed value of the land and of any moveable property which has been valued.[80] As with other time limits which apply to Ministers a failure to intimate by the valuer within the appropriate time limit will not affect the validity of the valuation.[81] Presumably in such a case the valuer would apply for an extension or a further extension. There does not appear to be any statutory bar to applying for more than one extension.

APPEALS

Appeals—registration of interest and exercise of right to buy

15–42 There are provisions which allow the owner of land or a community body to appeal to the sheriff against decisions by Ministers in relation to the consent to registration or non-registration of an interest or the consent to exercise of a right to buy. The owner of land may appeal by summary application to a sheriff against the decision by Ministers[82] that a community interest in the land is to be entered in the Register or a decision by Ministers[83] to give consent to the exercise by a community body of its right to buy land.[84] Similarly a community body may

---

[77] 2003 Reform Act, s.59(8) and (9).
[78] 2003 Reform Act, s.59(2).
[79] 2003 Reform Act, s.60(1).
[80] 2003 Reform Act, s.60(2) and (3).
[81] 2003 Reform Act, s.60(4).
[82] Under the 2003 Reform Act, s.37.
[83] Under the 2003 Reform Act, s.51.
[84] 2003 Reform Act, s.61(1).

by summary application appeal to the sheriff against a decision by Ministers[85] that its community interest is not to be entered on the Register or a decision by Ministers[86] not to give consent to the exercise by the community body of its right to buy.[87] It may be that certain members of the community are not in favour of the acquisition of the land by the particular community body. There may also be cases where, although the owner of the land is prepared to transfer to the community body without fuss other parties with subsidiary interests such as tenants may have different views. Accordingly there is provision for appeals to the sheriff by third parties.[88] A person who is a member of a community[89] or one who has an interest in land giving rise to a legally enforceable right may also by summary application appeal to the sheriff against the decision by Ministers that a community interest in land is to be entered in the Register or a decision by Ministers to consent to the exercise of the community body's right to buy land. This provision is rather odd in that it does not allow members of a community who may feel that their community body has not been organised or aggressive enough the right of appeal to the sheriff against a decision by Ministers not to register an interest or refuse to allow the community body to exercise its right to buy. Presumably it was felt that such a right of appeal could result in lengthy appeals by countless different members of a community who were not prepared to accept a rational and reasonable decision by Ministers not to allow the interest to be registered or the acquisition to go ahead. Any appeal must be lodged within 28 days of the date on which Ministers decided.[90] The sheriff in whose sheriffdom the land or any part of it is situated has jurisdiction to hear appeals.[91] Where an appeal is made by any of the competent parties then these parties must intimate the appeal to the other parties involved and Ministers. Where an appeal is by a member of a community intimation must be made to all three parties namely the community body, the owner and Ministers.[92] The decision of the sheriff in an appeal may require rectification of the Register, may oppose conditions upon the appellant, and is final.[93] It should be borne in mind that the reference to "the Register" is a reference to the Register of Community Interests in Land and not the Land Register.[94] Although the statutory provision states that the decision of the sheriff in an appeal is final no guidelines are given as to the factors which a sheriff should consider in determining an appeal against a decision of Ministers. However the appeal presumably must be based on a failure of Ministers to exercise their statutory obligations properly. As such it may take on the guise of a judicial review. It appears to have been conceded that despite the fact that the appeal is said to be final the Court of Session's jurisdiction to review the sheriff's

---

[85] Under the 2003 Reform Act, s.37.
[86] Under the 2003 Reform Act, s.51.
[87] 2003 Reform Act, s.61(2).
[88] 2003 Reform Act, s.61(3).
[89] As defined under the 2003 Reform Act, s.34(1)(a).
[90] 2003 Reform Act, s.61(4).
[91] 2003 Reform Act, s.61(5).
[92] 2003 Reform Act, s.61(6).
[93] 2003 Reform Act, s.61(7).
[94] 2003 Reform Act, s.46(1).

decision by way of judicial review procedure is not excluded. It has been held that the Court of Session can suspend or reduce any decision of a sheriff even in circumstances where the decision is stated to be final if that decision is *ultra vires* or in excess of jurisdiction. In *Brown v Hamilton District Council*[95] the House of Lords held that the sheriff had no jurisdiction to review a decision of a housing authority to the effect that a homeless person with a priority need for housing had become homeless intentionally within the meaning of section 17 of the Housing (Homeless Persons) Act 1977. The basis of the decision however was that the remedy of reduction or review was only competent in the Court of Session. There was no statutory provision which would have allowed the sheriff to review the decision of the local authority far less a statutory provision which indicated that any such decision would be final.

Appeals—valuation

15–43   The owner of the land or heritable creditor and the community body exercising the right to buy may appeal to the Lands Tribunal against the determination of the valuation by the valuer.[96] The appeal must state the grounds on which it is being made and must be lodged within 21 days of the date of notification[97] of the valuer's decision.[98] The Lands Tribunal may reassess the value of the land, any moveable property used in connection with and being sold with the land or both the land and such moveable property.[99] The valuer may be a witness in any appeal proceedings before the Tribunal.[1] The hearing of the appeal must begin not later than the first sitting day after the expiry of the period of four months beginning with the day on which the appeal was lodged and a sitting day is a day when the Lands Tribunal normally sits.[2] The Lands Tribunal must give reasons for its decision on an appeal and issue a written statement of these reasons within four weeks of the hearing of the appeal.[3] Nevertheless the validity of the appeal process and any decision will not be affected by the failure of the Lands Tribunal to comply with this time limit.[4] Ministers cannot be involved in the appeal by reason only that they appointed the valuer.[5] Ministers may make rules for appeals in front of the Tribunal in terms of the Lands Tribunal Act 1949.[6]

---

[95] 1983 S.L.T. 397(HL).
[96] 2003 Reform Act, s.62(1).
[97] Under the 2003 Reform Act, s.60(2).
[98] 2003 Reform Act, s.62(2).
[99] 2003 Reform Act, s.62(3).
[1] 2003 Reform Act, s.62(4).
[2] 2003 Reform Act, s.62(5) and (6).
[3] 2003 Reform Act, s.62(7).
[4] 2003 Reform Act, s.62(8).
[5] 2003 Reform Act, s.62(9).
[6] 2003 Reform Act, s.62(10).

Compensation

The legislation provides for the payment of compensation by Ministers **15–44** to persons except community bodies who have suffered loss or expense arising from the operation of the community right to buy.[7] Compensation is to be paid to such person (other than a community body) who have incurred loss or expense[8]:

(a) In complying with the procedural requirements relating to the community right to buy.

(b) As a result of failure by a community body to comply with an order of the Lands Tribunal requiring the community body to take action to rectify any delay relating to a transfer.[9]

(c) Attributable to a prohibition against the landowner and any heritable creditor from taking action to transfer the land or with a view to transfer following the receipt by Ministers of an application by a community body to have an interest registered,[10] or

(d) As a result of the provisions for fixing a date for entry.[11]

The amount of the compensation appears to be at the discretion of Ministers subject to an appeal to the Lands Tribunal which appeal must be lodged within 21 days of the decision of Ministers.[12] The heads of compensation are not cumulative but alternative. Where compensation is payable under head (d) the loss or expense incurred is restricted to the loss or expense incurred as a result of determining the date of entry where it is a type which would not normally be incurred had the sale of land been made to persons other than a community body.[13] If the community body and the owner of the land agree a date of entry and payment which is later than the last date on which the date of entry should have taken place in terms of the statutory provisions then no compensation will be payable for any loss or expense attributable to any period occurring after that statutory date.[14] The statutory provisions for the community right to buy may cut across an existing right of pre-emption, redemption or reversion which rights are suspended as from the date when the community body sends confirmation[15] to Ministers of its intention to buy the land.[16] A person holding such a right who has incurred loss or expense as result of the suspension of the right is also entitled to compensation from Ministers.[17] The procedure for calculation and recovering compensation may be prescribed by Ministers.[18]

---

[7] 2003 Reform Act, s.63.
[8] 2003 Reform Act, s.63(1).
[9] Under the 2003 Reform Act, s.57.
[10] Under the 2003 Reform Act, s.57(5)(e).
[11] Under the 2003 Reform Act, ss.56(3)(a) and 56(3)(b).
[12] 2003 Reform Act, s.64.
[13] 2003 Reform Act, s.63(2).
[14] 2003 Reform Act, s.63(3).
[15] Under the 2003 Reform Act, s.49(2)(a).
[16] 2003 Reform Act, s.65(1); and see para.15-45 below.
[17] 2003 Reform Act, s.63(4).
[18] 2003 Reform Act, s.63(5).

The effect of the right to buy on other rights

15–45 Where rights of pre-emption, redemption or reversion exercisable over land in which a community interest has been registered exist these rights are suspended as and from the date when the community body sent confirmation[19] to Ministers of its intention to buy the land.[20] The right of pre-emption, redemption or reversion is revived when the transfer is completed or at the point where the transfer is not completed because of a declinature[21] by the community body to proceed.[22] The effect here appears to be the same as where pre-emptions are suspended when a local authority residential tenant exercises a right to buy.[23] Other rights which parties may have in respect of land over which a community interest has been registered are also suspended. These rights include the rights of crofters or crofting communities to buy[24] and the right of sitting tenants to purchase from local authorities.[25] Again these rights are revived on completion of the sale or non-completion by reason of declinature by the community body.[26] However the community right to buy does not take precedence over an inhibition, an adjudication or the commencement, execution or operation of any other diligence.[27] Presumably therefore the owner of land will have to deal with an inhibition and will have an obligation to discharge that inhibition.

The role of the Land Register

15–46 There may be circumstances where the owner of land or a heritable creditor transfers land in circumstances where transfer may be prohibited because of the registration of an interest in land.[28] In such cases the Keeper must notify Ministers of the rejection of such an application on this ground and provide them with a copy of the application. The same would apply to a notice prohibiting the owner or heritable creditor.[29] The requirement on the Keeper to advise Ministers will not apply in a situation where the application has only been rejected because it has not been accompanied by the appropriate declaration that the transaction is exempt.[30]

---

[19] Under the 2003 Reform Act, s.49(2)(a).
[20] 2003 Reform Act, s.65(1)(a).
[21] Under 2003 Reform Act, s.54.
[22] 2003 Reform Act, s.65(1)(b).
[23] See *Patience v Ross & Cromarty District Council*, 1997 S.C. (HL) 46.
[24] Under s.12 of the Crofters (Scotland) Act 1993 or Part 3 of the 2003 Reform Act or under a new order by the Land Court in favour of a crofter.
[25] Under Part III of the Housing (Scotland) Act 1987.
[26] 2003 Reform Act, s.65(2).
[27] 2003 Reform Act, s.65(3).
[28] Under 2003 Reform Act, s.40(1).
[29] Under 2003 Reform Act, s.37(5)(e).
[30] Under 2003 Reform Act, s.43(2).

Partial transfers

References to the land in which a community interest has been regis-   **15–47**
tered include references to part of that land.[31] This however will not
apply to enable a right to buy land to be exercised by a community body
in relation to part of the land where they have registered interest in
respect of the whole of the land.[32]

Heritable creditors

References to creditors in a standard security with a right to sell land are   **15–48**
references to a creditor who has such right by virtue of the appropriate
statutory provisions relating to standard securities.[33]

THE CROFTING COMMUNITY RIGHT TO BUY

Introduction

Part 3 of the 2003 Reform Act sets out provisions conferring on crofting   **15–49**
communities the right to buy eligible croft land. These provisions differ
from the right of a crofter to purchase his or her croft.[34] As with the
general community right to buy there must be a community body and
this will be a company limited by guarantee.[35] However this right does
not depend on the owner taking a decision to sell or transfer; it is not
just a pre-emptive right. What is envisaged is that a crofting community
may buy up common grazings or croft land but not any croft which is
actually occupied or worked by its owner or a member of the owner's
family.

Definition of eligible croft land

Eligible croft land is defined[36] as land within the meaning of "croft"[37]   **15–50**
together with any land or right deemed to be a croft or a part thereof.
This would of course be subject to the exception in relation to a croft
occupied or worked by its owner or member of the owner's family.
Eligible croft land also includes any land in which a tenant of a croft
whether alone or in common with others has a right of pasture or
grazing and any land which is part of common grazing held by a tenant
of a croft or held runrig by such tenant which has not been apportioned
for exclusive use of a particular tenant.[38] Land which may be bought
includes salmon fishings and mineral rights. These can be bought either
at the same time as eligible croft land is being bought under which the

---

[31] 2003 Reform Act, s.67(1).
[32] 2003 Reform Act, s.67(2).
[33] Under ss.20(2), 23(2) and 24(1) of the Conveyancing and Feudal Reform (Scotland) Act 1970.
[34] Under the Crofters (Scotland) Act 1993.
[35] 2003 Reform Act, s.71.
[36] 2003 Reform Act, s.68.
[37] In terms of the Crofters (Scotland) Act 1993, s.3.
[38] Under the Crofters (Scotland) Act 1993, s.52.

mineral rights lie or from which the relevant salmon fishing can be exercised or during a relevant period following a successful application to purchase the eligible croft land. The period in relation to the purchase of salmon fishings is one year and in relation to mineral rights five years from the date on which the crofting community body bought the eligible croft land. A crofting community body which has bought eligible croft land may also buy eligible additional land which is contiguous to the eligible croft land originally bought and this includes eligible sporting interests.[39] Eligible sporting rights means the rights of a person other than the owner of the eligible croft land under any lease or other contract to shoot or fish own the land.[40] This does not however include any right under a lease of salmon fishings in inland waters within or contiguous to eligible croft land.[41]

Crofting community bodies

15–51   A crofting community body must be a company limited by guarantee and as with the general community right to buy the Memorandum and Articles of Association must include certain matters.[42] Ministers must be satisfied that a crofting community body has as its main purpose furthering the achievement of sustainable development.[43] A crofting community is statutorily defined as those persons resident in a crofting township situated in or otherwise associated with the croft land which the crofting community body has the right to buy. The definition also includes persons who are tenants of crofts in that crofting township but resident in any other place within sixteen kilometres of the township. In each case these parties must be entitled to vote in local government elections in the polling district or districts in which that township or as the case may be the other place within the sixteen kilometre distance is situated.[44] Ministers may adopt another definition if the statutory definition is inappropriate. A crofting township is defined[45] as any two or more crofts which share the right to use a common grazing together with that common grazing and any houses pertaining to or contiguous to those crofts or that common grazing or any combination of two or more crofting townships within that meaning.

Exercise of right to buy

15–52   Unlike the general community right to buy a crofting community right to buy is exercised as a right to buy without any requirement to register a preceding interest. Moreover the right does not depend on a decision by the owner to sell or transfer; it is not a pre-emptive right. The right can only be exercised with the consent of Ministers following on a written application by the crofting community body. The crofting com-

---

[39] 2003 Reform Act, s.70.
[40] 2003 Reform Act, s.70(4).
[41] 2003 Reform Act, s.70(5).
[42] 2003 Reform Act, s.71.
[43] 2003 Reform Act, s.71(4).
[44] 2003 Reform Act, s.71(5).
[45] 2003 Reform Act, s.71(6).

munity body must at the same time as it applies to Ministers send a copy of the application to the owner of the subjects and the heritable creditor.[46] This only applies where the heritable creditor has taken steps to enforce the security. Ministers will invite the owner or person entitled to the subjects of the application and the owners of contiguous land to give their views. Ministers must also invite the Crofter's Commission and any other person they consider to have an interest in the application to give views. Views must be given no later than 60 days after the sending of the invitation.[47] There are detailed provisions in relation to the process of the application, intimation, advertisement, criteria for giving consent by Ministers, ballots of the crofting community for approval and other matters in the 2003 Reform Act.[48] Where the owner of eligible additional land is involved matters may be referred to the Land Court if that owner does not consent. The Land Court may determine—

(a) That eligible additional land may be purchased by the crofting community body without the consent of the owner if the Court is satisfied that the purchase of the eligible additional land is essential for the development of the crofting community.
(b) That such development is compatible with furthering the achievement of sustainable development.
(c) That the purpose to which the land would be put cannot be reasonably achieved by any means within the power of the Court other than by its purchase.
(d) That where the land forms part of an area of land all of which is in the same ownership the purchase of the land will not seriously jeopardise the continued use and management of the remaining land, and
(e) That the land does not exceed in area whichever if the greater of ten hectares or five per cent of the combined area of land and any croft land being bought or which had previously been bought by the crofting community body.[49]

Additional land may be included at the request of the owner of that additional land. This would apply to eligible croft land and eligible additional land.[50] Ministers may make this decision themselves or they may refer the matter to the Land Court. If the owner of the land who wishes it to be purchased is unhappy with a refusal by Ministers to order the acquisition then matters must be referred to the Land Court.

Leaseback of sporting interests

Sporting interests are of considerable importance in rural communities. **15–53** Where an application is made by a crofting community body and the owner of the land is entitled to the sporting interests in the land and the community body has indicated that it proposes a leaseback of these interests Ministers shall within seven days of consenting to the application

---

[46] 2003 Reform Act, s.73(6).
[47] 2003 Reform Act, s.73(8).
[48] 2003 Reform Act, ss.73–76.
[49] 2003 Reform Act, s.77(3).
[50] 2003 Reform Act, s.79.

refer the question of what terms and conditions are appropriate for the lease to the Land Court. The Land Court determines the terms and conditions.[51] The owner must be willing to take a lease. The owner must within a period of 60 days notify Ministers in writing that he wishes such a lease. The terms and conditions must include the following:

    (a) A provision that the annual rent is nominal.

    (b) A provision that the duration of the lease is not to be less than twenty years.

    (c) A provision that the owner shall be entitled to assign the tenant's interest under the lease.[52]

The effect on other rights—pre-emption, redemption, reversion

15–54   As with the general community right to buy rights of pre-emption, redemption, reversion and options are suspended from the date Ministers receive the application to buy and are revived when the transfer is completed or withdrawn.[53] Similarly other statutory rights to buy such as the general community right to buy,[54] the crofter's right to buy his or his croft[55] or the right of a sitting tenant to buy from a local authority or other landlord[56] are suspended but revived.[57] Inhibitions, adjudications and other diligences are not affected by the crofting community body's right to buy.[58]

Completion of purchase

15–55   As with the general community right to buy it is for the crofting community to secure the expeditious exercise of its right to buy. There are detailed provisions in relation to documentation or production of titles, heritable securities and delays. The Land Court have rights to order the completion of a transfer.[59]

Valuation of croft land

15–56   The 2003 Reform Act contains detailed provisions in relation to the assessment of the value of the croft land to be acquired.[60] As with the general community right to buy Ministers must appoint a suitably qualified valuer who will not be acting on behalf of the owner or the crofting community body and will act as an expert and not an arbiter. The value to be assessed is the market value of the land or interest as at the date when Ministers consent to the application. Market value generally

---

[51] 2003 Reform Act, s.83.
[52] 2003 Reform Act, s.83(4).
[53] 2003 Reform Act, s.84(1).
[54] Under the 2003 Reform Act, Part 2.
[55] Under the Crofters (Scotland) Act 1993, s.12.
[56] Under the Housing (Scotland) Act 1987, Part III.
[57] 2003 Reform Act, s.84(2).
[58] 2003 Reform Act, s.84(3).
[59] 2003 Reform Act, ss.86 and 87.
[60] 2003 Reform Act, ss.88–93.

will be open market value between a willing seller and buyer but will also take into account depreciation of other land by injurious affection and disturbance. The valuation procedure is similar to the procedure in respect of the general community right to buy. There is provision for paying compensation to an owner or former owner who has incurred loss or expense in complying with the various procedures[61] and grants may be paid towards crofting community body's liabilities to pay this compensation.[62]

Appeals

Owners of land or persons entitled to sporting interests may, by summary application to the sheriff, appeal against Ministers' decisions to consent to an application from members of crofting communities. Other parties who may appeal are members of the crofting community, parties with subsidiary legal rights such as tenants and parties who were invited to give a view to Ministers. The crofting community body may appeal to the sheriff against a decision to refuse an application.[63] The Land Court does not appear to have a jurisdiction in this regard. Appeals in relation to valuation matters however do go to the Land Court.[64] **15–57**

Register of crofting community rights to buy

Although there is no provision for the registration of an interest of a crofting community the Crofter's Commission must set up and keep or secure that there is kept a Register of Crofting Community Rights to Buy which will be open for public inspection.[65] The Register will contain the name and address and registered office of the crofting community body which has submitted an application, a copy of the application and a copy of the Ministers' decision. Copies of notices of withdrawal, confirmation of intention to proceed and acknowledgements by Ministers must also be kept. **15–58**

Anti avoidance provisions

Where an owner of land or a person entitled to an interest to which an application relates has notification of that application then no disposal may take place after the consent date to any person other than the crofting community body.[66] The consent date is the date when Ministers consent to the application to buy the land.[67] There is no prohibition of a sale or disposal prior to the consent date even in circumstances where the owner may be aware that an application has or is to be made. The owner appears to be free to dispose of the land right up to the date on which Ministers consent. **15–59**

---

[61] 2003 Reform Act, s.89.
[62] 2003 Reform Act, s.90.
[63] 2003 Reform Act, s.91.
[64] 2003 Reform Act, s.92.
[65] 2003 Reform Act, s.94.
[66] 2003 Reform Act, s.95(1).
[67] 2003 Reform Act, ss.73 and 87(2).

The Scottish Land Court

15–60   The Scottish Land Court is given specific jurisdictions in relation to various matters but also a general jurisdiction to conduct hearings into and determine matters of fact in law relating to the exercise of the crofting community right to buy.[68] Appeal lies to the Inner House of the Court of Session by way of special case.[69] Otherwise the decision of the Land Court is final.

---

[68] 2003 Reform Act, s.97(1).
[69] 2003 Reform Act, s.97.

CHAPTER 16

HUMAN RIGHTS

INTRODUCTION

The dream of at least one prime minister was to create a property **16–01** owning democracy in the United Kingdom. Indeed it might be said that the need to own property is very deeply embedded in the British psyche. The right of property however is less than absolute in most western societies. It would take several volumes to comment on all the legal restrictions which apply to the right of property. The European Convention for the Protection of Human Rights and Fundamental Freedoms came into force on September 3, 1953 and was ratified by the United Kingdom before that in March 1951. At the time individual states still reeling from the Second World War were more concerned with the protection of human beings and their rights as persons than with the protection of property rights. Accordingly there was no mention of any human right in property in the original Convention. Moreover at the end of the war many states were actively taking a great many economic undertakings and utilities into public ownership. Accordingly to have included some sort of human right in property would have been problematic. The Convention itself has been amended five times by various protocols. A rather modified protection for human rights in property appears in the First Protocol.[1] In general terms Article 1 of the First Protocol provides that every natural or legal person is entitled to the peaceful enjoyment of his or her possessions. This right however is heavily qualified and indeed is weaker than the statement in the Universal Declaration of Human Rights which provides that everyone has the right to own property alone as well as in association with others.[2]

PROPERTY AND POSSESSIONS

Most jurisdictions draw a distinction between a right of property or **16–02** ownership and the lesser right of possession. For the purposes however of Article 1 of Protocol 1 the two terms have been treated as substantially the same.[3] The term "possessions" has been interpreted in a broad commercial way so that virtually all types of property, heritable and

---

[1] Protocol 1, Art.1; for a detailed discussion see Reed and Murdoch, *A Guide to Human Rights Law in Scotland*, Ch.8 and Greens *Scottish Human Rights Service* Div.C (Property).
[2] Universal Declaration of Human Rights 1948, Art.17.
[3] *Marckx v Belgium* (1979) 2 E.H.R.R 330.

moveable, corporeal and incorporeal are included in the term. Effectively what the Article seeks to protect are broad economic interests. Thus in *Gasus Dozier-Und Födertechnik v Netherlands*[4] the European Court of Human Rights took the view that it did not matter whether a particular property right was deemed a right of ownership or simply a right in security. A house,[5] an unregistered title,[6] a landlord's right to rent[7] and a real right of security[8] have all been held to be possessions for the purposes of the Article. The property rights or possessions must be existing ones and not contingent interests such as the right to succeed while the testator of a will is still alive.[9] The Article is essentially concerned with the protection of property rights and not peripheral or qualitative matters relating to property such as the environment.[10]

ADOPTION OF THE CONVENTION

16–03 The Convention was adopted into domestic law by the Human Rights Act 1998 and the Scotland Act 1998. A court or tribunal determining a question which has arisen in connection with any right under the Convention must apply the relevant law relating to human rights.[11] There is also an obligation to interpret primary and subordinate legislation in such a way as is compatible with the Convention.[12] So far as the Scottish Parliament is concerned there is separate provision in the Scotland Act 1998. There it is provided[13] that an Act of the Scottish Parliament is not law in so far as any provision is outside the legislative competence of the Scottish Parliament and this would include an Act of that Parliament which was incompatible with the rights which are created in the Convention. Similarly Scottish Ministers as members of the Scottish Executive have no power to make subordinate legislation nor do any other act which is incompatible with the rights under the Convention.[14]

THE WORDS OF ARTICLE 1 OF PROTOCOL 1

16–04 Article 1 of the First Protocol to the Convention is in the following terms:

"Every natural or legal person is entitled to the peaceful enjoyment of his possessions. No one shall be deprived of his possessions except in the public interest and subject to the conditions provided for by law and by the general principles of international law.

---

[4] (1995) 20 E.H.R.R. 403.
[5] *Akdivar v Turkey* (1996) 23 E.H.R.R. 143.
[6] *Holy Monasteries v Greece* (1994) 20 E.H.R.R. 1.
[7] *Mellacher v Austria* (1989) 12 E.H.R.R. 391.
[8] *Gasus Dozier-Und Födertechnik v Netherlands* (1995) 20 E.H.R.R. 403.
[9] *Inze v Austria* (1997) 10 E.H.R.R. 394.
[10] *S v France* (13728/88) (1990) DR 65, 250.
[11] Human Rights Act 1998, s.2.
[12] Human Rights Act 1998, s.3.
[13] Scotland Act 1998, s.29.
[14] Scotland Act 1998, s.57(2).

The preceding provisions shall not, however, in any way impair the right of a State to enforce such laws as it deems necessary to control the use of property in accordance with the general interest or to secure the payment of taxes or other contributions or penalties."

It is obvious even from the most superficial reading of Article 1 that the protection afforded to the individual is heavily qualified by reference in the first place to the public interest and in the second place to the general interest and the right of the State to act in that general interest. Accordingly where an issue arises in relation to the human right in property a balance between the right of the individual and the public or general interest has to be struck.

THE THREE RULES

In the leading case of *Sporrong & Lönnroth v Sweden*[15] the European Court **16–05** of Human Rights held that the human right in property involved three rules or principles. The first of these is the general principle that a person is entitled to the peaceful enjoyment of possessions or property. Secondly such a person should be protected against deprivation of these possessions or property. However thirdly states are entitled to control the use of property having regard to the general interest. Any analysis of the decisions of the European Court of Human Rights and indeed the decisions of domestic courts in applying Article 1 of Protocol 1 leads one inescapably to the conclusion that the second and third rules are of greater significance than the first. The first rule merely sets out a general guiding principle which is then heavily qualified. One of the leading cases involving the United Kingdom is *James v UK*[16] Any consideration of the human rights implications of the Scottish Executive's property law reform programme should be taken against this particular decision because it does relate to property rights of a heritable nature. The United Kingdom Parliament passed the Leasehold Reform Act 1967. The main thrust of the Act was to allow those who held residential property on leasehold tenure to obtain freehold tenure by buying out the lease from the landlord on payment of a sum of money by way of compensation. However, the compensation payable was not necessarily the market value of the land and the buildings thereon but in many cases simply the value of the land disregarding the value of the buildings. The justification for this was that the original landlord had simply leased a plot of land and the original tenant had erected the buildings at his or her expense. Accordingly, it was thought inequitable in these cases that the landlord pocket the value of the buildings as well as the land albeit that the landlord's and the tenant's interest might have changed hands on a number of occasions for value which might have included the value of the buildings. The Duke of Westminster's predecessor had acquired large tracts of land in Mayfair and Belgravia in London and granted ground leases. In the normal course of events when these leases came to an end the property including the buildings reverted to the landlord

---

[15] (1982) 5 E.H.R.R. 35.
[16] (1986) 8 E.H.R.R. 329.

who could negotiate either a new lease or sell at market value. The Leasehold Reform Act 1967 cut across these commercial and legal rights to the economic detriment of the Duke of Westminster's family. Accordingly an action was brought in the European Court of Human Rights in which it was alleged that the rights of the landlord to peaceful possession of his property in terms of Article 1 of Protocol 1 had been infringed. The United Kingdom defended the action on the ground that the legislation was necessary to control the use of property in accordance with the general interest. The European Court of Human Rights upheld the right of the United Kingdom to pass the legislation and decided against the landlord. Looking at the case in isolation the deprivation of the landlord's normal property right or at least the restriction of that right in economic terms is a clear breach of Article 1. In coming to its decision however the European Court of Human Rights appeared to take the view that there was a wide margin involving the economic and social policy of any state and that there could be a general or public interest in ensuring the fairness of private legal relations between individuals even where these were regulated by a private contract. A state could effectively take away a property right in pursuance of legitimate social or economic or other policies in the general interest even where the individual property concerned could not be said to be property in which the community at large had any rights of use or enjoyment. In other words there could be a public interest in a private contract or private property right. In *James v United Kingdom* it was held that the court must first determine whether the second and third rules were applicable before coming to a view as to whether or not the general right to peaceful enjoyment had been breached. For there to be a deprivation of possessions or property there need not be complete confiscation. It has been held that if a state places so many restrictions on the right of property as to make it virtually useless then there can be a breach of Article 1.[17] Recently it has been observed in the Judicial Committee of the Privy Council[18] that whether a law or the exercise of an administrative power amounts to a deprivation of property or possessions depends on the substance of the law rather than its form. In the past the European Court of Human Rights has looked at the spirit of legislation and not just the letter.[19] Not all deprivations of property will amount to a breach of the Article. The law of positive prescription in relation to heritable property will eventually deprive the true owner of the right of ownership notwithstanding the fact that the possessor may be relying on an invalid title and be in bad faith.[20] In England and Wales a party can lose ownership by adverse possession alone and it has been held that these laws of prescription are not breaches of Article 1 of Protocol 1.[21] The discharge of a land obligation without compensation to feudal superiors has been held not to be a breach of Article 1 of Protocol 1.[22]

---

[17] See *Papamichalopoulos v Greece* (1993) 16 E.H.R.R. 440; *Vasilescu v Romania* (1999) 28 E.H.R.R. 241.

[18] *Grape Bay Ltd v Att.-Gen. Of Bermuda* [2000] 1 W.L.R. 574 at 583 G.

[19] See *Stran Greek Refineries v Greece* (1994) 19 E.H.R.R. 293.

[20] Prescription and Limitation (Scotland) Act 1973, s.1.

[21] *J A Pye (Oxford) Ltd v Graham* [2001] 2 W.L.R. 1293.

[22] *Strathclyde Joint Police Board v Elderslie Estates Ltd*, August 17, 2001, Lands Tr.; 2001 GWD 7-1101

THE DOCTRINE OF PROPORTIONALITY

The right of the state to interfere with property rights in the general **16–06** interest can evolve a difficult balancing act. Obviously there will be no difficulty in relation to property taxes such as stamp duty land tax and other penalties. The delicate balance between the rights of the individual and the general interest is referred to as "proportionality". The term used in Article 1 is "control". The state has the right to control the use of property in accordance with the general interest. "Control" has been given a rather wide interpretation including the seizure of goods,[23] the control of rent increases,[24] planning control[25] and the revocation or suspension of a licence.[26] In coming to a view on whether or not the action of a state is proportionate the existence of compensation for the deprivation of a property right will always be a significant factor. However it is clear that the compensation need not be full compensation in the sense of meeting the open market value of the property right which has been lost or restricted.[27] It has been held that confiscation orders following a conviction for drug offences do not breach Article 1 of Protocol 1 because a fair balance is struck between the demands of the general interest of the community in combating drug trafficking and the protection of an individual's property right.[28]

HUMAN RIGHTS AND PROPERTY LAW REFORM

The new legislation

On November 28, 2004 the property rights of certain people will be **16–07** altered radically. The entire system of land tenure whereby a vassal holds land of a superior will cease to exist and estates of superiority including the paramount superiority of the Crown and the Prince and Steward of Scotland will be extinguished.[29] A new code dealing with real burdens will come into being and there will be radical changes in the law of the tenement. The use of land is also affected by the 2003 Reform Act.

Abolition of Feudal Tenure etc (Scotland) Act 2000

The rights of superiors to enforce real burdens, will for the most part, **16–08** cease subject to the rights to reallot and preserve. In general terms no compensation is payable for the simple loss of the superiority title and with it the loss of the right to enforce feudal conditions or waive them

---

[23] *Air Canada v UK* (1995) 20 E.H.R.R. 151.
[24] *Mellacher v Austria* (1989) 12 E.H.R.R. 391.
[25] *Pine Valley Developments v Ireland* (1991) 14 E.H.R.R. 319.
[26] *Tre Traktöre v Sweden* (1989) 14 E.H.R.R. 309; *Catscratch Ltd v City of Glasgow Licensing Board* (No.2) 2001 GWD 19-748; *Baird v Glasgow City Council*, Glasgow Sheriff Court, December 18, 2002.
[27] *Lithgow v UK* (1986) 8 E.H.R.R. 329; *James v UK* (1986) 8 E.H.R.R. 123; *Holy Monasteries v Greece* (1994) 20 E.H.R.R. 1
[28] *HM Advocate v McIntosh*, 2000 S.L.T. 1233; *HM Advocate v McSalley*, 2000 S.L.T. 1235; *HM Advocate v Burns*, 2000 S.L.T. 1242.
[29] 2000 Act, s.1.

in return for payment. At first sight the 2000 Act has all the appearance of confiscatory legislation. There is no doubt that an estate of superiority is a property right. Indeed it is a right of ownership and the 2000 Act extinguishes that ownership completely. The 2000 Act however seeks to address the issue of proportionality in a number of ways. In the first place the superior has certain restricted rights to reallot burdens or where there is no land capable of being a new dominant property, preserve them as personal real burdens.[30] In the second place the superior has the opportunity at least to attempt to agree with the vassal that the burden will stay alive with other land belonging to the superior being the dominant land.[31] In the third place where the vassal refuses to enter such an agreement the matter may be referred to the Lands Tribunal which will have the final say although that decision would be based, not on feudal principles, but on amenity issues having regard to any detrimental effect on the new dominant land caused by extinguishment.[32] The 2000 Act also caters for the situation where the price at which ground was feued in the past was nominal or non-existent because of the imposition of a particular burden, usually a restriction to some public spirited use or other. In such a case the 2000 Act contains provisions for very limited compensation.[33] The compensation bears no relation to any current development value of the burdened land. Nevertheless in human rights terms the compensation need not be at market value.[34] The fact that some limited compensation was payable to the landlord was a significant factor in *James v UK*[35] In so far as existing ground burdens are concerned the compensation which is payable[36] will be regarded as full compensation for the loss of a financial return. In any event it is difficult to see how the Scottish Parliament could have provided less generous terms for the compensatory payment on the extinction of feu duties than is already available for the voluntary and compulsory redemption of feu duties.[37] The author cannot see that a challenge under Article 1 of Protocol 1 in relation to the abolition legislation will succeed. There must be a public or general interest in the abolition of what most people would regard as an archaic and outmoded system of land tenure. Moreover the proportionality test has been met given the safeguards and the limited compensation rights which are contained in the 2000 Act.

Title Conditions (Scotland) Act 2003

16–09   In some ways it was supposed that the 2003 Act would give rise to less controversy than the 2000 Act. For some reason this has proved not to be the case although the 2003 Act does not raise so many human rights implications. Real burdens have been a feature of the land tenure system for some time and they were not restricted to the feudal context.

---

[30] 2000 Act, s.18.
[31] 2000 Act, s.19.
[32] 2000 Act, s.20.
[33] 2000 Act, ss.33–40.
[34] *Holy Monasteries v Greece* (1994) 20 E.H.R.R. 1.
[35] (1986) 8 E.H.R.R. 123.
[36] 2000 Act, ss.7–16.
[37] Under the Land Tenure Reform (Scotland) Act 1974, ss.4, 5 and 6.

They have not been abolished. There may of course be an argument that parties who might not have had enforcement rights in the past will now have them especially in respect in relation to community burdens applicable to related properties. There is also provision in section 57 (2) which does result in the imposition of burdens on land which had not been burdened because of a technical omission to nominate a benefited property in a deed which is clearly intended to create a common scheme. However if one takes the view that the burdens were always enforceable by one party it should not really matter for human rights purposes that they are now enforceable by another party or perhaps a number of parties; the burden on the land is essentially the same. The provisions in relation to the extinction of real burdens following on acquiescence,[38] the new five year negative prescription[39] and the notice of termination procedure[40] do not really offend against Article 1. The law of acquiescence has been with us for some time and he right to take action in respect of breaches of real burdens has always been subject to the long negative prescription of 20 years. The five year prescription is simply a shortening of the time period and not a matter of principle. It might be argued that the notice of termination procedure does impinge on human rights but proportionality is achieved by providing the benefited proprietor with a right to apply to the Lands Tribunal to have the burden renewed or varied.[41] The author cannot foresee any challenge under Article 1 of Protocol 1 in respect of any of the provisions of the 2003 Act being successful.

Tenements (Scotland) Bill

The scheme of the 2004 Bill is to leave the common law of ownership in so far as it relates to tenement properties intact. It has of course always been competent to alter the common law rules in the deeds. Admittedly in so far as maintenance obligations are concerned these will be altered for certain parties. Where the titles are silent the proprietor of a top flat will no longer have sole responsibility for maintenance of the roof because the roof is scheme property. Undoubtedly this is to the benefit of the top most proprietor but it is to the detriment of the proprietors of flatted units below because they will after a certain date have an increased burden of maintenance. There are no compensation provisions to deal with this shift in the balance of maintenance obligation. One could argue that the price that a ground flat proprietor paid for that particular flat was higher because, having regard to the state of the title to the particular tenement, there was no liability for maintenance of the roof. In practical terms however the price is often fixed by the market before the titles are examined. The 2004 Bill does not provide for any compensation to be payable to that ground floor proprietor to take account of a lowering in value as a result of the imposition of the statutory liability for maintenance of the roof. Accordingly the issue of proportionality here rests solely on the general interest argument. That

16–10

---

38 2003 Act, s.16.
39 2003 Act, s.18.
40 2003 Act, ss.20–24.
41 2000 Act, ss.21(4)(d) and 90(1)(b)(i).

general interest argument has to do with encouraging owners of tenemental property to maintain that property. The argument runs that provided owners see the apportionment of costs of maintenance as fair they are more likely to maintain the property, especially common parts. If because of a quirk of conveyancing or indeed an omission of a conveyancing solicitor the allocation of maintenance obligations seems unfair, an affected owner is less likely to be interested in maintenance. Given the fact that most other jurisdictions have extremely detailed statutory provisions in relation to flatted properties it is the author's view that standing the fact that the 2004 Bill does not alter ownership rights as such a challenge by such a ground floor proprietor under Article 1 of Protocol 1 is unlikely to succeed. One would also have to take on board that the vast majority of tenemental titles do indeed provide for common maintenance of all the major parts of a tenement such as the roof.

Management provisions

16–11   Both the 2003 Act and the 2004 Bill contain detailed provisions in relation to how property is to be managed. The 2003 Act provides for community burdens and manager burdens and the 2004 Bill provides a Tenement Management Scheme. The 2003 Act also makes provision for a Development Management Scheme. These provisions are however counterbalanced by rights to control and indeed dismiss managers and prohibitions of or restrictions on long term management monopolies. So far as tenemental properties are concerned common owners will lose their right to veto decisions relating to routine common maintenance but there are safeguards to protect dissenters. Where a party is liable for not less than 75% of scheme costs that party has an automatic right to annul a scheme decision. There is also a general power to appeal to the sheriff. It seems to the author that the balance of proportionality has been appropriately struck and there is unlikely to be any successful challenge to these management provisions in the 2003 Act and the 2004 Bill under Article 1 of Protocol 1.

Land Reform Act 2003

16–12   The 2003 Reform Act deals more with land use than with land tenure. As such a challenge under Article 1 of Protocol 1 might be seen to be more likely. The Act introduced statutory access rights, a community right to buy and a crofting community right to buy. The exercise of the rights of access however must be responsible and there is an access code. The management of land subject to the rights of access must also be responsible. There are also provisions in relation to excluded land.[42] There could be an issue in relation to how much land is necessary for reasonable privacy in relation to a house which is excluded from access rights. Nevertheless it does seem that the use of such words as "reasonable privacy" will be enough to comply with not only Article 1 of Protocol 1 but Article 8 of the Convention itself which deals with respect

---

[42] 2003 Reform Act, s.6.

for a citizen's private and family life and his or her home. The rights to buy for communities and crofting communities are only rights to buy at market value and there is provision for the appointment of an independent valuer. The community right to buy of course only arises when the landowner has decided to sell. Given the fact that the community will be a rural community one wonders whether or not the community right to buy would pass the public or general interest test. However Scottish Ministers must decide in the first place whether to allow registration of an interest and then must consent to the actual purchase. Moreover there are rights of appeal against ministerial decisions.[43] It is the author's view that the fact that the compensation offered here is full or market compensation will be sufficient to satisfy the proportionality test and that the community right to buy will not be deemed to be a breach of Article 1 of Protocol 1. So far as the crofting community is concerned there is no need to register an interest and it can be exercised whether or not the owner is proposing to sell. However the consent of ministers is still required before a crofting community body can actually exercise the right.[44] It is unlikely that any of the provisions relating to the crofting community's right to buy will be held to contravene Article 1 of Protocol 1.

Leasehold Reform

In *Mellacher v Austria*[45] the European Court of Human Rights held that rent control measures which effectively deprived the landlords of part of the rental income from their property did not contravene Article 1 of Protocol 1. The effect of the Austrian legislation was that there were substantial rent reductions in many cases despite the fact that the original rents had been agreed between landlords and tenants at the time and were in line with the then prevailing market rents. Accordingly the leases represented commercially agreed bargains voluntarily entered into between private persons the general public having no legal interest in these contracts. Nevertheless the court held that Austria could decide as a matter of social policy that the rents were unacceptable from the point of view of social justice. *Mellacher v Austria* is an example of how wide and general the right of the state to interfere with property rights can be if it can be shown in some way or other that there is a general or public interest not just in the legal sense but in the economic or social sense. The Leasehold Casualties (Scotland) Act 2001 received Royal Assent on April 12, 2001. Feudal casualties were abolished by the Feudal Casualties (Scotland) Act 1914. A casualty is a single payment due by a tenant to the landlord on the occurrence of a particular event such as the entry of a singular successor to the tenant's interest. Some casualties had provided for one years rent at current market value. The effect of the 2001 Act is to abolish all leasehold casualties with minimal compensation even where the casualty is for full market rent. Various parties appeared before the Justice Committee to give evidence during the Bills passage. One of the landlords who had recently acquired the

16–13

---

[43] 2003 Reform Act, s.61.
[44] 2003 Reform Act, s.73.
[45] (1989) 12 E.H.R.R. 391.

heritable interest gave evidence to the effect that the compensation terms were derisory in as much as they were based on the original nominal tack duties under the lease and not current market rents. There seems little doubt that the minimal compensation provisions were inserted in the Act purely to comply with Article 1 of Protocol 1. Again the question of proportionality arises. On one view one might say that if it is obvious that the compensation provisions are mere window dressing inserted purely to give the impression of human rights compliance then the legislation fails the proportionality test. However that is not the way in which the European Court of Human Rights and indeed domestic courts have chosen to interpret Article 1 of Protocol 1. All that really needs to be shown is that the state has addressed the question of proportionality including compensation in a reasonable manner. There has been no challenge to the Leasehold Casualties (Scotland) Act 2001 under Article 1 of Protocol 1 and in the opinion of the author a challenge would not succeed. The Scottish Law Commission has looked at leasehold tenure in general and their final report on the conversion of long leases to ordinary ownership, is likely to be produced at the end of 2004 or early in 2005.[46] The final report will have to decide on a definition of a long lease in terms of duration or in terms of years still to run. The Commission will also require to come to a view on whether it is appropriate for certain leases such as ground leases granted by local authorities for development to be excluded from the legislation. The scheme for conversion is likely to follow the same pattern as the scheme for the abolition of the feudal system with compensation based on the loss of rent or tack duty rather than market value of the land let and the buildings thereon. As with feu duties however compensation is only likely to be due if it is actually claimed. One of the difficulties with long leasehold tenure is that the identity of the landlord over the years becomes obscure there being little or no incentive to make up a title to a landlord's interest which produces a nominal annual income by way tack duty. There is of course a legislative precedent for the conversion of long leasehold title.[47] It is difficult to comment in detail on the human rights implications of any scheme until the legislation is drafted but assuming that it is drafted with some compensation provisions and reasonable exclusions it is unlikely to contravene Article 1 of Protocol 1.

---

[46] See discussion paper No.112, April 2001.
[47] Long Leases (Scotland) Act 1954 the provisions of which expired in 1959.

APPENDIX A

CONSTITUTIVE DEED OF REAL BURDENS

by

AB (Developments) Limited

2004

Subjects: Development at Ditch Farm, Anytown

Ref:
FAS2889

Harper Macleod The Ca'd'oro 45 Gordon Street Glasgow G1 3PE
Tel +44 (0)141 221 8888 **Fax** +44(0)141 226 4198
e-mail info@harpermacleod.co.uk **glasgow@thealliance.com**
www.harpermacleod.co.uk www.the**alliance**law.com **DX** GW86

Glasgow Berlin Dublin Düsseldorf Edinburgh Essen Frankfurt
Hamburg London Munich Paris

WE, AB (Developments) Limited, incorporated under the Companies Acts (Company No. 12345) and having our registered office at The Old Bank, Thirty Any Street, Erehwon heritable proprietors of ALL and WHOLE that area or piece of ground at Ditch Farm, Anytown being the subjects registered in the Land Register of Scotland under Title Number XYX 1234; WHEREAS we are about to erect dwellinghouses within that area or piece of ground comprising the Development shown outlined in green on the Plan annexed and signed as relative hereto (hereinafter referred to as "the Development") in separate plots for the erection of Detached Dwellinghouses and/or Semi-Detached Dwellinghouses, and/or Terraced Dwellinghouses and/or Cottage Flats and/or Flatted Dwellinghouses and that it is expedient to set forth and declare the various reservations, real burdens, conditions, servitudes and others affecting the Development which will apply to the said Development, and where appropriate a part or parts of the Development, and any building or buildings erected or to be erected thereon so that the same shall be constituted as real burdens within the meaning of Part I of the Title Conditions (Scotland) Act 2003; THEREFORE we do hereby provide, set forth and declare but that without prejudice to the addition in specific cases of further reservations, burdens, conditions and others or the real burdens and conditions as already affecting the Development as follows:-

FIRST	In this Deed:
Definitions	"The said Plan" means the Plan annexed and signed as relative hereto;
	"The 2003 Act" means the Title Conditions (Scotland) Act 2003;
	"Block" means a building containing Flatted Dwellinghouses the solum of which is owned in common by the Proprietors of the Flats or in respect of which each of the Proprietors has a right of Common Property;
	"Common Area" means the area outlined in green[1] on the said Plan annexed and signed as relative hereto, under exception of (1) all Plots and (2) any paths to which any individual Proprietor or Proprietors has/have been given a servitude right in the Disposition granted in their favour or by Deed of Servitude or otherwise, and (3) all parking spaces exclusively conveyed with any Detached, Semi-Detached, Terraced, Cottage Flat or Flat. The Common Area shall include the public open spaces, common or amenity ground or open spaces, any art features erected thereon, children's play area, the bicycle store and all storage equipment and/or racking system relating thereto and any bin stores, common access roads, pavements, footpaths, visitor

---

[1] It may not be appropriate to have all unsold parts of the Development part of the Common Area.

car parking spaces and all sewers, drains, pipes, cables, boundary fences, walls, retaining walls railings and hedges enclosing the same and common lighting, and generally all ground within the Development which is not disponed by the Developers for ownership by individual Proprietors or groups of Proprietors;

"Common Parts"[2] in relation to a Block on the Development means (i) the solum on which each Block is erected; the common foundations, outside walls, gables, roof and roof space and hatch or hatches leading thereto and any chimney vents and stalks of the Block, any internal division walls between any Flats, any internal ceilings, joists and floors separating flats and any of the other Common Parts, (ii) the drains, sewers, soil and rain water pipes, water supply pipes, tanks, common cisterns, rhones, gutters, conductors, gas and electric mains, and all pipes, cables, wires, flues and transmitters and connections so far as used in common by the Proprietors of more than one Flat in the Block, (iii) the entrance vestibule and canopy (if any), hall, stairs, staircase, passages, landings, walls and ceilings enclosing same; the hall, stairs and staircase lighting; the hall, stairs and staircase carpeting (if any) covering the same; the common electricity meter and any cables, pipes and connections thereto; the communal television aerial and satellite (if any); the bicycle racking system (if any); the communal bin stores (if any), (iv) the security telephone system regulating access to the Block (if any) (but excluding the actual equipment within each Flat) the door bells and letter boxes at the front entrance of each Block (if any) and any other part of the Block which is used in common by two or more Proprietors;

"Common Parts" in relation to a Cottage Flat Building shall mean (i) the solum on which the Cottage Flat Building is erected and the foundations of the said Cottage Flat Building; (ii) the roof and roof space and hatch or hatches leading thereto and any chimney vents and stalks serving the said upper and lower Cottage Flats and any other parts common to the respective Proprietors of the upper and lower Cottage Flats, declaring that the mutual wall separating two Cottage Flats shall be common on the upper floor between the two upper Cottage Flats and on the lower floor between the two lower Cottage Flats; (iii) the drains, sewers, soil and rain

---

[2] This deed cannot actually create or convey common parts; this must be done in a conveyance of a dwellinghouse either by listing the common parts *ad longum* or, by concession from the Keeper, by referring to the Deed of Conditions.

water pipes, water supply pipes, tanks, common cisterns, rhones, gutters, conductors, gas and electric mains, and all pipes, cables, wires, flues and transmitters and connections so far as used in common by the Proprietors of each upper and lower Cottage Flat;

"Community Burden" shall have the meaning assigned to it in accordance with Section 25 of the 2003 Act;

"Community" means the Development, Community having the meaning assigned to it by Section 26(2) of the 2003 Act;

"Cottage Community" means a Cottage Flat Building with the Plot on which it is erected;

"Cottage Flat Building" means a building comprising two upper flats and two lower flats each of which has a main door entrance;

"Cottage Flat" means an upper or lower flatted dwellinghouse forming part of a Cottage Flat Building;

"Detached Dwellinghouse" means a Detached Dwellinghouse situated on a plot owned exclusively by the Proprietor thereof;

"Developers" means us and our successors;

"Flat" means a Flatted Dwellinghouse located within a Block;

"Flatted Community" means a Block with the Plot on which it is erected;

"Manager" means a Property Manager or Factor appointed in terms of Clause TENTH of this Deed;

"Plot" means a plot of ground on which a Detached Dwellinghouse, Semi-Detached Dwellinghouse, Terraced Dwellinghouse, a Cottage Flat Building or a Block of Flatted Dwellinghouses is erected and the curtilage or garden ground appertaining thereto (if any), and includes any footpath or part of roadway within the Plot;

"Proprietor" means the owner for the time being of any Detached Dwellinghouse, Semi-Detached Dwellinghouse, Terraced Dwellinghouse, Cottage Flat or Flat and, where two or more persons own the same, includes both or all of them and any obligations hereby imposed on them shall bind them jointly and severally;

"Retaining Wall" means any wall indicated by a red line on the said Plan and shall include the foundations, support, projection and uplift of such retaining walls;

"Semi-Detached Dwellinghouse" means one of two Dwellinghouses joined one to each other by a common wall or gable;

"Service Strip" means the area of ground shown coloured yellow on the said Plan;

"Terraced Dwellinghouse" means a Dwellinghouse forming part of a row of three or more attached dwellinghouses;

"Visibility Splays" means the areas of ground shown coloured blue on the said Plan;

References to Dwellinghouses shall include Detached Dwellinghouses, Semi-Detached Dwellinghouses, Terraced Dwellinghouses, Cottage Flats and Flats;

References to the male shall include the female.

SECOND
General

(1) This deed is a constitutive deed creating real burdens within the

meaning of Sections 4 and 122(1) of the 2003 Act.

(2) The reservations, real burdens, conditions and others contained herein which apply to the whole Development as a Community shall be and are hereby created real burdens enforceable as community burdens by owners of all Dwellinghouses as units in the Community in terms of Section 27 of the 2003 Act.

(3) The reservations, real burdens, conditions and others which apply only to a Flatted Community or a Cottage Community shall be enforceable only by owners of Flats or Cottage Flats as units within such Flatted Communities or Cottage Communities as the case may be.

(4) Where servitudes are reserved or granted they shall have effect so far as individual Dwellinghouses are concerned on the registration of a separate title for such Dwellinghouse or Dwellinghouses in terms of Section 75(2) of the 2003 Act in so far as regards such Dwellinghouse or Dwellinghouses as both a dominant and servient tenement in relation to any such servitude.

(5) A Proprietor wishing to enforce a real burden contained herein shall require an interest to enforce within the meaning of Section 8(3) of the 2003 Act.

THIRD   (1) Each Plot shall be used solely for the purpose of
Buildings   the erection thereon of not more than one self-con-
                 tained Dwellinghouse, a Cottage Flat Building, or a
                 Block with relative offices.

Common Area   (2) The Common Area so far as not occupied by
                 buildings as aforesaid or roadways, access paths,
                 footpaths, visitor parking or children's play area
                 shall be laid out and maintained as ornamental
                 garden or pleasure ground with any art features
                 erected thereon and for no other purpose whatever
                 and shall be maintained as such in a neat and tidy
                 condition and when necessary renewed by all
                 Proprietors in all time coming. The Proprietors shall
                 be bound by the terms of any Planning Permission,
                 Tree Preservation Order, Woodland Management
                 Scheme, Core Paths Plan or Plan relating to trees,
                 plants or shrubs situated on any Common Area. Any
                 retaining wall shall be common insofar as same
                 forms part of the inside or outside face of a wall
                 which forms part of any boundary and the mainte-
                 nance thereof shall be borne equally by all
                 Proprietors. Any play area created by the Developers
                 shall be for the benefit of all Proprietors of the
                 Development and the cost of maintenance, repair
                 and replacement of any or all of the equipment, sur-
                 facing, boundary walls, fences or otherwise and all
                 other items and matters pertaining thereto shall be
                 borne equally among all of the Proprietors of the said
                 Development. Any art features erected on the
                 Development shall be for the benefit of all
                 Proprietors and as such shall be maintained,
                 replaced, repaired and renewed by all Proprietors,
                 the cost of such maintenance, replacement, repair
                 and renewal being borne equally among all of the
                 Proprietors of the Development. The Service Strip
                 and the Visibility Splays (if any) shall be laid out only
                 as garden ground with no construction or planting
                 other than grass or in the case of the Visibility Splays
                 plants not exceeding 900 millimetres in height.

Garden Ground   (3) Each Plot so far as not occupied by buildings as
                 aforesaid or roadways, access paths, drives or foot-
                 paths shall be laid out and maintained as ornamental
                 garden or pleasure ground in front and as such or as a
                 vegetable garden and drying green at the rear of the
                 Detached   Dwellinghouse,   Semi-Detached
                 Dwellinghouse or Terraced Dwellinghouse and for no
                 other purpose whatever, and shall be maintained as
                 such in a neat and tidy condition in all time coming.

Maintenance   (4) The Proprietor of each Plot shall maintain all
                 buildings and erections thereon in good order and
                 repair and if necessary rebuild in all time coming

and in the event of damage or destruction shall repair, restore and re-erect the same in all respects in accordance with the provisions of sub-clause (1) of this Clause.

(5) The Proprietor for the time being of each Cottage Flat shall maintain their Cottage Flat in good order and repair in all time coming and in the event of damage or destruction shall repair, restore and re-erect the same in all respects in accordance with the provisions of sub-clause (1) of this Clause.

The Proprietor for the time being of each Cottage Flat shall have an obligation along with the Proprietor of the adjoining Cottage Flat of mainte-nance, support and repair and, where necessary, renewal of all mutual walls. It is declared that where a stairway or staircase serves only one Cottage Flat then the responsibility for maintenance, support, repair, and, where necessary, renewal of that stair-way or staircase shall fall to the Proprietor served by that stairway or staircase.

(6) The Proprietors of each Block shall jointly main-tain all buildings and erections thereon in good order and repair and, if necessary, rebuild in all time coming and in the event of damage or destruction shall repair, restore and re-erect the same in all respects in accordance with the provisions of sub-clause (1) of this Clause.

(7) The Proprietor for the time being of each Detached, Semi-Detached Dwellinghouse, Terraced Dwellinghouse and Flatted Dwellinghouse shall have an obligation along with the Proprietor for the time being of the adjoining property of maintenance, support, repair and where necessary, renewal of all mutual walls, gables and fences except where the mutual gable wall or fence does not adjoin another Plot in which case the said gable wall or fence shall be maintained exclusively by the Proprietor.

FOURTH

So far as regards each Cottage Flat and the Cottage Flat Building of which it forms part and each Flat and the Block of which it forms part having been erected by the Developers:-

Common Parts-
Ownership[3]

(1) Each Proprietor of a Flat shall have an equal pro indiviso right of property in common with the other

[3] It has been common in deeds of conditions to narrate the common rights and that is why they appear here. It must be emphasised that it is not competent to create common rights in a deed of conditions or in any constitutive deed which only creates real burdens after November 28, 2004. The practice of the Land Register is to include common rights which have been narrated in such deeds provided they are either expressly conveyed in the first split off writ of a unit or there is reference to the common rights narrated in the deed of conditions or other constitutive deed in the split off writ.

Proprietors of the Flats in the same Block to the Common Parts of the said Block.

(2) Each Proprietor of a Cottage Flat shall have an equal pro indiviso right of property in common with the other Proprietors of the upper or lower Cottage Flats in the Cottage Flat Building to the Common Parts of the said Cottage Flat Building.

(3) The Proprietor of each of the Cottage Flats and Flats shall have the right of access to the roof and roof space thereof to carry out all necessary repairs, maintenance and renewal as required upon giving reasonable notice to the Proprietors of the upper Cottage Flats and upper Flats when access is required.

Maintenance of Common Parts of a Block and of Cottage Flat Building

(4) Each Flat shall be held by the Proprietor thereof in all time coming under the obligation jointly with the other Proprietors of Flats in Building in the same Block of upholding and maintaining in good order and repair and from time to time when necessary renewing and restoring the Common Parts of the said Block and of cleaning, repainting and decorating the said Common Parts subject to the provisions of sub-clause (1) of Clause FIFTH of this Deed. All expenses and charges incurred under the foregoing obligation and of any other work done or services rendered in respect of the said Common Parts shall be payable by the whole Proprietors of Flats in the same Block in equal proportions.

(5) Each Cottage Flat shall be held by the Proprietor thereof in all time coming and under the obligation jointly with the Proprietors of the other Cottage Flats in the Cottage Flat Building of upholding and maintaining in good order and repair and from time to time when necessary renewing and restoring the Common Parts of the said Cottage Flat Building and of cleaning, repainting and decorating the said Common Parts subject to the provisions of sub-clause (1) of Clause

FIFTH of this Deed. All expenses and charges incurred under the foregoing obligation and of any other work done or services rendered in respect of the said Common Parts shall be payable by the Proprietors of the Cottage Flats in the same Cottage Flat Building in equal proportions.

Reference to Manager/Factor

(6) In the event of any Proprietor of a Cottage Flat or any Proprietor of a Flat in a Block considering it necessary or desirable that any repairs or renewals or decoration or other works should be executed to the Common Parts of the Cottage Flat Building or to the Block or to the Plot on which it is situated and of the

other Proprietors of the Cottage Flats in the Cottage Flat Building or Block refusing to sanction such repairs, renewals, decoration or other works, he shall be entitled to refer the question to the Manager, and, in the event of the Manager deciding that all or any of such repairs, renewals, decoration or other works are necessary or desirable, the Manager shall have power to order them to be executed forthwith and the expense thereof shall be borne by all of the Proprietors of the Cottage Flats and Flats respectively in the said Cottage Flat Building or Block in equal proportions. The decision of the Manager shall be final and conclusive.

Maintenance of Flats

(7) Each Proprietor of a Flat shall maintain and when necessary renew the same and the fittings therein, the window frames and glass in the windows thereof and any stairs and stairway exclusively serving the same in a good state of repair and decoration and shall take all appropriate steps to prevent damage to the fabric of the Block of which the Flatted Dwellinghouse forms part, and in particular by control of vermin and immediate treatment of any wood rot or infestation in the floors, skirting boards, joists, doors, walls, ceilings, mouldings and others and by the repair of any damage to the water supply pipes, soil and water pipes and gas or electric cables, pipes or appliances within his own Flat and in the event of failure by any Proprietor to take timeous and adequate measures to prevent or repair such damage he shall be liable for any additional damage to other parts of the Block arising from such failure. There shall be reserved to each Proprietor of a Flat a heritable and irredeemable servitude right of access over the other Flats in the Block of which the Flat forms part for the purpose of maintenance, repair and renewal subject to the said right being exercised at reasonable times and upon reasonable notice except in the case of emergency and subject also to making good any damages caused by the exercise of such right. If in the opinion of the Manager it is necessary or desirable for the protection, appearance or general amenity of a Block that any works of repair, maintenance, renewal or decoration be carried out in or upon any Flat therein he may serve notice in writing upon the Proprietor thereof requiring the performance of such works as are specified in the notice within a period of not less than twenty one days. The Proprietor to whom such notice is sent shall be entitled within twenty-one days of its receipt to appeal to the Arbiter appointed in terms of Clause TWELFTH hereof to decide whether the works specified or any of them are nec-

essary or desirable for the purposes above mentioned and, if the Arbiter considers that such works or any of them are necessary or desirable, to determine the period within which they shall be performed. In the event of failure by the Proprietor to perform these works within the period stated in the Manager's notice or in the determination of the Arbiter, as the case may be, the Manager shall be entitled to have the work carried out and to have any access convenient or necessary for that purpose and to recover the cost thereof from the Proprietor.

Alterations to Dwellinghouses

(8) So far as regards all Dwellinghouses within the said Development[4]:-

(a) Subject to Clause (SECOND)(5) hereof no alterations, erections or additions shall be made on or to any of the Plots, Blocks or Cottage Flat Buildings or any of the Dwellinghouses thereon or on any part of the Development except alterations, erections or additions which conform in all respects to any Local Authority, Town and Country Planning or other relevant statutes and regulations in that behalf and all gas or electric installations shall comply with the requirements of the relevant Gas Authority or the relevant Electricity Authority.

(b) Only satellite dishes, television aerials or other usual forms of receiver for ordinary domestic use shall be attached, affixed, suspended or otherwise connected to any of the Plots or any Dwellinghouses therein or on any of the Common Parts of a Cottage Flat Building or a Block or the Common Area.

Curtilage or Garden Ground

(9) Any garden ground to be conveyed with any Plot shall be kept and used as ornamental or garden ground as hereinbefore defined under Clause THIRD (3) and for no other purpose except drives, footpaths, patios or roads. Each Proprietor shall be responsible for the maintenance and replacement if necessary of any trees, plants and shrubs on any Plot in accordance with any Planning Permission and any Tree Preservation Order or Woodland Management Scheme or Plan relating thereto. Save for any boundary walls or fences erected by the Developers, no fences, gates, division walls or any form of trellis or draught boarding or screening shall be erected thereon without the prior written consent of the rel-

---

[4] Thought should be given as to whether the creation of development wide user and amenity burdens is wise in every case. Although it is unlikely in most cases that anyone other than an immediate neighbour would have an interest to enforce in terms of the 2003 Act, s.8(3)(a) giving all proprietors in the community a title to enforce may result in difficulty in routine conveyancing. The burden (a) in relation to alterations and additions here only requires that the local authority requirements are met.

ative Local Authority and no vehicles of any kind shall be left or parked thereon. No clothes poles, clothes lines or rotary driers other than such as may be installed by us, the Developers, shall be erected on any part thereof nor shall clothes or clothes lines be attached to or suspended from any part of the exterior walls or down pipes, and no garbage cans, ash buckets or any other refuse receptacles shall be left or deposited on any part thereof other than in the designated bin storage/collection areas.

FIFTH
Use and
Prohibitions

(1) Each Dwellinghouse shall be used solely as a Dwellinghouse and for no other purpose whatever and none of the Dwellinghouses shall ever in any way be sub-divided or occupied by more than one family at a time. Each Garage (if any) shall be used only as a private garage for the sole use of a Proprietor or occupant of his Dwellinghouse and shall not be sold or let separately therefrom nor used for any commercial or trading purpose.

(2) The Proprietors and parties occupying any of the Dwellinghouses are hereby expressly prohibited from carrying on therein or in any other part of the Development any trade, business, manufacturing or profession, or from using them or any of them or causing them or any of them to be used for any purpose which might be deemed a nuisance and that whether or not such trade, business or profession is incidental to the ordinary residential use thereof, and notwithstanding any rule of law to the contrary[5]. Declaring that, without prejudice to the foregoing provision, no business name, trade, advertisement board, card or plate shall be fixed or adhibited to or in any part of any of the Dwellinghouses or Cottage Flat Building or Block of Flatted Dwellinghouses or on the ground whether common or otherwise or on any part of the Development. Declaring that the letting of Dwellinghouses for occupation as ordinary domestic residences is not a trade or business for the purposes of this Sub-clause.

(3) Nothing may be done on any part of the Development or in any building or erection thereon that may be deemed a nuisance or likely to occasion disturbance to other Proprietors of parts of the Development or proprietors of subjects adjoining the Development or their tenants or assignees.

(4) No Proprietor of any Dwellinghouse or Plot upon which it is erected shall permit any trailer, boat,

---

[5] This may now be an inappropriate burden; many people now work from home.

caravan or commercial vehicle (other than the normal tradesmen's delivery vans or removal contractors' vehicles) to enter or remain within the Development or to be parked upon any Plot or upon any car parking space within the Development. No motor vehicle shall be parked on any part of the Common Area so as to cause obstruction.

(5) Every Proprietor and his tenants and occupiers are hereby expressly prohibited from keeping in any Dwellinghouse or on the Plot on which it is erected poultry, ducks, pigeons, rabbits, bees or other livestock or from breeding animals but shall be entitled to keep domestic animals as pets provided that such animal or animals shall not prove to be a nuisance to other Proprietors; and it is hereby expressly provided that all dogs shall be kept under control within the Development and shall at no time be allowed to run unfettered within the same or to foul the footways, other footpaths or accessways, common amenity areas or public open spaces.

(6) It is hereby expressly provided that the roof and eaves spaces which form part of any Common Parts shall not be used for storage or in any other manner of way.

SIXTH
Insurance

(1)(a) Each Proprietor of a Detached Dwellinghouse, Semi-Detached Dwellinghouse or Terraced Dwellinghouse shall be bound to effect with a reputable insurance company and keep in force a policy of insurance against loss or damage by fire, explosion, flood, escape of water, storm and tempest for the full reinstatement value thereof to include site clearance charges and professional fees. Each Proprietor of a Dwellinghouse shall also be bound to concur with each other and with any Manager appointed in terms of Clause TENTH hereof in effecting a policy of insurance against the property owners' liability in the names of such Proprietors for their respective rights and interests for such reasonable sums as may be specified by the Developers or by any Factor or Person or Persons appointed in terms of Clause TENTH hereof.

(b)[6] In respect of Flats and Blocks of which they form part the Proprietors of such Flats shall be bound to concur with each other and with any Manager appointed in terms of Clause TENTH hereof in effecting a common policy or policies cov-

---

[6] Common insurance is sometimes the best option for flatted properties. These provisions may be stricter than required in some cases. In a Cottage Flat individual insurance may be preferred.

ering the whole Block in respect of the risks herein-before described. The cost of premiums for such common insurance shall be paid by the Proprietors of the Flats in the Block in equal shares.

In respect of Cottage Flats and Cottage Flat Buildings of which they form part the Proprietors of such Cottage Flats shall be bound to concur with each other and with any Manager appointed in terms of Clause TENTH hereof in effecting a common policy or policies covering the whole Block in respect of the risks hereinbefore described. The cost of premiums for such common insurance shall be paid by the Proprietors of the Cottage Flats in the Cottage Flat Building in equal shares.

(2) In the event of any Detached Dwellinghouse, Semi-Detached Dwellinghouse, Terraced Dwellinghouse, Cottage Flat, Cottage Flat Building, Flat, Block, Garage or any other buildings on the Plot on which it is erected being destroyed or damaged by any cause whether an insured risk or not the Proprietor or Proprietors thereof shall be bound to restore or rebuild the same and to repair the damage within one year of the occurrence of such destruc-tion or damage but without making any alteration in or deviation from the original design and dimen-sions of the said Detached Dwellinghouse, Semi-Detached Dwellinghouse, Terraced Dwellinghouse, Cottage Flat, Cottage Flat Building or Flat or Block or Garage. In the event that there is in existence a common policy of insurance the Proprietors con-cerned shall be bound to co-operate with each other and any Manager in the submission of any claim and reinstatement and repair. All sums which may be received from the insurance company or companies under a policy or policies in respect of loss or damage to buildings shall be applied forthwith in restoring or repairing such buildings. In the event of the cost of any such restoration or repairs exceeding the sum recovered from the said insurance company in respect of such loss or damage any further sum required to meet the said cost shall be paid by the Proprietor or Proprietors of the said Dwellinghouse or Dwellinghouses.

SEVENTH
Boundaries
and Fences

Fences or walls so far as forming divisions between adjoining Plots shall be erected as to one half of their width on each of such adjoining Plots and shall thereafter, except as herein provided, be maintained and kept in good order and repair by the adjoining Proprietors in all time coming, declaring that no Proprietor shall ever have a claim against the Developers in respect of the maintenance, restoration or re-erection of any such fences or walls. Where part of a boundary is formed by a wall of a Garage and there is no adjoining Garage on the adjacent Plot, the maintenance of such wall shall be the sole responsibility of the owner of the Garage. No alterations shall be made to boundary fences, walls or retaining walls except incidental to maintenance thereof and the erection of additional gates or accesses in boundary walls or fences is expressly prohibited.

EIGHTH
Roads and
Services

All necessary roadways, spaces and footpaths adjoining the same, visitor car parking and all sewers, drains, pipes, cables and other transmitters and connections shall be constructed by the Developers but once so constructed (a) the Proprietors within the Development shall be bound and obliged to maintain unbuilt on and in good order and repair to the full satisfaction of the Developers any such roadway, spaces, footpath and visitor car parking spaces so far as within the Development unless and until the same or any of them are taken over for maintenance by any public authority, in any application for which the said Proprietor or Proprietors shall be bound to concur, and (b) the Proprietor or Proprietors of a Plot shall be bound and obliged to maintain and repair such sewers, drains, pipes, cables and other transmitters and connections so far as the same do not become the responsibility of any public authority, the expense thereof being borne equally by the Proprietor or Proprietors of the property served thereby, and, where any of such sewers or others passes through another Plot or other Plots, the Plot or Plots through which the same passes shall be subject to a servitude right of wayleave for the same in favour of the Plot or Plots served thereby.

NINTH
Common Area

In respect that the Common Area has been designated by the Developers as public open space (including any art features erected thereon), amenity ground, roadway or footpath and visitor car parking spaces being such portions as are not included specifically with any Plot, the same shall be formed, laid out and as appropriate planted by the Developers and once so formed shall remain open and unbuilt upon in all time coming, each and every Plot being held under burden of each individual Proprietor thereof being liable for an equal share, or such other equitable share[7] as may be determined by the Developers or by the Manager of maintaining the

---

[7] This may be too vague to be enforceable.

same as public open spaces (including the cost of maintaining, repairing, replacing and/or renewing any art features erected thereon), amenity ground, roadway, footpaths and/or visitor car parking spaces in a neat, tidy and proper condition unless and until the said portions and others or any part of them are conveyed to or are taken over by any public authority or other party or parties for maintenance; declaring that no Proprietor shall have any claim against the Developers in respect of such maintenance.

TENTH
Residents'
Associations and
Managers

The Proprietors of all the said Dwellinghouses shall have the right jointly with all other Proprietors of the Dwellinghouses in the Community forming the Development to join an Association of all the residents of the Development and shall have power at any time to call a meeting of the Proprietors of all the said Dwellinghouses; The Proprietors of Flats in a Block and the Proprietors of Cottage Flats in a Cottage Flat Building may also call a meeting of all the residents in a Block or Cottage Flat Building as the case may be; all such meetings shall be held at such a reasonably convenient time and place as the convener of the said meetings may determine, and of which time and place of meeting at least seven days' notice in writing shall be given by or on behalf of the convener of the said meeting to the other Proprietors with an interest, and at any meeting so convened any of the Proprietors may be represented by a mandatory; the quorum of a meeting of (a) the Proprietors of all the Dwellinghouses in the Community shall be forty per cent of the total number of Proprietors, common owners of any Dwellinghouse counting as one Proprietor or their mandatories, (b) the Proprietors of Flats six Proprietors or their mandatories and (c) the Proprietors of Cottage Flats three Proprietors or their mandatories, and in such cases each Proprietor or mandatory will be entitled to one vote for each Dwellinghouse owned by him, her or them or his, her or their principal (declaring that in the event of any of the said subjects being owned by two or more persons only one of such owners shall be entitled to vote); the decisions of the majority of those Proprietors voting at any such a meeting shall be final and binding on all the Proprietors concerned. At the first meeting of the said Association of all Proprietors in the Development there shall be appointed a Committee consisting of a Chairman, Secretary and Treasurer and such other members of the Committee as the meeting shall determine and such Committee shall be authorised to carry out all the functions of the said Association as are referred to herein and such other functions as the members of the said Association may determine; the Committee shall be entitled to call annual meetings of the said Association at which time elections of new Committee members may be held with all previous Committee members being available for re-election. It shall be competent at any relevant meeting of Proprietors, Proprietors of Flats or Proprietors of Cottage Flats by a majority of the votes of those present, (First) to order to be executed any common or mutual operations and repairs, and any painting, decoration or repair of the subjects owned in common, (Second) to make any regulations which may be expedient or necessary with regard to preservation, cleaning and use or enjoyment of the subjects owned in common, (Third) to effect with a reputable insurance company and the keeping in force of same in respect of any Cottage Flat Building or Block and outbuildings pertaining thereto (i) a common policy of insurance against property owners' liability in the names of such Proprietors for their respective rights and interests for such reasonable sums as may be agreed or fixed by any Manager or Person or Persons appointed in terms of this Clause from time to time to be fixed at a meeting of the Proprietors concerned as provided for in this Clause and (ii) a common policy of insurance against loss or damage by fire, explosion, flood, escape of water, storm and tempest and such other risks as may from time to time be determined at a meeting of the Proprietors concerned as aforesaid for the full reinstatement value thereof to include site clearance charges and professional fees, (Fourth) to appoint any one qualified person or firm who may be of their own number (herein referred to as "the Manager") to have charge and perform the various functions to be exercised in the care, maintenance and management of the subjects owned in common, (Fifth) to fix the duration of the Manager's appointment and to appoint another Manager in his, her or their place; and (Sixth) to delegate to the said Manager the whole rights and powers exercisable by a majority vote at any relevant meetings, subject to such qualifications as the meeting may determine, and the right to collect from each Proprietor the proportions payable by him, her or them respectively of all common maintenance and other costs and management charges including, if thought appropriate by the said Committee or the said Manager, payment in advance by way of a float from each Proprietor of an appropriate sum towards the cost of maintenance and repair of the Common Parts the sum of such advancement by way of a factorial float to be determined from time to time by the said Committee or the said Manager; it is declared that the Manager, unless otherwise determined at a meeting, shall be entitled during the continuance of his appointment to exercise the whole rights and powers which may be competently exercised at or by a meeting of the Proprietors as aforesaid; and it is declared that all expenses and charges incurred for any work done or undertaken or services performed in terms of or in furtherance of the provisions of this clause or otherwise and the remuneration of the said Manager shall be payable by the respective Proprietors whether consenters thereto or not in equal proportions in the same way as if their consent had been obtained, and shall be collected by the said Manager or by any other person or persons appointed at any meeting convened as aforesaid, and in the event of any Proprietor or Proprietors so liable, failing to pay his, her or their proportion of such common maintenance charges, and others or such expenses, charges or remunerations within one month of such payment being demanded the said Manager or other person or persons appointed as aforesaid, such Proprietor or Proprietors shall bear interest at a rate equivalent to five per cent per annum above the base lending rate of the Bank of Toytown from the date of demand until payment and the Manager or other person or persons appointed as aforesaid shall (without prejudice to the other rights and remedies of the Proprietors) be entitled to sue for and to recover the same in his own name from the Proprietor or Proprietors so failing together with all expenses incurred by such Manager or other person or persons thereanent, provided always that it shall be in the option of the said Manager or other person or persons before or after taking any action to call a meeting of the Proprietors to decide if and to what extent, such action should be pursued and that in the event of failure to recover such payments and/or the expense of any action then such sums will fall to be paid by the other Proprietors; declaring that so long as the Developers remain the owners of any part of the Development the power to appoint a Manager shall be vest in us as Developers alone. The majority at any meeting convened in terms of this clause will not be entitled to dismiss any Manager appointed by the Developers in terms hereof without the consent in writing of the Developers for a period of five years after the date of registration hereof but subject to the terms of Section 64 of the 2003 Act.

ELEVENTH
Reserved rights

(a) There are reserved to the Developers and to any party to whom the Developers elect to convey or transfer any or all of the rights, benefits and others herein reserved and referred to and those Proprietors of Dwellinghouses erected on the Development having right thereto or served thereby servitude rights of access over and use of all roads, footpaths, rights of way, accesses, car parking areas but not individual car parking spaces owned exclusively with a Dwellinghouse, amenity ground and all other areas forming part of the Development and all drains, sewers, pipes, cables and services with power and liberty to us and our successors as Developers to make connections or to grant to the Proprietors of any Plot, Local Authority or Statutory Undertaker power and liberty to lay or to make connections with drains, sewers, electric, telephone or television cables, gas and water mains together with all necessary rights of access for the purpose of inspection, repair or renewal thereof subject always to an obligation to restore the surface of the ground damaged thereby.

(b) There are reserved to the Developers (one) all rights of access which may be necessary to complete building and other work and also to plant and thereafter maintain any trees or shrubs which may form part of the amenity scheme or which may already exist and which may be subject to a Tree Preservation Order or Woodland Management Scheme or Plan, (two) power to grant rights of access and egress and other servitudes or wayleaves to any party over any of the roads or footpaths.

(c) Where the Proprietor of any Dwellinghouse is entitled or obliged to maintain any part whether solely or in common with others he and his duly authorised tradesmen and others shall have all necessary servitude rights of access whenever reasonably required for the purpose of inspecting, maintaining and renewing the same, subject always to making good damage caused thereby.

(d) Without prejudice to the foresaid generality, all garden ground conveyed exclusively with any Plot shall be subject to a heritable and irredeemable servitude right of access in favour of the immediately adjoining Proprietor when reasonably required for the purpose of inspection, maintenance and repair of the adjoining subjects, subject always to making good any damage caused thereby.

TWELFTH
Arbitration

All questions, differences and disputes which may arise among the Proprietors or any of them regarding (1) their rights and interests in the Development or any part thereof, (2) the necessity for executing any works, whether common or not, or the liability for the cost thereof, (3) the reasonableness or expediency of any order, regulation, decision, determination or appointment made at any meeting of the Proprietors convened and held as aforesaid and (4) all other questions so far as depending upon or otherwise arising out of or in respect of these presents in any manner of way shall be referred to the amicable decision of the Sheriff Principal of North, South and East Glenshire or any of the Sheriffs at Erehwon Sheriff Court or any other suitable person appointed by the said Sheriff Principal or any of said Sheriffs as Arbiter, and whatever the said Arbiter shall determine shall be final and binding in all matters of law as well as of fact upon all concerned, and the Proprietors concerned shall be bound to implement and fulfil to each other the decisions, findings and decrees of the said Arbiter, with power to the said Arbiter to take skilled advice and order execution or performance of works and to apportion the cost thereof among the said Proprietors, to vary or annul any such order, regulation, decision, determination or appointment, and to find all or any of them liable in the expenses of the arbitration, and to descern accordingly. The application of Section 3 of the Administration of Justice (Scotland) Act 1972 is expressly excluded.

THIRTEENTH
Deviations

There is reserved to the Developers[8] full power to alter or even to depart entirely from the plans of and to deal with the Development or any part thereof and the development thereof as may be required by the Developers from time to time including alterations in types of Plot, Dwellinghouses, the layout, breadths, levels, gradients and the materials used for the construction of buildings, roads, footpaths, drains, sewers and others, and as regards the whole or any part of the Development to waive, alter, modify or dispense with observance of any conditions, restrictions and others herein set forth and in the event of such waiver, alteration or deviation by the Developers, no Proprietor shall have a right to object thereto or have any claim against the Developers in respect thereof.

---

[8] This must be of doubtful competence now and cannot affect rights and obligations created in Dispositions granted and registered prior to any alteration.

APPENDIX 2

TENEMENTS (SCOTLAND) BILL*

[AS AMENDED AT STAGE 2]

CONTENTS

Section

---

* This is the most up-to-date version of this Bill at time of going to press. Following enactment, the finalised text will be available on the HMSO website *www.scotland-legislation.hmso.gov.uk.*

300   *Contents*

TENEMENTS (SCOTLAND) BILL

[AS AMENDED AT STAGE 2]

An Act of the Scottish Parliament to make provision about the boundaries and pertinents of properties comprised in tenements and for the regulation of the rights and duties of the owners of properties comprised in tenements; to make minor amendments of the Title Conditions (Scotland) Act 2003 (asp 9); and for connected purposes.

Boundaries and pertinents

1 Determination of boundaries and pertinents

(1) Except in so far as any different boundaries or pertinents are constituted by virtue of the title to the tenement, or any enactment, the boundaries and pertinents of sectors of a tenement shall be determined in accordance with sections 2 and 3 of this Act.

(2) In this Act, "title to the tenement" means—
  (a) any conveyance, or reservation, of property which affects—
          (i) the tenement; or
          (ii) any sector in the tenement; and
  (b) where an interest in—
          (i) the tenement; or
          (ii) any sector in the tenement,
      has been registered in the Land Register of Scotland, the title sheet of that interest.

2 Tenement boundaries

(1) Subject to subsections (3) to (7) below, the boundary between any two contiguous sectors is the median of the structure that separates them; and a sector—
  (a) extends in any direction to such a boundary; or
  (b) if it does not first meet such a boundary–
          (i) extends to and includes the solum or any structure which is an outer surface of the tenement building; or
          (ii) extends to the boundary that separates the sector from a contiguous building which is not part of the tenement building.

(2) For the purposes of subsection (1) above, where the structure separating two contiguous sectors is or includes something (as for example, but without prejudice to the generality of this subsection, a door or window) which wholly or mainly serves only one of those sectors, the thing is in its entire thickness part of that sector.

(3) A top flat extends to and includes the roof over that flat.

(4) A bottom flat extends to and includes the solum under that flat.

(5) A close extends to and includes the roof over, and the solum under, the close.

(6) Where a sector includes the solum (or any part of it) the sector shall also include, subject to subsection (7) below, the airspace above the tenement building and directly over the solum (or part).

(7) Where the roof of the tenement building slopes, a sector which includes the roof (or any part of it) shall also include the airspace above the slope of the roof (or part) up to the level of the highest point of the roof.

3   Pertinents

(1) Subject to subsection (2) below, there shall attach to each of the flats, as a pertinent, a right of common property in (and in the whole of) the following parts of a tenement—
- (a) a close;
- (b) a lift by means of which access can be obtained to more than one of the flats.

(2) If a close or lift does not afford a means of access to a flat then there shall not attach to that flat, as a pertinent, a right of common property in the close or, as the case may be, lift.

(3) Any land (other than the solum of the tenement building) pertaining to a tenement shall attach as a pertinent to the bottom flat most nearly adjacent to the land (or part of the land); but this subsection shall not apply to any part which constitutes a path, outside stair or other way affording access to any sector other than that flat.

(4) If a tenement includes any part (such as, for example, a path, outside stair, fire escape, rhone, pipe, flue, conduit, cable, tank or chimney stack) that does not fall within subsection (1) or (3) above and that part—
- (a) wholly serves one flat, then it shall attach as a pertinent to that flat;
- (b) serves two or more flats, then there shall attach to each of the flats served, as a pertinent, a right of common property in (and in the whole of) the part.

(5) For the purposes of this section, references to rights of common property being attached to flats as pertinents are references to there attaching to each flat equal rights of common property; except that where the common property is a chimney stack the share allocated to a flat shall be determined in direct accordance with the ratio which the number of flues serving it in the stack bears to the total number of flues in the stack.

Tenement Management Scheme

4   Application of the Tenement Management Scheme

(1) The Tenement Management Scheme (referred to in this section as "the Scheme"), which is set out in the schedule to this Act, shall apply in relation to a tenement to the extent provided by the following provisions of this section.

(2) The Scheme shall not apply in any period during which the development management scheme applies to the tenement by virtue of section 71 of the Title Conditions (Scotland) Act 2003 (asp 9).

(3) The provisions of rule 1 of the Scheme shall apply, so far as rele-

vant, for the purpose of interpreting any other provision of the Scheme which applies to the tenement.

(4) Rule 2 of the Scheme shall apply unless—

    (a) a tenement burden provides procedures for the making of decisions by the owners; and

    (b) the same such procedures apply as respects each flat.

(5) The provisions of Rule 3 of the Scheme shall apply to the extent that there is no tenement burden enabling the owners to make scheme decisions on any matter on which a scheme decision may be made by them under that Rule.

(6) Rule 4 of the Scheme shall apply in relation to any scheme costs incurred in relation to any part of the tenement unless a tenement burden provides that the entire liability for those scheme costs (in so far as liability for those costs is not to be met by someone other than an owner) is to be met by one or more of the owners.

(7) The provisions of rule 5 of the Scheme shall apply to the extent that there is no tenement burden making provision as to the liability of the owners in the circumstances covered by the provisions of that rule.

(8) Rule 6 of the Scheme shall apply to the extent that there is no tenement burden making provision for an owner to instruct or carry out any emergency work as defined in that rule.

(9) The provisions of—

    (a) rule 7; and

    (b) subject to subsection (10) below, rule 8,

of the Scheme shall apply, so far as relevant, for the purpose of supplementing any other provision of the Scheme which applies to the tenement.

(10) The provisions of rule 8 are subject to any different provision in any tenement burden.

(11) The Scottish Ministers may by order substitute for the sums for the time being specified in rule 3.3 of the Scheme such other sums as appear to them to be justified by a change in the value of money appearing to them to have occurred since the last occasion on which the sums were fixed.

(12) Where some but not all of the provisions of the Scheme apply, references in the Scheme to "the scheme" shall be read as references only to those provisions of the Scheme which apply.

(13) In this section, "scheme costs" and "scheme decision" have the same meanings as they have in the Scheme.

Resolution of disputes

5 Application to sheriff for annulment of certain decisions

(1) Where—

    (a) a management scheme other than the development management scheme applies as respects the management of a tenement; and

    (b) a decision is made by the owners in accordance with the scheme,

any owner who, at the time the decision was made, was not in favour of the decision may, by summary application, apply to the sheriff for an order annulling the decision.

(2) For the purposes of any such application, the defender shall be all the other owners.

(3) An application by an owner under subsection (1) above shall be made—

    (a) in a case where the decision was made at a meeting attended by the owner, not later than 28 days after the date of that meeting; or

    (b) in any other case, not later than 28 days after the date on which notice of the making of the decision was sent to the owner for the time being of the flat in question.

(4) The sheriff may, if satisfied that the decision—

    (a) is not in the best interests of all (or both) the owners taken as a group; or

    (b) is unfairly prejudicial to one or more of the owners,

make an order annulling the decision (in whole or in part).

(5) Where such an application is made as respects a decision to carry out maintenance, improvements or alterations, the sheriff shall, in considering whether to make an order under subsection (4) above, have regard to—

    (a) the age of the property which is to be maintained, improved or, as the case may be, altered;

    (b) its condition;

    (c) the likely cost of any such maintenance, improvements or alterations; and

    (d) the reasonableness of that cost.

(6) Where the sheriff makes an order under subsection (4) above annulling a decision (in whole or in part), the sheriff may make such other, consequential, order as the sheriff thinks fit (as, for example, an order as respects the liability of owners for any costs already incurred).

(7) A party may not later than fourteen days after the date of—

    (a) an order under subsection (4) above; or

    (b) an interlocutor dismissing such an application,

appeal to the Court of Session on a point of law.

(8) A decision of the Court of Session on an appeal under subsection (7) above shall be final.

(9) Where an owner is entitled to make an application under subsection (1) above in relation to any decision, no step shall be taken to implement that decision unless—

    (a) the period specified in subsection (3) above within which such an application is to be made has expired without such an application having been made and notified to the owners; or

    (b) where such an application has been so made and notified—

        (i) the application has been disposed of and either the period specified in subsection (7) above within which an appeal against the sheriff's decision may be made has expired without such an appeal having been made or such an appeal has been made and disposed of; or

        (ii) the application has been abandoned.

(10) Subsection (9) above does not apply to a decision relating to work which requires to be carried out urgently.

6 Application to sheriff for order resolving certain disputes

(1) Any owner may by summary application apply to the sheriff for an order relating to any matter concerning the operation of—
  (a) the management scheme which applies as respects the tenement (except where that management scheme is the development management scheme); or
  (b) any provision of this Act in its application as respects the tenement.

(3) Where an application is made under subsection (1) above the sheriff may, subject to such conditions (if any) as the sheriff thinks fit—
  (a) grant the order craved; or
  (b) make such other order under this section as the sheriff considers necessary or expedient.

(4) A party may not later than fourteen days after the date of—
  (a) an order under subsection (3) above; or
  (b) an interlocutor dismissing such an application, appeal to the Court of Session on a point of law.

(5) A decision of the Court of Session on an appeal under subsection (4) above shall be final.

Support and shelter

7 Abolition as respects tenements of common law rules of common interest

Any rule of law relating to common interest shall, to the extent that it applies as respects a tenement, cease to have effect; but nothing in this section shall affect the operation of any such rule of law in its application to a question affecting both a tenement and—
  (a) some other building or former building (whether or not a tenement); or
  (b) any land not pertaining to the tenement.

8 Duty to maintain so as to provide support and shelter etc.

(1) Subject to subsection (2) below, the owner of any part of a tenement building, being a part that provides, or is intended to provide, support or shelter to any other part, shall maintain the supporting or sheltering part so as to ensure that it provides support or shelter.

(2) An owner shall not by virtue of subsection (1) above be obliged to maintain any part of a tenement building if it would not be reasonable to do so, having regard to all the circumstances (and including, in particular, the age of the tenement building, its condition and the likely cost of any maintenance).

(3) The duty imposed by subsection (1) above on an owner of a part of a tenement building may be enforced by any other such owner who is, or would be, directly affected by any breach of the duty.

9 Prohibition on interference with support or shelter etc.

(1) No owner or occupier of any part of a tenement shall be entitled to do anything in relation to that part which would, or would be reasonably likely to, impair to a material extent—

(a) the support or shelter provided to any part of the tenement building; or

(b) the natural light enjoyed by any part of the tenement building.

(2) The prohibition imposed by subsection (1) above on an owner or occupier of a part of a tenement may be enforced by any other such owner who is, or would be, directly affected by any breach of the prohibition.

10   Recovery of costs incurred by virtue of section 8

Where—

(a) by virtue of section 8 of this Act an owner carries out maintenance to any part of a tenement; and

(b) the management scheme which applies as respects the tenement provides for the maintenance of that part,
the owner shall be entitled to recover from any other owner any share of the cost of the maintenance for which that other owner would have been liable had the maintenance been carried out by virtue of the management scheme in question.

Repairs: costs and access

10A   Determination of when an owner's liability for certain costs arises

(1)   An owner is liable for any scheme costs (other than accumulating scheme costs) arising from a scheme decision from the date when the scheme decision to incur those costs is made.

(2)   For the purposes of subsection (1) above, a scheme decision is, in relation to an owner, taken to be made on—

(a) where the decision is made at a meeting attended by the owner, the date of the meeting; or

(b) in any other case, the date on which notice of the making of the decision is given to the owner.

(3) An owner is liable for the cost of any emergency work from the date on which the work is instructed.

(4) An owner is liable for any scheme costs mentioned in rule 4.1(d) of the Tenement Management Scheme from the date of any statutory notice requiring the carrying out of the work to which those costs relate.

(5) An owner is liable for any accumulating scheme costs (such as the cost of an insurance premium) on a daily basis.

(6) An owner is liable for any scheme costs arising from work instructed by a manager from the date on which the work is instructed.

(7) An owner is liable in accordance with section 10 of this Act for the costs of maintenance carried out by virtue of section 8 of this Act from the date on which the maintenance is completed.

(8) In this section, "emergency work", "manager", "scheme costs" and "scheme decision" have the same meanings as they have in the Tenement Management Scheme.

11 Liability of owner and successors for certain costs

(1) Any owner who is liable for any relevant costs shall not, by virtue only of ceasing to be such an owner, cease to be liable for those costs.

(2) Where a person becomes an owner (any such person being referred to in this section as a "new owner"), that person shall be severally liable with any former owner of the flat for any relevant costs for which the former owner is liable.

(3) Where a new owner pays any relevant costs for which a former owner of the flat is liable, the new owner may recover the amount so paid from the former owner.

(4) For the purposes of this section "relevant costs" means, as respects a flat—

- (a) the share of any costs for which the owner is liable by virtue of the Tenement Management Scheme;
- (aa) the share of any scheme costs (within the meaning of the Tenement Management Scheme) for which the owner is liable by virtue of any tenement burden; and
- (b) any other costs for which the owner is liable by virtue of this Act.

(5) This section applies as respects any relevant costs for which an owner becomes liable on or after the day on which this section comes into force.

11A Former owner's right to recover costs

An owner who is entitled, by virtue of the Tenement Management Scheme or any other provision of this Act, to recover any costs or a share of any costs from any other owner shall not, by virtue only of ceasing to be an owner, cease to be entitled to recover those costs or that share.

12 Prescriptive period for costs to which section 11 relates

In Schedule 1 to the Prescription and Limitation (Scotland) Act 1973 (c.52) (obligations affected by prescriptive periods of five years to which section 6 of that Act applies)—

- (a) after paragraph 1(aa) there shall be inserted—
    "(ab) to any obligation to pay a sum of money by way of costs to which section 11 of the Tenements (Scotland) Act 2003 (asp 9) applies;"; and
- (b) in paragraph 2(e), for the words "or (aa)" there shall be substituted ", (aa) or (ab)".

13 Common property: disapplication of common law right of recovery

Any rule of law which enables an owner of common property to recover the cost of necessary maintenance from the other owners of the property shall not apply in relation to any common property in a tenement where the maintenance of that property is provided for in the management scheme which applies as respects the tenement.

14   Access for maintenance purposes

(1) Where an owner gives reasonable notice to the owner or occupier of any other part of the tenement that access is required to, or through, that part for any of the purposes mentioned in subsection (3) below, the person given notice shall, subject to subsection (5) below, allow access for that purpose.

(2) Without prejudice to subsection (1) above, where the development management scheme applies, notice under that subsection may be given by any owners' association established by the scheme to the owner or occupier of any part of the tenement.

(3) The purposes are—

    (a) carrying out maintenance by virtue of the management scheme which applies as respects the tenement;

    (b) carrying out maintenance to any part of the tenement owned (whether solely or in common) by the person requiring access;

    (c) carrying out an inspection to determine whether it is necessary to carry out maintenance;

    (d) determining whether the owner of the part is fulfilling the duty imposed by section 8(1) of this Act;

    (e) determining whether the owner or occupier of the part is complying with the prohibition imposed by section 9(1) of this Act; and

    (f) where floor area is relevant for the purposes of determining any liability of owners, measuring floor area.

(4) Reasonable notice need not be given as mentioned in subsection (1) above where access is required for the purpose specified in subsection (3)(a) above and the maintenance requires to be carried out urgently.

(5) An owner or occupier may refuse to allow—

    (a) access under subsection (1) above; or

    (b) such access at a particular time,

if, having regard to all the circumstances (and, in particular, whether the requirement for access is reasonable), it is reasonable to refuse access.

(6) Where access is allowed under subsection (1) above for any purpose, such right of access may be exercised by—

    (a) the owner who or owners' association which gave notice that access was required; or

    (b) such person as the owner or, as the case may be, owners' association may authorise for the purpose (any such person being referred to in this section as an "authorised person").

(7) Where an authorised person acting in accordance with subsection (6) above is liable by virtue of any enactment or rule of law for damage caused to any part of a tenement, the owner who or owners' association which authorised that person shall be severally liable with the authorised person for the cost of remedying the damage; but an owner or, as the case may be, owners' association making any payment as respects that cost shall have a right of relief against the authorised person.

(8) Where access is allowed under subsection (1) above for any purpose, the owner who or owners' association which gave notice that access was required (referred to as the "accessing owner or association") shall, so far as reasonably practicable, ensure that the part of the tene-

ment to or through which access is allowed is left substantially in no worse a condition than that which it was in when access was taken.

(9) If the accessing owner or association fails to comply with the duty in subsection (8) above, the owner of the part to or through which access is allowed may—

(a) carry out, or arrange for the carrying out of, such work as is reasonably necessary to restore the part so that it is substantially in no worse a condition than that which it was in when access was taken; and

(b) recover from the accessing owner or association any expenses reasonably incurred in doing so.

Insurance

15 Obligation of owner to insure

(1) It shall be the duty of each owner to effect and keep in force a contract of insurance against the prescribed risks for the reinstatement value of that owner's flat and any part of the tenement building attaching to that flat as a pertinent.

(2) Where a tenement burden requires each flat to be insured by way of a common policy of insurance as respects the entire tenement building, then for the purposes of satisfying the duty imposed on an owner by subsection (1) above, the contract of insurance mentioned in that subsection shall be a common policy of insurance.

(3) The Scottish Ministers may by order prescribe risks against which an owner shall require to insure (in this section referred to as the "prescribed risks").

(4) Where, whether because of the location of the tenement or otherwise, an owner—

(a) having made reasonable efforts to do so, is unable to obtain insurance against a particular prescribed risk; or

(b) would be able to obtain such insurance but only at a cost which is unreasonably high,

the duty imposed by subsection (1) above shall not require an owner to insure against that particular risk.

(5) Any owner may by notice in writing request the owner of any other flat in the tenement to produce evidence of—

(a) the policy in respect of any contract of insurance which the owner of that other flat is required to have or to effect; and

(b) payment of the premium for any such policy,

and not later than 14 days after that notice is given the recipient shall produce to the owner giving the notice the evidence requested.

(6) The duty imposed by subsection (1) above on an owner may be enforced by any other owner.

Demolition and abandonment of tenement building

16 Demolition of tenement building not to affect ownership

(1) The demolition of a tenement building shall not alone effect any change as respects any right of ownership.

(2) In particular, the fact that, as a consequence of demolition of a

tenement building, any land pertaining to the building no longer serves, or affords access to, any flat or other sector shall not alone effect any change of ownership of the land as a pertinent.

17   Cost of demolishing tenement building

(1) Except where a tenement burden otherwise provides, the cost of demolishing a tenement building shall, subject to subsection (2) below, be shared equally among all (or both) the flats in the tenement, and each owner is liable accordingly.

(2) Where the floor area of the largest (or larger) flat in the tenement is more than one and a half times that of the smallest (or smaller) flat the owner of each flat shall be liable to contribute towards the cost of demolition of the tenement building in the proportion which the floor area of that owner's flat bears to the total floor area of all (or both) the flats.

(3) An owner is liable under this section for the cost of demolishing a tenement building—

   (a) in the case where the owner agrees to the proposal that the tenement building be demolished, from the date of the agreement; or

   (b) in any other case, from the date on which the carrying out of the demolition is instructed.

(4) This section applies as respects the demolition of part of a tenement building as it applies as respects the demolition of an entire tenement building but with any reference to a flat in the tenement being construed as a reference to a flat in the part.

(5) In this section references to flats in a tenement include references to flats which were comprehended by the tenement before its demolition.

(6) This section is subject to section 123 of the Housing (Scotland) Act 1987 (c.26) (which makes provision as respects demolition of buildings in pursuance of local authority demolition orders and recovery of expenses by local authorities etc.).

18   Use and disposal of site where tenement building demolished

(1) This section applies where a tenement building is demolished and after the demolition two or more flats which were comprehended by the tenement building before its demolition (any such flat being referred to in this section as a "former flat") are owned by different persons.

(2) Except in so far as—

   (a) the owners of all (or both) the former flats otherwise agree; or

   (b) those owners are subject to a requirement (whether imposed by a tenement burden or otherwise) to erect a building on the site or to rebuild the tenement,

   no owner may build on, or otherwise develop, the site.

(3) Except where the owners have agreed, or are required, to build on or develop the site as mentioned in paragraphs (a) and (b) of subsection (2) above, any owner of a former flat shall be entitled to apply for power to sell the entire site in accordance with schedule 2.

(4) Except where a tenement burden otherwise provides, the net proceeds of any sale in pursuance of subsection (3) above shall, subject to subsection (5) below, be shared equally among all (or both) the former

flats and the owner of each former flat shall be entitled to the share allocated to that flat.

(5) Where—
(a) evidence of the floor area of each of the former flats is readily available; and
(b) the floor area of the largest (or larger) former flat was more than one and a half times that of the smallest (or smaller) former flat,

the net proceeds of any sale shall be shared among (or between) the flats in the proportion which the floor area of each flat bore to the total floor area of all (or both) the flats and the owner of each former flat shall be entitled to the share allocated to that flat.

(6) The prohibition imposed by subsection (2) above on an owner of a former flat may be enforced by any other such owner.

(6A) In subsections (4) and (5) above, "net proceeds of any sale" means the proceeds of the sale less any expenses properly incurred in connection with the sale.

(7) In this section references to the site are references to the solum of the tenement building
that occupied the site together with the airspace that is directly above the solum and any land pertaining, as a means of access, to the tenement building immediately before its demolition.

20 Sale of abandoned tenement building

(1) Where—
(a) because of its poor condition a tenement building has been entirely unoccupied by any owner or person authorised by an owner for a period of more than six months; and
(b) it is unlikely that any such owner or other person will occupy any part of the tenement building,

any owner shall be entitled to apply for power to sell the tenement building in accordance with schedule 2.

(2) Subsections (4) and (5) of section 18 of this Act shall apply as respects a sale in pursuance of subsection (1) above as those subsections apply as respects a sale in pursuance of subsection (3) of that section.

(3) In this section any reference to a tenement building includes a reference to its solum.

Liability for certain costs

21 Liability to non-owner for certain damage costs

(1) Where—
(a) any part of a tenement is damaged as the result of the fault of any person (that person being in this subsection referred to as "A"); and
(b) the management scheme which applies as respects the tenement makes provision for the maintenance of that part,

any owner of a flat in the tenement (that owner being in this subsection referred to as "B") who is required by virtue of that provision to contribute to any extent to the cost of maintenance of the damaged part but who at the time when the damage was done was not an owner of the part shall be treated, for the purpose of determining whether A is liable to B as respects the cost of maintenance arising from the damage, as having been such an owner at that time.

(2) In this section "fault" means any wrongful act, breach of statutory duty or negligent act or omission which gives rise to liability in damages.

Miscellaneous and general

22   Amendments of Title Conditions (Scotland) Act 2003

(1) The Title Conditions (Scotland) Act 2003 (asp 9) shall be amended in accordance with subsections (2) to (5) below.

(2) In section 3(8) (waiver, mitigation and variation of real burdens), for "the holder" there
shall be substituted "a holder".

(3) In section 10 (affirmative burdens: continuing liability of former owner), at the end there shall be added–
"(5) This section does not apply in any case where section 11 of the Tenements (Scotland) Act 2004 (asp 00) applies.".

(3A) In section 11 (affirmative burdens: shared liability), after subsection (3) there shall be inserted—

"(3A) For the purposes of subsection (3) above, the floor area of a flat is calculated by measuring the total floor area (including the area occupied by any internal wall or other internal dividing structure) within its boundaries; but no account shall be taken of any pertinents or any of the following parts of a flat—

(a) a balcony; and
(b) except where it is used for any purpose other than storage, a loft or basement.".

(3B) In section 25 (definition of the expression "community burdens"), in subsection (1)(a),
for "four" there shall be substituted "two".

(4) In section 29 (power of majority to instruct common maintenance)—
(a) in subsection (2)—
(i) in paragraph (b)—
(A) for the words from the beginning to "that" where it first occurs there shall be substituted "subject to subsection (3A) below, require each"; and
(B) for sub-paragraph (ii) there shall be substituted—
"(ii) with such person as they may nominate for the purpose,"; and
(ii) paragraph (c) shall be omitted;
(b) after subsection (3) there shall be inserted—

"(3A) A requirement under subsection (2)(b) above that each owner deposit a sum of money—

(a) exceeding £100; or
(b) of £100 or less where the aggregate of that sum taken together with any other sum or sums required (otherwise

than by a previous notice under this subsection) in the preceding 12 months to be deposited under that subsection by each owner exceeds £200,

shall be made by written notice to each owner and shall require the sum to be deposited into such account (the "maintenance account") as the owners may nominate for the purpose.

(3B) The owners may authorise persons to operate the maintenance account on their behalf.";

  (c) in subsection (4), for "(2)(b)" there shall be substituted "(3A)";
  (ca) after subsection (6) there shall be inserted—
"(6A) The notice given under subsection (2)(b) above may specify a date as a refund date for the purposes of subsection (7)(b)(i) below.";
  (d) in subsection (7)(b)—
    (a) in sub-paragraph (i), for "the fourteenth" there shall be substituted "—
      (A) where the notice under subsection (2)(b) above specifies a refund date, that date; or
      (B) where that notice does not specify such a date, the twenty- eighth";
    (b) in sub-paragraph (ii), for "(4)(h)" there shall be substituted "(3B)";
  (da) after subsection (7) there shall be inserted—
"(7A) A former owner who, before ceasing to be an owner, deposited sums in compliance with a requirement under subsection (2)(b) above, shall have the same entitlement as an owner has under subsection (7)(b) above.";
  (e) in subsection (8), for "(2)(b)" there shall be substituted "(3A)"; and
  (f) after subsection (9) there shall be inserted—
"(10) The Scottish Ministers may by order substitute for the sums for the time being specified in subsection (3A) above such other sums as appear to them to be justified by a change in the value of money appearing to them to have occurred since the last occasion on which the sums were fixed.".
(5) After section 31 there shall be inserted—

"31A Disapplication of provisions of sections 28, 29 and 31 in certain cases

(1) Sections 28(1)(a) and (d) and (2)(a), 29 and 31 of this Act do not apply in relation to a community consisting of one tenement.
(2) Sections 28(1)(a) and (d) and 31 of this Act shall not apply to a community in any period during which the development management scheme applies to the community.".
  (6) In section 33 (majority etc. variation and discharge of community burdens)—
    (a) in subsection (1)(b), the words "where no such provision is made," shall be omitted; and

(b) in subsection (2)(a), at the beginning there shall be inserted "where no such provision as is mentioned in subsection (1)(a) above is made,".

(7) In section 35 (variation and discharge of community burdens by owners of adjacent units), in subsection (1), the words "in a case where no such provision as is mentioned in section 33(1)(a) of this Act is made" shall be omitted.

(8) In section 98 (granting certain applications for variation, discharge, renewal or preservation of title conditions), in paragraph (b)(i), for the words "the owners of all" there shall be substituted "all the owners (taken as a group) of".

(9) In section 99 (granting applications as respects development management schemes), in subsection (4)(a), for the words "the owners" there shall be substituted "all the owners
(taken as a group)".

(10) In section 122(1) (interpretation)—
(a) the definition of "flat" shall be omitted; and
(b) for the definition of "tenement" there shall be substituted—
""tenement" has the meaning given by section 23 of the Tenements (Scotland) Act 2004 (asp 00) and references to a flat in a tenement shall be construed accordingly;".

23   Meaning of "tenement"

(1) In this Act, "tenement" means a building or a part of a building which comprises two related flats which, or more than two such flats at least two of which—
(a) are, or are designed to be, in separate ownership; and
(b) are divided from each other horizontally,
and, except where the context otherwise requires, includes the solum and any other land pertaining to that building or, as the case may be, part of the building; and the expression "tenement building" shall be construed accordingly.

(2) In determining whether flats comprised in a building or part of a building are related for the purposes of subsection (1), regard shall be had, among other things, to—
(a) the title to the tenement; and
(b) any tenement burdens,
treating the building or part for that purpose as if it were a tenement.

24   Meaning of "owner", determination of liability etc.

(1) Subject to subsection (2) below, in this Act "owner" means a person who has right to a flat whether or not that person has completed title; but if, in relation to the flat (or, if the flat is held pro indiviso, any pro indiviso share in it) more than one person comes within that description of owner, then "owner" means such person as has most recently acquired such right.

(2) Where a heritable security has been granted over a flat and the heritable creditor has entered into lawful possession, "owner" means the heritable creditor in possession of the flat.

(3) Subject to subsection (4) below, if two or more persons own a flat

in common, any reference in this Act to an owner is a reference to both or, as the case may be, all of them.

(4) Any reference to an owner in sections 5(1) and (3), 6(1), 8(3), 9, 10, 14(1), (6) and (7), 15(5) and (6), 18, 20 and 21 of this Act shall be construed as a reference to any person who owns a flat either solely or in common with another.

(5) Where two or more persons own a flat in common—

    (a) they are severally liable for the performance of any obligation imposed by virtue of this Act on the owner of that flat; and

    (b) as between (or among) themselves they are liable in the proportions in which they own the flat.

25 Interpretation

(1) In this Act, unless the content otherwise requires—

"chimney stack" does not include flue or chimney pot;

"close" means a connected passage, stairs and landings within a tenement building which together constitute a common access to two or more of the flats;

"demolition" includes destruction and cognate expressions shall be construed accordingly; and demolition may occur on one occasion or over any period of time;

"the development management scheme" has the meaning given by section 71(3) of the Title Conditions (Scotland) Act 2003 (asp 9);

"door" includes its frame;

"flat" includes any premises whether or not—

    (a) used or intended to be used for residential purposes; or

    (b) on the one floor;

"lift" includes its shaft and operating machinery;

"management scheme" means—

    (a) the development management scheme;

    (b) the Tenement Management Scheme;

    (c) any tenement burden relating to the maintenance or management of the tenement or any combination of such tenement burdens; or

    (d) any combination of such tenement burdens and any provision of the Tenement Management Scheme;

"owner" shall be construed in accordance with section 24 of this Act;

"sector" means—

    (a) a flat;

    (b) any close or lift; or

(c) any other three-dimensional space not comprehended by a flat, close or lift, and the tenement building shall be taken to be entirely divided into sectors;

"solum" means the ground on which a building is erected;

"tenement" shall be construed in accordance with section 23 of this Act;

"tenement burden" means, in relation to a tenement, any real burden (within the meaning of the Title Conditions (Scotland) Act 2003 (asp 9)) which affects—

(a) the tenement; or
(b) any sector in the tenement;

"Tenement Management Scheme" means the scheme set out in the schedule to this Act;

"title to the tenement" shall be construed in accordance with section 1(2) of this Act; and

"window" includes its frame.

(2) The floor area of a flat is calculated for the purposes of this Act by measuring the total floor area (including the area occupied by any internal wall or other internal dividing structure) within its boundaries; but no account shall be taken of any pertinents or any of
15 the following parts of a flat—

(a) a balcony; and
(b) except where it is used for any purpose other than storage, a loft or basement.

25A   Giving of notice to owners

(1) Any notice which is to be given to an owner under or in connection with this Act (other than under or in connection with the Tenement Management Scheme) may be given in writing by sending the notice to—

(a) the owner; or
(b) the owner's agent.

(2) The reference in subsection (1) above to sending a notice is to its being—

(a) posted;
(b) delivered; or
(c) transmitted by electronic means.

(3) Where the name of an owner is not known, a notice shall be taken for the purposes of subsection (1)(a) above to be sent to the owner if it is posted or delivered to the owner's flat addressed to "The Owner" or using some similar expression such as "The Proprietor".

(4) For the purposes of this Act—

(a) a notice posted shall be taken to be given on the day of posting; and

(b) a notice transmitted by electronic means shall be taken to be given on the day of transmission.

26 Ancillary provision

(1) The Scottish Ministers may by order make such incidental, supplemental, consequential, transitional, transitory or saving provision as they consider necessary or expedient for the purposes, or in consequence, of this Act.

(2) An order under this section may modify any enactment (including this Act), instrument or document.

27 Orders

(1) Any power of the Scottish Ministers to make orders under this Act shall be exercisable by statutory instrument.

(2) A statutory instrument containing an order under this Act (except an order under section 29(2) or, where subsection (3) applies, section 26) shall be subject to annulment in pursuance of a resolution of the Scottish Parliament.

(3) Where an order under section 26 contains provisions which add to, replace or omit any part of the text of an Act, the order shall not be made unless a draft of the statutory instrument containing the order has been laid before, and approved by a resolution of, the Parliament.

28 Crown application

This Act, except section 15, binds the Crown.

29 Short title and commencement

(1) This Act may be cited as the Tenements (Scotland) Act 2004.

(2) This Act (other than this section) shall come into force on such day as the Scottish Ministers may by order appoint; and different days may be appointed for different purposes.

SCHEDULE 1

(introduced by section 4)

TENEMENT MANAGEMENT SCHEME

RULE 1 – SCOPE AND INTERPRETATION

1.1   Scope of scheme

This scheme provides for the management and maintenance of the scheme property of a tenement.

1.2   Meaning of "scheme property"

For the purposes of this scheme, "scheme property" means—
   (a) any part of a tenement that is the common property of two or more of the owners,
   (b) any part of a tenement (not being common property of the type mentioned in paragraph (a) above) the maintenance of which, or the cost of maintaining which, is, by virtue of a tenement burden, the responsibility of two or more of the owners, or
   (c) with the exceptions mentioned in rule 1.3, the following parts of a tenement building (so far as not scheme property by virtue of paragraph (a) or (b) above)—
         (i) the ground on which it is built,
         (ii) its foundations,
         (iii) its external walls,
         (iv) its roof (including any rafter or other structure sup-porting the roof),
         (v) if it is separated from another building by a gable wall, the part of the gable wall that is part of the tenement building, and
         (vi) any wall (not being one falling within the preceding sub-paragraphs), beam or column that is load-bearing.

1.3   Parts not included in rule 1.2(c)

The following parts of a tenement building are the exceptions referred to in rule 1.2(c)—
   (a) any extension which forms part of only one flat,
   (b) any—
         (i) door,

      (ii) window,
     (iii) skylight,
    (iv) vent, or
     (v) other opening,
  which serves only one flat,
(c) any chimney stack or chimney flue.

1.4 Meaning of "scheme decision"

A decision is a "scheme decision" for the purposes of this scheme if it is made in accordance with—

(a) rule 2, or

(b) where that rule does not apply, the tenement burden or burdens providing the procedure for the making of decisions by the owners.

1.5 Other definitions

In this scheme—

"maintenance" includes repairs and replacement, cleaning, painting and other routine works, gardening, the day-to-day running of a tenement and the reinstatement of a part (but not most) of the tenement building, but does not include demolition, alteration or improvement unless reasonably incidental to the maintenance,

"manager" means, in relation to a tenement, a person appointed (whether or not by virtue of rule 3.1(c)(i)) to manage the tenement, and

"scheme costs" has the meaning given by rule 4.1.

1.6 Rights of co-owners

If a flat is owned by two or more persons, then one of them may do anything that the owner is by virtue of this scheme entitled to do.

RULE 2 – PROCEDURE FOR MAKING SCHEME DECISIONS

2.1 Making scheme decisions

Any decision to be made by the owners shall be made in accordance with the following provisions of this rule.

2.2 Allocation and exercise of votes

Except as mentioned in rule 2.3, for the purpose of voting on any proposed scheme decision one vote is allocated as respects each flat, and any right to vote is exercisable by the owner of that flat or by someone nominated by the owner to vote as respects the flat.

2.3 Qualification on allocation of votes

No vote is allocated as respects a flat if—
  (a) the scheme decision relates to the maintenance of scheme property, and
  (b) the owner of that flat is not liable for maintenance of the property concerned.

2.4 Exercise of vote where two or more persons own flat

If a flat is owned by two or more persons the vote allocated as respects that flat may be exercised in relation to any proposal by either (or any) of them, but if those persons disagree as to how the vote should be cast then the vote is not to be counted unless—
  (a) where one of those persons owns more than a half share of the flat, the vote is exercised by that person, or
  (b) in any other case, the vote is the agreed vote of those who together own more than a half share of the flat.

2.5 Decision by majority

A scheme decision is made by majority vote of all the votes allocated.

2.7 Notice of meeting

If any owner wishes to call a meeting of the owners with a view to making a scheme decision at that meeting that owner must give the other owners at least 48 hours' notice of the date and time of the meeting, its purpose and the place where it is to be held.

2.8 Consultation of owners if scheme decision not made at meeting

If an owner wishes to propose that a scheme decision be made but does not wish to call a meeting for the purpose that owner must instead—
  (a) unless it is impracticable to do so (whether because of absence of any owner or for other good reason) consult on the proposal each of the other owners of flats as respects which votes are allocated, and
  (b) count the votes cast by them.

2.9 Consultation where two or more persons own flat

For the purposes of rule 2.8, the requirement to consult each owner is satisfied as respects any flat which is owned by more than one person if one of those persons is consulted.

2.10 Notification of scheme decisions

A scheme decision must, as soon as practicable, be notified—
  (a) if it was made at a meeting, to all the owners who were not present when the decision was made, by such person as may be nominated for the purpose by the persons who made the decision, or
  (b) in any other case, to each of the other owners, by the owner who proposed that the decision be made.

2.11 Case where decision may be annulled by notice

Any owner (or owners) who did not vote in favour of a scheme decision to carry out, or authorise, maintenance to scheme property and who would be liable for not less than 75 per cent. of the scheme costs arising from that decision may, within the time mentioned in rule 2.12, annul that decision by giving notice that the decision is annulled to each of the other owners.

2.12 Time limits for rule 2.11

The time within which a notice under rule 2.11 must be given is—
  (a) if the scheme decision was made at a meeting attended by the owner (or any of the owners), not later than 21 days after the date of that meeting, or
  (b) in any other case, not later than 21 days after the date on which notification of the making of the decision was sent to the owner or owners (that date being, where notification was sent to owners on different dates, the date on which it was sent to the last of them).

RULE 3 – MATTERS ON WHICH SCHEME DECISIONS MAY BE MADE

3.1 Basic scheme decisions

The owners may make a scheme decision on any of the following matters—
  (a) to carry out maintenance to scheme property,
  (b) to arrange for an inspection of scheme property to determine whether or to what extent it is necessary to carry out maintenance to the property,
  (c) except where a power conferred by a manager burden (within the meaning of the Title Conditions (Scotland) Act 2003 (asp 9)) is exercisable in relation to the tenement—
      (i) to appoint on such terms as they may determine a person (who may be an owner or a firm) to manage the tenement,
      (ii) to dismiss any manager,
  (d) to delegate to a manager power to—
      (i) decide that maintenance (costing no more than an

amount specified by the owners) needs to be carried out to scheme property and to instruct it, and

    (ii) arrange for an inspection as mentioned in paragraph (b),

(e) to arrange for the tenement a common policy of insurance complying with section of this Act and against such other risks (if any) as the owners may determine and to determine on an equitable basis the liability of each owner to contribute to the premium,

(f) to determine that an owner is not required to pay a share (or some part of a share) of such scheme costs as may be specified by them,

(g) to authorise any maintenance of scheme property already carried out by an owner,

(h) to modify or revoke any scheme decision.

3.2 Scheme decisions relating to maintenance

If the owners make a scheme decision to carry out maintenance to scheme property or if a manager decides, by virtue of a scheme decision, that maintenance needs to be carried out to scheme property, the owners may make a scheme decision on any of the following matters—

(a) to appoint on such terms as they may determine a person (who may be an owner or a firm) to manage the carrying out of the maintenance,

(b) to instruct or arrange for the carrying out of the maintenance,

(c) subject to rule 3.3, to require each owner to deposit—

    (i) by such date as they may decide (being a date not less than 28 days after the requirement is made of that owner), and

    (ii) with such person as they may nominate for the purpose,

a sum of money (being a sum not exceeding that owner's apportioned share of a reasonable estimate of the cost of the maintenance),

(d) to take such other steps as are necessary to ensure that the maintenance is carried out to a satisfactory standard and completed in good time.

3.3 Scheme decisions under rule 3.2(c) requiring deposits exceeding certain amounts

A requirement, in pursuance of a scheme decision under rule 3.2(c), that each owner deposit a sum of money—

(a) exceeding £100, or

(b) of £100 or less where the aggregate of that sum taken together with any other sum or sums required (otherwise than by a previous notice under this rule) in the preceding 12 months to be deposited by each owner by virtue any scheme decision under rule 3.2(c) exceeds £200,

shall be made by written notice to each owner and shall require the sum to be deposited into such account (the "maintenance account") as the owners may nominate for the 15 purpose.

3.4 Provision supplementary to rule 3.3

Where a requirement is, or is to be, made in accordance with rule 3.3—
  (a) the owners may make a scheme decision authorising persons to operate the maintenance account on behalf of the owners,
  (b) there must be contained in or attached to the notice to be given under rule 3.3 a note comprising a summary of the nature and extent of the maintenance to be carried out together with the following information—
    (i) the estimated cost of carrying out that maintenance,
    (ii) why the estimate is considered a reasonable estimate,
    (iii) how the sum required from the owner in question and the apportionment among the owners have been arrived at,
    (iv) what the apportioned shares of the other owners are,
    (v) the date on which the decision to carry out the maintenance was made and the names of those by whom it was made,
    (vi) a timetable for the carrying out of the maintenance, including the dates by which it is proposed the maintenance will be commenced and completed,
    (vii) the location and number of the maintenance account, and
    (viii) the names and addresses of the persons who will be authorised to operate that account on behalf of the owners,
  (c) the maintenance account to be nominated under rule 3.3 must be a bank or building society account which is interest bearing, and the authority of at least two persons or of a manager on whom has been conferred the right to give authority, must be required for any payment from it,
  (d) if a modification or revocation under rule 3.1(h) affects the information contained in the notice or the note referred to in paragraph (b) above, the information must be sent again, modified accordingly, to the owners,
  (e) an owner is entitled to inspect, at any reasonable time, any tender received in connection with the maintenance to be carried out,
  (ea) the notice to be given under rule 3.3 may specify a date as a refund date for the purposes of paragraph (f)(i) below;
  (f) if—
    (i) the maintenance is not commenced by—
      (A) where the notice under rule 3.3 specifies a refund date, that date, or
      (B) where that notice does not specify such a date, the twenty-eighth day after the proposed date for its commencement as specified in the notice by virtue of paragraph (b)(vi) above, and
    (ii) a depositor demands, by written notice, from the persons authorised under paragraph (a) above repayment (with accrued interest) of such sum as has been deposited by that person in compliance with the scheme decision under rule 3.2(c),

the depositor is entitled to be repaid accordingly, except that no requirement to make repayment in compliance with a notice under sub-paragraph (ii) arises if the persons so authorised do not receive that notice before the maintenance is commenced,

(g) such sums as are held in the maintenance account by virtue of rule 3.3 are held in trust for all the depositors, for the purpose of being used by the persons authorised to make payments from the account as payment for the maintenance,

(h) any sums held in the maintenance account after all sums payable in respect of the maintenance carried out have been paid shall be shared among the depositors—

  (i) by repaying each depositor, with any accrued interest and after deduction of that person's apportioned share of the actual cost of the maintenance, the sum which the person deposited, or

  (ii) in such other way as the depositors agree in writing.

3.5 Scheme decisions under rule 3.1(f): votes of persons standing to benefit not to be counted

A vote in favour of a scheme decision under rule 3.1(f) is not to be counted if—

(a) the owner exercising the vote, or

(b) where the vote is exercised by a person nominated by an owner—

  (i) that person, or

  (ii) the owner who nominated that person,

is the owner or an owner who, by virtue of the decision, would not be required to pay as mentioned in that rule.

RULE 4 – SCHEME COSTS: LIABILITY AND APPORTIONMENT

4.1 Meaning of "scheme costs"

Except in so far as rule 5 applies, this rule provides for the apportionment of liability among the owners for any of the following costs—

(a) any costs arising from any maintenance or inspection of scheme property where the maintenance or inspection is in pursuance of, or authorised by, a scheme decision,

(b) any remuneration payable to a person appointed to manage the carrying out of such maintenance as is mentioned in paragraph (a),

(c) running costs relating to any scheme property (other than costs incurred solely for the benefit of one flat),

(d) any costs recoverable by a local authority in respect of work relating to any scheme property carried out by them by virtue of any enactment,

(e) any remuneration payable to any manager,

(f) the cost of any common insurance to cover the tenement,

(fa) any costs relating to the calculation of the floor area of any flat, where such calculation is necessary for the purpose of determining the share of any other costs for which each owner is liable,

(g) any other costs relating to the management of scheme property, and a reference in this scheme to "scheme costs" is a reference to any of the costs mentioned in paragraphs (a) to (g).

4.2 Maintenance and running costs

Except as provided in rule 4.3, if any scheme costs mentioned in rule 4.1(a) to (d) relate to—

(a) the scheme property mentioned in rule 1.2(a), then those costs are shared among the owners in the proportions in which the owners share ownership of that property,

(b) the scheme property mentioned in rule 1.2(b) or (c), then—

(i) in any case where the floor area of the largest (or larger) flat is more than one and a half times that of the smallest (or smaller) flat, each owner is liable to contribute towards those costs in the proportion which the floor area of that owner's flat bears to the total floor area of all (or both) the flats,

(ii) in any other case, those costs are shared equally among the flats,

and each owner is liable accordingly.

4.3 Scheme costs relating to roof over the close

Where—

(a) any scheme costs mentioned in rule 4.1(a) to (d) relate to the roof over the close, and

(b) that roof is common property by virtue of section 3(1)(a) of this Act,

then, despite the fact that the roof is scheme property mentioned in rule 1.2(a), paragraph (b) of rule 4.2 shall apply for the purpose of apportioning liability for those costs.

4.4 Remuneration of manager

Any scheme costs mentioned in rule 4.1(e) are shared equally among the flats, and each owner is liable accordingly.

4.5 Insurance premium

Any scheme costs mentioned in rule 4.1(f) are shared among the flats—

(a) where the costs relate to common insurance arranged by virtue of rule 3.1(e), in such proportions as may be determined by the owners by virtue of that rule, or

(b) where the costs relate to common insurance arranged by virtue of a tenement burden, equally,

and each owner is liable accordingly.

4.6 Management costs

Any scheme costs mentioned in rule 4.1(fa) or (g) are shared equally among the flats, and each owner is liable accordingly.

RULE 5 – SCHEME COSTS: SPECIAL CASES

5.2 Redistribution of share of costs

Where an owner is liable for a share of any scheme costs but—
- (a) a scheme decision has been made determining that the share (or a portion of it) should not be paid by that owner, or
- (b) the share cannot be recovered for some other reason such as that—
    - (i) the estate of that owner has been sequestrated, or
    - (ii) that owner cannot, by reasonable inquiry, be identified or found,

then that share must be paid by the other owners as if it were a scheme cost for which they are liable, but where paragraph (b) applies that owner is liable to each of those other owners for the amount paid by each of them.

5.3 Liability for scheme costs where procedural irregularity

If any owner is directly affected by a procedural irregularity in the making of a scheme decision and that owner—
- (a) was not aware that any scheme costs relating to that decision were being incurred, or
- (b) on becoming aware as mentioned in paragraph (a), immediately objected to the incurring of those costs,

that owner is not liable for any such costs (whether incurred before or after the date of objection), and, for the purposes of determining the share of those scheme costs due by each of the other owners, that owner is left out of account.

RULE 6 – EMERGENCY WORK

6.1 Power to instruct or carry out

Any owner may instruct or carry out emergency work.

6.2 Liability for cost

The owners are liable for the cost of any emergency work instructed or carried out under rule 6.1 as if the cost of that work were scheme costs mentioned in rule 4.1(a).

6.3 Meaning of "emergency work"

For the purposes of this rule, "emergency work" means work which, before a scheme decision can be obtained, requires to be carried out to scheme property—

(a) to prevent damage to any part of the tenement, or
(b) in the interests of health or safety.

RULE 7 – ENFORCEMENT

7.1 Scheme binding on owners

This scheme binds the owners.

7.2 Scheme decision to be binding

A scheme decision is binding on the owners and their successors as owners.

7.3 Enforceability of scheme decisions

Any obligation imposed by this scheme or arising from a scheme decision may be enforced by any owner.

7.4 Enforcement by third party

Any person authorised in writing for the purpose by the owner or owners concerned may—
    (a) enforce an obligation such as is mentioned in rule 7.3 on behalf of one or more owners, and
    (b) in doing so, may bring any claim or action in that person's own name.

RULE 8 – GENERAL

8.1 Validity of scheme decisions

Any procedural irregularity in the making of a scheme decision does not affect the validity of that decision.

8.2 Giving of notice

Any notice which requires to be given to an owner under or in connection with this scheme may be given in writing by sending the notice to—
    (a) the owner, or
    (b) the owner's agent.

8.3 Methods of "sending" for the purposes of rule 8.2

The reference in rule 8.2 to sending a notice is to its being—
    (a) posted,
    (b) delivered, or
    (c) transmitted by electronic means.

8.4   Giving of notice to owner where owner's name is not known

Where the name of an owner is not known, a notice shall be taken for the purposes of rule 8.2(a) to be sent to the owner if it is posted or delivered to the owner's flat addressed to "The Owner" or using some other similar expression such as "The Proprietor".

8.5   Day on which notice is to be taken to be given

For the purposes of this scheme—
　　(a) a notice posted shall be taken to be given on the day of posting, and
　　(b) a notice transmitted by electronic means shall be taken to be given on the day of transmission.

SCHEDULE 2

(introduced by sections 18(3) and 20(1))

Sale under section 18(3) OR 20(1)

Application to sheriff for power to sell
　1 (1) Where an owner is entitled to apply—
　　(a) under section 18(3), for power to sell the site; or
　　(b) under section 20(1), for power to sell the tenement building,
the owner may make a summary application to the sheriff seeking an order (referred to in this schedule as a "power of sale order") conferring such power on the owner.
　　(2) The site or tenement building in relation to which an application or order is made under sub-paragraph (1) is referred to in this schedule as the "sale subjects".
　　(3) An owner making an application under sub-paragraph (1) shall give notice of it to each
30 of the other owners of the sale subjects.
　　(4) The sheriff shall, on an application under sub-paragraph (1)—
　　(a) grant the power of sale order sought unless satisfied that to do so would—
　　　　(i) not be in the best interests of all (or both) the owners taken as a group; or
　　　　(ii) be unfairly prejudicial to one or more of the owners; and
　　(b) if a power of sale order has previously been granted in respect of the same sale subjects, revoke that previous order.
　　(5) A power of sale order shall contain—
　　(a) the name and address of the owner in whose favour it is granted;
　　(b) the postal address of each flat or, as the case may be, former flat comprised in the sale subjects to which the order relates; and
　　(c) a sufficient conveyancing description of each of those flats or former flats.

(6) A description of a flat or former flat is a sufficient conveyancing description for the purposes of sub-paragraph (5)(c) if—

    (a) where the interest of the proprietor of the land comprising the flat or former flat has been registered in the Land Register of Scotland, the description refers to the number of the title sheet of that interest; or

    (b) in relation to any other flat or former flat, the description is by reference to a deed recorded in the Register of Sasines.

(7) An application under sub-paragraph (1) shall state the applicant's conclusions as to—

    (a) which of subsections (4) and (5) of section 18 applies for the purpose determining how the net proceeds of any sale of the sale subjects in pursuance of a power of sale order are to be shared among the owners of those subjects; and

    (b) if subsection (5) of that section is stated as applying for that purpose—

        (i) the floor area of each of the flats or former flats comprised in the sale subjects; and

        (ii) the proportion of the net proceeds of sale allocated to that flat.

Registration and recording of power of sale order

2 A power of sale order has no effect unless and until, within the period of 14 days after the day on which the order is made—

    (a) where the interest of the proprietor of the land comprising any flat or former flat comprised in the sale subjects to which the order relates has been registered in the Land Register of Scotland, the order is registered in that Register against that interest; and

    (b) where that interest has not been so registered, the order is recorded in the Register of Sasines.

Exercise of power of sale

3 (1) An owner in whose favour a power of sale order is granted may exercise the power conferred by the order by private bargain or by exposure to sale.

(2) However, in either case, the owner shall—

    (a) advertise the sale; and

    (b) take all reasonable steps to ensure that the price at which the sale subjects are sold is the best that can reasonably be obtained.

Distribution of proceeds of sale

4 (1) An owner selling the sale subjects (referred to in this paragraph as the "selling owner") shall, within seven days of completion of the sale—

    (a) calculate each owner's share; and

    (b) apply that share in accordance with sub-paragraph (2) below.

(2) An owner's share shall be applied—

    (a) first, to repay any amounts due under any heritable security affecting that owner's flat or former flat;

    (b) next, to defray any expenses properly incurred in complying with paragraph (a) above; and

(c) finally, to pay to the owner the remainder (if any) of that owner's share.

(3) If there is more than one heritable security affecting an owner's flat or former flat, the owner's share shall be applied under paragraph (2)(a) above in relation to each security in the order in which they rank.

(4) If any owner cannot by reasonable inquiry be identified or found, the selling owner shall
consign the remainder of that owner's share in the sheriff court.

(5) On paying to another owner the remainder of that owner's share, the selling owner shall also give to that other owner—

    (a) a written statement showing—

        (i) the amount of that owner's share and of the remainder of it; and

        (ii) how that share and remainder were calculated; and

    (b) evidence of—

        (i) the total amount of the proceeds of sale; and

        (ii) any expenses properly incurred in connection with the sale and in complying with sub-paragraph (2)(a) above.

(6) In this paragraph—

"remainder", in relation to an owner's share, means the amount of that share remaining after complying with sub-paragraph (2)(a) and (b) above;

"share", in relation to an owner, means the share of the net proceeds of sale to which that owner is entitled in accordance with subsection (4) or, as the case may be, subsection (5) of section 18.

Automatic discharge of heritable securities

5 Where—

    (a) an owner—

        (i) sells the sale subjects in pursuance of a power of sale order; and

        (ii) grants a disposition of those subjects to the purchaser or the purchaser's nominee; and

    (b) that disposition is duly registered in the Land Register of Scotland or recorded in the Register of Sasines,

all heritable securities affecting the sale subjects or any part of them shall, by virtue of this paragraph, be to that extent discharged.

APPENDIX C

S. I. 2003 No.453

The Title Conditions (Scotland) Act 2003 (Conservation Bodies) Order 2003

The Scottish Ministers, in exercise of the powers conferred by section 38(4) of the Title Conditions (Scotland) Act 2003 and of all powers enabling them in that behalf, hereby make the following Order:

Citation and commencement

1. This Order may be cited as the Title Conditions (Scotland) Act 2003 (Conservation Bodies) Order 2003 and shall come into force on 1st November 2003.

Prescribed conservation bodies

2. The bodies listed in Parts I and II of the Schedule to this Order are prescribed to be conservation bodies under section 38(4) (conservation burdens) of the Title Conditions (Scotland) Act 2003.

SCHEDULE

Article 2

CONSERVATION BODIES PRESCRIBED UNDER SECTION 38(4) OF THE TITLE CONDITIONS (SCOTLAND) ACT 2003

PART I

Local authorities

Aberdeen City Council
Aberdeenshire Council
Angus Council
Argyll and Bute Council
City of Edinburgh Council
Clackmannanshire Council
Comhairle nan Eilean Siar
Dumfries and Galloway Council
Dundee City Council
East Ayrshire Council
East Dunbartonshire Council

East Lothian Council
East Renfrewshire Council
Falkirk Council
Fife Council
Glasgow City Council
Highland Council
Inverclyde Council
Midlothian Council
Moray Council
North Ayrshire Council
North Lanarkshire Council
Orkney Islands Council
Perth and Kinross Council
Renfrewshire Council
Scottish Borders Council
Shetland Islands Council
South Ayrshire Council
South Lanarkshire Council
Stirling Council
West Dunbartonshire Council
West Lothian Council

PART II

Other bodies

Castles of Scotland Preservation Trust
Edinburgh World Heritage Trust
Glasgow Building Preservation Trust
Highland Buildings Preservation Trust
Plantlife—The Wild-Plant Conservation Charity
Scottish Natural Heritage
Solway Heritage
St Vincent Crescent Preservation Trust
Strathclyde Building Preservation Trust
The John Muir Trust
[1]The National Trust for Scotland for Places of Historic Interest and Natural Beauty
The Royal Society for the Protection of Birds
The Trustees of The Landmark Trust
The Trustees of the New Lanark Conservation Trust
The Woodland Trust

[1] As amended by SSI 2003/621, reg.2.

APPENDIX D

THE COMMUNITY RIGHT TO BUY (DEFINITION OF EXCLUDED LAND) (SCOTLAND) ORDER 2004

S. S. I. 2004 No. 296

The Scottish Ministers, in exercise of the powers conferred by section 33(2) of the Land Reform (Scotland) Act 2003, hereby make the following Order, a draft of which has, in accordance with section 98(5) of that Act, been laid before and approved by resolution of the Scottish Parliament:

Citation, commencement and interpretation

1.—(1) This Order may be cited as the Community Right to Buy (Definition of Excluded Land) (Scotland) Order 2004 and shall come into force on the day after the day on which it is made.

(2) In this Order—

"the Act" means the Land Reform (Scotland) Act 2003;
"designated maps" means the maps entitled "The Community Right to Buy (Definition of Excluded Land) (Scotland) Order 2004: Definitive Maps" deposited at the Offices of the Scottish Executive Environment and Rural Affairs Department, Pentland House, 47 Robb's Loan, Edinburgh, EH14 1TY; and
"the GROS report" means the General Register Office for Scotland publication "Scottish Settlements - Urban and Rural Areas in Scotland" which was published by the General Register Office for Scotland on 5th February 2001.

Excluded land

2.—(1) There is designated as excluded land for the purposes of section 33 of the Act, the land comprising the settlements listed in the Schedule to this Order, being settlements of over 10,000 people who are resident in the settlement areas defined in the GROS report.

(2) The boundaries of the settlements specified in the Schedule to this Order are the boundaries specified in the GROS report which are delineated on the designated maps.

(3) Foreshore which is adjacent to the settlements specified in the Schedule to this Order is excluded land for the purposes of section 33 of the Act.

Appendix D

SCHEDULE

Article 2

NAME

Aberdeen
Alloa
Arbroath
Ardrossan
Ayr/Prestwick
Bathgate
Blackwood (Cumbernauld)
Blantyre/Hamilton
Bo'ness
Bonnybridge
Broxburn
Buckhaven/Kennoway
Carluke
Carnoustie
Cowdenbeath
Dalkeith
Dumbarton
Dumfries
Dundee
Dunfermline
East Kilbride
Edinburgh
Elgin
Erskine
Falkirk
Forfar
Fraserburgh

NAME

Galashiels
Glasgow
Glenrothes
Greenock
Hawick
Helensburgh
Inverness
Inverurie
Irvine
Kilmarnock
Kilwinning
Kirkcaldy
Kirkintilloch/Lenzie
Largs
Larkhall
Linlithgow
Livingston
Montrose
Penicuik
Perth
Peterhead
St Andrews
Stirling
Stranraer
Troon
Whitburn

INDEX